Memory and Change in Europe

Studies in Contemporary European History

Editors:

Konrad Jarausch, Lurcy Professor of European Civilization, University of North Carolina, Chapel Hill, and a Director of the Zentrum für Zeithistorische Studien, Potsdam, Germany

Henry Rousso, Senior Research Fellow at the Institut d'histoire du temps present (Centre national de la recherche scientifique, Paris)

Volume 1
Between Utopia and Disillusionment: A Narrative of the Political Transformation in Eastern Europe
  Henri Vogt

Volume 2
The Inverted Mirror: Mythologizing the Enemy in France and Germany, 1898–1914
  Michael E. Nolan

Volume 3
Conflicted Memories: Europeanizing Contemporary Histories
  Edited by Konrad H. Jarausch and Thomas Lindenberger with the Collaboration of Annelie Ramsbrock

Volume 4
Playing Politics with History: The Bundestag Inquiries into East Germany
  Andrew H. Beattie

Volume 5
Alsace to the Alsatians? Visions and Divisions of Alsatian Regionalism, 1870–1939
  Christopher J. Fischer

Volume 6
A European Memory? Contested Histories and Politics of Remembrance
  Edited by Małgorzata Pakier and Bo Stråth

Volume 7
Experience and Memory: The Second World War in Europe
  Edited by Jörg Echternkamp and Stefan Martens

Volume 8
Children, Families, and States: Time Policies of Childcare, Preschool, and Primary Education in Europe
  Edited by Karen Hagemann, Konrad H. Jarausch, and Cristina Allemann-Ghionda

Volume 9
Social Policy in the Smaller European Union States
  Edited by Gary B. Cohen, Ben W. Ansell, Robert Henry Cox, and Jane Gingrich

Volume 10
A State of Peace in Europe: West Germany and the CSCE, 1966–1975
  Petri Hakkarainen

Volume 11
Visions of the End of the Cold War in Europe, 1945–1990
  Edited by Frederic Bozo, Marie-Pierre Rey, N. Piers Ludlow, and Bernd Rother

Volume 12
Investigating Srebrenica: Institutions, Facts, Responsibilities
  Edited by Isabelle Delpla, Xavier Bougarel, and Jean-Louis Fournel

Volume 13
Samizdat, Tamizdat, and Beyond: Transnational Media During and After Socialism
  Edited by Friederike Kind-Kovács and Jessie Labov

Volume 14
Shaping the Transnational Sphere: Experts, Networks and Issues from the 1840s to the 1930s
  Edited by Davide Rodogno, Bernhard Struck and Jakob Vogel

Volume 15
Tailoring Truth: Politicizing the Past and Negotiating Memory in East Germany, 1945–1990
  Jon Berndt Olsen

Volume 16
Memory and Change in Europe: Eastern Perspectives
  Edited by Małgorzata Pakier and Joanna Wawrzyniak

Memory and Change in Europe

Eastern Perspectives

Edited by
Małgorzata Pakier and Joanna Wawrzyniak

Published in 2016 by
Berghahn Books
www.berghahnbooks.com

© 2016, 2018 Małgorzata Pakier and Joanna Wawrzyniak
First paperback edition published in 2018.

All rights reserved. Except for the quotation of short passages
for the purposes of criticism and review, no part of this book
may be reproduced in any form or by any means, electronic or
mechanical, including photocopying, recording, or any information
storage and retrieval system now known or to be invented,
without written permission of the publisher.

Library of Congress Cataloging-in-Publication Data
Memory and change in Europe: Eastern perspectives / edited by Malgorzata Pakier and Joanna Wawrzyniak.
   pages cm. -- (Studies in contemporary European history; volume 16)
   Includes bibliographical references and index.
   ISBN 978-1-78238-929-3 (hardback: acid-free paper) -- ISBN 978-1-78238-930-9 (ebook)
   1. Memory--Social aspects--Europe, Eastern--History. 2. Collective memory--Europe, Eastern--History. 3. Social change--Europe, Eastern--History. 4. Post-communism--Social aspects--Europe, Eastern--History. 5. Europe, Eastern--Social life and customs. 6. Europe, Eastern--Social conditions. 7. Europe, Eastern--Relations--Europe, Western. 8. Europe, Western--Relations--Europe, Eastern. I. Pakier, Malgorzata, 1979- II. Wawrzyniak, Joanna, 1975-
   DJK48.5.M46 2015
   947--dc23
                                                                    2015007895

British Library Cataloguing in Publication Data
A catalogue record for this book is available from the British Library

ISBN 978-1-78238-929-3 (hardback)
ISBN 978-1-78533-816-8 (paperback)
ISBN 978-1-78238-930-9 (ebook)

Contents

List of Illustrations   viii

Foreword   ix
  Jeffrey K. Olick

Acknowledgements   xiii

Introduction   1
  Memory and Change in Eastern Europe: How Special?
  Małgorzata Pakier and Joanna Wawrzyniak

Part I   Memory Dialogues and Monologues

Chapter 1
  The Transformative Power of Memory   23
  Aleida Assmann

Chapter 2
  Political Correctness and Memories Constructed for 'Eastern Europe'   38
  Andrzej Nowak

Part II Eastern Europe as a (Unique) Memory Framework?

Chapter 3
The (non-)Travelling Concept of *Les Lieux de Mémoire*: Central and Eastern European Perspectives   59
Maciej Górny and Kornelia Kończal

Chapter 4
Ain't Nothing Special   77
Sławomir Kapralski

Chapter 5
Biographical and Collective Memory: Mutual Influences in Central and Eastern European Context   96
Kaja Kaźmierska

Part III Eastern European Memories Facing Historical Change and Cultural Transformations

Chapter 6
The Path of Bringing the Dark to Light: Memory of the Holocaust in Postcommunist Europe   115
Joanna Beata Michlic

Chapter 7
The Rise of an East European Community of Memory? On Lobbying for the Gulag Memory via Brussels   131
Lidia Zessin-Jurek

Chapter 8
Two Concepts of Victimhood: Property Restitution in the Czech Republic and Poland after 1989   150
Stanisław Tyszka

Chapter 9
Shared Memory Culture? Nationalizing the 'Great Patriotic War' in the Ukrainian-Russian Borderlands   169
Tatiana Zhurzhenko

Chapter 10
History, Politics and Memory (Ukraine 1990s – 2000s)   193
Georgiy Kasianov

Chapter 11
    Walking Memory through City Space in Sevastopol, Crimea   212
        Judy Brown

Part IV   Foci of Memories in Eastern Europe

Chapter 12
    The Second World War in the Memory of Contemporary Polish Society   231
        Piotr Tadeusz Kwiatkowski

Chapter 13
    Auschwitz and Katyn in Political Bondage: The Process of Shaping Memory in Communist Poland   246
        Jacek Chrobaczyński and Piotr Trojański

Chapter 14
    Germans in Eastern Europe as a Polish-German *Lieu de Mémoire*? On the Asymmetry of Memories   264
        Matthias Weber

Chapter 15
    Remembering Collectivization in Bulgaria   283
        Yana Yancheva

Chapter 16
    Uses and Misuses of Memory: Dealing with the Communist Past in Postcommunist Bulgaria and Romania   299
        Claudia-Florentina Dobre

Bibliography   317
Index   359

Illustrations

0.1. Warsaw. A prewar building at the United Nations Circle   2
0.2. A view from the other side of the United Nations Circle   3
9.1. Orthodox chapel with the Bell of Unity in front of Peter and Paul Cathedral   175
9.2. 'Belgorod – City of Military Glory', patriotic visual propaganda in the urban landscape   178
9.3. The Bell Tower on the Prokhorovka battlefield   180
9.4. The 'Third Battlefield of Russia' Museum with tank monument   182
9.5. The 'Soldier-Liberator' statue in Kharkiv   184
9.6. The Holocaust memorial 'Drobitskyi Yar'   185
9.7. Victory Day 2010 on the Marshall Konev Height   188
9.8. Orthodox chapel on the Marshall Konev Height   189
15.1. Map of Bulgaria   286

Foreword

Jeffrey K. Olick

Despite thirty putatively booming years, the discourse of memory that has galvanized scholars and public commentators during that time remains essentially unstable. There are, for instance, still some very good questions about what added value 'memory' provides in comparison to older discourses on tradition, heritage, identity and culture. It is also true that the topos of memory has often been profligate, pulling in commemoration, reminiscence and representation in ways that sometimes erase differences, and treating individual and collective phenomena as if one can assume they are part of the same epistemological and ontological universes. Additionally, as the editors of this fine volume point out, celebrations – and also eulogies – of the scholarly memory boom manifest a sometimes arrogant normativity, whereby the rest are measured by the West, and as usual are found to be backward.

The chapters in this volume, along with the excellent editorial introduction, provide a salutary corrective to these and other misconceptions about memory and the scholarship that has studied it, and are a clear demonstration of the field's importance. In the first place, it is clear that memory – with its undertones of trauma, manipulability and multiplicity – provides analytical purchase that some of the other phenomena under consideration – again, tradition, heritage, identity and culture – do not: among other things, these chapters show that memory is a way to link these other phenomena together in a single analytical framework, one that demonstrates that they are not independent of each other. So while historians may continue to object that memory studies was merely a fad that has passed its prime (though of course many claimed that already at the beginning of the so-called memory boom), in doing so they miss the essential and persistent reasons why the fad arose in the first place: namely, to explain the many different ways in which the past constitutes the present, and the many ways in which we understand – and misunderstand – that constitution. The problem of the past is not merely the challenge of getting it right or correcting those who do not, but of understanding how and why we produce both right and wrong versions, and the effects of both, and all sorts of other versions that cannot be judged on strictly epistemological criteria.

In the second place, the chapters in this volume show that while we cannot simply assume individual and collective memory are the same, nor can we assume that they are radically separate. While there is no such thing as collective memory separate from the people who participate in and carry it, there is equally no such thing as individual memory separate from the social and political frames that give rise to it. In this regard, the profligacy of 'memory' as a concept may in fact be a strength. The many different ways in which the concept is deployed, and the many different ways it is taken as an object of analysis and subject of discourse, in this volume is a clear demonstration of its power.

Finally, and perhaps most importantly, the focus on Central and Eastern Europe reveals that memory studies has not only not finished its work, but has got a great deal wrong because of its most common geographical starting points. The study of Central and Eastern Europe calls into question many of the assumptions about the politics of memory based on how they have unfolded in France and Germany; it shows not only that those other cases are not necessarily paradigmatic, but that at least some of our understandings of them may in fact be wrong: the models declared salutary and successful have clearly had their blind spots. We can thus now clearly see that there is more listening, and less instructing of others, to do in the West. Even more, the self-confidence of the avatars of Western memory models may in fact have caused – and may continue to be causing – disturbing effects elsewhere, for instance when model Germany's memory kit is packaged for export.

The meetings for which the chapters in this volume were originally written – and out of which this volume has emerged – were organized under the banners of 'genealogies of memory' and 'regions of memory', and it is perhaps worth explicating the latter label very briefly here as a preface to the outstanding work that the editors have guided and assembled. Although the focus of this volume is Central and Eastern Europe, in discussions among the conference conveners, the notion of regions of memory was formulated to exploit the productive tension between the specificity of memory discourses in different times and places and around different themes – e.g., in Western Europe about the Second World War and the Holocaust, or in the Southern Cone around authoritarian regimes and 'the disappeared', or in North-East Asia about Japanese imperialism and the Pacific War – and the generality of the issues. On the one hand, analysis of these different worlds of memory requires deep area knowledge and has thus often formed corps of specialists who know a great deal about their particular regions, but much less about the others. On the other hand, memory studies has become an international and generalizable enough discourse that some comparative perspective may now be possible. Within each world of memory, for instance, participants are often convinced that their problems with memory, or the memory dynamics in their particular cases, are like no other. By the same token, if one has the opportunity to travel intellectually between cases, one finds that many of the same issues and perspectives – including the firm belief in the uniqueness of the circumstances – is common across contexts. The idea was to bring experts in a number of different regions of memory – memory debates in different places around different events that occurred at different times – to see what cross-case insights might emerge. And the productivity of that dialogue is more than evident in the pages that follow.

The notion of 'regions of memory' also has some specific analytical content. In particular, it aimed to challenge and destabilize the taken-for-granted status of a number of predominant analytical frames within memory studies. In particular, memory studies has often been dominated by an emphasis on nation states as carriers of, and objects for, memory. To be sure, they are. But recent trends in memory studies and elsewhere have challenged the nation state as the predominant 'container' of memory and other important cultural phenomena. One solution has been to hypothesize global or universal memory discourses and dynamics, which certainly exist. Another has been to re-emphasize local or micro-frameworks of memory, for instance the family, which can travel in and out of various nation state containers. In these discussions, however, regional dynamics – the ways in which different nation states have been brought together in dialogical (or multilogical) discourses, the dynamics of which are not reducible to the participant nations while also not being mere instances of global discourse – have received less attention. There do indeed seem to be regions of memory discourse in which a particular event is framed in an irreducible relational geometry, the contours of which explain as much as the internal dynamics of each container. Examples, again, include Britain-France-Germany on the Second World War, Japan-China-South Korea on Japanese imperialism and the Pacific War, Australia-New Zealand-Canada and much less vigorously the United States on indigenous peoples, and of course Central and East Central Europe, though there are many others as well.

While the notion of regions of memory – discursive arenas above the level of the nation state but not fully universal – was meant to challenge both state-centric theory as well as the sense that cases are incommensurable, it was also meant as an addition to the arsenal of analytical constructs, in the hope of a possible systematic integration. In my own introductory remarks at the meeting on 'regions of memory', I thus emphasized multiple 'systems' of memory, of which region was one, along with the global system a level up, and nation states, localities, families and even individuals as other analytical – but not concretely – independent systems. And my main argument was that these are not merely nested like Matryoshka dolls, one inside the other, but that the flows and effects of memory can leap between different orders, from system to system, in a wide variety of ways: not only is the individual nested within the local, which in turn is nested in the national, regional and global; the global can work directly on the individual or local, and vice versa, just as the national can. I believe the chapters assembled here are an outstanding step, both towards providing the materials for such an analysis as well as having begun it already. Memory studies, it is thus clear, is not merely not done; it has a great deal left to do, though with these chapters there is perhaps a somewhat clearer agenda and better tools with which to do it. It was a great honour for me to participate in the excellent meetings that were a basis for the chapters, and to introduce the volume that has resulted.

Jeffrey K. Olick is professor of sociology and history at the University of Virginia and Sociology Department Chair. While he has published on a wide variety of topics, his interests focus particularly on collective memory, critical theory, transitional justice and postwar Germany. He is the author of several books and numerous articles and chapters on these issues. Among his best-known publications are *In the House of the Hangman: The Agonies of German Defeat, 1943–1949* (2005), *The Politics of Regret: On Collective Memory and Historical* (2007), and *The Collective Memory Reader* (2011, with V. Vinitzky-Seroussi and D. Levy).

ACKNOWLEDGEMENTS

This volume was prepared as a result of the discussions developed during two meetings: 'Genealogies of Memory in Central and Eastern Europe: Theories and Methods' from 2011, and 'Regions of Memory: A Comparative Perspective on Eastern Europe' from 2012. Both gatherings took place in Warsaw, in frames of the programme 'Genealogies of Memory in Central and Eastern Europe' conceptualized by the editors of this book.

Above all we wish to thank the programme's main sponsor and organizer, the European Network of Remembrance and Solidarity for their generous financial and institutional support. Thanks to the ENRS for making impossible into possible and enabling us to gather over a hundred distinguished international scholars for each meeting, as well as young researchers, for discussions about the state of research on memory, for which Central and Eastern Europe presented the main point of reference. We are especially grateful to Dr Burkhard Olschowsky, Rafał Rogulski, Professor Jan Rydel and Professor Matthias Weber from the ENRS, who supported this project from the very beginning, understanding the need to establish an international platform of intellectual exchange in Warsaw where a debate on memory, with special emphasis on the impact of the violent pasts of communism and Nazism, can take place. Special thanks to Hanna Gospodarczyk, Jan Kaczorowski and Agnieszka Nosowska from the ENRS for their tremendous organizational work at the programme. Without their skills and dedication the programme wouldn't have been a success.

We would also like to thank Dr Tadeusz Szawiel from the Institute of Sociology at the University of Warsaw, and Professor Gertrud Pickhan from Osteuropa-Institut der Freien Universität Berlin for the organizational commitment of their institutions in developing the programme. We are very grateful to Professor Jeffrey Olick (University of Virginia), who accepted our invitation to give a summary speech at the 'Genealogies of Memory' conference, and who inspired us and gave great conceptual support in the organization of the following discussions on 'regions of memory'. His ideas on the relation between history, memory and memory research have been at the core of our thinking about the concept of the programme and of this book. We would also like to express our gratitude to our colleagues from the Social Memory Laboratory of the Institute of Sociology at the University of Warsaw for all the inspiring discussions on the relevance of Central and Eastern Europe for memory studies today.

We also wish to express our appreciation to the contributors to this volume for their cooperation, goodwill and ideas, and to all other discussants, which prepared the ground for the conceptual structuring of this volume.

Special thanks from Joanna Wawrzyniak go to two excellent German academic institutions, Freiburg Institute for Advanced Studies and Imre Kertész Kolleg Jena, where she was a visiting fellow in 2012/2013 and 2013/2014, and where she had time to work on this book.

Last but not least, we want to thank Professors Konrad Jarausch and Henry Rousso who accepted our book proposal and agreed to publish it in their series *Studies in Contemporary European History*, as well as two anonymous reviewers for their helpful comments. We are also thankful to the copy editors for their hard work, and to Jan Pakier for his help with the index.

Małgorzata Pakier and Joanna Wawrzyniak

Introduction

MEMORY AND CHANGE IN EASTERN EUROPE
How Special?

Małgorzata Pakier and Joanna Wawrzyniak

In his seminal essay 'The Past is Another Country', the late Tony Judt (1992: 105) saw the East of Europe in the following way:

> The communist era … left a vacuum into which ethnic particularism, nationalism, nostalgia, xenophobia, and ancient quarrels could flow; not only were these older forms of political discourse legitimated again by virtue of communism's very denial of them, but they were the only real terms of political communication that anyone could recall, with roots in the history of the region. Together with religious affiliation, which in pre-1939 Eastern Europe was often itself the hallmark of nationality, they and the past they describe and represent have returned to haunt and distort postcommunist politics and memory.

This is the kind of archetypal statement that one comes across in literature. It treats Eastern European processes of remembering normatively and in terms of mnemonic pathologies, in which East European postcommunist societies have to catch up with the West European models of remembering the past. What was also typical until recently was to treat Eastern Europe as a marginal, supplementary, or in the best case scenario, an exceptional issue in the discussions of Europeanization of memory. The situation has changed in the last decade with flourishing political projects, cultural programmes and academic networks. Not only have European projects and globalization stirred identity debates and influenced changes in the perception of the past in the societies of the former Eastern Bloc, but the process is mutual. While previously the East Europeans found it difficult to draw the attention of their Western counterparts with regard to questions of their history and memory, the official commemorations and public controversies of the last few years show that Eastern Europe has

---

Notes for this chapter begin on page 19.

FIGURE 0.1 Warsaw. A prewar building at the United Nations Circle. Photo: M. Pakier.

become an important trigger for discussions about the content and form of a European narrative. Facing this important shift, which itself is part of a larger process of increasing awareness by the elite and the common people of both the flexibility and politicization of memory (Lebow 2008: 26), it is appropriate to ask then: are we at the climax of memory research, or are we entering the twilight? Or maybe rather still at the beginning, given the still unfulfilled demand for clarifications, memory textbooks, encyclopedias and other codifications of theory.

Everyday examples seem to confirm that the subject is still not passé. The mere space of the European city of Warsaw, and the layers of paint or graffiti on its prewar buildings and walls testify to that.

The image above shows one of the very few buildings in Warsaw to survive the war, now located at the United Nations Circle (*Rondo ONZ*). Prewar illustrations show it as part of a vibrant Jewish district, and during the war it belonged to the Jewish ghetto. In 2011 graffiti appeared on its wall, saying 'Immigration is not a crime' (*Imigracja to nie zbrodnia*). Today this part of Warsaw is also symbolic of the Polish systemic transformation since 1989; because the land was cheap in the 1990s and in a good location close to the city centre, it has been gradually evolving into a business district, and recently the United Nations Circle has also become a site for demonstrations defending immigration and multicultural society, the writing on the wall being one of the traces of such activities. It is significant that of all buildings in the neighborhood it was

FIGURE 0.2 A view from the other side of the United Nations Circle. Photo: M. Pakier.

this historical wall, once part of Warsaw's Jewish neighbourhood, which beckoned to the protesters to leave their remarks.

Paint on a wall is only the visible projection of a mental process. But what process? It could be argued that these are traces of activities that are merely recycling the already existing memory boom, confident of the audience they are going to receive. Or, alternatively, they might differ in quality from what we have already seen and known, and therefore merit a closer look. This example might guide us through questions about the use of history by non-state agents in the postcommunist context of the former Eastern Bloc countries. The painting on the wall is a sign of a free public space, liberated from the influence of the state that used to maintain a monopoly on interpretations of history. There is also the question of the coexistence of various layers of the past in a society going through dynamic social and cultural transformations. That carries implicit issues of forgetting, and of a rivalry of memories represented by various groups. Or, quite differently, it may be an example of a conscious use of the established global memory code, such as the Holocaust – with its strong moral connotations – in the new, post-transformation, multicultural context of a Poland that has already 'returned' to Europe. The political, social and cultural transformations after 1989 have changed the Polish ethnic and cultural landscape, wherein the prewar multiculturalism and the wartime fate of the Polish Jews has become a symbol to refer to when defending the 'others' of today.

The city space of Warsaw provides only a sample trace of social memory processes in Eastern Europe after 1989. Micro-histories like that of the Warsaw wall will provoke broader interpretative horizons and frameworks – local, national, regional, European and global. For memory scholars questions then arise as to whether we can inscribe such Eastern European puzzles amid the already existing matrix of concepts and theories – or do they deserve new categories to properly identify the social processes they are undergoing? To put it another way: do Eastern European data have the impetus for interrogating the paradigm of 'memory studies', as Blacker and Etkind (2013) recently suggested?

This book comments on two issues related to this marriage of 'memory studies' with the European identity debate. The first is on the memory studies aspect, and is connected to its immanent question on how collective memory changes or endures (Schwartz 1991, Olick 1999). In theoretical literature we find various views and discussions of factors such as time, trauma, generations, politics or media behind these processes (Assmann and Short 2012: 6–8). The quarter of a century that has just passed since the political breakthrough of 1989 and a decade of integration with the European Union, provide rich empirical material from Eastern Europe on the issue of collective memory change. This will be examined by the authors in this volume using various normative and theoretical approaches. The other central question is on the European identity aspect, and more particularly, it deals with alleged Eastern European specificity anchored in its history. This question, long discussed in the literature (e.g., Halecki 1980, Jedlicki 1999), will be scrutinized by the use of the interpretative tools of memory studies. The authors have different opinions on the matter. Some of them walk the path of Larry Wolff (1994) on the invented nature of Eastern Europe, while others see the differences in the content and the ways in which the past has been shaped in this region.

Unlike other volumes on Eastern European memories, this has been completed mainly (but not exclusively) by insiders, by multidisciplinary scholars from Eastern Europe. This offers the opportunity to see the sensitivity and identity of their research: how they use, understand, reinterpret or contest some of the memory concepts, but equally importantly it gives us access to rich data, often absent from the international agenda.

In the following introduction, we shall first discuss the present state of the European memory debate, mostly as represented in scholarship, and situate Eastern Europe within it both as an agent in the Europeanization processes as well as a subject of the debate on European memory. Next, we shall present the new wave of memory research, on and in Eastern Europe, which benefits from a broad use of comparative national and transnational cases, and propose some conclusions stemming from this research as an alternative to the more global framework of a pan-European memory.

Writing European Memory

European memory has become a popular subject of academic debate, vitally fuelling the discipline of memory studies. Usually supplied with a question mark – presented either as an impossibility, or as a desirable direction – European memory takes its impetus from the fundamental dilemmas defining Europe after 1945: Where are its borders? Can European societies be united – and if so, around what traditions and values? Is there a specifically European culture and tradition? How is it possible to shape a peaceful European future and to cultivate its pasts at the same time? Which pasts and which traditions should be cultivated, and which should be condemned? How is it possible to create unity and preserve the diversity of various heritages in Europe at the same time? The questions of European history and identity have necessarily involved the need to face both the internal and external others, and definitions of who the others are. This volume will provide a view on Europeanization from the perspective of East Europeans, and of their transformation from a peripheral status to one of the central subjects in the current debate on European history and memory.

Framing of the European narrative develops simultaneously within two academic fields. There are the efforts of historians aimed at rewriting European pasts in a new transnational fashion; the particular incentive for doing so has been the experience of mass violence in the twentieth century. Thus the historian Philipp Ther (2011, see also Ther and Siljak 2001) proposes supranational and regional frameworks to research forced migrations. Another historian, Timothy Snyder (2010), has constructed his own category of 'bloodlands' located in the East of Europe, in order to transgress the borders of traditional national historiographies when describing the phenomena of mass violence in the first half of the twentieth century. In their recently edited book, Omer Bartov and Eric D. Weitz (2013) reach further back in time, searching for the roots of the violence in twentieth-century Europe within the imperial processes of the nineteenth century characteristic of the continent. Following on from this, there have been some attention grabbing attempts to rewrite national master narratives into a 'European' history. Such endeavours, justified by current memory politics yet still transparent and comprehensive, are found in German historical writing (e.g. Frevert 2005).

Then there are those within the social and cultural studies on memory. Questions about the form and content of a shared European memory have been explicitly formulated and critically discussed in several recent English-language publications, such as by Jan-Werner Müller (2002), Konrad H. Jarausch and Thomas Lindenberger (2007b), Wulf Kansteiner et al. (2006), or Małgorzata Pakier and Bo Stråth (2010). Certain German publications, by Aleida Assmann (2006, 2012) and Claus Leggewie (2011), as well as those by French authors Georges Mink and Laure Neumayer (2007) or Sarah Gensburger and Marie-Clare Lavabre (2012) should also be mentioned in this context. Their authors seek to identify long-term and transnational patterns in dealing with the past in postwar Europe, indicating possibilities and challenges to a collective European historical narrative of the twentieth century.

Authors such as Daniel Levy and Natan Sznaider (2006), Gesine Schwan (1997), Aleida Assmann (2012), or Claus Leggewie (2010) typically play double roles – as scholars of memory and as memory agents, balancing between postulative-normative and analytical-descriptive tone and language. Common to their concepts of a shared European memory is an understanding of the importance of critical confrontations with shameful moments in the national past and a plea for a dialogue between formerly opposing parts – conflicted nations, victims and perpetrators – moving towards an empathic acknowledgement of the other's suffering, and of complex historical roles and various gray zones. It is easy to track the source for such a conceptualized European memory in the historical process of coming to terms with the Second World War and the Holocaust, begun by West Germany's reckonings with the Third Reich from the late 1960s. Some scholars assess these constructions skeptically, calling the new 'European' memory a product of the reunited German memory politics that has been developing since the 1990s (Müller 2010).

Many examples of European commemorations on the official level, as well as a simple look at the cultural memory landscapes (museums and monuments) in Europe, show how the Holocaust has become the canon of European memory (Karlsson 2010). Daniel Levy and Natan Sznaider (2006) describe a process in which the Holocaust has been transformed into a universal symbol of good and evil, helping to create a moral community of remembrance, which in a common effort of 'Never again!' transgresses any national boundaries. In a similar vein, Tony Judt (2005) observed for Europe that Holocaust memory, institutionalized through museums and official memorial days, has become a culmination of the postwar period. Reflecting on the ongoing discussion about Europe and its memory, Charles S. Maier (2002) commented that the Holocaust and Nazism have constituted the 'hot memory', while other experiences, like the Soviet atrocities and communism suffered by East Europeans, do not arouse similar emotions on the international arena, remaining Europe's 'cold memory'.

The enlargement of the European Union to include countries of the former Eastern Bloc made it apparent that the constructions of European memory and identity thus far reflected mainly the experience of the Western countries. This impression was augmented by certain discrepancies that emerged in official commemorations and public discussions about European history. Against the conceptual backdrop of a shared European memory that developed in the last few years, dissonant voices emphasized the incompatible character of the region's historical experience which would not easily fit into a pan-European memory conceptualized from the Western perspective. More urgent from the perspective of Eastern European societies was not a new memory as a cultural and political project, but rather a coming to terms with a surfeit of memories which had not hitherto been publicly articulated or acknowledged.

The multiplicity of memories, often mutually conflicted, is what, according to Polish intellectual historian Jerzy Jedlicki (1999) determines the specific character of Eastern Europe. It is, he states, historical memory that fuels animosities and conflicts in the present. It comprises the sanctification of certain historical events in the form of powerful symbols and myths, and the memory of collective wrongs and losses suffered in the past from other nations, together with an awareness of wrongdoings inflicted on the others. But instead of repeating Santayana's adage that those who cannot remember the past are condemned to repeat it, Jedlicki argues, with Claus Offe, that he 'who remembers history is condemned to repeat it' (ibid. 225–226). Another Polish scholar, Robert Traba, states to the contrary that what fuels present conflicts is not excessive remembering but rather an institutionalized forgetting of the preceding communist era (Traba 2007). He evokes the example of the inter-ethnic conflicts in the former Yugoslavia: '[a]ll those decades of attempts to deceive memory, to supplant it with the imposed ideology of brotherhood and to push it into the taboo sphere – if during those years there had been attempts to face the memory, to find a vent for it, even if it would have divided people, then maybe it would not have returned in such a violent and destructive way?' Despite these opposing views, both Jedlicki and Traba agree that memories of the twentieth century are still hot in Eastern Europe, to borrow Charles S. Maier's phrasing, and it is premature to expect them to cool off in the mould of a common European memory.

East Europeans with their experience of communism are, however, not the only European other. To be fair, there are more than two competitive pasts, Nazism and communism, on the market of European memories.

Pakier and Stråth (2010) name at least one more dark past that Europe has yet to reckon with – this being colonialism, both external and internal, regarding native minorities. Claus Leggewie (2010) sees the landscape of European memory as consisting of seven ever further horizons that he calls circles of memory: the Holocaust as Europe's negative foundation myth, the memory of Soviet communism, pan-European narratives of mass expulsions in the twentieth century, memories of two world wars, the experience of colonialism, Europe as the continent of immigration and finally Europe's postwar story of democratization, economic growth and integration.

Increasingly there are calls to develop institutional frames in Europe for such a culture of memory wherein these various narratives of the past can be rightfully articulated. The memory culture that has developed around commemorations of the Holocaust has been too monolithic, focused on victims but representing the perspective of the witnesses and perpetrators – since, unlike in the United States (see, for example, Diner 2010), there were few Jews in Europe who could play the role of postwar memory agents. This 'negative' European memory (Knigge and Frei 2002) has in its ethical dimension been based on the questions of guilt and moral responsibility for the fate of European Jewry. Aleida Assmann (2013, and in this volume) observes that the positive aspect of this model of memory is that it is more sensitive to the perspective of the other: the heirs of, or groups representing historical witnesses and perpetrators express their sorrow for the fate of the victims, as in the symbolic kneeling by Willy Brandt in Warsaw in 1970. According to Assmann, it is such a 'dialogic' memory model that is open to alternative narratives of the past to build a common culture of remembrance in Europe. This model draws on the postwar German memory culture that has emphasized the dark and shameful chapters in national history and called for a critical coming to terms with them. Other authors, however, see a void of a different kind in the ongoing Europeanization of memory: missing are not just narratives that disrupt traditionally heroic national views of history but also those representing the native voice of the multitude of historical victim groups in Europe, including the multitude of minority groups that have not been given proper attention. On the following pages, Sławomir Kapralski will discuss the problem from the perspective of Roma, giving one example of how minority memories may shape, or be ignored by, public memories. Robert Traba's (2007) concept of a 'polyphonic' memory shows how important it is to open the public space for the various voices of historical victims who were only allowed to articulate their claims with the fall of communism. Victims, or groups representing them, also speak for themselves in Michael Rothberg's (2009) concept of 'multidirectional' memory. The concept, similar in some respect to the earlier 'global' memory by Daniel Levy and Natan Sznaider (2002; 2006; see also Sznaider 2013) shows how the Holocaust may become a moral symbol to be endowed with multiple meanings by other groups and minorities who endured their own suffering in the past. In these two concepts, the Holocaust provides the frame of European public memories as a moral reference to invoke while articulating new narratives of victimhood.

In light of the rise of the many competitive claims to mark 'their' past in the European canon of history, what does a 'hot' memory really mean? Is the Holocaust indeed the hot memory of Europe, as Charles S. Maier wrote? With the EU enlargement and growing immigration to Europe from other continents, the proportions of and relations between various symbolic interests supported by particular historical narratives have changed significantly. Dominated by the 'negative' Holocaust memory, Europe is gradually becoming a hotpot of new rival historical narratives brought in by new agents of memory to include: memories of the Holodomor (the Ukrainian man-made famine), memories of the Balkan conflict in the 1990s, or memories of the Armenian genocide contested by the Turkish minority living in the EU, to name a few. These will not be easily melded into one. The conflict or tension between them, however, is what prevents those memories from becoming ritualized in the established and acknowledged public forms of commemoration, keeping their temperature at high level. Comparing public memories of the Holocaust in the Czech Republic and Poland after 1989 Stanisław Tyszka (2010) observed that, paradoxically, the accelerated process of acknowledgement of the Holocaust victims' status in the Czech public memory through a large-scale property restitution and compensation programme did not provoke any thorough historical debates in this country. In Poland, on the contrary, there was no legal solution to the problem of Jewish restitution, and it is this lack of symbolic closure, Tyszka argues, visible not just in the lack of restitution laws but in the public debate more generally, which is the guarantee that the Holocaust, and the broader context of Polish-Jewish historical relations, will continue for many years to shape historical debates in Poland, thus remaining the Polish 'hot' memory. Sławomir Kapralski in this volume observes quite similarly, referring to present Polish-Jewish encounters in Poland, that melancholic remembrance and 'un-mastered' past may well be a sign of a less visible, yet serious memory work.

What still fuels the debate on European memory is in fact the recognition of its internal divisions and exclusions. Gradually the landscape of memories in Europe is taking on more colours and shades. By discussing the particularities of the 'others' – East Europeans, immigrants, older minorities and non-European wannabes, and their status within a projected European memory – the process of Europeanization has not halted, but goes on. It is conflicts, controversy, discussion and the multitude of competitive memories that keep the debate on European history and memory alive and give it ongoing appeal.

Yet there is always the temptation of exceptionalism in the case of particular memory groups. It is a fact that East European memories are too willingly imagined by their construers and agents – scholars, politicians and other practitioners of memory – as a 'special' European case, slipping easily into the role of an *enfant terrible* of European memory. Sandra Kalniete's speech from 2004 has almost become paradigmatic, leading to rough formulations of differences in public memories between West and East such as Gulag contra Shoah (Droit 2007), or even volume titles, such as *Clashes in European Memory: The Case of Communist Repression and the Holocaust* (Blaive et al. 2011). As a new regional construct, the memory of Eastern Europe, based on the experience of two totalitarianisms, a more painful experience of the Second World War and decades of communism, often lashes out in polemics towards pan-European memory projects. In this process, Western Europe becomes an important incentive for identity building in Eastern Europe. The perceived cohesive and conflictless West invites constructions of self-indulging East European myths of uniqueness, based on convictions of a special kind of historical experience that is incomparable and of a fundamentally different character to that of the West. In this manner conceptualized history aims to juxtapose the East European historical experience with projects of a common European memory. This again pushes East European memory agents towards the peripheries of Europe, showing how important it remains for the former to observe themselves in the mirror of the latter.

The situation presents a challenge for memory scholars as well: how can they describe the memory processes taking place in Eastern Europe without neglecting their original, autonomous character by too easily referring to Western memory categories? And at the same time, how can they avoid the trap of constructing new myths of East European uniqueness? Finally, putting these two pleas together, how can they describe the meaning of memory phenomena in Eastern Europe so that the value of such studies is not purely anecdotal but preserves relevance for broader memory studies, and may be applied to other regions and contexts? In other words, can Eastern European memory research fruitfully draw upon global studies of memory, while at the same time avoid falling into an intellectually peripheral realm, and go on to fertilize broader theories and research with original findings and concepts? Below we propose to look at these questions in the context of the discipline development – the state of memory research in Eastern Europe and its position within global studies on memory.

Framing Eastern Europe – The New Wave of Research

A dominant current in memory studies is the fact that they have been largely shaped by a Western perspective. Put simply – in the domains of history, sociology, social psychology and cultural studies – this international English-language scholarship has referred to three main roots: French, German and Anglo-American writings,[1] and as we have argued elsewhere (Wawrzyniak and Pakier 2013), in the international field of memory studies, contributions by scholars from Eastern Europe have, until recently, mostly been lacking. Does this imply that memory issues have not been studied there? Quite the contrary, as is evident from bookshelves, special issues of journals and numerous conferences in these countries. The selected national states of research have been examined recently by several scholars, such as Doubravka Olšáková (2012) on the Czech Republic, Alina Kurhajcová (2012) on Slovakia, Ferenc Laczó and Máté Zombory (2012) on Hungary, Jörg Hackmann (2008, 2009) on the Baltic States, Piotr Filipkowski (2012), as well as Robert Traba (2011) on Poland. Such detailed overviews show that a respectable amount of work is being done in various disciplines: from micro-history, anthropology, political history, to the sociology of collective memory. Moreover, these efforts often share characteristics with their 'Western' memory studies counterparts as well as have long research traditions (Kończal and Wawrzyniak 2012; Kilias 2013; Tarkowska 2013). Yet this literature has remained largely unnoticed at the forefront of international memory studies.

The reason for the broader neglect of such regionally pursued Eastern European research seems apparent; local authors are not often cited internationally due to communication barriers: books and articles written in 'minor' languages are hardly recognized beyond national borders. Conversely, however, such locally produced scholarship has not always paid much attention to the counterpart literature in English, German and French, and only in rare instances to other authors from the region. Therefore, Laczó and Zombory (2012: 106) speak of a 'notorious time lag between international and local references' and Kończal and Wawrzyniak (2011: 11–40) of the lack of mutual recognition and selectivity.

Recently, however, new publications have appeared that allow us to speak of a new wave in memory research on Eastern Europe, represented both by East European and non-East European scholars. Characteristic of the new studies is that they treat Eastern Europe as their proper subject of research, using a broad range of methodological tools to describe the variety of narratives of the past, their functions and the historical contexts in which they were sustained or emerged in the public life of communist and postcommunist societies. Specific to the new wave is that scholars are better trained theoretically and employ tools that used to be only postulates, like the category of memory agents, the relations between biographical and collective memories, local memories, etc. In this new research Eastern Europe is not merely a supplement to discussions about European memory but becomes the very subject of comparative and transnational studies. Certainly the new opening was made possible by the earlier works on European memory named in the above section, as well as their growing reception and that of memory studies more generally by scholars in Eastern Europe. The new interest in the East European region has been also paralleled by the appearance of various multidisciplinary platforms (international projects, conferences, web pages) that facilitate exchanges of experience.[2]

Comparative scholars representing the new wave have found in Eastern Europe a suitable subject for studying relevant areas of memory studies, from general concern of cultures of memory, *Erinnerungskulturen* (Cornelißen, Holec, Pešek 2005), to more specific aspects, such as international and domestic policies and the political use of the histories of communism and the Second World War (Mink and Neumayer 2013; Miller and Lipman 2012; Mälksoo 2009), historiography versus memory (Kopeček 2008a), or sites of memory (Weber et al. 2011). Here are some leading examples of transnational research: the German historian Stefan Troebst (2005; 2013) works systematically on regional divisions of Europe in the tradition of Halecki (1950), Zernack (1977) and Szücs (1983), asking about transnational patterns of postcommunist cultures of remembrance in Eastern Europe versus similarly analytically distinguished Atlantic-Western European and German cultures of memory. In this respect, in Eastern Europe he identifies four clusters of countries: the first encompasses societies with a strong anticommunist consensus (e.g. Baltic States); the second includes societies characterized by an intense public debate on how history should be valued and commemorated (e.g. Hungary, Poland, Ukraine); the third comprises countries where public attempts to delegitimize the communist past were relatively weak (e.g. Bulgaria, Romania, Serbia, Albania); and the fourth cluster includes societies where communism has not suffered a loss of legitimacy (e.g. Belarus, Russia). Troebst (2010c) was also the leading scholar of a project comparing the memory cultures of Europe's southern and eastern semi-peripheries with regard to their coming to terms with dictatorial pasts, thereby extending Linz and Stepan's (1996) questions of the transitional politics and democratic consolidation in these regions.

The legacy of communist dictatorships was also a key topic of a book by British scholar James Mark (2010), whose research covered Poland,

Hungary, Romania, the Czech Republic, Latvia, Lithuania and Estonia. Significantly, Mark did not stop at examining the official memory of transitory politics in these countries, such as history commissions and institutes of national memory, nor did he omit analysing the cultural memory of communism at terror sites and in museums. Although these parts of his work are already appealing for their stress on the contingency, non-linearity and unpredictability of both commemorative narratives and aesthetics, the real breadth of his research lies in his analysis of oral history interviews with over a hundred representatives of Hungarian, Czech Republic and Polish intelligentsia, including party members and former oppositionists. With this example, Mark shows how individuals tend to 'write' themselves into public (conflicting) post-1989 narratives, using them as resources to shape their own biographies.

A Polish sociologist, Karolina Wigura (2011) uses the paradigm of reconciliation and the politics of regret to compare German-Polish and Ukrainian-Polish relations since the 1990s with regard to history. This paradigm refers to the international circulation of grammars of apologies and pleas for forgiveness (Mink and Neumayer 2013: 1). Wigura shows how the politics of reconciliation have played well in Poland's contacts with its Western neighbour. With Ukraine, however, while similar political rituals were employed in the commemoration of atrocities during the Second World War as mutually inflicted by the people of the two countries, the author describes the latter in terms of a 'reconciliation kitsch', stressing its inadequate character that has lacked any real political or social impact, in this example pointing to limits of the apology diplomacy.

In another comparative work, Małgorzata Pakier (2013) analyses German and Polish cinematic discourses on the Holocaust and the Second World War in the broad context of public debates in the two countries, including historical works, media and politics. In each country the social, cultural and political processes of Holocaust reckoning were subordinated to the commemoration of national pasts, being framed by categories such as heroism, defeat, victimhood and resistance. Yet also in both countries, newer narratives have been developed, especially in films, towards more universal interpretations. These are framed in terms of 'ordinary people' rather than nations, and they have presented a more critical challenge to national reflection.

An interesting conceptual innovation in memory studies was recently formulated by culture scholars working on the project 'Memory at War: Cultural Dynamics in Poland, Russia and Ukraine'. In a dialogue with Pierre Nora's concept of *lieux de mémoire*, which means material and non-material symbols of a given community that 'stop time', they propose a category of a 'memory event': 'deteritorialized and temporal phenomena that ... "start time" by endowing the past with new life in the future' (Etkind, Finnin et al. 2012: 10). This is not a language game, but a serious reconceptualization of a key memory studies concept in such a way that it can fit transnational agenda and the media society. The authors show how fruitful it can be by comparing and tracing the postwar circulation of representations of the Katyn mass murder (1940) in Poland, Ukraine, Belorussia, Russia and the Baltic States and show how this movement was fuelled by Andrzej Wajda's movie *Katyn* (2007) on the subject as well as by the Polish presidential plane crash in Smoleńsk in 2010.

This background is sketched mainly by political questions, whether going deeply into personal accounts as in Mark's book, or into the realms of ethics as in the book by Wigura, or of culture as in the study by Pakier, or Etkind, Finnin et al. Noteworthy too is work by scholars such as Maria Todorova, who point to the variety of genres of remembrance in postcommunist societies rather than to their consistency, including various forms of postcommunist nostalgia (e.g. Todorova and Gille 2010). Also distanced from the present context of contemporary politics is one of the largest bilateral Polish-German history projects of recent years, i.e. the 'Polish-German *lieux de mémoire*' (*Polsko-niemieckie miejsca pamięci*), led by Robert Traba and Hans Henning Hahn. The multi-volume bilingual project does not limit itself to the national, but points to the 'open-ended', trans-local symbols and patterns of meaning (Górny et al. 2012; see also Kończal 2012). In such works the ongoing dynamics and change, shifting categories, borderlands, changing borders and moving military fronts comprise the dominating rhetoric and the topoi recurring in the accounts of historical and mnemonic processes.

This new wave of transnational research on Eastern Europe with its focus on regional memory travels, borrowings and conflicts invites us to look for some integration, as we have argued elsewhere, and proposed to consider the East European region as one of the frameworks of memory (Wawrzyniak and Pakier 2013). In other words, to extend Halbwachs' (1925) concept of social frameworks of memory so as to include a region as one of them. A framework 'in essence ... is a series of images of the past and a set of relationships that specify how these images are to be ordered' (Middleton and Brown 2011: 35). Importantly, individuals locate their own processes of remembering in various frameworks, ranging from face-to-face interactions in primary groups, such as family, through local and national images up to such representations of the past that have achieved global recognition, such as the Holocaust. Which framework(s) they actually use to recall or narrate particular events depends on specific circumstances. What is more, it is possible to imagine that frameworks may interfere with one another without disrupting the actual processes of individual remembrance. In this context, we do not intend to replace 'family', 'occupational', 'national', 'European' or 'global' with 'regional' frameworks, but merely to indicate the latter's existence.

In this proposition, a 'regional' framework is not a predefined, essentialist, or purely geographical category. But it is understood as a set of discursive and physiognomic mechanisms beyond national frames, albeit of a limited, not global influence. That is, there are sets of representations which are only regionally intelligible and significant but are unlikely to attain global (or at least pan-European) importance. For instance, the French or Italians are not particularly interested in the Volyn massacre (1943), whereas it has become an important and conflicting transnational *lieu de mémoire* for Poles and Ukrainians by means of the activities of various memory agents (politicians, journalists, historians, NGO activities, victims' associations), as well as a point of reference for further discussion of the past. Moreover, it is important to stress that there is not one but rather multiple Eastern European frameworks of memory, depending on the historical event(s) which are remembered and the agents involved in commemoration. Still, making use of Eastern Europe as an umbrella concept makes sense since its societies were once influenced by a Soviet-type metanarrative and also by some resistance to it. Working through communism is thus very often a filter for other representations, especially for Fascism and Nazism (Mark 2010: 93–125). Therefore, it is not claimed here that individuals born and socialized in Eastern Europe remember in some 'special' ways in comparison to the rest of the world, but instead that there exists some specific set of discursive practices related to particular historical events that happened in this part of Europe.

Volume Overview – Meeting the Challenge of Regional Specificity and Socio-Political Changes

The subject of this volume is memories, and reflection on memories, of historical violence, in particular of the Second World War and communism in Eastern Europe, in the context of broader debate on European history, memory and identity. Rather than presenting a full and systemic overview of East European memory processes, we chose to emphasize those aspects that employ or question the regional specificity vis á vis the imagined Western European, or European, memory.[3] We use 'Eastern Europe' as an umbrella term to refer to the countries of the former Eastern Bloc, which in the twentieth century experienced double totalitarianism, wars and decades of communism (or real socialism) and Soviet dependency. Although the intention was not to bring up the Cold War as the only defining historical experience, the Iron Curtain dividing European societies in the second half of the twentieth century still represents a valid reference point when discussing European memories in the ensuing two-and-a-half decades. We do not examine memory processes in Russia, although Russia remains one of the major points of reference for discussions in many of the following chapters. The authors in this volume will refer to the geopolitical area of their research in various ways, sometimes as Eastern Europe, and in other places as Central and Eastern Europe, or Central-Eastern Europe. The choice of term depends not only on the subject of research itself, but also on the authors' position, which may be more global, thus inviting writing more generally about Eastern Europe, or more regional, inviting more nuanced phrasing.

The volume brings together scholars of various disciplines – historians, sociologists and anthropologists – to reflect on questions related to the specificities of research on memories in Eastern Europe, considered in its regional, broader European and global contexts. Contributors to the volume seek to establish the relevance of memory transformation in Eastern Europe for the overall debate on European memory, as well as to read the East European historical experience anew through the European debate.

Memory Dialogues and Monologues

The volume begins with Aleida Assmann and Andrzej Nowak's ideas on how European memory has been considered, and how it may yet be viewed. The two scholars represent two different perspectives. Aleida Assmann's subject is the development of traditional national narratives about the past towards inclusive memories, open to alternative perspectives represented by minority groups or other nations. She calls these 'dialogic' memories, while the processes that prepared the ground for them were the self-critical reckonings with national pasts that have taken place in various European countries, including in Eastern Europe, during the last two decades. Such dialogic memories allow for the development of a shared international memory culture, i.e., a European one. Andrzej Nowak detects an opposite trend, however, in which it is an already existing European consensus that is producing and imposing memory canons, that the author critically terms political correctness. This, according to the author, will not result in a shared historical awareness but instead equals a distortion of authentic memories of national communities. While providing different answers, both authors ask the same questions: What should the memory of Europeans look like? How should the differing, often conflicted, memories be organized? Can they co-exist? What memories have been overshadowed in the process so far of coming to terms with the twentieth-century past, both on national and international levels? These normative considerations provide a background for the following sections.

Eastern Europe as a (Unique) Mnemonic Framework?

The chapters in this section deal with the question of Eastern Europe as a potentially separate mnemonic region. They explore whether East European history has been unique, and whether the resulting mnemonic processes have developed along autonomous paths not comparable to the mnemonic processes of West Europeans. Kornelia Kończal and Maciej Górny open the section with a discussion of what challenges the region presents for memory scholarship, especially as regards the concept of *lieu de mémoire*, and how its premises have been formulated and may be further reformulated when applied to the region. Initially, scholars in this part of Europe did not see the need for its appropriation in their attempts at rewriting the national history, because this was done by means of other categories; however, contemporary scholarship from the region contributes to the reconceptualization of the notion beyond national frameworks, by acknowledging the internal diversity as inherently characteristic of the region. Another author in this section, Sławomir Kapralski, deals with the question of Eastern Europe's alleged uniqueness based on the example of the commemoration of the Jewish Holocaust and the Roma extermination. The author argues that these processes have not differed in Western and Eastern Europe, merely that their temporal situating was not synchronized. Both West and East have gone through periods of forgetting, as well as the opposite process of ritualization of memory. Despite this fact, myths were formulated about the special nature of memory in Eastern Europe which resulted from, and in turn contributed to an 'othering' of Eastern Europe. Next, Kaja Kaźmierska analyses the question of East European 'otherness' from the perspective of the relation between individual and collective memories. They mutually shape each other, national history becoming a frame for changes in perception of individual biographies, and vice versa, individual experience becoming a filter for the comprehension of national pasts. The individual and the collective are in constant communication, whereby the collective is dynamically reworked by the individual. In this way the author opposes another myth in scholarship on Eastern Europe which projects a one-way direction of influences in this process (individual-collective), as if based solely on power relationships.

The region's special condition, as reflected upon by the authors, is its dynamically changing history, resulting in shifting borders, the changed composition of local populations, ruptured institutional continuity and changing power centres. The question of change and transformation as framing memories in Eastern Europe, and how the latter face the change, is continued in the next part of the book.

East European Memories Facing Historical and Cultural Transformations

In this section the authors analyse processes of remembrance in various countries of Eastern Europe placed in the context of disruption of traditional cultural, political and institutional forms as a result of processes such as the collapse of communism, democratic transformation, globalization, growing multiculturalization, accession to the EU and growing integration of the European continent. In this part, cultural, political and social changes provide frameworks for memory processes that are subject of analysis. Joanna Michlic discusses how democratization after 1989 has influenced the shape of memory of the Holocaust, towards acknowledging the latter as the East European 'dark past'. Next, we find Lidia Zessin-Jurek's analysis of the reformulation of Gulag memories in the new context of Europe enlarging to the east. Subsequently, Stanisław Tyszka compares the Czech and Polish postcommunist public memories, and within this two different paths the two countries chose with regard to compensating the victims of property violations under previous regimes. In the next chapter, Tatiana Zhurzhenko studies the post-Soviet memory politics in the Ukrainian-Russian borderland region, including simultaneous processes of pluralization and nationalization of memories of the Second World War. Following this, Georgiy Kasianov discusses processes of formation of new Ukrainian memories and identities against the dynamically changing politics in the country between the 1990s and 2000s. The section closes with Judy Brown's analysis from the perspective of a Western ethnographer, and a tourist, of how the traditional historical narratives inscribed in the city space of Sevastopol can be read anew in the new context of globalization.

Foci of Memories in Eastern Europe

The last section of the volume deals with memories of selected events and phenomena in twentieth-century history and earlier that have provided the most studied topics of regional research, thereby defining Eastern Europe within memory studies. The contributors analyse these both in public realms and on the individual level. In this section are chapters by Piotr Kwiatkowski on the history of Polish memories of the Second World War; by Jacek Chrobaczyński and Piotr Trojański on Auschwitz and

Katyn as similar and competitive memory sites in Polish memory; then by Matthias Weber on memories of the German presence in Eastern Europe; next, by Yana Yancheva on memories of collectivization in Bulgaria; and finally, a comparative discussion by Claudia-Florentina Dobre of public memories of communism in Bulgaria and Romania.

Notes

1. With Maurice Halbwachs as the protagonist of the memory studies field as such, and Pierre Nora's concept of *lieux de mémoire* as an innovative push in the 1970s and 1980s towards its development. Among German authors Aby Warburg and Hermann Ebbinghaus are canonized as important founders in cultural studies and psychology respectively, then Jan Assmann and Aleida Assmann (cultural theory) and Harald Welzer (social psychology) as the leading contemporaries. Among the classics of Anglo-American writings one finds the psychology of Frederic Bartlett on the one hand and the sociology of George H. Mead, Charles H. Cooley, or W. Lloyd Warner on the other. Meanwhile among contemporaries there is a wide range of concepts, such as Jay Winter's sites of memory, Marianne Hirsch's postmemory, Daniel Levy and Nathan Sznaider's cosmopolitan memory, plus others, as enumerated by Conway (2010) and in readers by Olick et al. (2011), Erll and Nünning (2010), Boyer and Werstch (2009) and Radstone and Schwarz (2010).
2. Examples: 'Geschichtswerkstatt Europa' at the Remembrance, Responsibility and Future Foundation (www.geschichtswerkstatt-europa.org); 'Memory at War: Cultural Dynamics in Poland, Russia and Ukraine' – Cambridge, Bergen, Helsinki, Tartu, Groningen (www.memoryatwar.org); 'Genealogies of Memory in Central Eastern Europe' project at European Network of Remembrance and Solidarity (www.genealogies.enrs.eu); 'Colloquium Vilnense' (www.ehu.lt/en/events/show/colloquium-vilnense-2013-discussion-series-on-memory); 'Forum Geschichtskulturen' at Imre Kertész Kolleg Jena (www.imre-kertesz-kolleg.uni-jena.de/index.php?id=212).
3. The volume does not focus, for example, on museums, democratic opposition, or religion and churches. Those issues were recently examined by other authors. For an analysis of the role of museums and memorials in the East European memory processes, see Silberman and Vatan 2013, François et al. 2013, and Bogumil, Wawrzyniak et al. 2015. For democratic opposition, see Watson 1994, Mark 2010, and Von Plato et al. 2013. For religion and churches, see Buzalka 2007 and Ramet 2014. For the memory of 1989–1991 systemic transformation in particular, see Bernhard and Kubik 2014.

Małgorzata Pakier is a sociologist and historian, and head of the research department at the Museum of the History of Polish Jews in Warsaw. She received her PhD from the European University Institute in Florence, Italy. Together with Joanna Wawrzyniak she is the author and coordinator of the programme 'Genealogies of Memory in Central and Eastern

Europe', at the European Network of Remembrance and Solidarity. She is the author of *The Construction of European Holocaust Memory. German and Polish Cinema after 1989* (2013), and *A European Memory? Contested Histories and Politics of Remembrance* (co-edited with B. Stråth, 2010, 2012). Her research interests include: cultural memory and media of memory, including film and museums, Europeanization of memory, institutionalization of memory studies in Eastern Europe, Holocaust memory and representation and recently, Jewish involvement in the communist movement from biographical perspectives.

Joanna Wawrzyniak is deputy director at the Institute of Sociology, University of Warsaw, where she is also the head of the Social Memory Laboratory. Her academic interests are: politics of memory and memory cultures, including veteran and war victims' organizations and museums, history and theory of memory research in Central and Eastern Europe and the oral history of democratic opposition and deindustrialization processes in Poland. Among her recent publications are: *The Enemy on Display: The Second World War in Eastern European Museums* (co-authored with Zuzanna Bogumił et al., 2015), *Veterans, Victims and Memory: The Politics of the Second World War in Communist Poland* (forthcoming 2015) and numerous articles and book chapters on memory issues. In 2013/2014 she was a visiting fellow at Imre Kertész Kolleg Jena. Since 2012 she has been coordinator of the programme 'Genealogies of Memory in Central and Eastern Europe', together with Małgorzata Pakier.

PART I
Memory Dialogues and Monologues

Chapter 1

THE TRANSFORMATIVE POWER OF MEMORY

Aleida Assmann

The title of my chapter is double-edged. It refers to the power of memory that transforms people, societies and states, but it also looks at the transformations that memory itself undergoes over the years and under external influences. I will pursue this double activity in different realms and contexts. I will start with a shift in the cultural frameworks that has helped to create a new discourse on memory, then I will look at external and internal factors that change memory and finally I will inspect more closely the shift from old to new policies of remembering, which tap the transformative power of memory in situations of political and social change.

From the Modernist Frame to the Memory Frame

The idea that memory has transformative power is quite a new one and was developed only during the last thirty years. This shift in our thinking became manifest in a new term that surfaced in German discourse in the 1990s and has since become part and parcel of the trite stock of official and public rhetoric, namely *Erinnerungskultur* (memory culture). We have developed the great hope that memory can be conducive to changing human minds, hearts and habits and even whole societies and states in the process of overcoming a traumatic history of violence. Many people assume today that traumatic violence can be overcome by negotiating mutual strategies of memory and visions of the past. All over the world, the transformative power of memory is invoked to diffuse the pernicious fuel of violence. It is implemented after periods of autocratic and

---

Notes for this chapter begin on page 37.

genocidal violence (the Holocaust, Latin American dictatorships, South African apartheid, the Balkan War) as well as in response to the lasting impact of older genocides and crimes against humanity (such as European colonialism and slavery).

We must ask ourselves if this assumption is really true. What has made us so optimistic? What is our hope grounded on, or are we driven by an illusion? Let me start with a scholar who does not believe in the transformative power of memory. Historian Christian Meier (2010), for instance, has expressed his dissent and argues for forgetting rather than remembering as a transformative power that leads to overcoming a pernicious past and opening a new page of history. Meier argues as a historian, drawing attention to the policy of forgetting as an age-old strategy for containing the explosive force of conflicting memories. His examples are not only distant in time such as the Greek polis after the Peloponnesian War, or the peace treaty of Münster-Osnabrück 1648, after another civil war, which contains the formula: *'perpetua oblivio et amnestia'*.[1] This policy, which goes hand in hand with a blanket amnesty in order to end mutual hatred and achieve a new social integration of formerly opposed parties is not a thing of the past. Even after 1945 it was widely used as a political resource. It is true that the International Court at Nuremberg had dispensed transitional justice by indicting major Nazi functionaries for the newly defined 'crime against humanity'. This, however, was an act of purging rather than of remembering the past. In postwar Germany, the public sphere and that of official diplomacy remained largely shaped by what was called *kollektives Beschweigen* – 'a pact of silence' (Assmann and Frevert 1999: 76–78). The term comes from Hermann Lübbe who in 1983 made the point that maintaining silence was a necessary pragmatic strategy adopted in postwar Germany (and supported by the Allies) to facilitate the economic and political reconstruction of the state and the integration of society (Lübbe 2007). Forgetting, or the pact of silence, also became a strategy of European politics during the time of the Cold War, in which much had to be forgotten in order to consolidate the new Western military alliance against that of the communist bloc (Judt 2005). As an example, let me refer to a speech that Winston Churchill gave in Zurich in 1946 in which he demanded an end to 'the process of reckoning', declaring:

> We must all turn our backs upon the horrors of the past. We must look to the future. We cannot afford to drag forward across the years that are to come the hatreds and revenges which have sprung from the injuries of the past. If Europe is to be saved from infinite misery, and indeed from final doom, there must be an act of faith in the European family and an act of oblivion against all the crimes and follies of the past. (Churchill 1948: 200)[2]

Within the cultural framework of the 1940s to the 1960s, forgetting was considered to be a means to dissolve the divisive negative emotions of the past. As resentment and hatred are supported, continued and refuelled through memory, it was assumed that forgetting rather than remembering would help to overcome a violent past and open up a new future.

There are, however, two contrary ways of looking at forgetting: it can be seen as a positive resource for leaving a troubled past behind and creating the potential for a new future, or it can be considered as a form of suppression and continuation of violence. Whether it is remembering or forgetting that is credited with a transformative power depends on larger cultural frameworks and values that change over time. Moving from forgetting to remembering implied what I would like to call the shift from a *modernist* to a *moralist* perspective. The modernist spirit of innovation and orientation towards the future is based on a positive notion of temporal ruptures that contain the possibility of leaving the past behind. The moralistic or therapeutic perspective, on the other hand, prescribes a re-engagement with a traumatic past in order to work through and overcome it. During the last three decades, the general modernist trust in the automatic regenerative power of the future that had been a central value of modernism shared by European countries in both East and West has been eroded. In its stead, a new concern with the abiding impact of violent pasts has entered our thinking, feeling and acting, not only in Europe but in many other parts of the world as well. This is what I mean when I speak of a shift of attitude from the 'modernist frame' to the 'memory frame'.

External and Internal Factors of Change

There are various external and internal factors that can promote the transformative power of memory. Let me start with some external factors. Personal memory remains restricted, constrained and devalued if it is deliberately cut off from historical sources. The closing or opening of historical archives is therefore an important transformative factor. If sources are made publicly accessible and are recognized in public discourse, this can have a profound effect on a national memory. After the end of the Cold War, for instance, the opening of Eastern European archives changed the prevailing national maps of memory considerably. As the scope and complexity of Holocaust memory expanded, it challenged some firmly established positive national self-images. New documents about Vichy and the history of anti-Semitism in East Germany put an end to the self-image of France or the GDR as pure resisters; after the scandal around Waldheim and the book about Jedwabne, Austria (that had cultivated the comfortable self-image of being Hitler's first victim since the *Anschluss* in 1938) and Poland were no longer able to claim an exclusive victim status, and even the seemingly neutral Swiss were confronted with their own 'sites of memory' in the form of their banks and borders. As new evidence documenting collaboration or indifference towards this crime against humanity ushered in heated debates, the clear and simple structure of dominant national narratives had to become more complex and inclusive. As long as archives remain closed, political power exerts control over memory and the national self-image.

Another important external factor is the impact of media. Books or films – if they are innovative, carry an effective charge or are well-timed – can stimulate public debates and change the social climate of discussion. An example of a powerful media intervention into German memory was the American TV series *Holocaust*, which was televised in Germany in 1979. It is now generally agreed that this series managed to do what public Holocaust education had hitherto not been able to do: to tap the emotions of a wide range of the population and to open up the blocked channels of empathy for Jewish victims. While many critics denigrated the quality of the series as a trivial product of American mass culture, historians such as Saul Friedländer and sociologists like Daniel Levy and Natan Sznaider (2005) have emphasized the transformative power of this televisual event. (I learned later that many younger Germans were forbidden by their parents to watch the series, which, of course, only stimulated their interest in this topic.)

This brings me to a third factor that is of paramount importance for the transformation of memory. With this factor we are moving from external to internal influences. Memory exists not only in the shape of external media, archives and monuments, but also as embodied memory that is communicated across *generations* living together and interacting in a synchronic relationship. According to sociologists who have investigated this field, each generation is shaped by its decisive lifetime experiences that influence its thinking and feeling. Values, affections, loyalties and a specific weight of the past colours their consciousness, their mindset and emotions. This generational memory is not only transmitted from generation to generation but also periodically challenged, questioned and refuted by the younger one. In this way, generational memories are exposed to continuous conflict and contestation within a society.

Inter-generational dynamics are a central factor in changing the course of memory. A common and even normative pattern in Western cultures is the revolt of sons and daughters against the hegemony of their parents. The young protestors are allowed and expected to deviate from, and break with, prevailing traditions and values. In Germany this generational tension, which is built into the dynamics of Western culture, was reinforced by the 1968 generation's desire to break with their parents' continuing silent loyalties with the Nazi period. In their revolt, they enacted a violent cultural break in which they cut themselves off from the contaminated legacy of the past. The sociologist Rainer Mario Lepsius has coined the term 'externalization' which can be applied to this desire to break away and start anew (Lepsius 1989). Twenty years later, when the 1968ers had themselves become fathers and mothers, they changed this attitude considerably towards what Lepsius would call 'internalization'. It took the form of reconnecting with the family and working through the national past in a more empathetic and self-critical way, taking into account their own place in the generational chain.

The generational change can be of great importance for the introduction of a new perspective in national memory. One example is the famous speech of West German president Richard von Weizsäcker in 1985 in which he taught the Germans to think of 8 May 1945 no longer in terms of defeat and occupation but rather in terms of liberation. He gave this speech at a moment when there was a dwindling number of people who belonged to the generation that had actually experienced a defeat and experienced shorter or longer terms of imprisonment. The younger generations, on the other hand, had grown up in a democracy that had become an integral part of Western Europe in which the spirit of liberation had spilled across national borders.

The crucial importance of generations as carriers of memory can also be seen in the aftermath of the Spanish Civil War. In Spain there was indeed a 'pact of silence', or forgetfulness, which, however, did not come about immediately at the end of the Civil War (1936–1939), but was postponed for almost four decades until Franco's dictatorship ended with his death in 1975. The pact of silence in 1977 was intended to underpin the transition (*transición*) from autocracy to democracy. This transition has been characterized as 'the birth of democracy out of the spirit of dictatorship' (Schüle 2003: 22). All political crimes prior to 1977 were granted an amnesty by the unwritten law of silence. The option of forgetting was in accord with a widespread consensus in society at the time. Nearly forty years after the end of the Civil War, the Spanish were prepared to let the problems of the past be kept in the past, so as not to endanger their fragile democracy. It was the second generation after the Civil War that bypassed issues relating to guilt or mourning in the interests of consolidating a common future. Starting in the mid-1990s and culminating in the years after the turn of the century, the layers of silence enshrouding the violent past became increasingly porous; Republican counter-memory began rediscovering the hidden past through an exhumation project, skeleton by skeleton.

This new memory impulse originated in the third generation, which went looking for the bodies of their lost grandparents and found them dispersed throughout the country. What their parents had chosen not to do – to act on behalf of the first generation of victims – the grandchildren took up as their specific generational projects; identifying Franco's dead and working as self-declared advocates of historical memory with the help of archaeologists, anthropologists and geneticists. The pact of silence that the second generation had endorsed enabled a transition to democracy, but it did not dissolve the traumatic legacy of violence. Instead, it consolidated a deep division within society, materially preserved in the earth and in family memories.

In 2007, nearly seventy years after the end of the Civil War and three decades after the second generation's pact of silence, another shift in the Spanish policy of forgetting occurred. Prime Minister José Luis Zapatero, himself the grandson of a Republican grandfather who was murdered and whose body disappeared, rescinded the amnesty law after thirty years, which amounts to the time span of a generation. He passed the 'Law of Historical Remembrance' (*Ley de Memoria Histórica*) in parliament which condemned the fascist dictatorship for the first time, assuring its victims of recognition and restitution. Zapatero not only conceded here to the internal pressure of Republican family memories, he was also responding to changes in the general political climate of remembrance which favoured recalling the crimes of states and dictatorships even after such an extended period of time. In a landscape saturated with Franquist symbols, the hidden and hitherto neglected sites where the victims were unceremoniously disposed of have become the most significant *lieux de mémoire* for Republicans. The need for recognition that is felt by family members and their descendants encompasses the rehabilitation and propitiation of the dead. Within the time span of communicative memory, it is obviously the task of the third generation to mourn and to bury the dead, performing this last ritual duty of commemoration for their grandparents. The act of recovering and laying to rest the hidden and forgotten dead refers us to an important transformative power or memory that is rooted in the cultural dimension of religion and ritual.

From Monologic to Dialogic Memory Policies

From these personal and private acts of ritual remembrance let me come back to the public and political context and discuss in more detail the paradigmatic shift from *forgetting* to *remembering* in terms of the new memory policies that we have seen emerging. Before addressing these new policies, let me first say a few words about the old ones, which – alas – appear to be still thriving and continue to be in active use. Edward Said (2000) characterized this traditional memory policy succinctly when he wrote: 'Memory and its representations touch very significantly upon questions of identity, of nationalism, of power and authority' (ibid. 176). In this context of power and politics, he added, the past has always been 'something to be used, misused and exploited' (ibid. 179). Such transformation of history into memory is based on two important dimensions: political myths and national *lieux de mémoire*. Said defined myth in this context as the 'power of narrative history to mobilize people around a common goal' (ibid. 184). He argued that in a world of 'decreasing efficacy of religious, familial, and dynastic bonds ... people now look to this refashioned memory, especially in its collective forms, to give themselves a coherent identity, a national narrative, a place in the world' (ibid. 179).

Lieux de mémoire are more diverse than political myths; it is their function to provide the nation with a sense of its distinct identity, rooting it in symbolic time and space, emotionally charged common references and shared cultural practices. Pierre Nora's concept is today also undergoing changes that reflect a shift from monologic to more complex memory constructs. Nora's inventory of common historical and cultural references reflected a strong French cult of the national. In the meantime, his concept has been widely imitated but also transformed with each new context in which it is applied (Kreis 2008/2009). In addition to many national variations,[3] new transnational models are currently being explored and tested, such as Heinz Duchardt's European *lieux de mémoire* (Boer et al. 2011–2012) or Hans Henning Hahn and Robert Traba's (2012–2013) impressive collaboration project on German and Polish memory sites. The new projects are often less normative and self-affirming and more self-reflexive and critical, including also traumatic and contested sites. Nora's holistic notion of the nation has also been exchanged for a new emphasis on different social milieus and ethnic experiences. This open and inclusive approach is of special significance at a time when nation states are undergoing a structural change and reconfiguring their memories to make room for the experience of migrant minorities. The lasting success of Nora's concept seems to lie in its great flexibility and adaptability. Its updated versions are doing much more justice to the diversity of social and regional groups and counter-memories, pointing even to gaps of oblivion or what is chosen not to be remembered.

As Said emphasized, there is a direct connection between historical memory and nation building. The power of such a memory lies not in an event but in the effective narrative rendering of the event, which aims at creating a distinct profile and positive self-image 'as part of trying to gain independence. To become a nation in the formal sense of the word, a people must make itself into something more than a collection of tribes, or political organizations' (Said 2000: 184). Said wrote this from the point of view of the Palestinians and their 'inability to produce a convincing narrative story with a beginning, middle and end' (ibid. 185) and who as a consequence, according to him, have remained 'scattered and politically ineffective victims of Zionism' (ibid.).

In the old framework, national memories were mainly constructed around heroic actions and heroic suffering. They are highly selective and composed in such a way that they are identity-enhancing and self-celebrating. National memories are self-serving and therein closely aligned with political myths, which Peter Sloterdijk has appropriately termed modes of 'self-hypnosis' (Sloterdijk 2006: 247–248). With respect to traumatic events, these myths provide effective protection shields against those events that a nation prefers to forget. When facing negative events in the past, there are only three dignified roles for the national collective to assume: that of the victor who has overcome the evil, that of the resistor who has heroically fought the evil and that of the victim who has passively suffered the evil. Everything else lies outside the scope of these memory perspectives and is conveniently forgotten.

The new memory policy that I am dealing with in this chapter differs from the old one, not in abolishing national memory but in rethinking and reconfiguring it along different lines. The new memory policy has undergone a shift from a monologic to a more dialogic structure. It no longer evolves exclusively around a heroic self-image but also acknowledges historical violence, suffering and trauma within a new framework of moral and historical accountability. It was the cumulative process of the returning Holocaust memory in the 1980s that laid the ground for a profound cultural change in sensibility which in many places in the world also triggered new approaches to dealing with other historic traumas. Against this background of a new transnational awareness of the suffering of victims, forgetting was no longer considered as an acceptable policy for overcoming atrocities of the past. Remembering became a universal ethical and political claim when dealing with the dictatorships in South America, the South African regime of apartheid, colonial history or the crime of slavery. In most of these cases, references and metaphorical allusions were made to the newly established memory icon of the Holocaust. In all of these cases, remembering rather than forgetting was chosen for its transformative power and implemented as a therapeutic tool to cleanse, to purge, to heal, to reconcile in the process of transforming a state or reintegrating a society.

Reconciliation is often proverbially represented by the two verbs 'forgive and forget'. In these new cases, however, this is no longer the case. In the new policy, forgiving is no longer connected to forgetting but to remembering. Remembering here means recognition of the victims' memories. It is agreed more and more that without working through the atrocities of the past from the point of view of those who suffered, the process of social and political transformation cannot begin. This transformative power of memory plays a crucial role in the Truth and Reconciliation Commissions (TRC) that were invented in South America when countries such as Chile, Uruguay, Argentina and Brazil transitioned from military dictatorships to democracy in the 1980s and 1990s. In this process, it was the ethical concept of human rights that supported the demands to investigate a hidden past and restore it to social memory. By enforcing the moral human rights paradigm, new political and extremely influential concepts were coined such as 'human rights violations' and 'state terrorism'. This led to the establishment of investigative commissions, which became the antecedent of later Truth Commissions. The aim of TRCs is first and foremost a pragmatic one: they are designed as instruments for 'mastering' (rather than memorializing) the past (Hazan 2007). They emphasize the transformative value of truth and stress the importance of acts of remembrance. '"Remember, so as not to repeat" (emerged) as a message and as a cultural imperative' (Jelin 2003). The new human rights framework replaced the older frameworks within which power struggles had been constructed in terms of ideologies, class struggles, national revolutions or other political antagonisms. By resorting to the universal value of bodily integrity and human rights, the new terminology depoliticized the conflict and led to the elaboration of memory policies (ibid. 6). In the new framework of a human rights agenda and a new memory culture, other forms of state violence could be addressed such as racial and gender discrimination, repression and the rights of indigenous people. When decades and sometimes centuries have passed after traumatic events, and justice in the full sense is no longer possible, memory was discovered as an important symbolic resource to retrospectively acknowledge these crimes against humanity. What the transnational movement of abolition was for the nineteenth century, the new transnational concept of victimhood is for the late nineteenth and early twentieth century. The important change is, however, that now the victims speak for themselves and claim their memories in a globalized public arena. The dissemination of their voices and their public visibility and audibility has created a new 'world ethos' that makes it increasingly difficult for state authorities to continue a repressive policy of forgetting and silence.

We have learned in the meantime that a new beginning can no longer be forged on a *tabula rasa*. The road from authoritarian to civil societies leads through the needle's eye of facing, remembering and coming to terms with a burdened past. This insight pushed the shift from the modernist frame to the memory frame that occurred in the last decades of the twentieth century. It was accompanied by a return of the old memory policy, but it also brought with it a shift from monologic to dialogic memory constructs. Dialogic memory transcends the old policy by integrating two or more perspectives on a common legacy of traumatic violence. Two countries engage in a dialogic memory if they face a shared history of mutual violence by mutually acknowledging their own guilt and empathy with the suffering they have inflicted on others.

It is true that what I call 'dialogic memory' is not yet backed up by a consolidated consensus but is still most conspicuous in its absence. It has, for instance, become especially manifest in the relations between Russia and some Eastern European nations. While Russian memory is today centred around the Great Patriotic War and Stalin is celebrated as the national hero, the nations that broke away from Soviet power maintain a strikingly different memory of Stalin that has to do with deportations, forced labour and mass killings. The triumphalist memory of Russia and the traumatic memory of Eastern European nations clash at the internal borders of Europe and fuel continuous irritations and conflicts. 'With respect to its memories', writes Janusz Reiter, previous Polish ambassador in Germany, 'the European Union remains a split continent. After its extension, the line that separated the EU from other countries now runs right through it' (Reiter 2005). It must be emphasized, however, that the European Union creates a challenge to the solipsistic constructions of national memory and provides an ideal framework for mutual observations, interactions and thus for dialogic remembering. As we all know, the European Union is itself the consequence of a traumatic legacy of an entangled history of unprecedented violence. If it is to develop further from an economic and political network to a community of shared values, the entangled histories will have to be transformed into sharable memories. On the occasion of the sixtieth anniversary of the liberation of Buchenwald, the former prisoner of the concentration camp and late writer Jorge Semprún said that one of the most effective possibilities to forge a common future for the EU is 'to share our past, our remembrance, our hitherto divided memories'. He added that the Eastern extension of the EU can only work 'once we will be able to share our memories, including those of the countries of the other Europe, the Europe that was caught up in Soviet totalitarianism' (Semprún 2005).

There are dark incidents that are well known to historians and emphatically commemorated by the traumatized country but utterly forgotten by the nation that was immediately responsible for the suffering. While in the meantime the Germans have learned a lot about the Holocaust, younger generations today know next to nothing about the legacy of the Second World War and the atrocities committed by Germans against, for instance, their Polish and Russian neighbours. The Warsaw uprising, a seminal event commemorated in Poland, is unknown to Germans because it is fully eclipsed by the Warsaw ghetto uprising. Germans have rightly reclaimed the area bombing of Dresden for their national memory, but they have totally forgotten a key event of Russian memory, namely the Leningrad Blockade (1941–1944) by the German Wehrmacht, through which 700,000 Russians were starved to death.[4] This event has never entered German national memory due to a lack of interest, empathy and external pressure.

Within the new memory frame, there are promising beginnings between teachers and historians of neighbouring countries working on shared textbooks and mutual perceptions. Dialogic memory has a special relevance for Europe; it could produce a new type of nation state that is not exclusively grounded in pride but also accepts its dark legacies, thus ending a destructive history of violence by including the victims of this violence into its own memory. Only such an inclusive memory, which is based on the moral standard of accountability and human rights, can credibly back up the protection of human rights in the present and support the values of a civil society in the future.

Dialogic memory, of course, can be extended also to other regions of the world. My last example is the conflict between Israelis and Palestinians. National memory not only crystallizes in narratives, but also around places. Sites of antagonistic and violent history are always overdetermined and become contested spaces for which new narratives have yet to be created. Said had suggested that the Palestinians fell short in the process of national integration through myth making, which deprived them of mobilizing symbols and rendered them helpless victims of Zionism. How could memory in this case unfold its transformative power? The Israeli writer Amos Oz has no hope whatsoever in such a power. He once remarked: 'If I had a say in the peace talks – no matter where, in Wye, Oslo or where ever – I would instruct the sound technicians to turn off the microphones as soon as one of the negotiating parties starts talking about the past. They are paid for finding solutions for the present and the future' (Oz 1998: 83). Oz obviously argues from the point of view of the modernist frame which neatly separates the future from the past. In a conversation at Konstanz, Avishai Margalit made a similar point to me on a more pragmatic level. He summed up the problem in the formula: 'No introduction of memory before the consolidation of political structures!'[5] Obviously both Oz and Margalit have little regard for the transformative power of memory. There is, however, an Israeli NGO that is built on exactly this hope in the transformative power of memory. It is called Zachrot, which is the female form of '*Zachor*', meaning 'Remember!' This imperative is a central obligation in the Hebrew Bible and the key to Jewish tradition and identity. The female analogy of this emphatic word was created as the name of a group of Israelis who take remembering out of a religious context and place it in a political context. Their goal is to construct a more inclusive memory on the basis of a dialogic remembering that includes Israeli memory of the Holocaust and also the Palestinian memory of the Nakba, a term for the traumatic expulsion from their homes during the war of independence in 1948. In contrast to Oz and Margalit, the group that calls itself Zachrot considers this dialogic and inclusive memory an important basis for citizenship and a common future with Palestinians. This is how they summarize their position on the internet:

> Zachrot works to make the history of the Nakba accessible to the Israeli public so as to engage Jews and Palestinians in an open recounting of our painful common history. We hope that by bringing the Nakba into Hebrew, the language spoken by the Jewish majority in Israel, we can make a qualitative change in the political discourse of this region. Acknowledging the past is the first step in taking responsibility for its consequences. This must include equal rights for all the peoples of this land, including the right of Palestinians to return to their homes.[6]

Conclusion

Memories, to sum up, are dynamic and thus transformed over time. What is being remembered of the past is largely dependent on the cultural frames, moral sensibilities and demands of the present. In retrospect, we can identify a shift from the modernist frame to the memory frame which occurred in the late twentieth century. During the Cold War, the memory of the Second World War was very different from what it is today; the Holocaust has moved from the periphery to the centre of West European memory only during the last two decades, but also other historic traumas went through shorter or longer periods of latency before they became the object of remembering and commemoration. While the old heroic and monologic memory policy continues to be in use, it is now also challenged in a new transnational if not global arena, where the two coexist in a web of mutual reactions, observations, imitations, competitions and other forms of interaction.

During the last decades, *the theory and use of memory have acquired a new meaning* where it became obvious that memory can be both a force for refuelling hatred and violence and thus maintaining and hardening divisions, as well as a therapy for integration. Depending on the use and quality of memory, the former fronts of violent conflict can be preserved or overcome. Although history has occurred and is irreversible, our knowledge and evaluation of events can be transformed in hindsight, if we reassess them in the light of retrospective knowledge and values.

The way trauma is remembered has to evolve between the extremes of keeping the wound open (or 'preservation of the past') and looking for closure (or 'mastering the past'). But we should not forget that *remembering takes place simultaneously on the separate but interrelated levels of individuals, families, society and the state*. Its transformative power works in different ways on the psychological, the moral, the political and – last but not least – the religious level, when it comes to the proper burying as a prerequisite for the memory of the dead. It is precisely this cultural and religious duty of laying the dead to rest that is so shockingly disrupted after periods of excessive violence. In the case of millions of Jewish victims, there are no graves because their bodies were gassed, burnt and dissolved into air. For this reason this wound cannot be closed. At other places the victims were 'disappeared' or shot and hidden in anonymous mass graves. Some of these, relating to the Spanish Civil War, are being reopened only now after almost eighty years (Ingendaay 2008). While the politicians and society have still not found a consensus for introducing these victims into a shared or sharable memory, it is up to individual family members to recover their dead and to perform these last acts of reverence.

Let me close with a final question. In an essay with the title 'Nightmares or Daydreams?' Konrad Jarausch looked back at sixty-five years of European memory. He saw a strong preponderance of negative memories, but what he missed were positive values:

> The impressive catalogue of human rights included in the document has therefore derived its significance more from a general realization of past evils that needed to be avoided than from a specific delineation of common values that would bind the community together in the present. This failure is regrettable, because it tends to lock thinking about Europe into a negative mode. Europe has become a kind of insurance policy against the repetition of prior problems rather than a positive goal, based upon a shared vision for the future. (Jarausch 2010: 314)

In his assessment of European memories, Jarausch uses two categorical distinctions. The first is the neat divide between past and future that resonates clearly with the modernist frame of thinking. As I tried to show, this simple binary has been replaced in the memory frame by a more complex interaction: in order to move forward, we have to make a detour via the past. The second distinction is the opposition between negative lessons and positive values. As I hope to have shown, this neat distinction does not work in the case of recent European history where the positive values of human rights, recognition of suffering, respect for the 'other' and historical accountability were obviously distilled from negative lessons. Since the Europeans gained these values in the course of their history, remembering this history including its errors, violence and unmeasurable crimes, is their way of adopting and ascertaining these values. This new form of remembering deviates strikingly from the old (and I would even say, default) monologic mode that focuses exclusively on national heroism and national suffering by embracing one's own guilt and also the suffering of others. It is this twist that transforms a negative history into a positive memory built on values that open up a new common future. I would like to claim that the specific European heritage lies in this civil transformation of its own violent history into transnational orientations and new connecting bonds. I fully support Adam Michnik's definition of this European heritage:

> The European Union emerged out of the negation of totalitarian dictatorships which were full of atrocities and barbarism. The European values are humanism and tolerance, equal dignity for all citizens, freedom of the individual, solidarity with the weak and political pluralism. It is this testimony and value system that Europe can bring to the world. (Michnik 2011: 6)

For my generation the unexpectedly long peaceful phase in Europe comes as an unexpected and, especially from the point of view of Germans, an utterly undeserved gift. I am deeply grateful to the Europeans for their collective effort in transforming the nightmare of their history into a vision which they now have the potential to make real. The history they look back on is a particularly heavy burden and a great challenge to commemoration. This is true, above all, of the trauma of the Holocaust, which has created a national, European and trans-European memory. Appreciation of the value of human dignity was won from the most extreme destruction of that human dignity, the positive significance of this value remains linked to its negative genesis (cf. Joas 2009). The same applies to war and postwar traumas, for the joint remembrance of a violent history is the most effective way of overcoming the conditions that made it possible in the first place. Historical violence has driven the nations of Europe apart; dialogic forms of remembering can – in spite of lingering tensions and invisible barriers – bring them closer together. The shared house of Europe gains in stability in proportion to the commitment that Europeans display in becoming inhabitants of their shared history.

Notes

1. The peace treaty ('Instrumentum Pacis Osnabrugensis' of 24 October 1648) contains the following article: 'Both sides grant each other a perpetual forgetting and amnesty concerning every aggressive act committed in any place in any way by both parties here and there since the beginning of the war' (Buschmann 1994: 17).
2. Thanks to Marco Duranti for drawing my attention to this speech.
3. Denmark 1991/92, Netherlands 1993, Italy 1987/88, Austria 2000, Germany 2001 and Luxembourg 2007.
4. To quote from a recent historical account, the siege of Leningrad was 'an integral part of the unprecedented German war of extermination against the civilian population of the Soviet Union ... Considering the number of victims and the permanence of the terror, it was the greatest catastrophe that hit any city during the Second World War. The city was cut off from the outside world for almost 900 days from September 7th 1941 to 27th January 1944' (Ganzenmüller 2005: 20; see also Jahn 2007).
5. Conversation with Avishai Margalit in the Inselhotel, Konstanz in November 2006 where he gave the opening lecture of a conference on 'Civil Wars'.
6. http://www.nakbainhebrew.org/index.php?lang=english (accessed 20 March 2007).

Aleida Assmann was professor of English literature at the University of Konstanz from 1993 to 2014. She was a visiting professor at the universities of Princeton, Yale, Houston, Chicago and Vienna. She holds numerous awards and honours. In her numerous books she has introduced ideas and concepts that have proved fundamental for memory studies. Her writings are characterized by an interdisciplinary approach, employing literary and cultural perspectives. Publications in English include *Cultural Memory and Western Civilization: Functions, Media, Archives* (Cambridge University Press, 2011) and *Shadows of Trauma: Memory and the Politics of Postwar Identity* (Fordham, 2015).

Chapter 2

POLITICAL CORRECTNESS AND MEMORIES CONSTRUCTED FOR 'EASTERN EUROPE'

Andrzej Nowak

History has been narrated as a discourse of power since the times of Ssu-ma Ch'ien and Polybius. The new concept of memory as counter-history, developed so effectively in past decades, has not escaped the logic of power discourse. It has become the dominant discourse itself, propped up with the help of 'memorial' laws and bans introduced in many European countries (Nowak 2009a, 2009b). Different ideological centres and instruments enforce elements of 'memorial policies'. Not just governments, but also non-governmental media, churches preaching reconciliation ideology, academic elites and prominent representatives of so-called critical art – all of them form more or less obligatory frames for narratives of public memories, with the result that they reduce a great variety of different experiences and realities into binary oppositions: 'new' and 'old', 'correct' and 'to-be-corrected'. This is where the concept of symbolic violence, proposed a few decades ago by Pierre Bourdieu (1984), might be revealing. But this is also a situation where another concept, less sophisticated, but broadly recognizable – that of political correctness – seems worth revisiting (Domańska 2006: 15–17, 229–230).[1] The aim of this chapter is to present a few questions concerning the limits of top-down (and, as I claim, equal to West-East) public memory constructions in contemporary Europe. How, after the EU enlargement to the east, have conflicting patterns of memories become objects of proscriptive regulations and prescriptive models? Is it possible to achieve 'a democratic consensus' between different memories in Europe? These two questions form the axis of further argument.

Notes for this chapter begin on page 55.

PC and Eastern Europe: Definitions and Dangers

The Oxford Dictionary of New Words defines political correctness (PC for short) as 'conformity to a body of liberal or radical opinion on social matters, characterized by the advocacy of approved views and the rejection of language and behaviour considered discriminatory or offensive'. In practice, hard right-wing forces use the concept of 'political correctness' to justify racist, antifeminist or homophobic concepts. Geoffrey Hughes in his profound analysis of the history and semantics of PC puts it somewhat more mildly but nonetheless succinctly: 'Political correctness inculcates a sense of obligation or conformity in areas which should be (or are) matters of choice' (Hughes 2009: 4, 13; Lessing 2004: 72–78). I would like to stress three elements in these definitions: 'conformity to...', 'advocacy of approved views' and 'the rejection of...', as well as acknowledging the best intentions of those who want to dissuade us from inappropriate language or behaviour. What about our memories? Do they belong to social matters which might form another object of PC? But first, before we begin to ponder these questions seriously, we have to determine what this 'we' or 'our' means. Who is asking here about PC and constructed memories? Well, I am just one of some 105 million so-called 'new Europeans' from the east of the continent. One of 170 million 'Eastern Europeans', if one adds non-Russian, post-Soviet, and yet non EU-members from the geographical continent of Europe. Finally, I am one of just over 300 million 'Eastern Europeans', if one were to add all the inhabitants of the Russian Federation to the previous number.

We differ from each other in our memories and yet ever since the concept of Eastern Europe was invented, we have been lumped together. We have a common generic name: Eastern Europeans. As Larry Wolff reminded us in his brilliant book, eighteenth-century Western intellectuals, predominantly French and German, arranged a European concept of Eastern Europe according to one general perspective. On their mental maps they united countries and peoples under one rubric, where they were able to analyse these countries and peoples' position between 'barbarism' and 'civilization' – evaluated with respect to a standard set by *les philosophes*. All of these peoples offered themselves up to the gaze of Western observers as helpless victims, sacrifices to the observers' irrepressible analytic and standard-creating energies. 'One thinks of Michael Foucault, who philosophized historically about the gaze that made vision into knowledge and knowledge into power' (Wolff 1994: 20). The lands of Eastern Europe had 'wrong' histories – to be forgotten or rewritten. They had to import institutions and arts, they had to borrow brains and stability. Voltaire developed a conception of mastery in Eastern Europe as a civilizing process: everything remains to be undone and redone there, according to plans prepared in the centres of the Western mind.

Many legal, economic and institutional standards together make up the formal conditions for membership of the European Union. In the case we intend to analyse there is, however, more: namely a risky intrusion into the sphere of people's imagination, particular experiences and their mental processes of dealing with them. It began, like PC, within the 'Western/Western European'-born phenomenon of therapeutic culture. Starting with Gordon Allport's (1954) concept of semantic therapy, it developed into a full-scale social policy that aims to inform people what to believe and how to think. Imperceptibly, the model of protecting children from misleading commercials and bad dreams has been extended to cover their elders. From warnings against 'hurtful/offensive/illegitimate' speech, to protecting people from 'harmful' memories and the demand that they be censored, along with the stigmatization of scepticism. As Frank Furedi (2011: 132, 140) warns, 'Therapeutic censorship both patronizes and infantilizes people', and he insists that it 'plays an essential role helping individuals to make the "right choices". … The project of remoulding the way people think and act [and remember] requires a significant erosion of people's right to assent to, or reject, policies. This approach clearly presupposes the elimination of a two-way process of discussion between citizens and their rulers'. They are not citizens and their (democratically elected) rulers any more, but just patients and therapists. The latter know better how to protect the former from 'the wrong choices' in words and memories (still nurtured by the deviant national past), and how to protect people from themselves. Governments and intergovernmental, 'European' task forces take an ever-increasing part in this process, playing the role of a caring Big Brother (Furedi 2011: 142).

Now the care is extended to others: 'Powerful institutions value some histories more than others, provide narratives and exemplars of how individuals can and should remember and stimulate memory in ways and for reasons that have nothing to do with the individual or aggregate neurological records' (Olick 2007: 28–29). This general remark applies not just to 'old' nation state memorial practices; it applies to contemporary Europe as well.

Unequal Memories in 'Enlarged' Europe

The centre of European memorial therapy formed, quite naturally, in Germany. Horrors and traumas of the Second World War concentrated in experiences stemming from that centre of Europe. The construction of the memory of the war began right after the war ended. 'Everyone had an interest in this affair, the context of which ranged from private score-settling to the emerging international balance of power' (Judt 2002: 160). The uniqueness of the mass murder of European Jews has been accepted in Germany (three to four decades after the war) as the central experience to be remembered. It has since prevailed in the construction of New Europe as the main *memento*, not just against Nazism, but against the recurrent danger of national hatred, and nationalism itself. The Holocaust came to be treated as a negative new European founding myth. Germans in the Federal Republic were the first to acknowledge this. 'To Europeanize German memory politics might seem pretentious', as Claus Leggewie stated (2011: 123). 'But it is a fact that anti-Semitism and fascism were pan-European phenomena'. This fact (or rather awareness of this fact) coincided with a growing acknowledgement of different historical traumas, dramatic experiences of collective victimhood created by wars, colonialism, mass expulsions and ethnic cleansings. This turn from triumph (of the victorious powers in the Second World War) to trauma (Giesen 2004) has strengthened the tendency to institutionalize a common memory for the growing European Union based precisely on collective traumas and effective ways of overcoming them. At the core of this turn is acknowledgement of the collective guilt stemming from wars, the Holocaust as the paradigmatic horror and trauma, and colonial crimes. The guilt that Europe is ready to acknowledge in order to build a new, safer, not national, but rather transnational community. But is it possible to build a guilt culture of memory from above? Maybe, to use an old dichotomy by Ruth Benedict (2005 (1946): 222–227), it would not be a guilt culture but rather a shame culture, motivated not by private judgement of individual consciences but by conformity to enforced rituals.

The institutional structure of this memory community was formed by the International Task Force for International Cooperation on Holocaust Education, Remembrance and Research which was announced in January 2000 in Stockholm. The new initiative openly aims to create a supranational memory community with a specific political agenda.[2] As Aleida Assmann (2010: 112) notes, 'In spite of its self-description as an NGO, the full package of ITF (International Task Force for International Cooperation on Holocaust Education, Remembrance and Research) membership conditions entails practical commitments at national level, including top-down regulations for Holocaust school education, museums and commemoration days'.

The new construction of European memory – the effect of several decades of intellectual and memorial evolution taking place predominantly in the

Western part of the continent – was, at the moment of its institutional triumph, confronted with a different set of collective memories formed from the past experiences of the new EU members from Eastern Europe. This confrontation led the community of Western European memorial activists quite abruptly from triumph to trauma, again. A new EU Commissioner from Latvia, Sandra Kalniete, ignited this trauma with her appeal during the Leipzig Book Fair in 2004 to accept another commemorative culture, that of 'Eastern Europe', based on the experience of the Gulag. In May 2005, with the great show of the Russian Federation's memory politics organized around the sixtieth anniversary of 'the victory over fascism', yet another chasm within 'Eastern European' commemorative culture exhibited itself. Russia intended to take responsibility for the lion's share of the great victory, which was partly understandable due to their Western commemorative culture, though based more on heroic memory of the Red Army veterans than on any sensibility for the victims (other than Red Army soldiers). For numerous sections of society in many other 'Eastern European' countries, however, especially in Latvia, Lithuania, Estonia and Poland (all members of the EU), 1945 symbolized not liberation by the Red Army, but also the new partition of Europe and subjugation to another imperial occupation, the Soviet one. 'Yalta' rather than liberated Auschwitz, or 'Yalta' along with liberated Auschwitz, symbolized the most important experience and source of collective traumas (Zhurzhenko 2007).[3]

Has a new 'Yalta' loomed on the memorial horizon, a new *Ausgleich* of European memories, divided into two partially overlapping zones: Holocaust and Gulag? Must a renewed effort be made to reassert the hegemonic position of the commemorative model produced for Europe somewhere between Berlin, Stockholm and Brussels before 2005? Or to organize and sanction a hierarchy of European memories, from the most fundamental to those which are more or less marginal? These possibilities have begun to penetrate discussions of 'Western European' memorial activists, provoking a state of their 'commemorative anxiety'[4] in the last decade.

The situation has been aggravated by a more general phenomenon which Pierre Nora (1996a: 8–9) called a 'hypertrophy of memory', while Geoffrey Hartmann (1993: 147–150) gave it an even broader name of 'information sickness' – a 'sensory and information overload'. We are informed every day about dramatic experiences and traumas that vie for our recognition. There seems to be a shrinking amount of attention for new memories. The interrelation between the production and reception of memories becomes not just an acute cognitive problem but also a social one (Kansteiner 2002: 179–197; Cubitt 2007: 242–256).

Gavriel D. Rosenfeld (2009: 142–146) acknowledged that the way the Federal Republic of Germany faced the most important trauma of all – that of the Holocaust – 'sets a standard of reckoning with the past that others have been forced to confront'. And yet, in his provocative essay he questions the future of this standard, 'so perfectly institutionalized and commercially organized', or rather its position in our reflection on the past. It will wane, that is inevitable, he suggests. From a New York perspective, after 9/11, he declares a state of commemorative crisis, to be accepted with the simple consequence that there are no more memories worth listening to and no more 'important' traumas to be acknowledged. 'After more than two decades' intensive work done on the Holocaust and the unearthing of historical injustices all across the globe – from the Aboriginals' "stolen generation" to apartheid – we have now arrived at a point of saturation with "memory". Instead of continuing to deal with memory and the past, we should start looking at the present and future' – that's how Astrid Erll (2011: 172) synthesized Rosenfeld's position.

There are many possible consequences and reactions to such a projection. We can briefly explore the one that stems from non-recognition of those 'new' memories and traumas which have not found their way to the standard accepted as the final one. Different personal and group 'Eastern European' memories of communist power and terror, as well as those of Russian imperial dominance, were suppressed and stigmatized by that power between 'Yalta' (1945) and *Annus Mirabilis* (1989). They retrieved their 'freedom of speech' after 1989. The problem – for the victims with traumas so far unspoken – was that they have not had the audience they hoped for. Privatization of the past and decentralization of history has been quite a natural reaction to the previous state of public memory, strictly controlled by the communist regimes. That reaction coincided with general civilizational changes of the late twentieth century which led to a quick emotional and memorial overload, described above. Even though different political regimes in the postcommunist countries of Eastern Europe set up different institutional devices to create new national standards of memory, some of them anticommunist, some of them anti-Russian, they were nowhere near as systematic or effective as the previous (pre-1989) system of public memory control. And this is probably one of the very few generalizations that can be made about them. Besides, they differed among themselves.[5] Perhaps there is one more general difference between Russia on the one hand, and all these eastern countries that have either already joined the EU or have been seriously preparing themselves for accession. The former has kept its national political centre for organization of public memory more rather than less monopolistic, while the latter have been institutionally influenced by memorial standards emanating from Brussels.

To sum up: there was no time for the many dramatic (different and conflicting) memories of the inhabitants of Eastern Europe, suppressed or marginalized before 1989, to find a place in the public space – unlike in Western Europe, where the Nazi occupation horrors, collaboration and Holocaust supplanted previous more 'heroic' or individual national memorial narratives after only three to five decades of evolution. There was no time for many of them, meaning hundreds of thousands of victims (and living mourning communities of these victims), to reach recognition – and only after that a 'healing' stage (Koresaar, Kuutma and Lauk 2009; Kiss 2009; Vukov 2009; Assmann 2012: 61–62). They were to be 'healed' without recognition. They have met with the demands of a new centralizing memory politics, one which has come – once again – from 'outside', from Europe.

If you want to belong, you must remember: you must remember what your community demands from you to be remembered. This eternal appeal of every constructed community is also repeated at the gate of the EU. It has its obvious negative side: if you want to belong, you must forget. You must forget exactly what constituted your previous (collective) identity. Both sides of this appeal are theoretically illuminated by two studies on forgetting: by Frank Ankersmit (2001) and Paul Connerton (2008). The latter puts this case under the rubric of 'forgetting that is constitutive in the formation of a new identity', while Ankersmit brilliantly analyses it as the fourth, and the most dramatic type of forgetting in his system(atic). It 'involves the transition from a former to a new identity. Here the traumatic loss truly is the loss of one's (former) self. And what loss could possibly be greater – for is this not as close to death as one may come?' – asks the Dutch historian (Ankersmit 2001: 303). What neither he nor Connerton takes into consideration is a possibility that such a vital (or rather suicidal, as Ankersmit reminds) change in memory might be – at least to a degree – backed or forced from 'outside' or 'above'. Connerton enumerates in his systematic a type of forgetting which he calls 'repressive erasure', dating back at least to Roman criminal law as *damnatio memoriae* (condemnation of memory). He reminds us that it need not always take malign forms or be identified with totalitarian regimes, but 'can be encrypted covertly and without apparent violence', as for example is done with the help of historical master narratives organizing even the spatial dispositions of modern art galleries (Connerton 2008: 60–61).

This type of forgetting is rarely, if ever, connected to relations between the Western European contemporary model of memory and Eastern European deviant pasts. It is however, just like in Connerton's systematic, well understood that such a repressive erasure, forcing a suicide of the former self, has happened many times in relations between 'the West' and 'the rest': Africa, Asia, Pacific, Latin America, Native Indians – all subjects of Western European-centred practices of colonialism and imperialism. Now, the West is there to remember its own shame *vis-à-vis* the non-European, formerly colonized communities. What is reserved for Eastern Europe, still in the process of Western construction since the time of Voltaire and Rousseau to the present day, is just the reminder of memories that were repressed in this region as too painful to be admitted, the third type of forgetting in Ankersmit's systematic, or identified by Connerton as 'humiliated silence', brought about by a particular kind of collective shame.

Setting European Memorial Standards: Model One (Aleida Assmann)

In the opening of an important contribution to one of the most recent volumes on European divided memory, Aleida Assmann (2013) begins with a story of her meeting with a student from Poland who represents a new generation of memory – one in the process of reconstruction on the basis of collective shame. The Polish student contrasts himself (or is contrasted by the author of the story) with his father – a man with 'wrong' historical memories. These memories are easily translated into his politically 'wrong' opinions: he would never think of travelling to Germany and is a staunch opponent of the European Union, which he perceives as just another version of German imperialism.

Mnemonology possesses its demonology – and here is one of the demons identified. A demon of politically incorrect memory – the one from Eastern Europe, still not accepting its place within the frame of memorial references already built by those who set standards of reckoning with the past. There are, of course, other voices from 'Eastern Europe' which are audible in commemorative projects sanctioned by Western European hegemonic elites. They are the voices who form an echo of the memorial standard, confirming its full applicability to Eastern European experiences. The rest is (usually) silenced. One is tempted to repeat the question of Dipesh Chakrabarty: Who speaks for Eastern European (not 'Indian' in our case) pasts, for Eastern European memories?

In another essay on European community of memory, Aleida Assmann (2007: 11–26) quotes the Hungarian writer, Peter Esterházy: 'To conceal one's own guilt by referring to Germany's crimes is European habit. Hatred for the Germans is the foundation of the postwar period'. This is the only voice from Eastern Europe she quotes in her text – approvingly. She comments on Esterházy's statement, denouncing a specific Eastern European memory block and 'defensive memorial strategies', as opposed to Western Europe, where 'national myths were challenged and debunked'. There are many national myths which constitute still visible elements of an Eastern European memorial landscape. There are real tragedies and traumas to be remembered, to be connected with the role of perpetrator, such as those symbolized by the murder of the Jews in Jedwabne by their Polish neighbours. And there are, fortunately, voices struggling with 'unmastered pasts' in the region. They do represent a real effort to cope with what Frank Ankersmit described as the third type of forgetting: when the memory of some dramatic, sometimes even criminal aspect of our past is too painful to be admitted to our collective consciousness. And they should not be blocked by glorious memories of heroic deeds generalized for the construction of a national identity. The question is, however, whether the opposite situation is satisfactory, when only voices like the one presented by Esterházy, or by those who draw 'the trajectories of bringing the dark to light', or by those who deplore 'asymmetry of memories' in Germany and some Eastern European countries, are accepted on the Western side of a European memorial dialogue? When a memorial yardstick, firmly in the hand of a 'Western European' teacher, is easily transformed into a political stick (Tunander 1997: 25–27)?

I will give just two examples of what might be called contemporary European identity formation and a politically correct collective memory produced by this process. The first is well documented in Aleida Assmann's studies of the subject, and took shape immediately after the EU was enlarged. 'Today, we see that the future has lost much of its power to integrate, while the past is becoming increasingly important in the formation of identity.' This pessimistic observation, made by the author of *Der lange Schatten der Vergangenheit*, served as a starting point for a series of proposals that aimed at dealing effectively with the problem of expanded European memory, both in cultural space and political importance. The next example is a concept of 'European guiding culture', quite correctly exposed by a German Muslim, Bassam Tibi (1998), the political scientist. Among the standards it sets for European identity there are such premises as 'precedence of individual human rights over communal rights', 'universally recognized pluralism as well as mutually effective tolerance' (quoted after Assmann 2007: 12). At the same time various actions have been taken to create something like a common historical memory for the growing European Union. 'Indeed, steps have been taken to institutionalize this common memory as the core of European identity.' One could ask: what about an individual human right – the right to have individual memory? Does it take precedence over communal, even pan-European memory? What about 'recognized pluralism' and 'effective tolerance' in terms of memory? Aleida Assmann (2007: 19) exhibits her best intentions to bridge these gaps when she proposes 'some practical guidelines that might help to regulate the use and banish the abuse of collective memories'. She reminds us for example of Christian Meier's (1987) warning about the possibility of 'negative privileging' of one crime or trauma against another one: 'Have not atrocities like those which we perpetrated against Poland and Russia ... disappeared under the shadow of the Holocaust?' Among similar practical, commonsensical and compassionate insights there is however always this daunting task: to guide, to regulate and to banish.

Six years later Aleida Assmann commented on the visible consequences of a specific clash of memories in an enlarged Europe: 'European memory is still divided'. The very first premise for her answer to this situation, taken as the political-cultural challenge, is still the same. Memory is too important to Europe to be left to vagaries of individual and different group choices. 'Memory' there means the forms and content of Second World War remembrance – this traumatic experience is treated as the beginning of Europe. What came before is not worth remembering except as the way to the catastrophe. A typically Manichean opposition is still in use: 'modern Europe rose from the ashes of the old Europe ... the EU has helped to transform most of Europe from a continent of war to a continent of peace'. The old (evil, condemned) and the new (good, blessed), war and peace. The new, good and peaceful is endangered now by the influx of the old – from the east, from Eastern Europe: 'the memory of Stalinism and Soviet occupation that formed the centre of the national narratives of the new states that claimed political independence after the collapse of Communism' (Assmann 2013).

Aleida Assmann reminds us how European institutions, such as ITF or a European commission at Brussels which met in May 2011 have tried to answer this challenge. To guide and to regulate now means to put safely different memorial phenomena under two, spatially ascribed and organized 'rubrics'. One is the Western memory of Nazism/Holocaust; the second would be the Eastern memory of the Gulag/Stalinism. This is exactly where a concept of new *Ausgleich*, or new 'Yalta' emerges – this time in terms of a memorial agreement.[6] It is easier to construct a new pan-European memory from two blocs than to deal with a real plethora of cultural memories that do not fit the already established pattern. Would it be enough to pass a resolution in the European Parliament, adding to 27 January (liberation of Auschwitz) another day of remembrance – that of 23 August, the signing of the Molotov-Ribbentrop Pact – to commemorate the victims of both Nazism and communist totalitarian regimes? Assmann gives a warning there, quoting Heidemarie Uhl, who has not only 'pointed out that the problematic levelling of the two forms of totalitarianism is at odds with current historical research', but also that it could 'undermine the ethical standards of Western memory culture' (Uhl 2009a: 172–173; Assmann 2013).

This strong statement is evidently aimed not only to 'guide and regulate', but also to 'banish'. But what to do with such examples of 'current historical research' as Norman Naimark's (2010) latest study of Stalin's genocides, or Timothy Snyder's (2010) monumental history of 'Bloodlands', or Hiroaki Kuromiya's (2007) study on Stalin's Great Terror, just to quote a few world-renowned scholars? There is also a problem with the tendency to eliminate the national aspect from post-traumatic memories in Eastern Europe. How to read, for example, a central chapter in Norman Naimark's study, 'Removing Nations', with what he calls 'one of the most unambiguous cases of genocide in the history of the twentieth century' (Naimark 2010: 92)?[7] The Nazi and Soviet regimes turned people into numbers. 'It is for us as humanists to turn the numbers back into people' – reminds Snyder. While returning identities to the victims, we cannot avoid remembering an element that was sometimes especially important to them, and vitally important to their totalitarian perpetrators: we cannot dismiss their nationality. Stalin selected victims for his totalitarian machine not randomly, and not only according to 'social class' definitions, but also by nationality. Sometimes it meant the executions of hundreds of thousands of people chosen on exactly the same basis as the Jews or the Gypsies were chosen by Hitler and his willing executioners. And as German women were raped by the Red Army soldiers in 1944–1945 – precisely because they were identified as German. Can the acknowledgement of these facts really 'undermine the ethical standards of Western memory culture'? And where is this 'West' exactly? Where does this particular 'memory culture' end, whom does it comprise, what countries, and what social groups within these countries? Where does the East begin in these terms? Again – many questions, (most of) which cannot be answered by any other discourse than that of power.

There is a transformative power of forgetting, not just that of remembering. Who is ordering a policy of silence? Who is ordering a policy of memory? These twin questions are always legitimate when top-down memory changes are advocated, obliterating some memories from the public sphere. 'The crucial question must always be: who profits, who suffers from forgetting?' This question, posed so appropriately by Aleida Assmann (2011) in her polemic with a proposal to forget rather than remember the crimes and misdeeds of the past, is worth restating here too.

Drawing European Memorial Circles:
Model Two (Claus Leggewie)

Some of the Western European (German in this case) specialists are well aware of this problem and try to cope with it by proposing a more nuanced view of the Eastern European memorial landscape. Stefan Troebst effectively develops Oskar Halecki's eighty-year-old paradigm of different historical 'zones' of experiences to the east of Germany. In his development of the *Erinnerungsräumen* concept he evades a Manichean opposition between Western and Eastern cultures of remembrance, as well as escaping happily from a proposal for a new *Ausgleich* between 'Holocaust' and 'Gulag' as the final solution for European memorial problems. It is an important step beyond the rigid borders of politically correct answers for complex historical, political and cultural questions, a step towards reality where there are not just two memorial foci in Europe – Holocaust and Gulag – but a multitude of them, functioning in complicated relations, created by complicated histories and individual experiences (Troebst 2011: 145–154; Troebst 2005).

Aleida Assmann however (2013: 38), seems to reject such a perspective:

> The European Union is premised on difference, as we have heard so often, so why not accept and abide by different historical perspectives, narratives, and memories? Such relativism, however, implies a trivialization of the problem, as we are not just dealing with different historical narratives and memory policies, but also with different and irreconcilable values.

She adds very appropriate questions to her verdict on 'memorial pluralism'. However, she perceives the problems addressed in these questions only in 'them' – in the 'wrong' national memories: 'Is a national memory constructed to affirm and glorify the collective or does it do justice to those who have been wronged and abused in the past? ... Does it allow complexity or does it enforce unity? Does it repress or integrate minorities?' (ibid.). One could add other variants of the same questions. Is a Central European, transnational memory, such as is envisaged in this case (and contrasted with 'old', Eastern European national memory), constructed to affirm and glorify the collective – now the EU and its policies? Does it allow complexity or does it enforce unity? Does it repress or integrate (memorial) minorities – especially those from the 'inferior', and still memorially 'underdeveloped' Eastern Europe, the 'forgotten cousins' from the former Soviet bloc?

Keeping these questions in mind, we can now move to a second interesting example of a politically correct system of European memory, that proposed by Claus Leggewie. His starting point is close to the one described above: the moment when 'Holocaust memory' met that of 'the Gulag memory'. He is ready to acknowledge the fact that the representatives of post-Soviet Russia have neither apologized nor paid reparations for mass deportations and murders, loss of freedom and forced Russification 'to which the Eastern European satellite states had been subjected under their communist governments'. He identifies reasons for the asymmetry of European memory, reminding that 'assumption of the singularity of the Holocaust ... combined with the acknowledgement of Russian suffering in World War Two, has caused a blindness to "red totalitarianism"'. He contests another reason for this asymmetry when he mentions 'far greater visibility', 'iconization of and media attention to' the Holocaust, in contrast to so many cases of mass murder by communist regimes. The account that is usually offered to somehow justify this difference, namely that 'the Nazi Germans predominantly killed other people, the Communists in Russia and China predominantly killed their own' is again contested by Leggewie, when he sets forth the persecution of the populations of Eastern Central Europe, Central Asia and Tibet by Russian and Chinese 'colonial powers'. He mentions 'the identity-forming function that anticommunism had in Western Europe for many years' as another obstacle for pan-European recognition of the importance of 'Eastern European' traumatic memories of communism. Leggewie endorses a perspective where Europe would be able to develop a collective memory 'as diverse as its nations and cultures', and confirms that 'Memory cannot be regulated mnemotechnically, let alone through official acts of state or routinized commemorative rituals such as May 8 and 9 or January 27' (Leggewie 2011: 127).

And yet he decided to propose a magical number of 'Seven Circles of European Memory'. After 'Holocaust' and 'Gulag', there are the following five circles: 'Expulsion as a Pan-European Trauma', 'War and Wartime Memory', 'Black Book of Colonialism', 'Europe as a Continent of Immigration' and 'Europe's Success Story After 1945'. Seven circles are of course more than just one obligatory memory, or even two (Holocaust and Gulag). There is more space for memo-diversity. It is worth stressing that in such an important element of this memorial construction as 'Expulsion', Claus Leggewie offers a good example of Eastern and Western European collaboration by providing a real forum of memorial 'exchange': the European Network of Remembrance and Solidarity, an educational-cultural entertainment created by the ministries of culture of Germany, Hungary, Poland and Slovakia. 'War and Wartime' memories, I may add, recently had a temporary, but very effective forum for such an exchange, namely the project 'Memory at War', run in Cambridge, by

Alexander Etkind with Uilleam Blacker and Julie Fedor, dealing with 'cultural dynamics in Russia, Poland, and Ukraine'.[8] Other 'circles', however, still seem deprived of such instruments. How interesting it would be, for example, to debate different perspectives, both from Eastern and Western Europe, on colonialism before it is made a common, pan-European memorial focus, as obligatory in Bratislava, Sofia or Vilnius, as it should be in Brussels, London or Marseille.

The only point where I do see an element of proscriptive (political) correctness in Claus Leggewie's concept is this risky generalization, shared with Aleida Assmann and many other specialists in European memory studies: 'Awareness that this [European] memory dominated by a history of crime and trauma is common to all Europeans' (Leggewie 2011: 140). Is it, really? To all of us? Or is it rather – at least to a degree – symbolically enforced and politically encouraged? Nothing else, but traumas and guilt-ridden cemeteries, already too full to accept new bodies? Just two circles short of the full Dante's *Inferno*? I mention the great Italian and – yes, European – poet, not by chance. In Claus Leggewie there are actually six circles of memorial hell – and one representing paradise, at the end: Europe after 1945 (constructed in its Western part), the only thing worth showing in the House of European History. So we are left with what is called (not without a specific pride) a 'negative memory' of all that was before 1945 plus an appraisal of the actual status quo. How typical for so many examples of historical politics, beginning with Qin Shihuangdi.

So where would Dante be in this memory? Where is the memory of all European culture, developing from south and west over centuries, reaching Eastern Europe with its inspirations, and giving us 'Easterners' our aspirations to be a part of, to participate in this cultural adventure? I am from Krakow, an old Polish city, which is proud of its magnificent monuments built over centuries for Polish kings and magnates, as well as for multinational burghers by Italian, German, Dutch, Czech and Polish architects, sculptors and engineers. Why deprive our public memory of such a visible, such an omnipresent element of European common cultural heritage? This is also visible in smaller towns and even villages, in church architecture, from Gothic, through Renaissance and baroque. Maybe it is for the new members of the EU, as well for those Eastern European countries that are not included (yet?) – to remind some of our Western European mentors about their (and our) common cultural memory? It seems to be a past not yet addressed in the politically correct European memory of the last twenty years. Maybe it can be readdressed again?

Is Peaceful Coexistence of Memories Possible?

We are dealing here with a perspective of obligatory European memories. It is dominated by the enumeration of circles of a historical hell, and presents political corridors to the EU as necessary mnemonic purgatory, leading to the final stage of static paradise, achieved in the Noble-Prize awarded Union. Such a perspective provokes not the preparation of any alternative list of memories or guidelines to organize them, but rather a reflection upon the important consequences of the sociocultural application of this perspective.

There are three such consequences with which I intend to close. The first is really a fundamental one, something like a fatal choice: to be or to fear? Centrally organized memory of Europe is now built on fear rather than hope for better times. 'The future has lost much of its power to integrate, while the past is becoming increasingly important in the formation of identity', to repeat Aleida Assmann's formula, already quoted above. The goal is clear: to control the past in order to avoid chaos, and all these nightmares that happened in one, two or six circles of the European past, all leading to 1945. There are obvious reasons for such vigilance. The 'Never again!' memorial policy is based on unprecedented horrors. And yet – not by horror alone do identities live. Ewa Domańska (2012: 136–141) does not contest the tide of trauma-centred memorial practices in her new book because they have any specific consequences for Eastern Europe and its place in contemporary memorial debates and hierarchies. There is something more important at stake: human agency, or rather its constant training to become weaker and weaker, its ever-increasing fragility and strengthened need for protection. This is how we turn strong subjects of democratic process into patients waiting for their therapists, be it in Western or Eastern Europe. If there are only traumas to be cured, only fear stemming from the past, we are confirming our 'incapacity to entertain transformative political projects for the future', as Charles Maier (2003: 303) observed more than ten years ago.

The second consequence of memorial correctness is connected more strictly with 'Europeanism' – that is, a visible tendency to construct a common memorial identity for an institutionally united Europe, just like the old nation states had constructed identities for their subjects. This is a danger of a typically top-down construction, undermining the divergence of memorial realities – of different experiences in different social and cultural groups. The goal of transnational memory formation could provide such boring and predictable effects as those of a Treitschke-type historiography in the nineteenth and early twentieth-century European states.

Konrad H. Jarausch and Thomas Lindenberger (2007a: 16–17) who have described this 'temptation' eloquently, appeal to contemporary organizers of a common memory culture to be self-critical, not just to advertise 'cute advertising symbols from Brussels', but rather to prepare the best intellectual conditions for 'a long process of talking and listening to each other'. Henry Rousso (2007: 23–56), while certain of the necessity to still confront 'a murderous past dominated by national passions', also warns against 'the illusions of a tabula rasa and the construction of an artificial memory without genuine historical foundations'.[9]

Probably no one has pinpointed more precisely the third consequence of contemporary European top-down (or rather West-East) memory construction than an outside commentator, the Israeli specialist in memory studies, Natan Sznaider. He contests the very concept of memories divided along territorial borders, and an extension of this concept into a perspective on Eastern Europe as a closed space with its own rules and regulations of memory. The 'positive model' created in Western Europe by its best specialists and the 'negative' one – frozen in the east of the continent – have ceased to appear as projects and have become instead regarded as something natural:

> A binary discourse celebrating Western universal post-nationalism and condemning the persistence or return of ethnic, religious, and/or national particularism in large parts of Europe (or anywhere else). The central problem with the prevalent visions of Europe is that they tend to denigrate all particularism as an affront to its post-national vision of politics. European identity politics operates with a highly cultural bias in which culture (such as Jewish contributions to Europe) is celebrated at the expense of the experience and memories of those who belong to it. … This tries to obliterate the political memory of Europe and replace it with a tamed cultural approach as if divided political memories would undermine the unification of the European process of integration, which is, of course, possible. However, more is at stake here. (Sznaider 2013: 62–63)

What is at stake, exactly? The problem of non-recognition of the divergent historical memories of new Europe recalls a much broader question of constant negotiation between the particular and the universal – as represented by Western European heirs of Kant. As Sznaider (2013: 64) warns, dreaming of rationality beyond here and now, such universalism denies cultural difference, and dignity along with it. 'This dream can also turn into nightmare', he says (ibid. 74). Maybe a bit of Herder could help to avoid such a dangerous perspective? Born in Mohrungen (today: Morąg) in East Prussia, now Poland, and beginning his intellectual career in Riga, Johann Gottfried Herder in his curiosity and respect for the particular, for what makes others different, might be a useful patron of a corrective to a stiff, universalist (or rather politically correct) model of European memory.

Natan Sznaider proposes another counter-proposal: one stemming from the Jewish experience where universalism and particularism cease to be mutually exclusive categories. From this perspective he offers his verdict:

> Despite the tendency to privilege the mostly Western European conception that situates the origins of the memory boom during the 1980s, a concept that developed in response to a late reaction to the events of World War Two, this should not be mistaken for the sole or preferred form for how the past should be commemorated. This is an important point to 'remember': What is officially remembered is not identical to the memories particular groups carry; a unified European memory should recognize that divided memories result inevitably from different experiences. And there is nothing wrong with divided memories or narratives. They are not 'noise' in an integrated system. They do not need to be overcome and become united. Common narratives are not common in the sense that everybody should tell the same story. Instead, the recognition of the different narratives is the crux of the matter here. It primarily involves a kind of conflict ridden history, in which various groups, linked across national boundaries and cleavages, seek to live with the conflict without necessarily trying to overcome it, engaged in the quest for a common narrative but without ever hoping to actually reach it. In doing so, to a certain extent they change their own identities and create new opportunities for political action. (2013: 62–63)

Should we give up the dream of a rational consensus in such an important area as the one where the memory of Europe is debated? Not only Natan Sznaider, but also other thinkers see an element of provisional hegemony in any consensus, proposing instead 'agonistic pluralism', reciprocity and openness as more important discursive principles (Mouffe 1999: 745–758). A Polish political scientist and active participant of memorial debates in his country, Aleksander Smolar (2008: 56–57), reminds us that there are memorial cleavages not only and not even predominantly along the national frontiers, nor between East and West, but rather within these boundaries. He has proposed an interesting systematic of possible models for a politics of memory: 1. politics of conquest (when one side of the debate just conquers the other with its memorial practices, hierarchies and symbols); 2. politics of the internal Cold War (when the power of one side is too weak to conquer the other, but the goal of the memorial conquest is still the same); 3. politics of a stabilized difference and peaceful coexistence of memories; 4. politics of a restricted democratic consensus between different memories. This systematic has been formed on the basis of Polish internal struggles for memories after communism. It might be applicable, I presume, to the contemporary situation of the memory establishing business in Europe. Maybe we can concentrate our efforts in moving from the conquest theory and practice, and from a new East-West European Cold War, such as declared after Sandra Kalniete's 2004 'Gulag speech' in Leipzig, towards the model of stabilized difference and peaceful coexistence in European memories? Maybe only then would a 'restricted democratic consensus' be achievable?

Only when we speak, listen and learn different languages and different genealogies of our individual memories does such a goal seem at least imaginable. But is it really within our human range to freeze any consensus for a longer time?[10] Political correctness in memory construction tries to instil exactly such a sense of permanence, a sense of utopia of the status quo, the meanest utopia of all, according to Robert Musil and his *Man without Qualities*. Memories are changing, they are connected with many different experiences and directions, not just this one: from triumph to trauma. If there is any common direction in human memories, the one always worth reminding to (probably) all memory students, especially all those who try to organize the memories of others, is the shortest summary of all our efforts:

> *Uns überfüllts. Wir ordnens. Es zerfällt.*
> *Wir ordnens wieder und zerfallen selbst.*
> [It spills over us. We order it. It falls apart.
> We order it again and fall apart ourselves.]
> (Rainer Maria Rilke, *Duineser Elegien, Die achte Elegie*)

Notes

1. Another Polish specialist in historical theory, Jan Pomorski (2008: 107–166), has suggested that even the very tendency to escape from history towards memory is an element of contemporary political correctness.
2. Task Force for International Cooperation on Holocaust Education, Remembrance and Research, http://www.holocausttaskforce.org/about-the-itf/stockholm-declaration.html (accessed 12 February 2013).
3. As Stefan Troebst (2011: 148) observed perspicuously, President Putin intended to stress the imperial character of the 2005 commemoration of 'the victory' with a double invitation to Polish presidents. He had to invite Acting President of Poland, Aleksander Kwaśniewski, but he also decided to invite General Wojciech Jaruzelski, the man who proclaimed martial law in Poland in 1918 in order to save power for the Communist Party. 'So on May 9 [2005], two Polands were present on Red Square; the democratic republic as well as the Soviet vassal.'
4. An expression used by Aleida Assmann in an unpublished discussion in Cambridge, July 2011.
5. For different views and opinions on the subject, see: Hayashi 2003; Nowinowski, Pomorski and Stobiecki 2008; Nowak 2010; Miller and Lipman 2012.

6. See an interesting development of this perspective by Yamashita 2005.
7. For a more detailed picture of the problem see Martin 2001.
8. See the project page: www.memoryatwar.org, and its newsletter: *East European Memory Studies*, available on that page.
9. For a stronger critique of a 'Euro-formative' politics of memory and history, see Pocock 2005: 259–310.
10. Aleida Assmann (2010: 109) gives a very penetrating critical assessment of such a perspective in her recent essay on global extensions and limits of a new memory community based on the Holocaust. She deplores an 'Americanization' of the Holocaust which tends to 'disregard the local sites and contexts, rendering events more and more abstract' and she asks the question whether 'non-Western nations have to enter the realm of universalist morals through the needle's eye of the Holocaust or whether there are multiple trajectories that can lead to the same level of moral standards?' Maybe these critical questions are worth answering not only in the global context of 'Western' versus 'Non-Western' memories, but also when we are dealing with efforts aimed at creating a unified European collective memory?

Andrzej Nowak, Polish historian and public intellectual, born in Krakow, is professor of Eastern European history at Jagiellonian University and in the Institute of History of the Polish Academy of Sciences, Warsaw. Between 1994 and 2012 he was editor-in-chief of political-cultural bimonthly *ARCANA*. He is the author of twenty books, as well as co-author and editor of several others, mostly on Eastern European political and intellectual history. Among his recent publications are: *Imperiological Studies: A Polish Perspective* (Krakow, 2011), *Imperial Victims/Empires as Victims: 44 Views* (ed., Warsaw, 2010), *History and Geopolitics: A Contest for Eastern Europe* (Warsaw, 2008), *Russia and Eastern Europe: Applied 'Imperiology'* (Krakow, 2006).

PART II
Eastern Europe as a (Unique) Memory Framework?

Chapter 3

THE (NON-)TRAVELLING CONCEPT OF *LES LIEUX DE MÉMOIRE*
Central and Eastern European Perspectives

Maciej Górny and Kornelia Kończal

The migration of ideas, concepts and research perspectives from one province of thought to another continues to attract scholarly attention. Since in the 'ongoing process of travel, exchange and transfer' concepts are 'invested with new meanings' (Neumann and Nünning 2012: 3) researchers exploring their history ask why certain tools and approaches are susceptible to 'exportation'; which mechanisms and actors enable them to cross borders; and how do changing contexts of reception and appropriation shape their original design? Less attention, however, has been paid so far to the lack of transfer – understood both as an explicit, as well as implicit, refusal to engage with some analytical tools and categories. Why are certain concepts pursuing a transnational career in many regions of the world of very limited interest or even not appealing at all for scholars from other countries? Which features of a given setting can explain the fact that scholars anchored in that setting are not engaging with approaches that proved to be successful and stimulating in other research traditions? Can a closer look at the non-reception of a research perspective reveal something new about it, and can it help us to better understand the peculiarities of the non-receptive research context? Inspired by these questions, this chapter will explore the weak reception of the concept of *lieux de mémoire* in Central and Eastern Europe – a phenomenon that contrasts sharply with its success in most Western European countries.

The transnational career of the category coined in the 1980s by French historian and series editor at Gallimard Pierre Nora, was all but predictable. Nora's intention was to create a new tool that could be useful in rethinking the history of France. In the beginning, the originator and

---
Notes for this chapter begin on page 76.

editor of the seven volumes of *Les Lieux de mémoire* (1984–1992) was even convinced that his concept could only be applied to the French past. However, the last twenty years have proved that the concept of realms of memory – to use the problematic English translation of *les lieux de mémoire* preferred by Nora himself – can be applied with success in a variety of geographical and temporal settings. Consequently, there can be no talk of French 'exclusiveness' of *les lieux de mémoire*, if only because from the mid-1990s onwards historians from many Western European countries have been conceptualizing large-scale research projects inspired by Nora's idea (Audigier 2003; Boer 2008; Kończal 2012) and some attempts have been made at applying this tool to a new reading of the history of Europe (Boer et al. 2011–2012; Étienne and Serrier 2012).

In comparison with its Western European reception, the popularity of Nora's approach in Central and Eastern Europe leaves much to be desired: in the last twenty years, up to the most recent period, in no country east of Germany has any attempt been made to reconsider national history through the lens of *lieux de mémoire*. The aim of this chapter is to explore obstacles to the 'travelling' of Nora's concept to Central and Eastern Europe. For this purpose, the presence (and absence) of Nora's writings in Central and Eastern European languages will be addressed, and the main reasons for the weak reception of his tool in this part of Europe will be clarified. After some new instances of the application of Nora's category by historians and social scientists from Central and Eastern Europe, selected memory-related approaches formulated by sociologists and historians from the region (long) before 1989 as well as in the last twenty years will be presented. Finally, the last part of the chapter will enlarge the perspective by demonstrating that it is precisely the history of this part of Europe that can provide particularly stimulating ideas for reconceptualizing Nora's approach beyond the nation.

The chapter revolves therefore around two principal arguments. First, it assumes that Nora's approach was less useful for researchers from Central and Eastern Europe than for their Western European colleagues. But despite the marginal interest in Nora's concept in countries east of Germany, the general question of the relationship between history and memory has been a lively debated topic in local humanities. Moreover, even though there was no direct 'importation' of the particular concept of *lieux de mémoire* to this part of Europe, the perspective on history as conceptualized by Pierre Nora – albeit under other labels – was and still is present in Central and Eastern European humanities. Second, it shows the specific Central European contribution to the further development of Nora's tool. As a matter of fact, some stimulating attempts at a transnational reconsidering of the notion of *lieux de mémoire* have already been made by scholars from Central Europe. In this regard, the large-scale research project dealing with Polish-German *lieux de mémoire* gives the opportunity to move beyond methodological speculations and to formulate some assumptions about the concept's future prospects.

Le Nora imaginaire

In 2006, Maria Todorova discussed the question of how to employ the category of *lieu de mémoire* beyond its original French context. She saw three possible modes of transfer. First, the French example can be treated as a sort of norm and applied to different contexts, as happened with such notions as feudalism or modernity. Second, it can be 'naturalized', so that the 'original context would … revert to the status of a case study (although one with a temporal priority), one hypostasis of a multiple phenomenon'. Third, 'one can stick to the most conventional, everyday, literal, commonsense use of the term "places of memory", consciously disregarding the fact that the category has become invested with a particular meaning in a particular historiography' (Todorova 2006: 382–383).

It would be an oversimplification to claim that the 'memory turn' in French historiography has passed unnoticed in the former Soviet bloc. Throughout the 1990s, almost all the regional historiographies referred to it, albeit rather marginally. It was during this decade that the first translations of parts of Nora's work into local languages started to appear. In 1996, Nora's introduction to *Les Lieux de mémoire* was translated into Czech (Nora 1996b). Three years later, the Hungarian translation was published (Nora 1999a). Also in 1999, an anthology was edited in St Petersburg (Nora 1999b). Thanks to the cultural journal *Novoe Literaturnoe Obozrenie*, Nora's essay on generation was made known to the Russian public in 1998 (Nora 1998). In the subsequent decade, fragments of *Les Lieux de mémoire*, as well as short essays by the editor, were published in Poland (Nora 2001a; 2007a; 2008), Romania (2001b; 2002a; 2004a) and – as an anthology close to the Russian edition – Bulgaria (Nora 2004b). Incidentally, mostly in conference volumes, Pierre Nora's articles have appeared in other countries of the region (Nora 2007b). Finally, over a decade after the Czech and Hungarian translations, Nora's introductory essay appeared in Polish (2009; 2011).

The consequence of the scarcity of translations combined with the ritualistic invocation of Nora's name and the reduction of his approach to a small set of slogans is that, in Central and Eastern Europe, the knowledge of the concept of *lieux de mémoire* remains rather limited. Therefore, Étienne François's (2005: 8) assessment of an 'imagined Nora' (*le Nora imaginaire*), i.e., a clear contrast 'between an appreciable recognisability of Pierre Nora and his concept of *lieux de mémoire*, and, the insufficient, not to say very limited and distorted, at times, knowledge of his work as such' refers not only to France and Germany but can be seen as a pan-European phenomenon that also hints at Todorova.

The relative scarcity of translations did not, however, play a decisive role in the interrupted 'travel' of the concept of *lieux de mémoire* to the East of Europe. Only rarely does a translation policy regulate the pulse of humanities so rigidly as in the case of Ukraine with its 'peculiar diktat of translations when the decisions taken by a publishing company and sponsoring organizations determined the reading audience' (Portnov 2009: 439). In most countries of the region, there are multiple channels of intellectual transfer so that the scientific communities subscribe to many different discourses at the same time. Furthermore, English, German and – last but not least – Russian translations of (parts of) *Les Lieux de mémoire* create yet another potential opportunity for scholars from Central and Eastern Europe to get in touch with Nora's concept.

The question of non-existent translations becomes all the more vexing if one looks at the closest Polish equivalent to the French *Les Lieux de mémoire* project, i.e., the series of books entitled *A to Polska właśnie* (*This is Poland*) published since the mid-1990s and now numbering over sixty volumes. Even though it does not directly refer to Nora's concept, the scope of the project is indeed comparable to his perspective. The volumes vary in theme including historical phenomena (cabaret, cuisine, the Polish language, monasteries and convents, pilgrimages), individuals and groups (Gombrowicz, John Paul II, Miłosz, Napoleon, Słowacki, the Jews), regions (Galicia, Silesia, Warmia and Masuria or the former Eastern provinces called *Kresy*) and cities (e.g., Wrocław). In short, this book series deals with the history and memory of many historical phenomena that were or still are contributing to the feeling of belonging to Polish culture.

As mentioned above, the series *A to Polska właśnie* does not refer to Nora's tool. Yet, there are some other regional attempts at reinterpreting national history through the lens of collective memory which, in contrast, are directly inspired by Nora's project. At the University of Debrecen, a project on '*Magyar emlékezethelyek*' (Hungarian *lieux de mémoire*) started in 2011, resulting (so far) in a demo-webpage with a collection of forty entries devoted to such historical phenomena as the Golden Team (of Hungarian football players in the 1950s), *gulyás* or Trianon.[1] The *emlékezethelyek* give access to printed documents and visual sources that played (or are still playing) an identity-shaping role in Hungarian society. Thus the intention of the project is to collect media of collective memory rather than to analyse their social and cultural functions. A similar agenda is characteristic of the Polish project '*Polska – węzły pamięci zbiorowej*' ('Poland – knots of collective memory') also initiated in 2011 by the literary historian, former member of the democratic opposition and director of the Polish section of Radio Free Europe, Zdzisław Najder. The intention of the project, which was conceived with a clear reference to the concept of Pierre Nora, is to 'rescue' the memory of interwar Polish society from oblivion.

There are some striking similarities between both projects under construction – the Hungarian '*Magyar emlékezethelyek*' and the Polish '*Węzły pamięci zbiorowej*'. They illustrate quite well the process of a relatively superficial transfer of a research concept, as observed by Todorova; their teams do not express much interest in methodology (Láczo and Zombory 2012:108–109), and both endeavours testify to the discontinuity of local traditions of memory studies, which will be addressed in the next part of the chapter.

As the Hungarian case shows, besides translations of Nora's texts into lesser and more widely-spoken languages, there were also other routes that led to *Les lieux de mémoire*. In Hungary, the reception of Pierre Nora and his approach to memory followed a somewhat unusual path: its beginnings long preceded the translation of his works. The overall enterprise of *Les lieux de mémoire* and its key concepts were more earnestly discussed first in relation to the exhibition 'Hungarians between "East" and "West": National Symbols and Legends' held at the Museum of Ethnography in Budapest in 1994 (Laczó and Zombory 2012: 108).

In a publication related to the exhibition, Tamás Hofer (1994) opened a debate about the possibility of adopting the French concept in Hungary. Yet his argument revolved around the question of whether Hungarian realms of memory could be exhibited. Consequently, in contrast to countries such as Italy, Germany, Austria, the Netherlands, Luxembourg, Belgium and Switzerland, the Hungarian reference to Nora's idea did not transform into a large-scale research project on *lieux de mémoire*.

In some cases, for instance in Romania and to a lesser extent in the Czech Republic, the middle generation of historians and 'Francophile' scholars from other disciplines still cultivate intellectual ties with French colleagues. Yet this academic exchange did not induce any Czech or Romanian project on *les lieux de mémoire*. As far as Poland is concerned, historically speaking, French thought has exerted the largest foreign impact on Polish humanities in general, and memory studies in particular (Kula 2010; Pleskot 2010). Striking in this regard, however, is the selective reception of concepts and theories developed by French scholars. Despite the fairly long tradition of quoting Maurice Halbwachs, whose *Social Frames of Memory* appeared in Polish in the late 1960s (Halbwachs 2008 [1969]), there are still no Polish-language editions – or, for that matter, full readings by Polish historians and sociologists – of his *The Legendary Topography of the Gospels in the Holy Land* (1941) or *La mémoire collective* (1950). And even though some important books have been translated from French into Polish – for example those by Paul Ricœur (2006), Jacques Le Goff (2007) and Marc Augé (2009) – the reference to the concept of collective memory in Polish historiography remains rather disparate[2] and as far as the specific concept of *lieux de mémoire* is concerned, some Polish historians are even convinced that this tool 'does not bring anything new or essential to the study of history' (Wiszewski 2008: 123) and is therefore of no use to historians. Polish sociologists have shown more interest in collective memory than historians, for example Barbara Szacka[3] and her colleagues, yet their main methodological references were not of direct French origin.

What is more, even the newest research agendas dealing with the relationship between memory and space do not refer to the French concept of *lieux de mémoire*. This is illustrated by projects originated and conducted by psychologist Maria Lewicka on identity and memory formation of the inhabitants of some (former) Polish cities and regions (Lewicka 2011, 2012; Wójcik, Bilewicz and Lewicka 2010); works on geopoetics written by literary scholars (Marszałek and Sasse 2010; Rybicka 2008: 19–31); and some projects conducted by cultural scientists – e.g., Jacek Małczyński's (2009) study in progress about trees as 'living monuments' on the territory of the former extermination camp in Bełżec, or Magdalena Saryusz-Wolska's (2010) monograph on collective memory in some Central European cities. Moreover, there have been some attempts to establish concepts that could represent an alternative to Nora's category (Nijakowski 2006; Bednarek 2010). How to explain the tension between the interest in memory and space on the one hand and the reserved attitude towards the research perspective developed by Pierre Nora on the other?

The Burden of Language and the Weight of Politics

It seems that two regional implications of memory discourse can help to explain this paradox. The one goes back to a purely linguistic aspect that has apparently played an important role in the non-reception of Nora's concept in this part of Europe; in fact, in some countries in the region this may be the primary reason. The other is rooted in a specific political imprint of memory-related debates on Central and Eastern European history.

In some languages – for instance in Polish – it is impossible to make a distinction between the symbolic and the geographic dimension of *le lieu de mémoire* – as can be done in French (*lieu de mémoire* versus *site de mémoire* or *lieu de souvenir*) or in German (*Erinnerungsort* versus *Gedenkstätte* or *Erinnerungsstätte*). The Polish term *miejsce pamięci* can be the linguistic equivalent of both – *le lieu de mémoire* (as a symbolic realm of memory) and *le site de mémoire* or *le lieu de souvenir* (as a geographic site of memory). In practical language use, however, the Polish phrase *miejsce pamięci* is more likely to be understood in its purely topographic sense referring to monuments, statues and memorial plaques, which are also often associated with the Second World War. That is to say, the term *miejsce pamięci* is marked by a strong connection with patriotic memory and the history of mass violence. The phrase 'places of memory and martyrdom' is commonplace rhetoric, whose meaning blends in completely with the French *lieux de mémoire*. Thus, for the majority of Poles, the first association connected to the words *lieu* and *mémoire* are monuments (if not cemeteries). The impossibility of liberating the phrase *miejsce pamięci* from its topographical imprint might explain difficulties encountered with the concept of *lieu de mémoire* in Polish historiographical discourse. Similar developments can be observed in the Czech case. Since the late 1990s, mainly due to the activities of the non-governmental organization Antikomplex, the notion 'sites of memory' (*místa paměti*) is increasingly associated with cities in the region of Sudetenland where the German inhabitants fled or were expelled in the 1940s (Mikšíček et al. 2004).

Akin to the linguistic obstacle to the use of the term *lieu de mémoire* in other contexts than the topographical one is the problem of a regional 'politics of history', which is common to the entire postcommunist space. In the early 1990s, there was a general expectation that the new state structures would 'tell the truth' about the history of the Second World War as well as investigate and judge the communist dictatorships. In Czechoslovakia, the lustration law was introduced as early as 1991 (six years before similar Polish legislation) and was followed in 1993 by a declaration of lawlessness of the communist regime (Kopeček 2008b). These processes were accompanied by the postulate to 'come to terms with the past' – primarily the communist one (Gluza 1997). The (then) Gauck Institute (*Die Behörde des Bundesbeauftragten für die Unterlagen des Staatssicherheitsdienstes der ehemaligen Deutschen Demokratischen Republik*) was a norm commonly referred to in Central and Eastern Europe. The first of the Eastern European 'Gauck Institutes', the Polish Institute of National Remembrance (*Instytut Pamięci Narodowej* – IPN) was created in 1998, and 2003 saw the creation of the Slovak Nation's Memory Institute (*Ústav Pamäti Národa*).

Until the mid-2000s both institutes concentrated first and foremost on redressing the victims of the dictatorship. In the following years, the 'politics of history' played a crucial role in public discourse about the past, leading to a strong politicization of the 'memorial' institutes. Both the Slovak (Ivan Petranský) and the Polish (Janusz Kurtyka) directors of the respective institutes were criticized for their role in the public debate: the Slovak institute contributed to the 'rehabilitation' of the wartime pro-German Slovak state, an act difficult to combine with the official commemoration of the anti-German uprising of 1944, which was directed both against Nazi Germany and its Slovak allies; the Polish IPN launched an attack on the symbol of *Solidarność*, Lech Wałęsa. Neither institute abstained from introducing their subcutaneous political agenda to their programmes of civic education. Meanwhile, the very idea of 'national memory' as well as the need to pursue an official politics of history were (and still are) being questioned (Stola 2012). Similar doubts apply to several other Central and Eastern European public institutions unifying research tasks and civic education, such as the House of Terror (*Terror Háza*) in Budapest, the Occupation Museum in Tallinn (*Okupatsioonidemuuseum*), a similar one in Riga (*Latvijas Okupācijas Muzejs*) or the Genocide and Resistance Research Centre of Lithuania (*Lietuvos Gyventojų Genocide ir Rezistencijo Styrimo Centras*).

At first glance, the creation of Central and Eastern European 'Gauck Institutes' and similar establishments, as well as their politicization, can seem rather distant from the issue addressed in this chapter. Yet, in addition to their role in the public debates of the last decade, they have also been shaping the language and content-driven, as well as emotional setting, in which 'memory' is referred to. For a long time, they have even been successful in monopolizing the very notion of memory, making it extremely difficult to break through with a different narrative. A good illustration of this phenomenon is an attempt made more than ten years ago by the Polish art historian Andrzej Tomaszewski (1934–2010). Already in 2001 Tomaszewski tried to initiate a discussion on Polish *lieux de mémoire*. Referring to Nora's project, he proposed a list of eighty entries that could form the backbone of a future publication (Tomaszewski et al. 2001; Tomaszewski 2005). Despite the enthusiasm of a group of (art) historians, the predominant reaction to the proposal was colored by skepticism. Eventually, Tomaszewski dropped his idea after the parliamentary elections of 2005, arguing that the new political climate was not conducive to serious debates on collective identity.[4]

The dilemma faced by Andrzej Tomaszewski in Poland addresses a general problem with (discussions of) history in Central and Eastern Europe: the twentieth century's domination over the notion of collective memory and often antagonistic interpretations of the major events that took place during the short century. Insightful in this regard is Gábor Gyáni's analysis of the Hungarian discourse on the 1956 revolution. He describes the clinch between contradictory readings of the past and argues that the different interpretations of the revolution are irreconcilable:

> even within the frames of memory work conducted on a scholarly basis under the aegis of institutionalized craftsmanship. This is due only in part to the natural divergences that mark discursive practice, and much more to the domination of the plural historical narratives based on personal recollection or other forms of collective memory. The case ... seems to suggest there is some validity in the postmodern belief that everyone can be his or her own historian, in line with the democratization of the past, even if such a belief causes anxiety among the professionals who still hold a near-monopoly over the memory of the past. (Gyáni 2006: 1206–1207)

The same could be said not only about the 1956 revolution in Hungary, but also about the events in Czechoslovakia, Poland and Romania in 1968, in Poland in 1956 and 1980 as well as in Romania in 1989.

All the phenomena addressed in this section of the chapter – the semantics of memory marked by a close connection between memory and mass violence, the regional debate on the communist past and the politicized memory of postwar revolutions – indicate that in Central and Eastern Europe the notion of collective memory is not an empty shell but has been and still is the object of intensive and highly politicized debate. In consequence, it could not be easily filled with a set of concepts 'imported' from Western European memory studies. However, the burden of language and the weight of politics were not the only reasons for the durability of the conceptual iron curtain.

The 'Forgotten' Traditions

Writing about the history of Polish philosophy, Jan Skoczyński summarizes that it is characterized by the discipline's 'multi-storeyedness, entanglement, frequent lack of clear solutions, uncertainty. Its edges are dominated by an unceasing movement, the borders are constantly changing, and nothing lasts for very long; that which is built up is quickly destroyed' (Skoczyński and Woleński 2010: 519). Basically the same can be said about many Central and Eastern European approaches to memory studies. As for this point, it is worth noting on a more general level that memory-related research concepts 'travelled' to Central and Eastern Europe only from the West. This contention implies a threefold meaning. First, it means that Western knowledge about works conceived in less widely-spoken Eastern European languages which could be inspiring for scholars analysing the history of memory is almost non-existent – incidentally, this is not only characteristic of the field of memory studies. Second, it means that, for most countries in Central and Eastern Europe, one can observe striking discontinuities and ruptures within local research traditions. Third, it means that ignorance is not only confined to the national framework of research but also relates to the broader context of the region – consider the fact that research concepts have been travelling *from* the West *to* the East and not *within* Central and Eastern Europe. A closer look at some memory-related research perspectives advanced by Central and Eastern European scholars in the past century demonstrates that this research topic has a long, though scattered and partly forgotten, tradition. Furthermore, it yields yet another tenet, which affords an explanation of the weak reception of Nora's concept in Central and Eastern Europe.

Seminal works by Polish sociologist Stefan Czarnowski (1879–1937) from the 1920s containing some striking anticipations of Nora's insights, or those written by Czarnowski's student, Nina Assorodobraj-Kula (1908–1999), in the 1960s which are reminiscent of concepts conceived later by Jan and Aleida Assmann are known merely in their country of origin, if at all. Other research traditions originating on Central and Eastern European ground and of paramount importance for the interdisciplinary field of memory studies are confronted with the same problem.

Possibly the most prominent example of non-reception is the Tartu-Moscow Semiotic School. Formed in the mid-1960s by – among others – Juri Lotman (1922–1993) and Vladimir Toporov (1928–2005), this school of thought proposed an original reading of cultural history through the lens of semiotics. Even though direct references to the terminology of memory in the works of Russian and Estonian semioticians are rather scarce (Lotman 1990) many of their monographs are in fact devoted to historical phenomena where, according to the definition of *lieux de mémoire*, 'memory crystallizes and secrets itself' (Nora 1989: 7). Yet the valuable insights of scholars from the Tartu-Moscow Semiotic School only rarely represented a source of inspiration for Central and Eastern European cultural scientists (rather than historians) exploring the processes of collective identity building. If Central and Eastern European researchers referred to the works of their Russian and Estonian colleagues, they did so mostly in analysis of national myths and stereotypes. From the 1970s onwards, in the humanities of many Central and Eastern European countries, these issues have belonged to the most popular research topics. In what follows, this research trend will be illustrated with selected monographs written by Czech, Polish and Romanian scholars concerning the nineteenth-century national movements.

One of the very few instances of direct inspiration by the Tartu school is the work of Czech literary scholar Vladimír Macura (1945–1999). His *The Czech Dream* (1998; see idem in English 2010) is an analysis of 'national myths' as a system of signs generating symbolical meanings. According to Macura, the process of the Czech national revival driven by a strong intellectual energy was a set of interconnected 'dreams' directed towards an imagined national future, rather than a response to Bohemian reality in the nineteenth century. Macura's focus on the discursiveness of national culture goes as far as the self-referential question about the role of the literary historian in the construction of his object of inquiry.

The same issue – in contrast to the approach of Macura, without any reference to the works of Estonian and Russian semioticians – has been addressed in studies by other literary scholars from the region: to mention just two of the most prominent Polish historians of ideas, literature and collective imagination Maria Janion (1990, 1998, 2006) and Andrzej Mencwel (2006). The crucial questions of their work, that of imagined Polishness (*polskość*) and the discursive formation of the nation in the nineteenth and twentieth centuries, are also of interest for Polish historians – especially those working on the history of ideas, like Jerzy Jedlicki (1988, in English 1999), Tomasz Kizwalter (1999) and Andrzej Walicki (1982, 1994). The broad field of collective identities, national myths and stereotypes has been also repeatedly visited by historians from the research school that was opened at the University of Łódź in the 1960s by Marian Henryk Serejski[5] (1897–1975) and further developed by Andrzej Feliks Grabski (1934–2000) (1983, 1985) and Andrzej Wierzbicki (1993). Two features of Grabski's definition of the history of historiography are of interest here. First, he defined it as 'an analysis of various forms of thinking about the past, not restricted to those which contain the so-called scientific reflection on history referring to the modern concept of historical research'. Second, he emphasized 'a holistic view of historiography' including 'organizational structures, theoretical fundaments, and interpretations of the past' (Stobiecki 2003: XIII). A pitfall of this broadened perspective on the history of historiography, however, is the lack of a strict methodology. Indeed, a comparison of Serejski's or Grabski's works with the 'German' type of the history of historiography represented e.g. by Jörn Rüsen (1993) reveals a crucial difference: the focus of Polish historians on such 'soft' categories as 'interpretations of the past', 'historical consciousness' and 'historical identity' contrasts sharply with the question of rhetoric and aesthetics – central for Rüsen's understanding of German historicism. In light of this 'distance' from methodological strictness, it is perhaps not surprising that the works of Polish historians of historiography are also free of methodological references to the line of research developed by Estonian and Russian semioticians.

Another example of Central and Eastern European historians' interest in national mythologies is the Romanian case – and especially works written since the 1980s by Lucian Boia on the construction, cultural significance and socio-political functions of some myths that the Romanian collective identity is based upon. Focusing on Romanian history in the nineteenth and twentieth centuries, Boia examines myths as 'an imaginary construction (which, once again, does not mean either "real" or "unreal", but arranged according to the logic of the imaginary), which serves to highlight the essence of cosmic and social phenomena, in close relation to the fundamental values of the community, and with the aim of ensuring that community's cohesion' (Boia 2001: 29; see also ibid. 1987, 1998).

The intense preoccupation of Central and Eastern European historians with the discursiveness of national history, especially with the formation of collective identities and shared interpretations of the past in the form of myths, represents the main regional approach to the issues addressed in France and other Western European countries under the label of *lieux de mémoire*. In addition to the circumstances discussed in the previous sections of this chapter, this feature might explain why in Central and Eastern European humanities there was neither a 'memory turn' nor a *trente mémorieuses* – to employ the phrase coined by Jean-Pierre Rioux (2006) as description of the memorial awakening in France from the mid-1970s onwards.[6] Much more likely, a reverse turn could be spotted in the 1990s. Some of the most interesting native research traditions have been either marginalized or interrupted. For the same reason, important and sometimes still very inspiring works of local historians and sociologists on tradition, historical consciousness, collective identity or historical culture, written in the first half of the twentieth century and in the 1960s and 1970s are far less successful in the field of memory studies in today's Central and Eastern Europe than recent works by American, French and German authors. In short: whereas local research traditions have fallen into oblivion and since the interest in collective memory has been centred upon questions of war and the communist past, the new wave in humanities looks for inspiration in the West rather than in regional traditions.

Beyond the Nation

These circumstances create the context in which, at least in the last few years, the increasing interest of Central and Eastern European scholars in the concept of *lieux de mémoire* can be observed. It is true that apart from the Polish and Hungarian projects under construction mentioned above, in no country east of Germany has any attempt at defining local *lieux de mémoire* been made. Consequently, there are no multi-volume publications on, for instance Czech, Slovak or Romanian history conceived as a symbolic topography of *lieux de mémoire*. Yet there are a number of monographs on single historical phenomena written by Central and Eastern European researchers, inspired by Nora's approach. Interestingly enough, all of them share certain features that were less visible in Nora's project as well as in most Western European projects drawing on his approach to the history of memory.

Mostly due to the complex ethnic structures of the region and the weak centralizing power of the states, Central and Eastern European *lieux de mémoire* divide communities more often than they unite them. The points of crystallization of collective identities are therefore filled with contradictory meanings. For this reason, in Central and Eastern Europe the same *lieu* can serve the *mémoire* of different social, ethnic or religious groups and cannot therefore be analysed in purely national terms – as the Central European historian Moritz Csáky rightly observed, criticizing the nationally foreshortened perspective of the history of memory (Csáky 2003; 2004). In what follows, the recent application of the French research concept in Central and Eastern Europe will be illustrated with the examples of a monograph, a research agenda and a large-scale Polish-German research project proposing a transnational approach.

In her book devoted to the mountain Devín, the Slovak ethnographer Gabriela Kiliánová (2005, in German 2011) examines the history of Slovak, Magyar and German appropriations of the symbolic space referring directly to the concept of *lieux de mémoire* as the main methodological instrument (translated as *pamätne mesto*, i.e., 'memorable place' rather than 'place of memory'). In the discussion with her reviewers (Stekl and Mannová 2003), Kiliánová refers implicitly to a joint Austro-Slovak comparative project on heroes, myths and identities as well as to '*Deutsche Erinnerungsorte*' as her principal sources of inspiration. The author perceives the mountain Devín in particular and the history of Slovakia in general as predominantly fitting the theoretical approach of Moritz Csáky. Due to the complex interplay of Slovak, Magyar, German, Jewish, Czech and Czechoslovak identities it is a paradigmatic instance of hybrid, transnational and heterogeneous territories (Kiliánová 2006).

The other examples are publications by Ľubomír Lipták and Elena Mannová dealing with the complex interplay of state and ethnic symbols in urban and rural settings. In the extremely interesting (though by no means exceptional in the region) case of Slovakia this means 'changes of changes' from Hungarian, through Czechoslovak, Slovak, Czechoslovak again and, finally (for the time being), Slovak statehood again. Of note here especially is the early essay on memorialization of the Slovak

National Uprising published by Lipták in 1995 (Lipták 1995a: 363–365). He discusses not only the politics of memory, but also the transformation of spontaneous acts of commemoration into an official symbol of the historical event. On another occasion, Lipták – the unquestionable leader of Slovak historiography in the 1990s – pointed at the embeddedness of historiography in the framework of collective identities:

> A deeper analysis of the course of the great changes in the twentieth century shows that historical analysis always played only a supportive role. A reinvigorated, recalled history gave to movements, events and their representatives an ethical dimension and emotional charge, a higher and timeless legality, a consecration in antiquity and a kind of inevitability. (Lipták 1995b: 13)

Yet, the 'recalled history' – as Lipták puts it – has seldom been analysed by Slovak historians, since throughout the 1990s many of them were engaged in a struggle between 'national' or 'conservative' and 'cosmopolitan' or 'liberal' current (Hlavičková 2007: 263). Meanwhile, particularly inspiring impulses came from Slovak ethnographers, to bring up just the aforementioned work by Kiliánová (2005).[7] The relative openness of Slovak memory studies, however, does not only go back to their interdisciplinary character (and for a short time the lack of interest by historians). Two other possible causes seem worth at least mentioning: they could be called 'the structural' and 'the situational' setting. The first is based on the observation that recent Slovak references to the French, Austrian or German authors are not only a matter of choice or intellectual fashion, they also testify to the scarcity of 'native' research traditions,[8] which proves to be stimulating for the relatively swift transfer of methodological concepts from abroad into the Slovak humanities. The 'situational' setting, in turn, lies in geography. Bratislava's proximity to Vienna, which is, thanks to the research group around Moritz Csáky, possibly the most innovative centre of memory studies in Central Europe, is certainly very advantageous for intellectual transfers. Some Slovak scholars were even involved in international research projects conducted at the Viennese Academy of Sciences. Others have personal contacts to Hannes Stekl, one of the co-editors of *Memoria Austriae* (Brix, Bruckmüller and Stekl 2004–2005) and to Moritz Csáky himself.

The Slovak examples of a fruitful adaptation of Nora's research concept to local history concentrate upon the multiplicity of competing collective memories. It was a question of time for a more ambitious endeavour subscribing to this perspective to appear. The first attempt to overcome the national view on the history of memory within a large-scale research project was carried out between 2006 and 2013 at the Centre for Historical Research of the Polish Academy of Sciences in Berlin in cooperation with

Carl von Ossietzky University in Oldenburg (Hahn and Traba 2012–2013). The aim of 'Polish-German *Lieux de Mémoire*' is to go beyond the national framework in a bid to rethink Polish-German history through the lens of two approaches tied together: the history of Polish-German relations (*Beziehungsgeschichte*) and the history of collective memory (*Erinnerungsgeschichte*). Of the nine volumes in total (five in German and four in Polish), three contain essays on common, shared and parallel Polish-German *lieux de mémoire*. The last type of *lieu de mémoire* addressed in the Polish-German project is a new category referring to two (or more) completely different historical phenomena. Yet although the 'real' objects of remembering are completely separate, there are many parallels in their identity-building functions in both societies – for instance as symbols of betrayal or success, as memorial embodiment of paradise lost or imperial ambitions, or other figures constituting a sense of belonging to the community.[9] This is not to say that *Polish-German Lieux de Mémoire* is the first ever publication to aim at transcending national borders in the examination of *lieux de mémoire* (Raphaël and Herberich-Marx 1991; Hudemann 2002; Le Rider, Csáky and Sommer 2002; Adriansen and Schartl 2006; Henningsen, Kliemann-Geisinger and Troebst 2009). Yet in contrast to manifold rather disparate conference volumes or purely editorial undertakings, it is the first large-scale research project proposing the practical application of a new research design inspired by Nora's concept. And it surely has the potential to serve as a reference for other regional rather than national projects on multiple collective memories.

The innovative approach of the Polish-German project confirms that the entangled history of Central and Eastern Europe aspires to reconsider the hitherto prevailing focus on national cultures of remembrance. This, in turn, encourages a reversal of the main question of the present chapter 'What does the concept of *lieux de mémoire* mean for Central and Eastern Europe?' by asking rather 'What does Central and Eastern Europe mean for *lieux de mémoire*?' Taking up the thought-provoking account of Moritz Csáky (2003), Jörg Hackmann listed:

> various types of places related to transnational memory. A typology might comprise: first, places of memory with national connotations that are situated beyond contemporary national borders; … second, places that refer to an imperial, pre-national past; third, places where shared or divided memories of several groups, nations and societies concur; fourth, places that have been re-interpreted and filled with new contents; and finally, places of memory that compete with each other. (Hackmann 2008: 386)

Hackmann's typology of transnational Eastern European *lieux de mémoire* can certainly be further developed or reformulated. But the basic assumption – i.e., the aspiration to go beyond the national framework – is by no means restricted to the symbolic topography of Central and Eastern Europe. On the contrary, it may and, as a matter of fact, actually does shape the very category of *lieux de mémoire*. While the initial idea of Pierre Nora referred to historical phenomena where French national identity crystallized, some subsequent applications of his notion in Western Europe tried to gradually 'open' the category.[10] Yet, as Hartmut Kaelble (2006: 114–155) rightly pointed out, dealing with the history of Central and Eastern Europe sharpens researcher's sensitivity for changing borders, entanglements, tensions and conflicts. The same applies to the examination of the history of collective memory.

Concluding Remarks

At the beginning of this chapter, we argued that in Central and Eastern European academia, knowledge about the concept of *lieux de mémoire* remains limited. Then, the main reasons for the non-travelling of Nora's idea eastwards were identified. First, the initial moment of Nora's appearance in Central and Eastern European historiographies coincided with heated debates on recent history, which involved the instrumentalization of the very notion of memory (and, at times, also that of *lieux de mémoire*). Therefore, the intellectual potential of Nora's concept was largely unnoticed and the first instances of its application did not emerge prior to 2000. Second, the main components of Nora's approach were present in Central and Eastern European humanities already, long before 1989, albeit under different names. Although there are almost no large-scale research projects on *lieux de mémoire* in Central and Eastern Europe, recent years have brought some insightful monographs on selected places, individuals and historical events interpreted through the lens of Nora's concept. Moreover, specifically a Central European scholar – Moritz Csáky – raised the most extended criticism of the purely national view of the history of memory. Finally, it was in this European region where the first project was conceptualized – 'The Polish-German *Lieux de Mémoire*' – which tries to go beyond the national perspective. Three concluding remarks can be drawn from this account.

First, Central and Eastern European scholars were interested in memory issues long before the memory boom was diagnosed in Western Europe and the USA. We find plentiful evidence for it already at the beginning of the twentieth century as well as in the 1960s and 1970s (Kończal and Wawrzyniak 2012). Yet whereas Nora's concept of *lieux de mémoire* pursued an unparalleled career in many Western European historiographies, it did not generate any large-scale research projects on national *lieux de mémoire* in Central and Eastern Europe. In the 1990s and 2000s, historians in this region did not see the need for its appropriation for a holistic reinterpretation of national history, because the processes of the discursive formation of collective identities and historical consciousness had already been analysed in this part of Europe by other means. In addition, two decades after the collapse of communism saw a shift of the very category of collective memory into the sphere of recent history and politics of history.

Nevertheless, it is not accurate to see the lack of large-scale research projects on *lieux de mémoire* in Central and Eastern Europe as a peculiarity of this region. It is not the task of this chapter to formulate any hypothesis that could explain why neither Danish, Finnish, Norwegian nor Swedish historians have hitherto initiated any large-scale research projects on their *lieux de mémoire*. It is worth noting that there is no publication inspired by Nora's idea in Great Britain (Collini 1994) – a country with an outstanding tradition of inquiry into national myths, to mention just a few: Eric Hobsbawm (1917–2012) (1991), Raphael Samuel (1934–1996) (1989) or Anthony Smith (1986, 1999, 2003). Their exploration of national mythologies and corresponding Central and Eastern European studies on historical consciousness, national stereotypes and other identity-related discursive phenomena confirm the obvious fact that there are many 'constructionist themes in the historiography of the nation' (Stråth 2008) besides the French concept of *lieux de mémoire*.

Finally, since the majority of Central and Eastern European *lieux de mémoire* are focal points for conflicted memories, they are characterized by contradictory interpretations of the same historical phenomena by different social, religious or ethnic groups. This 'militant' aspect of collective memory might be the most important lesson from the encounter between Central and Eastern Europe and Nora's concept. However, this is not to say that Central and Eastern European shared *lieux de mémoire* represent a regional 'peculiarity'. Contrary to the received wisdom, this particular region is not exceptional in its troublesome ethnic, cultural, religious and political heterogeneity. It is rather to say that the main inspiration from Central and Eastern Europe for further reflection upon Nora's concept could be a higher sensitivity for memory discourses beyond the nation. The Central and Eastern European challenge for Nora's concept is all the more stimulating as it is free of the teleological trap characterizing much of the current discussions on the European *lieux de mémoire*.

Notes

1. See http://deba.unideb.hu/deba/emlekezethely/ (accessed 17 April 2013).
2. Important books in this respect include those by Bronisław Baczko and Krzysztof Pomian, scholars belonging to the so-called Warsaw school of the history of ideas and, after their emigration, closely connected to the humanities in France. The numerous works of Marcin Kula are also of note, and bear signs of highly personal inspiration by the *Annales*.
3. A good summing-up of her memory-related research projects: Szacka 2006.
4. In conversation with Kornelia Kończal, 24 October 2009.
5. Among his numerous publications of significance in the context of this chapter are especially Serejski 1973 and Serejski 1965.
6. Rioux formulated this phrase in analogy to the well-known term '*Trente Glorieuses*' (The Glorious Thirty) coined by the French demographer Jean Fourastié to characterize the three first decades of postwar history in France, a period of unparalleled economic prosperity.
7. For detailed bibliographic information on recent Slovak memory research see Kurhajcová 2012.
8. Lipták argues that the discontinuity of national history corresponds to the discontinuity of the Slovak historiography (1995b: 14).
9. About virtues of this approach: Czapliński 2012: 29–33.
10. Possibly the most visible attempt to overcome the purely national perspective of *lieux de mémoire* was the German publication on *Deutsche Erinnerungsorte* whose editors succeeded in including within the three volumes some shared *Erinnerungsorte* (François and Schulze 2001; see also François 2001).

Maciej Górny is professor at the Historical Institute of the Polish Academy of Sciences. Currently he is also visiting professor at the German Historical Institute in Warsaw. He was a research associate at the Centre for Historical Research of the Polish Academy of Sciences in Berlin from 2006 to 2010. His research interests are Central and Eastern Europe in the nineteenth and twentieth centuries, the history of historiography, discourses on race and the First World War. His publications include *The Nation Should Come First: Marxism and Historiography in East Central Europe* (2013, Polish edition 2007, German edition 2011).

Kornelia Kończal is a PhD student at the European University Institute in Florence, Italy. Her project explores the postwar reconstruction of social order in Central Europe through the lens of the plundering of German property. Until 2012 she was the coordinator of the project on Polish-German *lieux de mémoire* undertaken by the Centre for Historical Research of the Polish Academy of Sciences in Berlin. She is co-editor of a volume on the politics of history in Europe after 1989 (*Strategien der Geschichtspolitik in Europa nach 1989. Deutschland, Frankreich und Polen im internationalen Vergleich*, Göttingen 2013).

Chapter 4

AIN'T NOTHING SPECIAL

Sławomir Kapralski

In this chapter the author presents two intertwined lines of argument. First, it is argued that the thesis that the 'special nature' of social memory and frames of remembrance in Eastern Europe is based on a false generalization of the fact that 'Western' and 'Eastern' memories have been 'desynchronized': that the same motifs appear in both types of memory, although at different times. In addition, it is argued that the popularity of the thesis can be accounted for by an 'orientalizing temporal othering'. Second, the chapter presents a review of the processes of silencing and erasing the memory of the atrocities experienced by the Roma/Gypsies in Europe to show that similar mechanisms of remembrance/forgetting have been employed in both parts of the continent. The author's standpoint in this discussion can be summarized by the lyrics of Duncan Sheik's song *Nothing Special*, from which the title has been borrowed, and which helped to structure the argument:

> *You ain't nothing special*
> *You're no more celestial than anyone else*
> *As far as I can tell I call it mythology*
> *We see what we want to see*
> *And I'm the snake who bites his own tail.*
>   Duncan Sheik

Ain't Nothing Special

It has often been argued that historical experience, memory and remembrance in the postcommunist countries of Eastern Europe are essentially

---

Notes for this chapter begin on page 95.

different from their Western European counterparts. Of course, in a very basic sense such a claim is banally true (at least for those more familiar with human diversity) and reflects the different historical paths of the two parts of the continent as well as a mutual lack of knowledge regarding the history of the 'others'. When it comes to a more detailed description of the difference, however, the thesis often turns out to be a critical evaluation. Moreover, the message is contradictory regarding what the difference actually is. For example, for Tony Judt, Eastern Europe can be characterized by the abundance of (conflicting) memories: in his approach we simply have 'too much memory, too many pasts on which people can draw, usually as a weapon against the past of someone else' (Judt 1992: 99). The abundance of memory is believed here to be potentially dangerous and it is especially Eastern European nationalism that uses images of the past in acts of real and symbolic violence. Radical nationalism in postcommunist countries can therefore be interpreted as the result of 'cultural forces that are beyond rational comprehension' and as an eruption of the 'ancient ethnic and religious hatreds, dormant for centuries' until the 'iron hand of the communist state was lifted' (Delanty and O'Mahony 2002: 152).

Shari J. Cohen (1999), on the other hand, argues that the origins of postcommunist nationalism are relatively recent and of a political nature. Postcommunist nationalism is therefore, in this approach, the 'product of the absence of history, not its return' (Delanty and O'Mahony 2002: 152). What is particularly absent in Eastern Europe is the memory of peaceful multicultural coexistence in the past, because it is not the kind of symbolic resource that may be easily employed in recent political conflicts. William Outhwaite and Larry Ray (2005: 188) refer to Freudian psychoanalysis to say that while the West of the continent is a domain of 'mourning', possible because of the 'memory work that enables reconciliation with loss', the remembrance in the East is shaped by 'melancholia', responsible for the fact that the 'loss is continually revisited, is vital, intrusive, and persistent'. 'Melancholic remembrance' leads to 'repression of grief followed by repetition of trauma that cannot be expurgated' and this in turn may authorize violence targeting the other communities of memory.

When Richard Esbenshade, for example, emphasizes the absence of the Holocaust in the East European memoryscapes and official discourses of the past and presents it as a conscious manipulation of remembrance to erase uncomfortable memories of involvement in past events or silencing the memories of victimized groups (Esbenshade 1995: 80), we may doubt whether this is an expression of mourning or rather an outcome of a melancholic inability to deal with trauma (of victims, bystanders or perpetrators). On the other hand though, a number of authors emphasize that the liberation of the debate from the constraints of the communist state resulted, in Poland for example, in the series of important and agonizing discussions of the time of the Holocaust in which the 'whole of Polish society was convulsed by an extraordinary self-examination' (Weinbaum 2002: 132).

Perhaps melancholic convulsion, and a too easy mourning through erasure, are both wrong answers to the problem of memory of the Holocaust? Diana Pinto, for example, has asked postcommunist Poland to think of the Holocaust in terms of a 'Europe of tolerance', a heterogeneous, pluralist and multicultural Europe, the incarnation of which Jews once were (Pinto 1996: 176). This could be, according to Andrea Tyndall, a more effective symbol of the union of European citizens than political treaties. The question of whether the citizens of Eastern Europe can be included, however, seems to be open since in the opinion of this author the memory of the Holocaust would 'serve to connect European values with other *Western* nations' value systems' (Tyndal 2004: 121, emphasis mine), and it is by no means clear who, according to this particular author, belongs to that category.

We may also ask whether that appeal should not be directed precisely at the 'Western nations'. Saul Friedländer has observed that in the last fifty years Western societies can be characterized by an 'abundance of deliberate evocations of the past via media productions, museums, and memorials' which did not contribute to reconciliation but rather made the past irrelevant (Friedländer 1993: 58–59). Eva Hoffman comments, in a similar way, that the Holocaust has been threatened by an 'inflation of rhetoric' and 'exaltation of memory', which have led to the dissolution of its actual meaning into abstraction and the 'convenient hypnosis' that prevents us from knowing what it actually is to remember (Hoffman 2004: 174).

These theoretical considerations are confirmed by anthropologist Erica Lehrer. Her experience shows that melancholic remembrance may well be a matter of chance for a serious memory work:

> Thinking back to my time in Germany, my hyper-consciousness of my own Jewishness was generally met with stony silence. The monuments and Holocaust education were in place. Any surfeit beyond these neat, formulaic terms felt unmentionable. There didn't seem to be any space in German homes or classrooms to acknowledge the ways that the past still swirled around me – that I was its continuation. In Poland, by contrast, strangers would take one look at my face and begin to bleed history … [I]n Poland, the relative homogeneity of society means Jews (however imaginary) are still the significant other. And the past – my past, our past – there is an open wound, in which people constantly, uninhibitedly poke their fingers. While this can be ugly and uncomfortable at times, there is something welcoming and cathartic in the acknowledgment that the past is not over. Whether in the form of accusations

or apologies, fascination or simply a desire to reconnect with something tragically, violently, but incompletely lost, Poles approached me in train stations, post offices, or on village streets to say, in some way, I remember. (Lehrer 2012: 230)

Poland can therefore offer a sort of memory without commemoration, a living memory that may well be lost if the past is closed in formulas and rituals of remembrance. The latter, according to Saul Friedländer (1994), is not a realm of deep experience of the Holocaust: it is the realm of public, ritualized commemoration, which gives an intellectual closure, an elegant explanation that glosses over what is indefinite and escaping conceptualization, erases the specific nature of the Holocaust and offers its redemptive narrative, which contradicts the Holocaust as living memory (see also Stone 2003).

Memory in Eastern Europe appears to be an ambiguous phenomenon. It is characterized as a special form of memory, distinct from those that prevail in the West. But when it comes to the presentation of this specificity, the accounts are ambiguous: too much and too little memory; mourning and melancholia, erasure and commemoration may serve as an example of that ambiguity. Moreover, we can also find interpretations that present Western memories along very similar lines. The excess of commemoration that coexists with the atrophy of memory, for example, has been discussed on the occasion of Pierre Nora's famous distinction between *lieux* and *milieux de mémoire*. Saul Friedländer casts doubt on the efficiency of memory work when it comes to the remembrance of the Holocaust: melancholia is therefore not only a feature of memory in Eastern Europe. Eventually, the erasure of uncomfortable memories is a universal phenomenon, the memory of the Holocaust was for a long time marginalized in the West as well (Novick 2001), and the suffering of some groups (Roma being the most notable example) has been addressed only recently and not without hesitation.

Julia von dem Knesebeck writes that it has taken thirty years since the Holocaust for scholars to seriously approach the Roma in a way that would not constitute part of the institutional persecution. According to her, in that period the Roma 'were doubly forgotten: largely ignored by the authorities immediately after the war, and absent from the public and historical memory of the Holocaust in West Germany and elsewhere' (Knesebeck 2011: 2). The few rather concise texts and testimonies that expressed compassion for the fate of the Roma published shortly after the end of the war (like those by Dora Yates [1949], Frederick Max [1946] or Miriam Novitch [1968]), did not influence academic interest, nor did they have an impact on popular consciousness (Asséo 2005: 88).

Roma were generally perceived as not being a part of the Holocaust, which meant for example that they were denied the status of victims of the National Socialists' racial persecution:

> One of the main reasons for this lack of recognition was the absence of a clear break in attitudes towards, and perceptions of, Roma in the aftermath of the third Reich ... The general population in West Germany ... remained ignorant of the genocidal policies towards the Roma. In the decades immediately following the war, the racial nature of the Roma's persecution was not acknowledged by the Allies, German politicians and historians, or by the German public as a whole. (Knesebeck 2011: 23; see also Trumpener 1992)

Anna Marie Reading writes in that in the 'heartland of Europe there has been a critical amnesia' about the fate of Roma which, contrary to the Holocaust of the Jews or the Stalinist terror, has not been voiced and commemorated in a way that would inform a broader audience and become a part of public memory (Reading 2012: 121). The 'heartland of Europe' mentioned in the sentence quoted, is for Reading a vast area that includes Germany, Romania, the Czech Republic and Turkey (and, by and large, the Holocaust Memorial Museum in Washington with its misleading and limited presentation of Roma as victims of National Socialism).[1] Following Asséo (2005), if we add France to the list, we conclude that the amnesia regarding the fate of Roma is a universal phenomenon and that the assumed difference between Western and Eastern types of memory does not perform any significant role in this respect.

Of course some forms of Eastern European amnesia concerning the Roma may have different causes from the ones behind the silence in the West. In Western Germany before unification, Gilad Margalit (1999) argues that the silence can be attributed to the persistence of the 'Nazi-like' narrative, according to which the persecution of Roma had not been racial and could be justified by the alleged 'criminal lifestyle' of the persecuted. In communist Eastern Europe 'the memory of the Nazi Holocaust was de-ethnicized and the particular targeting of Roma and Jews by the Nazi regime was largely ignored in communist propaganda that sought to represent the struggle of the Red Army against fascism' (Reading 2012: 127).

One must add, however, that within the communist discourse there was a place for commemorating the Roma – precisely those who had struggled against fascism in the ranks of the Red Army (Bessonov 2010) or those who, as the artists of the Moscow theatre Romen, supported military efforts with their artistic performances for soldiers (Lemon 2000), or those who joined the communist resistance (Kenrick 2006). That Jews and Roma were the target of genocide, or that the racially motivated genocide was the crucial part of the Second World War, have not been fully understood in the postwar reality, neither in the West, nor in the East (Novick 2001; Roskies 1984). The crimes committed against groups who had been the target of genocidal policies have been dissolved in the postwar years into an undifferentiated category of 'crimes against humanity' and this perception only changed in the 1960s.[2]

Unfortunately, in Eastern Europe this was precisely the time of merging the communist perception of history and nationalist interpretations of the past, which was a part of the new legitimizing strategies of communist regimes. The categories of 'crime against humanity' or 'fascist terror' were therefore largely replaced in commemorative discourses by the 'martyrdom' of particular nations. The process of national-communist internal homogenization has therefore excluded those categories of victims who were perceived as not belonging to the ethnically understood nation. But even then it was possible to commemorate Romani victims of the Holocaust, although not exactly under their own names. In 1965, in Szczurowa, a village near Tarnów in Southern Poland, a memorial to the Roma victims was ceremonially unveiled; this was probably the first official commemorative ceremony of its kind in Europe. In Szczurowa, on 3 July1943, ninety-three Roma – including women, children, and the elderly – were killed by the German police.

The memorial was a local initiative, although it had to be approved by higher authorities, which was a typical communist practice. The text on the memorial says that this is a 'mass grave of the ninety-three inhabitants of Szczurowa murdered by the Hitlerites'. The victims have not been identified as Roma but as 'locals' which, according to Adam Bartosz (2010) could mean that the Roma in Szczurowa had been well-integrated, and their being 'Szczurowians' was more important for the local population than being Roma. Although the ties between Roma and the majority in Szczurowa before the Second World War were indeed close (including mixed marriages), and the execution of the local Roma was witnessed by horrified local Poles, the absence of a reference to the identity of the victims and to the nature of their victimization (genocide) indicates that such a reference would not fit the national-communist vision of history.

The unveiling ceremony, on the other hand, in which one of the Roma survivors of the Szczurowa massacre participated, made clear what had always been obvious to the locals: that the victims were Roma. The Szczurowa memorial and related commemorative practices indicate that memory of Roma and their specific fate could be preserved on the local level, while at the same time in the nationwide discourse it could disappear in a national-communist narrative of Polish 'martyrdom', or the international-communist narrative of 'peaceful people, workers and peasants, suffering at the hands of imperialist fascists'.

Although it is true that, as Alaina Lemon observes (2000: 167), communist authorities 'censured war memorials that singled out any ethnic category as having suffered in particular', even the censured memorials could have an impact on the local level, perpetuating the memory of the victims. Such local memories have coexisted with the general silence about Roma, constituting the realm of alternative memories or 'counter-memories', silenced or forbidden by the political regime that controlled the process of remembrance. They have, however, resurfaced after the collapse of communism, with the help of a newly established polycentric network of remembrance, Roma themselves having been a part of it as the agents in the process of voicing their experience (cf. Pine, Kaneff and Haukanes 2004).

No More Celestial

It is often argued that the alleged specificity of East European memory is a result of its peculiar 'frame', which is constituted by myth and ritual, not by a reflexive and rational appropriation of the past. The region, notorious for its ruptures and discontinuities of history and largely disempowered, was indeed prone to mythological explanations of its fate. In a devastating description by Tismaneanu (1998: 6) this myth is anti-Enlightenment (that is, anticapitalist and antidemocratic), racist, xenophobic, nationalist and authoritarian. Its main elements are: the image of a Golden Age, salvation through martyrdom, historical-religious mission, or election of a particular nation or group to perform a crucial role in history. Such mythological frames are not subject to critical reflection and are responsible for very strong forms of collective memory, able to justify any form of violence as part of a mission or as compensation for martyrdom. In this way Serbian ethnopolitical myth presents Serbs as forming a 'celestial' or 'heavenly' kingdom, rejecting life and material values and choosing martyrdom and eternal, spiritual glory (Čolović 2002). Similarly, the vision of Poland as Christ of Nations, developed in the nineteenth century by the Polish romantic poets, delivers a frame for remembering Polish history as a sacrifice and victimization at the hands of the enemies (Davies 1997). Being a 'celestial martyr' justifies in this mythological frame all wrongdoings and crimes committed against others as a justified self-defense.

This understanding of the Eastern European myth can easily account for the erasure of memories of those who do not form the core of the local nations and, more generally, for the image of Eastern Europe as a place where memories (and sometimes their bearers) disappear. Mythological images are, however, generally perceived as an inevitable part of any construct of memory and identity, and Eastern Europe is no exception. The image of a nation crucified by enemies can be found in the older American political pamphlets, while the myth of historical mission or election, adjusted to the global economy and consumer culture, can take the form of a credo that might be found inscribed inside a pair of blue jeans: 'Created by Levi Strauss in 1873 – has become an American tradition, symbolizing the vitality of the West to people all over the world'.[3]

As a matter of fact there are no forms of memory that would be free of mythological frames (Margalit 2002). Only certain forms of expert knowledge about the past can be to some extent demystified, but their role in the process of forming social memories and identities is rather limited. Moreover, the distinction between myth and rationality is untenable: there are not only anti-Enlightenment myths, there are also myths that the Enlightenment has called into being (Bauman 1991). The Roma genocide was not carried out by the bloodthirsty, irrational, anti-Enlightenment 'celestial people' but, with few exceptions, by rational bureaucrats with the help of lawyers and medical doctors trained in the best universities of the (Western) world. It is precisely there, in the mythological framework of Western modernity, where we must look to discover the origins of the racial persecution of Roma.

The deep roots of the Nazi persecution of Roma can be seen in the changes that took place in the perception of this group, together with the beginning of the process of modernization in European society. At that time Roma became the embodiment of cultural elements contrary to modernization and as such were either excluded or discriminated against by the dominant ideology of modernity, or were idealized by romantic currents. Modernity from the cultural point of view means growing control, discipline, standardization and homogenization of social life. Work, property, accumulation and growth become the basic values. The process of modernization also meant the repression of groups whose way of life did not fit within the sociocultural framework, and this repression sometimes served as a deterrent example of what could happen to others if they did not subordinate themselves to the demands of modern discipline, and did not recognize the values of the modern epoch as their own. This is asserted by Herbert Heuss (1988: 58), putting forward an interesting although controversial hypothesis saying that Roma were the 'surrogate victims' of modernization. The point of departure for this hypothesis is the observation that anti-Gypsy activity undertaken by the apparatus of the state, at the beginning at least, did not have support in the form of developed popular 'anti-Gypsyism'. Marginalization of the Roma was then part of a state programme of political unification and social homogenization, and in its way a warning directed at those who dropped out of the main current of social life, for example as a result of unemployment or proletarianization (Heuss 1997: 22).

This concerned in particular nomadic groups (although of course not all Roma, not even a majority of them, followed a wandering way of life): as Michel Foucault wrote (1991: 207), nomadism meant in essence being outside the obligatory classifications and social structures, outside the newly introduced discipline. As a consequence the Roma became marginalized in modern society. Their life was not just one of several alternative ways of existence, as in pre-modern times, but became the synonym for difference and backwardness, and thus a pathology that should be eliminated.

Something very characteristic of the modern exclusion of Roma was their treatment as a people not from Europe, and culturally foreign to Europe. This has remained into the present and can be seen in the unfortunate sentence at the start of various reflections about Roma: 'Roma come from India'. As already noted, sentences of this type do not begin the narrative of the histories of other European peoples, each of which at some time came to Europe from somewhere else. The tendency to exclude penetrates modernity to such an extent that it can be found in otherwise great minds. Reflecting on the essence of 'European-ness' Edmund Husserl wrote that 'in a spiritual sense the English dominions, the United States and so on belong in an obvious way to Europe, but not ... the Gypsies who constantly wander around Europe' (Husserl 1965: 155). Gypsies, then, were excluded by Husserl from a Europe understood as 'a unity of spiritual life and creative activity' (ibid.). Husserl put forward this thesis in 1935, the year of the proclamation of the Nuremberg Laws. A year later Husserl's name was removed from the list of lecturers of Freiburg University, since it turned out that the vision of the European spirit guiding the Nazis had no room in it for his philosophy.

A change of outlook led to a change in attitudes and strategies applied to Roma. Modern times brought the beginning of subjecting Roma to ever greater control e.g., in identity checks and forced settlement, the elimination of their traditional culture by a process of assimilation and forbidding the use of their language, as well as attempts to interrupt cultural continuity by forcible removal of Roma children from their families in order to be brought up by non-Roma families. It is worth noting that the trend towards control and limitation of Roma wanderings was carried out in a situation in which, for example in Germany, freedom of movement had become one of the gains of modernity that to a large extent transformed the hitherto stable picture of society. As Herbert Heuss wrote (1997: 21), after the lifting of the limitations in the second half of the nineteenth century 'millions of men took to the road: Germany became a mobile society'. Such a change can mean a serious infringement of 'ontological security' and requires legitimization by distinguishing desirable from undesirable migration. 'Jews and Gypsies', wrote Heuss, 'were put forward in a short time as the archetypes of undesirable migration and its consequences' – of a feeling of chaos (ibid.). Gypsies then became one of the scapegoats of modernity.

In turn, social movements against modernization idealized Roma as bearers of the spirit of freedom and traditional communal values threatened by the development of modern society. In a certain sense that symbolic construction of Roma can be regarded as a rejection of the traumatic cost of modernization (i.e., the reverse of treating Roma as 'scapegoats', as the phenomenon was described by Heuss), as the 'bad conscience' of modern Europe, but also as a nostalgic projection of sentiments excluded by modernity (see Trumpener 1992: 860–868). From this approach comes an array of literary portraits of Roma in European culture, in which they are genuinely treated with sympathy, nonetheless, just as in the case of the approach mentioned previously, also as people fundamentally unsuited to life in modern society.

Katie Trumpener (1992: 854) asserts, rightly in my view, that the negative vision of Roma as being not up to modern standards and the Romantic idealization of Roma as rejecting those standards constitute two halves of post-Enlightenment ideology and frequently appear at the same time, but separately, in various cultural and political discourses. This inconsistent mythology, that in many ways created the background for the Nazi persecution of Roma, together with its incoherence, is still present in the public discourses and private attitudes. Its influence has clearly marked the economic/political transformation in Eastern Europe, which was nothing else than a delayed modernization. It was in the 1990s that attitudes towards 'Gypsies' radically changed for the worse. The 'modernizers' perceived them as a burden to the economy and as 'free-riders' who had broken the newly established social covenant. The 'romantics', on the other hand, were too insecure to idealize Roma: instead, they employed xenophobic exclusion as a means of strengthening their 'ontological security'. But nevertheless, Eastern Europeans have not invented anything new here: they have just repeated the pattern that characterized the Western part of the continent in the past and which returns now, with the economic crisis, and influences the radically anti-immigrant, anti-Roma policies of several Western European countries.

I Call it Mythology

What I would call a real mythology is the image of memory in Eastern Europe as something radically different from memory in the West. As with most forms of myth, this image is constructed out of a number of binary oppositions: rational – irrational, modern – traditional, reflexive – taken for granted, pluralistic – monocentric, liberal – authoritarian, peaceful – belligerent. It is a consequence of the most fundamental opposition between 'modern West' and its 'other', the 'pre-modern East'. This temporal 'othering', to use Johannes Fabian's expression (1983), maps the temporal opposition into space: dynamic West opposed the static Orient; the enlightened versus the benighted. The other of Western modernity represents everything that is alien to the West and its project of development. Thus the idea of a special Eastern European memory is constructed as a projection of the modern Western idea of the 'East' as the enchanted, pre-modern world, built as an opposition to modern forms of Western self-identity and remembrance (Robins 1996).

Katrin Simhandl provides interesting evidence for the process of 'othering' Roma as a problem of Eastern Europe, and, we may add, Eastern European memory. The very term 'Roma', advocated by Romani activists as an umbrella term that may serve as a political endonym for various groups with their particular ethnic self-descriptions, has been employed in Western European discourse as a means of separating the Western 'Gypsies' (and their countries of residence) from the Eastern European 'Roma' (and their problems). Such a 'discursive separation between "Western Gypsies and Travellers" and "Eastern Roma" allows the people and their situation in the "old" Member States to be rendered invisible' (Simhandl 2006: 110). Nando Sigona and Nidhi Trehan develop that thesis, stating that with the arrival of Eastern European Romani migrants the approach of governments to the Western 'indigenous Gypsies' become worse, for example 'the process of the denial of Italian Romani and Sinti political subjectivities through their conflation with foreign Roma' (Sigona and Trehan 2009: 10).

This process has coincided with the attempts by leaders of international Romani organizations, usually with East European roots, to search for a collective identity for various Roma/Gypsy groups. This has been presented as a transnational unity of diasporic population or as a political nation, based on the common history of persecution that affected all Roma people and culminated in the time of the Holocaust (Vermeersch 2006; van Baar 2011; Kapralski 2012). Chronologically, the Nazi persecution was first invoked in political discourse in the 1970s as part of the German Sinti struggle for compensation and enfranchisement but without an attempt to politically unite all Roma/Gypsies.[4] It was later, after the establishment of a pan-Romani transnational ideology, with the help of the East European Roma political activists and traditions, that the memory of Roma genocide during the Second World War was integrated into a general Roma identity project (Asséo 2005: 87).

This coincidence may strengthen the assumption that persecution and genocide are pertinent to East European Roma, especially that 'anti-Gypsyism' is indeed widespread in the Eastern part of the continent.[5] It is often presented, both by Roma leaders and human rights activists, as a continuation of the wartime persecution, which creates an impression that the latter is also a problem for East European memory and responsibility. The mytho-logic here is as follows: Roma genocide during the Second World War is associated with the contemporary acts of violence against Roma; these acts of violence happen to take place in Eastern Europe; ergo, Roma genocide must be associated with Eastern Europe. It is one of the general functions of myth to remove the evil to outside the community, to externalize it and present it as an alien intrusion. Thus, in the mythological framework massacres, genocides and atrocities are the 'things that happen in the East', at least as a rule. If they by any chance happened amidst us, the role of myth is to show that our community, contrary to many others out there, can intellectually process the evil: take the right attitude, properly commemorate and draw a lesson from the past to ensure that it will never happen again.[6]

We See What We Want to See

The boundary responsible for the mythological perception of Eastern European memory was constructed during the Enlightenment, but it was solidified and made less permeable during the Cold War when it became synonymous with 'iron curtain'. As a result, the countries behind the curtain have been left in shadow. And in the shadow, Larry Wolff writes, 'it was possible to imagine vaguely whatever was unhappy or unpleasant, unsettling or alarming, and yet it was also possible not to look too closely, permitted even to look away – for who could see through an iron curtain and discern the shapes enveloped in shadow?' (Wolff 1994: 1).

It was therefore Western Europe 'that invented Eastern Europe as its complementary other half' and invented it as a complementing opposition to the notion of 'civilization' – as backwardness and barbarism (ibid. 4). This in turn may be interpreted with the help of Zygmunt Bauman's concept of 'differential deprivation of history'. If we substitute 'memory' for 'history', we could say that it is an attempt to appropriate the (proper) memory for 'us' and to make other people 'have no (proper) memory of their own', which deprives them of the right or possibility to 'demonstrate the lasting visibility of their own past' in terms of their own choosing (Bauman 1992: 55).

What then follows is the 'obliteration of a people's actual and tragic history' which, as Katie Trumpener (1992: 861) observes, may be attributed to the 'European myth of the Gypsies' that animated the traditional ethnography of the Roma. However, the reverse seems to be equally true: the myth has emerged and is perpetuated as a consequence of the processes of marginalization, subjugation and obliteration of Romani history.

These processes run parallel to the historical deprivation of Eastern Europe: both Roma and Eastern Europe are perceived as 'non-historical' and as not fully belonging to the true European narrative. As a consequence, the Roma could not have been easily incorporated into the narrative of the Holocaust. The reason lies in the fact that the Holocaust has been a part, or even a key element, of European history, a history from which Roma have been removed. Thus, it has been difficult to break disciplinary and mental boundaries that are responsible for the fact that the entry of 'Roma' has invoked associations with 'pollution taboos', 'kinship' and 'traditional law', rather than with the central event of European history.

One of the key issues on the political agenda of some Roma political activists is to change this perception. In their discourse the Roma appear as a people 'with history', which is largely the history of their interactions with European societies and the persecutions the Roma suffered from them. The Holocaust may be perceived here as the culmination of the persecutions that the Roma experienced after their arrival in Europe and as a condensation of the different forms of discrimination to which they were subjected. As such, the Holocaust creates the linearity of Romani history, dividing it into periods 'before' and 'after', and gives this history meaning as a continuous unfolding of the persecution pattern (Hancock 1991).

In this way the political discourse can be interpreted, first, as an effort to show the Roma as a people in the centre of the most important events in Europe's modern history, not as a marginalized people vegetating outside of history. Second, a historical narrative of the fate of the Roma during the war can become a means to unite the different groups into which Roma are divided, by making them aware that in certain historical situations their differences did not matter: they were treated the same (at least in principle) because they were 'Gypsies'. Uniform narrative of the Holocaust allows the members of different Romani groups, who often do not feel closely associated, to envision the commonality of the fate of the Roma, and this can have important consequences for the forms their political cooperation takes now and in the future.

This opportunity, created by the Holocaust discourse, brings some scholars and activists to claim that the Roma genocide:

has become the central component of Romani national identity. It is important to note that most Romani intellectuals and activists use the word Holocaust for the mass murder of Roma and other Gypsy ethnic groups during the war. Thus, they seek to create a parallel between Nazi policy toward extermination of the Jews and destruction of the Roma, namely, the notion of annihilating a people. (Stauber and Vago 2007: 123)

This claim, however, is untenable as a description of the reality of Roma communities in Europe. The experience of genocide is definitely a part of the social memory of some groups. Some of them, but not all, make efforts to transform that memory into a new, (trans)national (pan-)Romani identity. Some, however, reject those efforts. Moreover, there are groups who either did not experience genocidal policy or, if they did, prefer not to refer to it in their identity constructs. There are also groups without the experience of genocide which, nevertheless, choose the status of Holocaust victims as a part of a strategic identity that allows them to build links with other Romani communities (Marushiakova and Popov 2006).

This situation is to a large degree conditioned by the inconsistent and decentred nature of the Roma genocide. 'National-Socialist Gypsy policy', writes Michael Zimmermann, the most eminent historian of Roma genocide:

> evolved over the six pre-war years of Nazi rule and was later radicalized into genocide during World War Two. There was no unified central plan that guided this persecution; rather, it differed depending on geographical region and administrative area of authorization. Conflicts of interest arose with the system of Nazi rule, and sometimes policy proceeded down bureaucratic blind alleys. As a result, both in the Reich and the occupied areas in the Europe, Gypsy persecution under the Nazis was disjointed, marked by non-simultaneities and contradictions. (Zimmermann 2001: 112)

In Germany, Austria, Bohemia and Moravia, and to a certain extent in the Netherlands, persecution of the Roma was better organized and prepared by many years' practice of police registration. In successive stages the Roma were further excluded from society, both by means of legal regulations and by internment in special 'Gypsy camps' or imprisonment in concentration camps. From there the road frequently led through Jewish ghettos in occupied Poland to the gas chambers of the death camps. On the territory of the USSR Roma died in mass executions organized by units of the SS, the Wehrmacht and the police, while in Poland both methods were used. In the satellite states the situation of the Roma was very varied: from Bulgaria where the Roma, in comparison with their kinsmen from other countries were practically free of persecution, to Romania where part of the local Roma had been deported and died from hunger and disease while the other part lived relatively unaffected, having even been drafted in to the military units that fought together with the Wehrmacht against the Red Army, to Croatia where Roma met their death in the Jasenovac camp at the hands of criminals armed with knives. In Western Europe, except Germany and the Netherlands, Roma were mostly interned in special camps and those from Spain, Portugal, the United Kingdom and Scandinavia did not suffer.

The disjointed character of persecution could also mean that one and the same German Sinto[7] could be deported to the occupied territories of Poland in 1940, to be later allowed to return, drafted and sent to the Eastern front, then, as a consequence of Himmler's Decree, arrested and deported at the beginning of 1943 to Auschwitz where he could meet his family in the 'Gypsy Family Camp' at Birkenau, be subsequently transported to Dachau, Ravensbrück or any slave labour camp in Germany, and eventually, in the last moments of the war, be forced into the ranks of the Waffen-SS to fight against the approaching Soviets while the ashes of his wife and children were diffusing in the killing grounds of Auschwitz (Zimmermann 2001).

Scholars are divided regarding the definition of the fate of the Roma. Just as Ian Hancock (2001) or Wolfgang Wippermann (2005) hold that there was no difference between Nazi persecution of Jews and Roma, so Yehuda Bauer (1978 and, to a lesser degree, 2001), Gilad Margalit (2000) and Guenther Lewy (2000) decidedly contradict this. While those such as Michael Zimmermann (2007b) state that there were similarities in Nazi treatment of Jews and Roma, there were also significant differences, and the task of the historian is to investigate them, not to resolve conflicts about, at bottom, values. Even Zimmerman (2006), however, has a tendency to build a hierarchy of the victims to prove that the Gypsies were a less important target of the Nazi terror. Zimmermann emphasizes, however, the racial motivation behind the crimes against Roma which had also been applied to Jews. They were crimes committed against individuals 'whom the National Socialists declared to be members of a "race", but who did not see themselves either as a unitary people or a nation in the modern sense of the term' (ibid. 136). In both cases the factor decisive for recognition of someone as a Jew or Gypsy respectively 'was the image rather than the identity of those affected' (ibid.).

The main difference between Jews and Gypsies was defined by the different positions they held in the Nazi racial hierarchy. 'Gypsies were labelled as an "alien race" and at the same time as an "anti-social element" from the point of view of "racial hygiene". But the Jews were regarded by the Nazis to be the main problem. Unlike the Gypsies they [Jews] were presented as an "anti-race" competing with the Aryans for dominance over the world' (ibid. 84). So while Jews were an eschatological evil, the absolute enemy, destroying the most important institutions of social life, Gypsies only weakened them, acting at lower levels of the social structure (Zimmermann 2007a: 14).

Another important difference but also an important similarity between Jews and Gypsies was related to the problem of intention to murder the whole people and the existence of a pre-planned, precise programme of extermination. Here Zimmermann tries to synthesize the intentionalist and functionalist standpoints that we may find in reflections on the Holocaust. He retains an intentionalist approach claiming that – contrary to the situation of the Jews, the 'murder of the Gypsies ... was not linked to an intention to kill the whole group' but he comes closer to a functionalist position when he claims that neither in the case of Roma, nor in the case of Jews 'was there a plan already prepared and awaiting implementation in 1933 or 1939' (Zimmermann 2007b: 50). According to Zimmermann, we can speak here rather of a 'situational decision-making process' in which various institutions and levels of the Nazi hierarchy participated, together forming, sometimes in a disconcerted way, the policy of genocide.

This standpoint has been developed by Michael Stewart (2010) who emphasizes that instead of intention we should rather speak of a 'consensus' of the individuals and institutions involved in the Roma genocide, which was based on the assumption that Gypsies were generally a category that needed to be eliminated. Within this consensus, that was – according to Stewart – so obvious that it did not require a precise formulation; partial decisions and daily administrative procedures were enacted to contribute to the efficient mass killing amounting to genocide.

In addition, according to Zimmermann, Jews in German-occupied Europe were persecuted in a far more radical manner than Gypsies. 'While the latter were fortunately not threatened with extermination in every region occupied by the Germans, nor in all countries that were allied to Germany, Jewish lives were threatened across the whole continent, from Norway to Greece, from France to Russia' (Zimmermann 2007b: 50). At the same time however, Zimmermann asserts that we should avoid belittling the tragedy of the Roma by treating the Holocaust as the only adequate measure of evil. Nevertheless, the word 'Holocaust' is in Zimmermann's work reserved for the tragedy of European Jews.

Contrary to that, some Romani leaders and intellectuals, as well as some non-Roma authors prefer to speak of the Roma genocide within a narrative that Gilad Margalit describes as 'Jewish-like': 'it perceives the Gypsy persecution in the same way as the persecution of Jews was perceived by many in the English-speaking world. This narrative ... shaped the Gypsy victim of Nazism in the image of the Jewish victim' (Margalit 1999: 226).

The Roma genocide has been presented in this narrative as a 'total extermination in gas chambers according to a predetermined plan' (ibid. 239), which largely ignores the complex nature and differential outcomes of the persecution from which the Roma suffered.

It does, however, perform very well as a myth that may unite different groups of Roma by providing them with a cultural frame in which they can develop their communicative memory of Nazi persecution, or – if such memory is absent – with a prosthetic memory or postmemory of suffering (Landsberg 2004; Hirsch 1999) that may strengthen the political construct of Roma as a people with history which, and this is the crucial point, is the same as the history of other European nations and is paradigmatically exemplified by the narrative of the Holocaust. Apart from having been a useful (which does not mean efficient) tool for building a pan-Romani identity, the myth patterned after the Holocaust discourse is also a means of empowerment. It helps Roma activists to claim the power of representation in a cultural sense: 'the power to give a human community a symbolical representation of itself – that is, an identity which subsumes its inner divisions' (Doyle 2011: 90).

The Snake Who Bites His Own Tail

If Eastern Europe represents in Western mythology an earlier stage of historical development that the West has already passed through, then the criticism of the Eastern European forms of remembrance can be described with the help of an image of a snake who bites his own tail. It is a criticism that, in due course, could have been applied to Western forms of memory as well. Having been applied to the Eastern European remembrance and commemoration, it reconfirms the two modes of memory as desynchronized, in other words belonging to different temporal orders.

A good example of such desynchronization is the memory of the Holocaust. Western discourse of memory has projected its own postwar silence regarding the Holocaust onto Eastern Europe precisely at the moment when Eastern Europeans started to deal seriously with the memory of the Holocaust. Regarding the Roma genocide we may say that the dynamics of remembrance and forgetting of Roma suffering in the East was similar to that in the West, and that the recent wave of commemoration and practices of remembrance related to the fate of the Roma has been largely possible because of the existence of the Romani past as an alternative memory in communist Eastern Europe and the interactions of the Eastern and Western European Romani leaders after the collapse of communism.

By making Holocaust discourse a tool of identity building, Roma leaders refer to the mythologized 'Jewish-like' narrative from which they claimed to be excluded, while scholars are divided into those who support the leaders in their attempts to unite Roma around the Holocaust and those who follow other, equally mythologized, narratives that exclude or marginalize the victimization of Roma during the Second World War.

The metaphor of the snake biting its own tail means therefore, first, that when the West criticizes the East, it criticizes its own past and its own mythology and, second, that when the Roma leaders construct their visions of history they are strongly influenced by myth present in the non-Roma historiography and in the tradition of Eastern European nationalism. Eventually it means that when memory focuses that much on past persecution it forms a circle that it is difficult to break and creates an obstacle to seeing the real problems of the present. Shimon Samuels (2013) rightly observes that the 'massive investment in memory has neither prevented nor mitigated the resurgence of anti-Semitism, gypsophobia, homophobia or even skinhead violence against the disabled. Dare one suggest that mourning for the victims of seventy years ago is so much easier than defending the same victim groups of today?' As a matter of fact it is this ease which makes some Roma activists reject the Holocaust discourse together with the whole issue of 'identity politics' as not contributing to the solution of the most vital problems of Roma communities.

Political activists have recently found an ally in the groups of Roma intellectuals of a younger generation,[8] who critically reflect on those leaders who impose a ready-made identity of Holocaust victims on all Roma, in spite of the fact that many of them may prefer to identify differently. Behind this criticism there is a rejection of fixed identities having been imposed by some sort of external authority, regardless of whether they are a Roma political activist or a non-Roma scholar. At the same time, new Roma intellectuals assert the primacy of self-ascription in the field of identity-building processes, which makes identification with the Nazi persecution possible even for those whose ancestors did not suffer from it, but also secures for the descendants of the victims the right to identify themselves differently. In such a way, memory of the Holocaust would be retained as one among many factors that may be used in building contemporary Roma identities, but not as the exceptional one.

Notes

1. Reading in a similar way criticizes the 'Roma section' of the State Museum of Auschwitz-Birkenau, or rather repeats critical remarks of Huub van Baar (2011), apparently without having noticed that this part of the museum has been designed and arranged by the organization of German Sinti and Roma and thus represents a (one among many) 'Romani perspective' in representing the Romani past. This confirms, first, that the Roma take an active role in the commemoration of their suffering and by doing this they advance their own agenda regardless of whether non-Roma scholars like it or not; and second – that 'Roma memory' is in fact a very diversified, polyphonic entity, or, rather, a dynamic process of interactions between the images of the past held by various Romani (and non-Romani) groups.
2. That does not mean a 'silence' regarding the Holocaust, which was appropriately remembered by most survivors. Their voices, however, have not been heard, and the popular culture of remembrance has not – until a certain point in time – developed. I think that the recent critical attacks on the idea of 'silence about the Holocaust' (e.g., Diner 2009; Cesarani and Sundquist 2012) confuse these two levels on which memory exists.
3. Often followed by 'Made in Pakistan' which perhaps symbolizes the 'vitality of the West' even more.
4. Although already in the 1960s Ionel Rotaru (also known as Vaida Voevod) combined the claims for compensation with a pan-Romani agenda and was issuing 'Roma passports' of the Romani state to be located on the territory of Somalia that he demanded from the UNO.
5. The other half, however, is quickly catching up if we bear in mind the attitudes and institutional actions targeting the immigrant Roma communities.
6. The notorious 'Polish death camps' in the Western media can be similarly interpreted as a 'Freudian slip' that reveals the mythological mechanism of the externalization of evil.
7. Male member of the Sinti which is an ethnonym of those who descend from the first Gypsies who arrived in the German lands in the fifteenth century.
8. The names of Brian Belton (2005), Damian Le Bas (2010) and Gregor Dufunia Kwiek (2010) should be mentioned here.

Sławomir Kapralski is a sociologist and social anthropologist. He is professor of sociology at the Pedagogical University in Krakow. He is the author of *A Nation from the Ashes: The Memory of the Genocide and Roma Identity* (2012, in Polish), and numerous articles on memory and identity, nationalism and ethnicity, the Holocaust and the problems of Roma communities. His ongoing projects include research on the strategies of remembering Jewish culture in Poland and on the Holocaust as a frame of memory for the Roma political movement.

Chapter 5

BIOGRAPHICAL AND COLLECTIVE MEMORY
Mutual Influences in Central and Eastern European Context

Kaja Kaźmierska

The history of Central and Eastern European societies has been shaped by complicated events of the nineteenth century, twentieth-century wars and the time of communism.[1] This general statement refers to very complex phenomena rooted in the historically grounded processes of creating the idea of nation, collective (national) identity, the role of culture, the idea of the state and modern society.[2] In this respect we can talk about a specific historical and cultural background forming different aspects of social reality, for example scientific discourse, artistic output or commonsense knowledge about community roots and collective identity. Regarding academic discourse, as a sociologist, I shall refer here to the intellectual tradition established by Polish sociology, especially studies on culture and identity elaborated by William I. Thomas and Florian Znaniecki (1918/20), Józef Chałasiński (1968) or Stanisław Ossowski (1967, 1984) and recently by Antonina Kłoskowska (1996, Eng. 2001). According to this perspective, national consciousness is connected with the process of building knowledge *of* and identification *with* national culture. The nation emerges as the result of awareness of commonly shared culture, defined and identified by a community as its heritage. Thus, cultural and historical aspects are pivotal in the process of creating national identity '[a] common national culture ... is a basis for social solidarity uniting the people to share it' (Znaniecki 1973 [1952]: 15). This approach has been continued in further studies on culture and national identity understood as 'the entire body of texts of the national culture creating its syntagma, especially its canonical core' (Kłoskowska 2001: 88).[3]

The cultural concept of nation, characteristic to Central and Eastern European thought, is usually contrasted with the definition of nation as a

---

Notes for this chapter begin on page 110.

political community, where the idea of state and citizenship is considered as fundamental to the process of creating collective identity. Different interpretations of social and historical processes are influenced by the differences between Western and Eastern European histories of states and societies and the dynamic of creating the idea of modern nations. This difference has influenced other related fields of academic reflection, and the concept of memory should be considered as one of them. Memory, especially in its social aspects, became a vivid topic of academics' attention only a couple of decades ago. Concurrently, this attention is connected to a renaissance of national studies (Szacki 2004) and biographical method (Kaźmierska 2010). It is often pointed out that sociology, especially in English-speaking countries, up to the 1970s has neglected reflection on these issues (Szacka 2003). When it comes to studies on memory, a serious gap in sociological thought resulted from, firstly, a lack of interest in the achievements of psychology, and especially psychoanalysis, and secondly, no reflection on the ideas of the classics, for instance Maurice Halbwachs (Hirszowicz and Neyman 2007), whose work gained unexpected acclaim only several decades after its publication (Ricoeur 2004: 124). As a result of these briefly described changes in social sciences, memory studies has become an influential perspective in various kinds of human sciences like history, sociology, psychology and cultural anthropology. This shared interest, though percolated by the theoretical approaches of each discipline, enables the construction of a common field for interdisciplinary discourse that is so welcome in postmodern science. At the same time memory has become a key word or better a key concept for studying different aspects of social reality. Whereas in the field of history the reflection on memory seems to be naturally related to the discipline, the 'memory shift' in such sciences as sociology is far more complicated. For example, this could be considered as an innovative aspect of reflection in the last decades of the twentieth century in Western European academic discourse, and what is conceptualized under the general label of memory studies has been the subject of reflection for Polish sociologists due to their intellectual tradition focused of studies on culture, though they did not allude to memory as a pivotal concept. Here the more general question arises: To what extent should sociological reflection and studies undertaken in this field, even when related to the past, belong to memory studies? In my opinion there is no such 'obligation' and the problem lies in the distinction between the substantive and the formal level of theoretical reflection (Glaser and Strauss 1967). In many sociological studies problems of memory relate to the substantive area, but theoretical reflection based on the formal level is related to a wider frame, e.g., theory of culture. From this perspective memory remains a part of culture and not vice versa, and labelling some research as memory studies can be considered as over-interpretation.[4]

The aim of these introductory remarks is to explain the frames of interpretation for the main topic of this chapter. Although I am going to focus on the mutual influence between biographical and collective memory in the Central and Eastern European context, I treat memory as a social construct aimed at interpretation of the present and subjected to certain cultural and social frames. As a sociologist practising in the field of biographical research, I am especially interested in social aspects of biographical experiences and memory. Though not in its psychological sense when focusing on psychological mechanism of remembering and forgetting (Conway and Pleydell-Pearce 2000), but in its social construct based on experiences that gain meaning and are (re)interpreted by an individual through the prism of his/her social actions. I begin by describing the phenomenon of biographical memory and I then present two excerpts from autobiographical narrative interviews where I show mutual interferences between biographical and collective aspects of memory. I refer to different social and biographical contexts in which the phenomenon of asymmetry or symmetry between biographical and collective memory gains specific meanings and results in a complicated process of work on individual and collective identity undertaken from the perspective of biographical experiences.

Biographical Memory

To systematize the reflection upon memory, first its different levels need to be distinguished (Kaźmierska 2008: 2012). These are: the collective memory (formal or official), the social memory of a given community and the individual memory that I will henceforth refer to as the biographical memory. Each of those levels is connected to the corresponding 'subjects of memory'. And so the collective memory is formed mostly by the institutions that belong to the governing system, both national and local; the social memory by the institutions of the civil society; and the biographical memory by non-institutionalized agents, such as groups of friends, informal groups and families (Ziółkowski 2002: 9–10). This division is but one of many. It allows us to organize reflections on the mutual effects that specific subjects of memory have on each other. These effects can be compared to the phenomena occurring at a macro-, mezzo- and micro-social scale, respectively. Since the term collective memory is frequently used in sociological literature, I will pay more attention to biographical memory. I will also skip the description of an 'in-between' level – the social memory characteristic to local communities, especially important where spectacular events in the past took place (e.g., in the case of wartime it may be local ethnic relationships – Kaźmierska 2008, 2012).

The term 'biographical memory' suggests that its resources comprise personal experiences that an individual gathers in the course of life. However, 'biographicality' does not only equal acquiring the individual perspective, but it also suggests constant work on the experiences that undergo (re)interpretation. Thus, biographical memory does not only mean the images of the past or the course of past actions stored in our thoughts, but it is always a version of these, conditioned by the individual course of life, as well as by a broader sociocultural context. This context shapes the way one memorizes events and, more importantly, it influences the way one recalls biographical experiences. Memory, which is first and foremost a communicative activity, becomes an exchange of narrations about the past. This is why the build-up of memory through intergenerational transfer (that involves both great and small narrations) combines the perspectives of at least a couple of generations – 'therefore the meeting of memory and history stretches across no less than a century' (Ricoeur 1995: 22). This mode of memory Jan and Aleida Assmann call communicative memory after Jan Vansina (Assmann 2006: 1–30), transmitted by witnesses to the next generations. Communicative memory finishes with the death of the third generation. The biographical memory becomes the basis for intergenerational discourse, where the borderline between our actual experiences and what we have been told about may be blurred:

> What is difficult to achieve in one's childhood gains in value. A story about childhood often seems, therefore, an initiation quest, whose difficulties become a subject of special scrutiny. The memory is divided, the recollections evaporate, loose at the beginning, of course if there is any beginning, but then a shuttle will weave them together, although there will always remain a doubt as to its circumstances and details. An autobiographer will express his or her doubts. This doubting discourse will slightly rattle, but not shatter the credibility of the memories. Authenticity of an autobiography, which is a most fundamental issue, results, to some extent, from memory's *hesitation*, whereas the value of a memory results from its frailty. (Lejeune 2001: 242)

As Philippe Lejeune suggests, from the perspective of an individual – a biography incumbent – knowledge about the past incorporated into one's biography may be defined as fundamental for constructing biographical memory and individual identity.[5] Thus biographical memory appears to be not only an experience *of*, but also knowledge *about* the past. This phenomenon is also very well characterized by Polish philosopher Barbara Skarga (1995: 6):

I always have a story which can be told and whose hero I am. The story has some specific characteristics, which can cause a conflict and destroy the 'selfness' which is being created. The reasons can be different. Firstly, the beginning of a story does not coincide with the beginning of my life, as I do not remember this, other people were its witnesses, it is from them that I gather the knowledge about it. My own story begins where my memory can reach, although it is possible that those first days or years could have weighed on its entire course. Therefore it is an imperfect story, its imperfection originates from the very nature of memory. Imperfect, uncertain and readily manipulated.

Another aspect of biographical memory is its dynamic character, which frames the relation between biographical and collective memory, both in its diachronic and synchronic aspects. Memory, as being always an attribute of a particular group, is subject to the constant process of (re)interpretation. This is a result of the special role that memory plays in the process of creation and maintenance of identity. In this context, the core of the memory is not so much the content of the memorized experiences, as rather their interpretation. Therefore the answer to *what* the subject of the memory is, should be preceded by the explanation of *how* and *why* that particular vision of the past has been constructed (Szacka 1995: 71), because memory is not about what happened in the past, but how this memory is used by the current generation (Ziółkowski 2000). Therefore arguments about the content of collective memory are only superficially conflicts about the past, because the way the past is interpreted shapes the interpretation of the present.

On the one hand then, we have a dynamically, diachronically changing structure of each generation's memory constructed on the basis of biographical experiences, and on the other, this cultural memory, to use Assmann's term (2008), allows us to sustain the sense of a particular community's continual presence in time. This phenomenon can be regarded also in synchronic order, in two aspects. First, memory is ahistorical. While historical discourse acquires the linear perspective of time, the collective memory uses mythical time. 'Its past has no direction. The distances between the people who populate it and the events that fill it are defined not by the dates, but by the relations between the values they symbolize' (Szacka 2000: 14). Therefore, memory is affective and magical, it belongs to the *sacrum*, while history belongs to the *profanum* (Nora 1989: 8–9). In the case of the latter, the truth is the truth of the reason, in the case of memory – it is the truth of the heart that strengthens in turn the effective relation between its collective and biographical levels.

Secondly, it should be noted how particular levels of memory affect one another vertically at a given moment in time. The collective memory is most of all a communicative and ritual activity, through which the biographical memory transforms into the collective one (Kapralski 2010). The collective memory provides us with codes and categories for the interpretation of individual biographical experiences, and vice versa, the individual experiences constitute the content of the collective memory. However, the nature of those mutual relations is very complex, because they are conditioned by historical, social and biographical circumstances. And so we return to the basic question about memory, namely: *how* and *why* the relations between particular levels of memory are shaped the way they are at a given moment in time. One of the core relations is the symmetry or asymmetry between the collective and the biographical memory.

Symmetry or Asymmetry between the Collective and the Biographical Memory

The community of memory is built upon the schemata and categories typical for its cultural universality. As I have already observed, the formation of images of the past has its foundations in the institutionalized activities and the collective memory; it is not a sum of individual experiences, but it results from a more or less intentional, but always in some sense selective, interpretation of the past. The most general point of reference for this selectivity is the way an individual/community/state respectively perceives their own culture and society. It draws the borders of both memory and of oblivion. Thus, the formation of images of the past is always connected with the ideologization occurring on each memory level that results from the relation between the collective memory and the collective identity. Sometimes the ideologization is highly intentional and leads to the build-up of an official, institutionalized version of the past that cannot be interpreted by individuals. Especially in authoritarian regimes, controlling the contents of collective memory is considered the means to control biographical memory, which in turn leads to control of people's way of thinking and as a consequence control of their lives. Although this 'Orwellian' scenario fortunately rarely becomes real, we can find examples of the effective influence of a regime's propaganda, like Russian children denouncing their parents in the Soviet system or in a recently reported case in North Korea. However, more frequently we encounter falsified versions of the past that are used instrumentally to validate the existing order. As a result we can observe that ideological pressure may lead to a phenomenon that I call asymmetry between biographical and collective memory, when the official image of the past does not correspond with biographical experiences of individuals.

The asymmetry of memory can have various consequences. Usually it results in a certain tension caused by the inability to include one's own biographical experiences in the community of memory. Depending on the circumstances, this state may incite social marginalization or even alienation, and it may result in an attempt to reject a part of one's own biography. In such a case individuals are confronted with a socially 'unnatural' situation when generation members – 'subjects of memory' cannot/are not expected to join the process of exchanging memories in the mode of communicative memory. The alternative is symmetry of memory, which as the desirable option would mean correspondence between biographical and collective memory in terms both of their condensed and discursive activity. However the symmetry between the collective and the biographical memory may encourage a joint effort to work on the memory, as well as on oblivion when some aspects of the past are facilely omitted in public and private discourse or falsified. Let me now illustrate the above mentioned interdependencies by commenting on particular instances of them.

Overcoming Asymmetry between the Collective and the Biographical Memory: The *Kresy* and Katyn Narratives

Between 1991 and 1992, as part of the project 'Biography and the National Identity' (1997) financed by the State Committee for Scientific Research in Poland, I gathered biographical narrative interviews with the residents of the former Polish Eastern Borderlands – *Kresy*. Since *Kresy* have played a specific and significant role in Polish history and culture, a short explanation is required in order to contextualize the excerpts of narratives presented below. The term *Kresy* refers to a former territory of the eastern provinces of Poland which today lie in Eastern Lithuania, Western Ukraine and Western Belarus. Historically the territory was included within the Polish-Lithuanian Commonwealth (sixteenth to eighteenth century) and the Second Polish Republic (1918–1939), until the Second World War. As a consequence of the Molotov–Ribbentrop Pact,[6] on 17 September 1939, the *Kresy* territories were annexed by the Soviet Union and occupied. As a result of the Soviet occupation a significant part of the ethnic Polish population of the *Kresy* was deported to other areas of the Soviet Union, mainly to Siberia and Kazakhstan, where thousands died of hunger and exhaustion caused by slave labour and terrible living conditions (Gross 1988). In 1945, Poland's eastern frontier was imposed by Soviet policy. According to international agreements, settlements along the eastern border of Poland were moved and Polish inhabitants of *Kresy* had to leave their homeland. This process of displacement was called in the language of communist propaganda 'a repatriation', whereas those who had to move recognized this term as a false and imposed category since they had a deep feeling of leaving their homeland and the land that for centuries was considered in Polish collective memory as a part of the state – *patria* (Kaźmierska 2000). In this respect Norman Davies' comment on the issue of Polish borders seems to be very relevant:

> People who lived on islands, or on half-continents of their own, find difficulty in comprehending the territorial obsession of landlocked nations. Never having faced the prospects of ceding Kent to Germany, or California to the USSR, they tend to look with quizzical unconcern, if not with contempt, on those who would lay down their lives for an inch of ground or for a dotted line on a map. In this respect, the passions concerning the history of modern Polish frontiers are far removed indeed from the main concerns of the Anglo-Saxon world. They are all the greater, since, with one signal exception, the Poles have not been permitted to fix their frontiers for themselves. (1981: 492)

Though the Eastern Borderlands are no longer a part of Polish territory, the memory of a Polish *Kresy* has been cultivated especially by the generation born there. Yet it is not only a question of communicative memory (which, as I will explain later, was not easily expressed during the time of communism) but also a spectacular role that *Kresy* have played in Polish culture, being considered as a 'center of Polish life, the very center of Polish thought, tradition and spirit. From *Kresy* come Polish dreams and myths' (Lisicki 2012: 3). Distinguished Polish artists, poets and writers born in *Kresy* have developed an artistic, mythologized and nostalgic image of this land incorporated into collective identity and often built in opposition to the Eastern borderland's neighbours – Imperial Russia and then the Soviet Union. Thus up to now *Kresy* have remained a specific memory figure, a symbol of both martyrdom and heroism, a symbol of collective identity focused on cultivation of Polishness.

Let me now return to the research. The beginning of the 1990s was a time of feverish rediscovery of history, of filling in its 'blank spaces'. For the first time in their lives, my interviewees, previously inhabitants of the Eastern Borderlands, could freely talk about their past, including their wartime biographies dominated by the experiences of the Soviet occupation. After the war displaced people quickly realized that it was taboo to disclose the entire war history of Poland. Before1989, coming from *Kresy* was a kind of stigma in itself, let alone having engaged in clandestine activities or underground fighting. Many people, including some of my narrators, were under surveillance by the communist security simply because of their background (Kaźmierska 2000). After 1989, carefully protected and preserved memories that had only been shared within families and sometimes not even there, could finally become a part of the public discourse.[7] However, the propaganda of the Polish People's Republic incited such an asymmetry between the collective and the biographical memory that it influenced the narration as well. My interviewees, when talking about their wartime biographical experiences, would not only talk about 'what happened', but most of all they would give arguments to justify their experiences by relating them to the official image of the war. And so their experiences would always be contrasted with the German occupation and related to the official image of war that functioned for decades, according to which Polish society was victimized by a single occupant. Therefore the narrations were rich in argumentative structures, where the narrators tried to explain or justify the tragedy of their experiences from the period of the Soviet occupation. The biographical need to narrate after years of silence and the awareness of its social function, which has always given a witness, was thus confronted with the general frame of reference that had been formed by the official collective memory. Thus it could be said that those narratives are above all the documentation of a certain period of time, when the new social discourse about the past was being created, and the asymmetry between the collective and the biographical memory was being broken.

It could be considered that the last twenty years constitute a whole epoch in the process of restructuring this part of the collective memory. I remember vividly my high school history lessons at the beginning of the 1980s. With the satisfaction typical of young and restless, rebellious minds, we would interrogate our teacher about *Kresy* war history. In those days Katyn was a symbol of the Soviet oppression. Katyn Forest near Smoleńsk in Belarus, though only one of many sites of mass graves, is the place where the corpses of about four and a half thousand Polish officers were found by Germans in April 1943. Katyn has become a symbolic *lieu de mémoire* of the martyrdom of over 15,000 Polish officer-prisoners, professionals and reservists, captured by Soviets and disappeared in the spring of 1940, whose fate was otherwise unknown. They were recognized as outstanding representatives of the prewar Polish intellectual, professional and military elites. All of them were killed in the same manner, having their hands tied behind their back and a German bullet in the base of their skull. For years the Soviets claimed that the crime had been committed by the Nazi Germans (Davies 2000; Etkind at al. 2012).

So we asked our teacher about Katyn. She knew that we knew. She was not so ideologically biased as to present the strictly official version of the history promoted by the communist propaganda supported by the Soviet Union, but she was afraid to go beyond the political correctness of that time. What during my school years was considered a discovery of the forbidden areas of history and influenced our image of the Soviet occupants as a 'disguised' enemy,[8] today constitutes the canon of collective memory, and for the younger generation it became one of the historical facts that create knowledge about the Second World War.

Here we have to refer to the obvious, though crucial issue related to the concept of generations. According to Karl Mannheim (1952: 286–320) generations form a community of experiences and their interpretations. Each generation is positioned in a specific social and historical space. So if we in turn consider the generation raised in the time of communism (namely born in the 1940s–1950s) to whom the time of the war was part of collective and not biographical memory, we would see that at least to some people who did not have access to the communicative memory of those who experienced the Soviet occupation at least for some time, the problem of asymmetry between biographical memory of war witnesses and official collective memory did not exist, whereas it was experienced by those coming from *Kresy*. To illustrate this tension I will relate a fragment of a narrative interview with a woman who was born and spent the war in Vilnius, the city recognized before the war as one of the most outstanding Polish cities of *Kresy*:

> We knew about Katyn. Of course we didn't have any illusions that was [done] by Germans, any illusions. It was clearly marked in letters of our different friends, from ladies who lost their husbands transported to Russia. And everywhere letters stopped on a specific date and it was clear so we didn't have any doubt that Katyn was [done by] Russians ...
>
> And I always say that I had no illusions and that my opinions had been formed on the 17th of September 1939[9] and then they were simply developed and now I look at it from the perspective of my whole life but the awareness that bolshevism is and has always been the same ... my opinions have only been [for years] strengthened. In the high school where I worked [the narrator is a retired teacher] there was a charming teacher, a very nice man and wise, now he obviously shares our viewpoint but when he started working at school he was very pro-Soviet. And once we talked and he said 'You are so happy that you did not experience your eyes open' [to the truth] and I answered 'I experienced it but in 1939'.

The first part of the quotation comes from the main storyline, the other from the last fragment of the interview when the narrator was summing up her story. The first excerpt illustrates two aspects of the narrator's experience which I have already pointed out: the meaning of the Soviet occupation in biographies of those who were on the Eastern Borderlands, and relating those experiences to official memory 'we had no illusions that it was [done] by Germans' (as has been discussed, according to the Soviet and postwar propaganda the murder in Katyn was performed by

Germans). The narrator alludes to these aspects in the second part of the quotation. In this context the figure of her colleague – a history teacher – is introduced (he represents a younger generation than the narrator). He started his professional career as a supporter of the official ideology and then changed his opinions.

The recalled interaction illustrates very well the dynamic character of collective memory and the tension between the biographical and collective dimensions when constructing images of the past. For this man discovering a new version of the past was a deep biographical experience, a form of ideological conversion. Though there is no evidence for it in the quoted fragment, I should add that this teacher was well known in the 1980s for his courage in contesting the official version of history in his lessons. Although the time of the war was not a part of his biographical memory, the process of redefinition of resources of the collective image of the past became an important biographical challenge to build asymmetry between the official and authentic discourse about the past – so here the symmetry has evolved into asymmetry.

The case of *Kresy* illustrates very well the process of democratization and decolonization of memory (Nora 2002c) when liberated from totalitarian ideologies. From this perspective the *Kresy* case is one of a few examples in the postcommunist reality of overcoming the asymmetry of memories. It also shows how effective and relatively quick this process can be. Within a decade the history of the prewar Eastern Borderland was incorporated into collective memory, supported by school curricula.[10] However there are other topics related to wartime that have not been easily accepted and incorporated into a commonly shared image of the past. A particularly good example in the context of the war experiences is the symmetry of Polish collective and biographical memory, or better yet, oblivion, when it comes to the wartime fate of Polish Jews. There is no room here to discuss this complex issue, but I do so elsewhere (see Kaźmierska 2012).

Constructing Asymmetry of Memory by Overcoming Its Symmetry: The Great Patriotic War Narrative

The case described in the last section may be considered quite a common pattern in a formal sense. Taking into account the social meaning and power of collective memory as one of the main means of constructing and sustaining collective identity, we may usually observe the process of building symmetry or overcoming the symmetry between collective and biographical memory especially when democratization of memory takes place. However, the process of democratization leading to undertaking work on both biographical and collective experiences may also result in the opposite phenomenon, of (re)constructing the asymmetry of this relation. The case I will discuss here shows this other, more complex aspect of the relationship between biographical and collective memory. I refer to the fragment of a narrative interview with a Belarusian woman:[11]

> You see, it wasn't even openly imposed, it was done surreptitiously, stealthily encroached like some foreign matter through all our pores. It was not put straightforwardly that Russians were better, not at all. The winners of the war were the Russians, as simple as that, casualties were mostly among the Russians and on the whole Russia, that is Russia and Russians won the war … In shops let's say when Lithuanians had already broken off and Latvians too and Belarus started mentioning its independence and all of a sudden old Russian acquaintances of yours, the ones you've known for more than twenty years, well it all started with war veterans; I can remember myself queuing and a veteran saying we liberated you and I suddenly recalled that my dad aged nineteen when the Soviet troops arrived here, was called to arms and literally four months later on the territory of Poland he lost his right leg, he ended up as a second group invalid with an artificial limb but initially he was walking on crutches. He spent liberation day in Lvov in hospital, a chunk of flesh torn off his right arm, huge pieces off his back, in short he barely survived. He was lying in a cast for months and worms grew under the plaster, a nurse nursed him back to health, anyway he recovered. And I suddenly told this veteran I'd remembered it all surprisingly and about the Russian weapons and Russian victory, and I'm telling him 'You know what, I was personally liberated by my own father, a Belarusian national, and he personally left his very own right leg there, and as regards the fact that you liberated us I'm sorry but liberators liberate and leave', that's it, well yes like an insult, it was disgusting.

The quoted part of this biographical narrative interview shows a complexity of both biographical and collective memory work. The background is collective memory indoctrinated by the Soviet system. It is official memory, created in the Soviet Union in order to build a common space of discourse but, as the narrator stresses, this commonality is based on monoethnicity: it is dominated by the Russian perspective. The woman rebuilds its image retrospectively – from the contemporary point of view she analyses its mechanisms, whose aim was to favour the image of Russians. Although she had not reflected on it earlier she realized that the effects of this strategy influenced her biographical memory relating to her family history. She 'suddenly recalled' the tragic history of her father. Of course it is not the case of suppressing, or fading out of awareness of experiences due to their traumatic potential or discovering facts that had not been known (the woman's father was handicapped for the rest of his life and everybody knew the reason). The point is in a symbolic exclusion of the father's fate from the image of the Great War shaped by an ideological discourse in which 'on the whole Russia and Russians won the war'. It is a very interesting example of a specific asymmetry of biographical and collective memory, where biographical memory is colonized in a very sophisticated way, which is not based on forbidding the recounting of her father's war experiences but on incorporating them into the image of the war so that his own history is instrumentally interpreted, even by his family. In such a way an apparent symmetry between biographical and collective memory is built. From the present perspective of the narrator the main tension in discourse is the target of sustaining asymmetry of both levels of memory, which in its biographical dimension is related to Belarusian identity being in opposition to the official discourse of the collective memory dominated by the Russian perspective.

Just as memory is indispensable in the creation of identity, so identity influences and conditions the process of creation and maintenance of memory. Both phenomena are rooted in time: memory animates the past; identity, in turn, is based on the sense of continuity, and thus also on awareness of our existence in time. The meaning of memory in the process of creation of identity is not restricted to treating it as a source of knowledge about the past, but also, perhaps even more importantly, it is connected to this specific experience linked structurally with our presence in time. The process of restructuring the collective memory is entangled in the process of creation of the collective identity. The sense of being rooted in the past increases one's self-esteem, it allows one to pass on values and models of behaviour and it constitutes the symbolic language of a group (Szacka 2000: 16–18). In the presented example (re)construction of collective identity is done on the basis of biographical and not collective memory. The latter is crucial in the process of creating and supporting national or ethnic identity. In the case discussed this type of memory has been totally conquered by totalitarian ideology, which above all is interpreted as part of the national ideology once represented by the Soviet Union, now by Russia. That is why the strategy to sustain an asymmetry of biographical and collective memory remains; at least in those days, it was the main means by which to strengthen Belarusian identity. As we know, as a long-term strategy in the case of collective identity it may not be effective, especially in a Central and Eastern European context, since it is the collective memory which builds the feeling of group solidarity and identification with the nation. In addition:

> [u]nder the existing authoritarian rule, there is no arena for the unrestrained exchange of autobiographical memories or collective memory work in Belarus,

as no democratization of public discourse is underway. The highly censored national Belarusian memory circulates within clandestine milieus and is, in the best case, transmitted in the form of personal accounts from generation to generation within families. (Mamul 2009a: 146)[12]

Conclusions

A specific sensitivity to history influenced by the difficult process of creating national identities in the nineteenth and twentieth centuries was suppressed on the one hand and strengthened on the other during the time of communism. The process of democratization after 1989 'awoke' people's national and ethnic identities, made them think about collective belonging in terms of a rich, previously suppressed or neglected cultural and historical heritage. As a result, this specifically strong historical consciousness and awareness of national failures or victories of Central and Eastern Europeans influenced discourse about the past and its role in contemporary collective identity. 'It seems that wherever national aspirations have been frustrated for a long time, the nation is an exceptionally prominent theme of all reflection on society although, of course, it is in fact a very universal topic' (Szacki 2004: 3). This discourse in Central and Eastern Europe is diverse due to specific 'local' histories, though common, and it is specifically defined in Western Europe. From the occidental perspective, using historical and memory references as a means of constructing collective identity is often interpreted as a premodern way of thinking. 'The inhabitants of Central and Eastern Europe (let us call them *Eastropeans*) well know and feel that as a rule they are looked down upon by the *Westropeans*' (Jedlicki 2005: 45). The dichotomy constructed between Western and Eastern Europe in terms of a Western and 'non-Western' approach towards the issues of e.g., collective (national) identity, nations and memory (see Kohn 1955) has influenced the perspective of many Western scholars representing the human sciences. The difference conceptualized in such a way often leads to a distinction between civic (Western) and ethnic (Eastern) nationalism (Jaskułowski 2010; Kymlicka 2001). 'Many works in the field we are discussing here typically begin with an expression of the author's amazement with the manifestations of belligerent nationalism. Recently, the events in former Yugoslavia and the disintegration of the Soviet Union have probably had the greatest impact' (Szacki 2004: 5). From this point of view Europeanization means overcoming national sentiments rooted in tradition and historically grounded patterns. Such an approach often 'stresses the importance of forgetting for the emergence of the politics of a global citizenship' (Misztal 2010:

27). This occidental perspective relates not only to scientific discourse but also to public discourse on European identity and memory, and it has recently been criticized by some sociologists who discuss the idea of Europeanization in institutional frames of the European Union where the definition of being European is constructed only from a Western European perspective (e.g., Kohli 2000; Calhoun 2004; Hansen 2000, 2002, 2009) and illegitimates other possible ways of constructing collective identities that are estimated as not modern, thus not suited to (post)modern society.[13] The examples presented of personal narratives illustrate how dynamic the nature of the relation between collective and biographical memory may be and what an important role it may play in the process of construction of contemporary identity. At this point the past meets the present. Different understanding of *what, how* and *for what reasons* collective memory is (re) constructed may stimulate work not only on Central Eastern European memory, but also on deconstructing the universalism of the occidental frame of interpretation.

Notes

1. Timothy Snyders's recently published book *Bloodlands* (2010) shows how important it is to analyse the dramatic history of this region while taking into account different perspectives and complex circumstances moulding political and social frames of ongoing events and phenomena.
2. In the case of Polish history those phenomena are vividly characterized by Norman Davies (e.g., 1981, 2000).
3. Recently the concept of culture and collective identity has been seen from the range of biographical sociolinguistic and discourse analytical perspectives of interpretative sociology in Poland (e.g., Czyżewski et al. 1997; Rokuszewska-Pawełek 2002; Mamul 2009a, b; Kaźmierska 2012; Waniek 2012; Wygnańaska 2011).
4. For example, such an approach can be recognized in a very systematic and elaborate overview presented by Kończal and Wawrzyniak 2011.
5. We can learn how important this aspect of biography is when analysing biographical stories of individuals who, for different reasons, do not know their roots since they do not have access to their family history, e.g., children who survived the Holocaust but who were not brought up with the memory of grandparents and parents.
6. The Molotov-Ribbentrop Pact or Nazi-Soviet Pact was a non-aggression pact signed on the 23rd of August 1939. It included a secret protocol that divided territories of Romania, Poland, Lithuania, Latvia, Estonia and Finland into Nazi and Soviet 'spheres of influence', anticipating potential 'territorial and political rearrangements' of these countries (Davies 1981).
7. It is worth mentioning that at the end of the 1980s when people started to be more eager to share their life stories, KARTA started to collect first testimonies; the Eastern Archive

– a social movement documenting the concealed and distorted history of *Kresy* was established in 1987, and was developed in the 1990s as a regular project.
8. These differences in 'educational upbringing' might have influenced to some extent popular reactions in Poland after the plane catastrophe in Smoleńsk in 2010 when all ninety-eight passengers including the president of Poland and many prominent politicians died. The generation raised in the time of asymmetry of memories was more skeptical about the possibility of honest cooperation with the Russian authorities considering investigating the catastrophe. When analyzing narratives with inhabitants of *Kresy* who experienced the Soviet occupation I found that in interactional scenes which they recalled in their stories the suspicion awareness context defining identity of the other (the Soviets) was dominant. (Acording to Glaser and Straus 1964 a suspicion awareness context is one of four distinguished modes regulating interaction between actors according to their assumed identity by an interaction partner; in suspicion awareness context the interaction partner assumes that the identity presented by the other is not his true identity). Narrators always described Soviets as 'disguised' enemies, who in interactions presented themselves as a friend, and mistrust was always considered as a main interaction frame (Kaźmierska 1999). The same pattern of interpretation of the other's action appeared in 2010 and afterwards was to some extent strengthened along with Russian involvement in the Smoleńsk investigation. Additionally, the symbolic meaning of catastrophe intensified those associations – the plane was transporting the official Polish delegation to commemorate the seventieth anniversary of the Katyn crime.
9. See note 6. The main theme of this interview is the comparison between the Soviet and German occupations (see Kaźmierska 2000).
10. Interesting analysis of school books is presented by Gołębiewska.
11. The quotation comes from research by Mamul (2009a, b) from her PhD dissertation on national identity in biographical experience of Belarusian-speaking intelligentsia.
12. The very issue of the role and the image of the Second World War in Russia is quite interesting. Monopolizing its image refers not only to the Soviet/Russian perspective but also to the gender context. The war has been defined as a 'men's job' whereas about one million women living in the Soviet Union took active part in military action, not only as nurses or liaison officers but also as snipers, pilots and tank crew members. Swietlana Aleksiejewicz (2010) – a journalist and writer – describes the process of revealing this part of Russian war memory and introducing it into the discourse dominated by men's stories. When collecting women's war stories she realized how much they differ in terms of language, details and meaningfulness of experience. The hegemonic discourse created by men as well as the cultural image of the war placing women in subordinated positions influenced women's attitude towards their war experiences. There was no social need to listen to their stories; on the contrary, being a soldier was a social stigma – finding a husband or a good job was quite difficult when the women revealed their war biographies. It is a very interesting example of social and cultural exclusion from the collective memory in a situation where others (men) having similar biographical experiences gained a privileged position – veterans of war.
13. As an example of this type of discourse constructed from the occidental perspective we can refer to the case of Balkan countries that are expected to overcome strong ethnic and national sentiments in a situation where the whole region is symbolically constituted on the basis of historically defined ethnic and national heritage (Wygnańska 2011). This is a key perspective for understanding contemporary social, cultural and political processes related to the former Yugoslavia, but they are rather neglected by Western European discourse.

Kaja Kaźmierska is an associated professor and head of the Department of Sociology of Culture, Institute of Sociology, Faculty of Economics and Sociology, University of Łódź, Poland. Her research interests include: biographical analysis, collective/national identity and memory, migration, borderland and European identity formation and studies on Jewish identity. Her recently published titles include: *Biography and Memory: The Generational Experience of the Shoah Survivors* (Boston: Academic Studies Press, 2012). She was recently the main coordinator of the project: 'The People's Republic of Poland and the German Democratic Republic in Memory and Biographical Experiences of People Born Between 1945–1955', funded by the Polish-German Foundation for Science (2012–2014).

PART III
Eastern European Memories Facing Historical Change and Cultural Transformations

Chapter 6

THE PATH OF BRINGING THE DARK TO LIGHT
Memory of the Holocaust in Postcommunist Europe

Joanna Beata Michlic

In 1945, only a few grasped the extent of the destruction of Eastern European Jews with their civilization and the implication of this loss for the region. Today, the Holocaust has become the European paradigm of *lieu de mémoire* (Diner 2007a) and the universal icon of evil. Most recently some have claimed the Holocaust as an international paradigm of human rights. These developments have evolved in different directions, creating greater understanding of the impact of the Holocaust on the one hand, and on the other making poor analogies and producing competing narratives of martyrdom.

In Europe, despite the establishment of the International Day of Holocaust Remembrance (27 January), the memory of the Holocaust does not cease to cause tensions between the West and the postcommunist countries. In the latter states, the Holocaust as a matter of public discourse arrived late, and its arrival has been greeted with a kaleidoscope of reactions ranging from poignant reflection about the loss, a moral and social obligation to remember, new scholarly interest, nostalgia for the lost pre-1939 East European Jewish civilization, to political instrumentalization, relativization, trivialization and rejection. Moreover, the memory of the Gulag and strong reluctance to come to terms with the dark wartime past in relation to local Jewish communities that go hand in hand, plays a significant role in the manner in which the Holocaust is approached and commemorated today. In addition, in Belarus, Ukraine and Romania, where millions of Jews were shot and executed and then buried in mass graves, the Holocaust is today manifesting itself in an extraordinarily tangible manner, demonstrating that the wartime past is still part of the present. In the 2000s, in small villages and towns of this region, corpses of

---

Notes for this chapter begin on page 129.

the murdered Jews began to be uncovered with the help of local eyewitnesses, many of whom were children during the Second World War, and only given a proper burial more than sixty years after their killings. The project has been carried out by the French priest Father Patrick Desbois with the cooperation of some Jewish religious authorities.

1989–1990s: The Outburst of Competing and Discordant Memories

When communism collapsed in Eastern Europe in 1989 and in the Soviet Union in 1991, coming to terms with the Holocaust was one of the political, moral and cultural challenges that encumbered postcommunist Europe's 'return' to the rest of Europe. If the citizens of the postcommunist bloc aspired to the new European values, then they were obliged to adopt the thinking about the Holocaust that prevailed in Stockholm, London and Brussels. In the initial euphoria of the 'end of history', the difficulties in reconciling the two Europes' understandings of the Holocaust did not seem to loom large. But as time passed, it became clearer that postcommunist Europe was not finding it so easy to accept the Western model of the Holocaust; in fact, there was considerable resistance, often taking on similar forms in different countries. Today, in the middle of 2015, this resistance has not diminished, but in fact has been increasing, in spite of the 'discovery' of the Jews and the Holocaust in the region.

In Eastern Europe, the late 1980s and the beginning of the 1990s witnessed what the historian Padraic Kenney (2002) calls a 'carnival of revolution',[1] remarkably peaceful in Central Europe, and violent in the Balkans. The carnival was marked by the explosion of a plethora of memories. This period opened the floodgates to memories of the past, both the precommunist and communist pasts.[2] As a result, various skeletons from the national closets were exposed to the light of day for the first time since 1945. Hence the restoration of memory has not been a smooth, unifying and unified process.[3] And at present it is still undergoing many dynamic transformations of competing and discordant remembering.

So far we can differentiate two major stages in the process of restoration of memory. This is central to understanding how the national communities – the political and cultural elites as well as ordinary members of societies – have related to, remembered and commemorated the Holocaust throughout the postcommunist period. This is also crucial to understand the continuities and *discontinuities* of the major narratives about the Holocaust and Jews that had emerged prior to and during this time, and the continuing redesigning and refashioning of these narratives.

The first phase, which occurred immediately after the fall of communism, took on a more (ethno)nationalist form. During this phase a powerful dichotomy of 'we' the nation and 'they' the communist regime was strongly emphasized at the expense of a more nuanced representation of the past, whilst the ethnic vision of the past that was prevalent excluded the memory of the local Jewish communities and other ethnic and national minorities. Moreover, the memory of the Holocaust continued to be repressed in public discourse, and defensive attitudes toward the difficult past in relation to the destruction of the Jews played a more significant role in public discourse than the newly emerged narratives aiming at exposing the 'dark past'. At the same time, a new wave of recycled and modified nationalistic and anti-Semitic narratives about the Jews as perpetrators vis-à-vis the nation during the communist period (Judeo-communism) have also re-emerged. The theme of Judeo-communism, in its various versions, is the key narrative in the repertoire of the right-wing ethnonationalist politicians, journalists and historians in Eastern Europe. Judeo-communism is one of the most durable modern scapegoating and victimization myths directed against Jews. The aggressive hate speech of the Jobbik party that entered the Hungarian parliament in 2010, vulgar and intense exchanges on mainstream social media in postcommunist Baltic states, Poland or Ukraine, represent good and alarming examples of the varied range and proliferation of this myth in the last two decades. This powerful, pan-European, anti-Semitic stereotype crystallized in the long nineteenth century, and by the first decade of the twentieth century its disseminators were responsible for causing widespread, transnational Judeo-Bolshevik panic by suggesting that Jews as a collectivity aimed to destroy the order of nation states and Christianity in Europe. Judeo-communism reached its zenith in terms of its political, social and cultural scope and impact during the interwar period, 1918–1939, when Europe was engulfed in real and imagined fear of the first newly established communist entity, Soviet Russia (1917), and the swift rise of communist movements and political parties in individual European nation states. Lay people, conservative and nationalistic politicians, journalists and writers of both secular and religious ideological provenance, and Christian clergy began to constantly use terms such as Judeo-bolshevism, Judeo-masonry and 'Red Jews' to describe what they perceived as the chief enemy of Christian European civilization and their respective nation states and national interests.

Today, in the postcommunist period, the myth of Judeo-communism serves to justify and minimize any wrongdoing against the Jews during the Holocaust and to reinforce the narrative of one's own victimhood during the Second World War and in the post-1945 communist period. A good illustration of the still potent nature of the myth of Judeo-communism in postcommunist Poland, for example, was the debate about the anti-Jewish violence of the summer of 1941, which was triggered by the publication of Jan T. Gross's *Sąsiedzi (Neighbours)* in May 2000 (English 2001). Individuals and groups that strongly opposed Gross's theses about Polish participation in the collective massacre of the Jews of Jedwabne on 10 July 1941 used the stereotype of the Jew as anti-Polish and pro-Soviet to prove that his theses were wrong. In the most extreme version, which is advocated by marginal radical groups only, even the late Karol Wojtyła (Pope John Paul II) is considered a member of the Judeo-communist conspiracy and is portrayed as a servant of Jews. However, as the subsequent debates about Jan T. Gross's other publications such as *Fear: Anti-Semitism in Poland after Auschwitz* (2006) and *Golden Harvest* (2012) demonstrated, the narrative of Judeo-communism constitutes a premise for historical thinking characteristic of the new ethnonationalistic or 'monumental' historiography claiming to defend the good name of Poland. Its leading representatives are Marek J. Chodakiewicz, Piotr Gontarczyk, Leszek Żebrowski, Bogdan Musiał, the late Tomasz Strzembosz, Igor Cyprian Pogonowski and Krzysztof Jasiewicz.[4] Some of these historians are considered members of the established mainstream historical schools. In the case of Krzysztof Jasiewicz, he underwent a radical transformation in his professional interpretation of the role of Polish Jews in Polish history in less than a decade. In 2002, Jasiewicz published *Pierwsi po diable. Elity sowieckie w okupowanej Polsce, 1939–1941 (First after the Devil: Soviet Elites in Occupied Poland, 1939–1941)*, which is a detailed study of the participation of different ethnic groups in the Soviet state apparatus and administration in the entire region of Western Belarus during the Soviet occupation between September 1939 and June 1941. Jasiewicz's in-depth statistical analysis of Soviet primary sources demonstrated that collaboration with the Soviet regime was cross-ethnic, and that it encompassed not only the Jewish and Slavic national minorities of the *Kresy*, but also ethnic Poles. His textual analysis of wartime testimonies of Polish soldiers of the Anders Army, which are housed in the Hoover Institute of Stanford University, confirmed Gross's thesis about the prejudicial nature of their content with regards to the image of Polish Jews and Polish-Jewish relations, especially Jewish collaboration with the Soviets, manifested in the cliché of Judeo-communism. In his monograph, Jasiewicz directly and forcefully criticized historians for treating the stereotype of pro-Soviet, pro-communist and anti-Polish Jews as a historical fact and not as an anti-Semitic cliché.

However, since the publication of his review, in January 2009, of Edward Zwick's acclaimed feature film *Defiance*, based on Nechama Tec's book of the same title, Jasiewicz has changed his tune entirely: he himself 'resurrected' the myth of Judeo-communism as a historical truth. Moreover, he accused Western historiography of unjustified preoccupation with the Holocaust, of unfairly placing the event in the centre of inquiries into the human condition of the twentieth century, and the Jews of focusing solely on their own sufferings and forgetting about the sheer number of human beings who had perished in all wars throughout history.[5] Jasiewicz's case is perhaps a striking illustration of a powerful dynamic tension in one individual between the desire to find out uncomfortable truths about one's own history and the desire to foster 'false' pride in the community to which one belongs. Individuals such as Jasiewicz do not only reside in their countries of origin, but also in the West; the Romanian intellectual Paul Goma, living in Paris, is a good example of the latter.

The Arrival of 'Dark Pasts' in Eastern Europe

The second phase of restoration of memory was gradually crystallized by the late 1990s and the first years of the new millennium. It can be called progressive, pluralistic and civic because it aims at exploring the complex, painful memory of the Holocaust and other uncomfortable events in a nation's history. The key characteristic of this phase is increasing awareness that national history is more complicated than a black and white vision opposing the communist version of the past. Other main features are the elasticity and multiplicity of the representations of the Jews and the Holocaust, the fusion of official and private memories absent during the communist era, and the variety of participants in memory and commemoration projects, including Holocaust survivors and their descendants living in postcommunist societies, and in Israel and the West.

During this phase, new information and new interpretations of the past, previously absent and ignored both under communism and in émigré circles, have been entering public discourse. It is during this phase that the dark, discomforting past of the majority of nations with regard to the treatment of Jewish communities during the Holocaust has become a subject of historical awareness, history writing, artistic performances and public discourse on a limited or broad national scale, depending on the state.

The impetus for the development of this phase springs from two different current cultural and political factors that intersect. The first is the emergence of the genuine culture of nostalgia for the multi-ethnic past in some sections of societies in the region, accompanied by interests in 'all things Jewish' and the emergence of what the acclaimed writer Ruth Ellen Gruber has called 'virtual Jewish culture'.[6] On a smaller local scale, this process has even led to the emergence of 'the self-proclaimed carriers of the lost East-European Jewish civilization',[7] such as Janusz Makuch, director of the highly successful annual international Jewish Festival in Krakow who proclaimed in May 2007:

> People have to realize the dimensions of the enormous evil that was done here and understand that it is important to cleanse themselves of it. The festival creates a confessional space that should help people realize what happened here and what we have lost. We have to ask ourselves the question why we lost it, what our guilt is, what our Polish complicity is in the fact that this Jewish world is not only gone, but will never return. (Makuch 2008: 232)

The second factor is the pragmatic realization that the Holocaust has become the contemporary European entry ticket, as discerningly observed by the late Tony Judt in *Postwar* (2005: 803). As a result, the countries that had already joined the European Union in May 2004 and some of those that are awaiting admission have discovered that it is far better politically to commemorate the Holocaust and that it is more profitable commercially to celebrate their multi-ethnic past than to deny it. Politicians of these countries recognize that endorsing multiculturalism is a means of gaining respectability and visible international status in the West. Therefore, their new endorsed reconceptualizations of Jews and the Holocaust tend to perceive 'the perished Jews as good citizens and Jewish survivors and their descendants living in the West as welcome visitors'.[8] On many occasions, however, state officials utter pronouncements that contradict the new stance on Jews, as various speeches of Romanian, Hungarian and Baltic state representatives have demonstrated in the 1990s and throughout the beginning of the twenty-first century. Hungary, with the largest Jewish minority today in Central Europe, represents the most notorious case. The language of hatred towards Jews and the old anti-Semitic myths about Jewish conspiracies and desire to control the world have been on the increase in the mainstream Hungarian political culture and public discourse since 2010.

Memory of the Gulag and Memory of Jews and the Holocaust

The Holocaust has no doubt arrived in postcommunist countries, but the temptation to tell the past in a comforting way, as Tony Judt (2002) correctly predicted, is persistent in the region. Perhaps it is out of this temptation that 'the double genocide theory' or the symmetry between Nazi and communist crimes was born, which is most pronounced in the

Baltic states, Hungary and the Ukraine. This theory makes a powerful tool in the hands of local right-wing ethnonationalists, and might have a detrimental impact on the process of coming to terms with the 'dark past' in those countries. Ethnonationalists employ this theory to minimalize the wartime crimes against Jews and to undermine the discourse about legal, historical and moral responsibilities for the Holocaust. In their eyes, the Holocaust is a purely 'exaggerated' historical event that basically obfuscates the suffering of other people.[9] To reinforce their negative evaluation of the Holocaust, the radical ethnonationalists skilfully employ the above-mentioned theme of Judeo-communism. They also weave a refashioned theme of Israel as the present embodiment of the Nazi state into the narrative of what they consider to be their own unacknowledged and forgotten suffering juxtaposed with the well-known suffering of the Jews. Responsible criticisms of Israeli policies are valid, but the comparisons of Israel to the Nazi state are perverse, as noted by Shlomo Avineri, a political scientist, Israeli statesman and public intellectual, himself a critic of specific policies of the current Israeli governments (Avineri 2010).

Putting on the mantle of martyrdom and unacknowledged suffering of one's own nation and mixing them with anti-Semitic themes of Judeo-communism and 'Nazi Israel' in order to undermine the memory of the Holocaust creates a highly volatile mixture that could not only have a lasting effect on the integration of the 'dark past' into mainstream historical consciousness and history writing, but also on the popular memory of the Second World War in general.

The Senate of the Czech Republic endorsed the theory of double genocide in a resolution of 3 June 2008, and the European Parliament passed a similar resolution on 2 April 2009, declaring 23 August, the date in 1939 on which the infamous Ribbentrop-Molotov agreement was signed between Nazi Germany and the Soviet Union, as a date of remembrance for victims of both regimes. Yehuda Bauer, the eminent Israeli Holocaust historian, protested against the comparisons between Nazi Germany and the Soviet regime, arguing that 'World War Two was started by Nazi Germany, not the Soviet Union, and the responsibility of the 35 million dead in Europe, 29 million of them non-Jews, is that of Nazi Germany, not Stalin. To commemorate victims equally is a distortion.'[10] A minority of local public intellectuals also strongly protested this comparison as some of the chapters in *Bringing the Dark Past to Light: The Memory of the Holocaust in Postcommunist Europe* (Himka and Michlic 2013) reveal. But perhaps one of the most adamant voices against political calls for the Soviet Union's crimes against Lithuania to be named an act of genocide is that of Lithuanian philosopher Leonidas Donskis. In his article 'The Inflation of Genocide', published in July 2009, Donskis argues:

> We are living in an era of not only monetary inflation, but also of the inflation – hence devaluation – of concepts and values … After all, we cannot regard the history of all our civilizations as one ongoing crime and one endless genocide of some group or other. Whitewashing a concept benefits no one … No matter how cruel the Soviet terror that was visited upon the Baltic states, a large segment of Lithuanian, Latvian and Estonian society, by going over to the other side, by becoming collaborators, was not only able to save itself, but also secure for itself successful careers in the administration of the occupying regime. This group was able to wreak havoc on and settle scores with its own people, doing so with impunity. (Donskis 2009)

The Extent and Limits of the Second Restorative Phase: Poland as a Paradigm

Contemporary Poland is the best illustration of a postcommunist country where the second phase of restored memory has reached a sophisticated and advanced level, as demonstrated during the Jedwabne debate, 2000–2002, and the post-Jedwabne era, 2002–2013. Whereas Ukraine, on the other hand, can be seen as the best example of a postcommunist country where the first phase of restored memory still dominates over the second phase, which is trying, with great difficulty, to make its mark on public discourse and history writing. In Ukraine, as Anatolii Podol's'kyi, Director of the Ukrainian Centre for Holocaust Research in Kiev, sharply summarized in 2008, 'remembrance culture has reached a dead end', since there is 'no desire to accept the "other" as well' (Podol's'kyi 2008: 278).

Examining the discourse on the Holocaust in most postcommunist countries, one is inclined to argue that all of them are still awaiting their own 'Jedwabne debate' that would install the Holocaust and the uncomfortable aspects of relations with the Jewish minority at the centre of public debate, that would pose salient questions about contemporary national identity and the status of various ethnic and national minorities in the past and present, and that would lead to the emergence of empathic memory for the Jewish minority, that historical 'other' perceived formerly as the chief enemy.

'Jedwabne debates' are necessary triggers of national inquiry into the present and future nature of society, 'who we are', 'who we want to be' and 'how we relate to the "other"'. Yet they may not necessarily make the nation tell its past anew. In Poland of the post-Jedwabne era, in spite of the booming theatre of memory of Jews and the Holocaust, there is still a visible split between groups of politicians, historians, public intellectuals, journalists and artists, in the way they evaluate the dark aspects of Polish relations with the Jews before, during and after the Holocaust, and where they place this 'dark past' in national history and culture. The central issue here is how much of the 'dark past' is acceptable to contemporary society, and how much of it is perceived as excessive and thus not acceptable. Today, more than one decade after the discovery of the Jedwabne crime, it is clear that sections of the public are either uninterested or have difficulty in accepting the sheer depth of the 'dark past' still being uncovered by historians, and are inclined to believe in and preach the more socially acceptable narrative where only a small minority within Polish society wronged the Jews during the war. The latter is a continuation of the hegemonic narrative from the communist era, skillfully 'dressed up' and 'repackaged' to suit the present social and political needs. In other words, there is evident continuing social and cultural resistance to fully integrating the most painful and discomforting layers of this 'dark past' into public memory and popular historical consciousness. This is despite impressive ongoing historical research carried out by historians in Poland representing a critical school of history writing and scholars abroad, the endorsement of the difficult past by sections of mainstream political and cultural elites, and sophisticated, fact-based educational programmes in Polish high schools from the mid-2000s onwards.

During the communist period, scholars in Poland and elsewhere in communist Eastern Europe did not investigate the dark past, and historical data on the subject was not publically known nor accessible to professional historians. In the postcommunist era, this is no longer true; instead, many Poles seem to be looking at something but refusing to properly see it. Goethe's saying, 'Everyone hears only what he understands', captures how different groups and individuals, including professional historians, approach inconvenient dark historical truths differently. This is, of course, by no means exclusively a problem for Polish society or East European postcommunist societies.

The old Goethe saying recently echoed in Umberto Eco's latest novel, *The Cemetery of Prague*, might be viewed as one plausible interpretation of the presence of conflicting and disparate evaluations of inconvenient dark historical truths. Here the key issue is how much of the dark truth is 'too much truth' for Polish history, collective memory and identity, how much of it could be channelled into the collective historical awareness and national mythology, and how much of it is 'indigestible', overwhelmingly frightful, alien and disturbing not only to the old, but also to the younger generations.[11] Another key issue is the problem of dissemination of the dark truth in an effective and productive manner that will not trigger strong self-defence mechanisms and painful, unbearably negative feelings about one's own collective. What would be the best manner to disseminate the subject? How can it be successfully implemented and practised at schools and non-governmental institutions? Under what conditions could it reach broader social circles organically without causing highly emotionally negative reactions? What are its limits in terms of modifying collective history writing, national mythologies and social memory? Could it be dependent on the scope of the transformation of national traditions and mythologies? How could one create sustainable levels of openness towards and empathy for the Jewish minority (and other minorities) past and present? Manifestos such as Jan T. Gross's *Neighbors* constitute an important first step in this process (not only in Poland but in the entirety of Eastern Europe), but building and sustaining empathy for the Jews and disseminating and deepening knowledge about the Holocaust cannot be achieved only by constantly confronting the public with new manifestos that do not necessarily represent the same intellectual and moral power as *Neighbors*. What needs to be considered is other means and activities that would link and interweave positive aspects of modern Polish history and Polish-Jewish relations with the dark ones in a broader historical and comparative context. This began to be realized in grass-roots educational projects such as the Dialogue School with Polish youth, in which they learn both positive aspects of their national history in relation towards Jews, such as the history of dedicated and genuine rescuers of Jews, and the dark history of these relations that reflect negatively on the Polish collective.[12]

However, in light of the current opposition to the full integration of the dark past of Polish-Jewish relations, rooted in psychological and cultural self-defence mechanisms, we should realize that the splits over history could once again become a fixed landmark of the difficult process of memorializing Jews and the Holocaust. This seems the most likely scenario in Poland, despite the most advanced second stage of memory restoration in the country in comparison to other nation states in the region.

It might prove to be difficult for Polish society as a whole to come to terms with the dark past soon and fully because of the deeply shameful nature of this past and the emotive power of fundamental Polish national myths about the Second World War, and the political manipulation of that past by right-wing politicians and pundits. As exemplified in a number of polls conducted since 2000, Polish society still perceives the Second World War as a central event in the country's history and as one embodying national heroism, pride and victimhood. According to the first poll conducted a few months before Poland joined the European Union in early May 2004, only 3 per cent of those who were interviewed felt ashamed about negative attitudes toward Jews in the Second World War.[13]

None of the interviewees mentioned the name Jedwabne in their own statements, and the researchers concluded that memory of the massacre had been embraced only by the Polish intelligentsia for whom Jedwabne represents a moral and historical problem. The second poll, conducted in 2009, on the eve of the seventieth anniversary of the outbreak of the Second World War, confirmed the results gathered five years earlier (see Szacki 2009a, b). According to this poll, 73 per cent of those interviewed were convinced that Poles had many reasons to be proud of their conduct during the war, including the rescue activities extended to Jews, whereas only 17 per cent stated that there were wartime events about which Poles should feel ashamed. Though Jedwabne is recalled by many of those interviewed, a cognitive confusion is widespread about who the real perpetrators of the massacre were; many attributed the crime to the Germans and not to the local Poles.

The recent report by Antoni Sułek in which the author discusses polls conducted in 2002 and 2011 about the Jedwabne massacre confirms the results of the aforementioned polls. Sułek, who was the author of both questionnaires, concludes that Jedwabne as a historical event has not entered long-term social memory and that poll respondents continually show a great deal of confusion with regard to identifying the perpetrators of the crime (Sułek 2011: 43–44). It is basically very hard for the Poles to accept that the history of their nation is full not only of heroes and victims, but also of perpetrators of crimes against others. Sułek argues that one of the main reasons for the persistence of such beliefs lies in the lack of public commemoration of the massacres of Jews, in places other than Jedwabne, which also occurred in the summer of 1941. Another reason for this unawareness, he contends, lies in the weaknesses of the Polish educational system. High school history textbooks in which Jedwabne is given proper attention, he notes, are rare. Yet, in his conclusions, Sułek optimistically points out that another poll, one conducted in 2010 by the prestigious *Centralny Ośrodek Badań Społecznych* (Public Opinion Research Centre), CBOS, demonstrates that 5 per cent of respondents named attitudes of Poles toward Jews during the Second World War as shameful, and 5 per cent declared they felt ashamed of Poland's anti-Semitism. In this same poll, the number of respondents who felt ashamed of any events in Polish history numbered 31 per cent. This indicates that changes in historical awareness about national history and national mythology are possible, even if the transformation is slow. However, according to another quantitative study conducted in Poland over the entire political transformation period with: 'the passing of time and the disappearance of war-time generation, Polish representation of the past has increasingly moved away from historical truth: the number of Poles who claim that ethnic Poles were more victimized than Jews during the Nazi occupation has systematically increased' (Bilewicz and Winiewski 2014: 214).

Notwithstanding the improvements in historical knowledge about the Holocaust, the number of Poles who perceive Jews as the primary victims of the Holocaust is decreasing (ibid. 212). The same report also stresses that the thesis of declining anti-Semitism in postcommunist Poland is not supported by empirical data and that in fact one can observe the relative stability of anti-Semitism and that it targets 'real' Jews (ibid. 213–214). Similarly another poll studying intolerance, prejudice and discrimination in Europe as a whole, published in Germany in 2011, also offers rather troubling insights. It found that 49.9 per cent of Polish (and 69.2 per cent of Hungarian) respondents believe that Jews in their countries have too much power; 72.2 per cent of Polish respondents also believe that Jews try to take advantage of having been victims during the Nazi era, this in comparison to 68.1 per cent of Hungarian and 52.2 per cent of Portuguese respondents who think that way. By the same token 51.2 per cent of Polish, 57.3 per cent of Hungarian, and 51.9 per cent of Portuguese respondents agreed that Jews bring enrichment to their culture (Hövermann, Küpper and Zick 2011: 57–58).

Looking at post-Jedwabne Poland, I differentiate three key dimensions in the landscape of memory. In my view, these three dimensions are useful not only for understanding the dynamics of memory of the Jews and the Holocaust in Poland today, but also for comparative analyses of the dynamics of this memory in the entire postcommunist region – where these countries stand at present, and the commonalities and differences amongst them. I call these dimensions: 'remembering to remember', 'remembering to benefit' and 'remembering to forget'. 'Remembering to remember' is a process that underscores, on both the cognitive and moral levels, the void left after the genocide of the Jewish people, and the majority-nation-to-Jewish relations in all its aspects, including all the wrongs done to the Jewish minority before, during and after the Holocaust. The intention of the advocates of 'remembering to remember' is to mourn and commemorate the loss of prewar Jewish citizens, and to come to terms with the 'dark past' in relation to the Jewish minority, by making this past an integral part of national history, present historical consciousness and public memory. They insist not only on integrating the history of the Jews and other ethnic and national minorities into national history, but also on treating the Jews and members of other ethnic and cultural minorities as members of the nation in a civic sense. On a cultural level, their major goal is to create both a 'community of identification' with, and an empathic memory for the 'other'. Thus they are engaged in building a forward-looking, open and inclusive society based on the civic model of national belonging, with a respect for multiculturalism and humanitarian values.

In the 'remembering to benefit' dimension, the key intention behind the recalling and commemoration of the Jews and the Holocaust is the achievement of tangible goals on individual, regional and national levels. Here the focus is not so much on the past *per se*, or on an identification with, or empathic memory for the 'other', but rather on making use of the past in the pursuit of tangible benefits such as elevated status and respectability in the international arena. With regard to the history of the Jews in their nation, they emphasize that the Jewish minority has long been present, and that the descendants of this minority living abroad are today welcome to become part of and to invest in the new postcommunist entity. They posit that Israeli and Western Diaspora Jews should view the country of their ancestors with a completely fresh eye. They insist on treating the present moment in history as a 'zero point' in forging new and mutually beneficial relationships with Jews in the West and in Israel. Though they acknowledge the 'dark past' in the history of their nation, for them that past is a completely closed chapter, on which one should not dwell, but should instead look to the future. In the name of this 'bright' future, they claim it is better to concentrate on those chapters in the history of the majority nation's relations with the Jews that cast a good light, rather than on the dark history of anti-Semitism and the Holocaust. Giving a positive spin on the past in Polish-Jewish relations is the key to understanding the thinking, policies and practices within this group.

In 'the remembering to forget' dimension, the third category, the memory of the Jews and the Holocaust is understood as an awkward problem that does not fit well with the conservative, religious and ethnonationalist model. Here, interest in the Jewish past and the Holocaust is greeted with tension, and is disdainfully referred to as 'an imported fashion for Jews'. The advocates of 'remembering to forget' view the painful 'dark past' as an unjust insult to national history and memory, and as a threat to the nation's identity and future, and therefore they attack advocates of 'remembering to remember'. In 'remembering to forget', the archaeology of the dark and uncomfortable past provokes an upsurge of old anti-Jewish prejudices and stereotypes, carefully modified and repackaged to suit particular current political and social situations, and depending on the particular disseminators, the new/old anti-Jewish messages are delivered either overtly or covertly. Calling for the right *polityka historyczna* (historical policy) that would put an end to the archaeology of the difficult past is the key to understanding the thinking, policies and practices within this group.

Each of these three dimensions is dynamic, and manifests itself in subtly different versions, depending on the key actors. Some versions of 'remembering to remember' overlap with variants of 'remembering to benefit', and are sometimes difficult to differentiate.

In *Triumph and Trauma*, Bernard Giesen observes that today in the West the Holocaust has acquired the position of 'a free-floating myth or a cultural icon of horror and inhumanity' (2004: 142). But in postcommunist Eastern Europe, approaches towards the meanings of the Holocaust still have a rather more specific local character, embedded in wartime and postwar communist history, though Western influences are also visible and important. Characteristically, any acceptance of the 'remembering to remember' dimension, with its new rituals of commemorating the 'dark past' and advocacy of memory of empathy with the Jews, usually provokes counter-rituals. The rise of 'critical history' writing about the 'dark past' similarly provokes a counter-history – clinging to the 'monumental national history'. Thus, at present, it is impossible to speak about a rupture between the past and the present. Instead, one can observe a fusion of the past and the present, which produces modifications of traditional narratives designed to suit current political and social needs.

The multitude of approaches towards the Jews and the Holocaust, and the painful dynamic of the 'dark past' in postcommunist countries, also suggests that cultural heritage and tradition exert an enduring power over national identity, memory and professional historical writing. On the other hand, some transformations in the realm of national memory, identity and history are possible because of new global conditions, Western/international demands and pressures, the culture of multiculturalism and genuine nostalgia for the multi-ethnic past. On the one hand the memory of the Holocaust and the Jewish past in postcommunist Eastern Europe cannot be understood without a careful study of the history of anti-Semitism, ethnonationalism and the impact of ethnonational and religious prejudices towards the Jews past and present in the region. The old prejudicial myths about Jews skilfully repackaged in new forms have not ceased to be an integral aspect of the discourse about national identity in the region.

No doubt, the memory of Jews and the Holocaust in Eastern Europe constitutes an exceptionally interesting case for the study of the painful process of coming to terms with 'the dark past', whilst on the other, of getting the past wrong, thus making both the past and present not only bearable, but also predominantly positive and 'bright'. It demonstrates that in significant segments of mainstream historical consciousness and public memory the painstakingly 'uncovered' accounts of the 'dark' pasts are still perceived in a category of 'too much truth' that can hardly be accepted on a larger social scale. It shows too that in public memory, remembering is not necessarily about getting the past right, but rather about maintaining the positive collective self-image and soothing national myths. Thus, 'the dark past' is perceived as a 'spoiler'. What is therefore certain is that the project of integration of the memory of the Holocaust, with all its painful and uncomfortable aspects, will require intense work on the part of more than one generation of scholars, public intellectuals, educators and local enthusiasts, both within the postcommunist region and in its diasporas.

Notes

1. On subsequent right-wing ideological interpretations of peaceful revolutions in Central Europe as 'stolen' or 'unfinished', see Rév 2005: 304–336.
2. On postcommunist intellectual discourse about the communist past and national identity, see for example, Esbenshade 1995: 72–96.
3. On memory as never unitary, but continually changing in time and place, see the important comparative analysis by Olick 2003.
4. On the use of Judeo-communism as a historical fact in history writing, see Michlic 2007.
5. For Jasiewicz's total transformation from his earlier position, see Jasiewicz 2010a and 2010b.
6 On the concept of virtual Jewishness, see Gruber 2002 and 2009.
7. On specific unconventional ways of encountering and interpreting Jewish identity by non-Jewish Poles as an integral part of their own identity in a city such as Krakow, see Lehrer 2007.
8. By comparison, on the recent reconceptualization of the Holocaust in Austria, see Maier 1993.
9. In his keynote lecture titled 'Genocide and the Holocaust: What Are We Arguing about?' delivered at the Eleventh Biennial Lessons and Legacies Conference on the Holocaust, Omer Bartov convincingly argued that the notion that the Holocaust presents an obstacle to a larger understanding of genocide is not a uniquely East European phenomenon, but is also evident in the writings of some mainstream scholars of comparative genocide in the West. I would like to thank Prof. Bartov for sharing the lecture with me.
10. Yehuda Bauer, 'Memo to the ITF on Comparisons between Nazi Germany and the Soviet Regime'. I would like to thank Prof. Yehuda Bauer for sharing this article with me.
11. On the problem of refusing to accept the dark truth, and the lack of empathy towards Jewish victims and survivors of the Holocaust among Polish youth, see Bilewicz 2011.
12. On the importance of grass-roots educational projects with Polish youth through which they learn both positive aspects of their national history in relations towards Jews, such as the history of rescuers, and the dark history of these relations that reflect negatively on Polish collective see Bilewicz and Witkowska. I would like to thank the authors for sharing this work with me.
13. See the report on the poll 'Duma i wstyd Polaków – sondaż' 2004.

Joanna Beata Michlic is a social and cultural historian, and founder and director of the Hadassah-Brandeis Institute Project on Families, Children and the Holocaust at Brandeis University. Since 2013, she has been teaching contemporary history in the Department of Historical

Studies at Bristol University, UK. Her major publications include *Neighbors Respond: The Controversy about Jedwabne* (2004, co-edited with A. Polonsky), *Poland's Threatening Other: The Image of the Jew from 1880 to the Present*, and *Bringing the Dark to Light: The Reception of the Holocaust in Postcommunist Europe* (2013, co-edited with J.-P. Himka). She is also the editor of the forthcoming *Jewish Families in Europe, 1939 – Present: History, Representation and Memory* (2015). Her current research topics are the history of rescuers of Jews and East European Jewish childhood, 1945–1950. She is the recipient of many academic awards and fellowships, most recently the Fulbright Senior Scholar Award, Haifa University, Spring Semester 2013/2014.

Chapter 7

THE RISE OF AN EAST EUROPEAN COMMUNITY OF MEMORY?
On Lobbying for the Gulag Memory via Brussels

Lidia Zessin-Jurek

The white steppes of Siberia have for long remained an empty space on the mnemonic map of Europe, a 'blank spot' in the history of the twentieth century. Yet they were the scene of imprisonment for hundreds of thousands of deportees to the Gulag. This past belongs to Eastern Europe's heritage, and recently more and more voices have insisted on dealing with it in a new way, such as the author of the Pulitzer Prize-winning volume on that topic, 'If we go on forgetting half of Europe's history, some of what we know about mankind itself will be distorted' (Applebaum 2003: 576).

Anne Applebaum made her claim just before the 2004 European Union enlargement, which indeed brought challenges in terms of integrating Eastern representations of the past into Western memories. The memory of the Gulag, touched by the state-enforced discursive cleansing after 1945 and a motif of initially illegal, later official, literature ever since, did not establish a strong foothold among postcommunist communities of memory after 1989. It grew in prominence only in the mid-2000s in the context of memory discourses being forged in Brussels. There it serves to foster an emerging cosmopolitan memory of Soviet terror, which clashes, however, with the Western European metanarrative, which has been moving in the direction of embracing national guilt rather than perpetuating discourses of self-perceived victimhood. At the same time, this metanarrative has been informed by the motto 'no more totalitarianism in Europe', which creates the space for the new member states to plea for inclusion of communism, often recounted by them as their second totalitarian experience, into European memories (Bonnard and Meckl 2007). Against this backdrop, the question arises of whether it is possible to

---

Notes for this chapter begin on page 147.

speak about the emergence of an East European community of memory built around one of the symbols of the Stalinist crimes – the Gulag.

Mapping Eastern Europe

History

There is a common view that Eastern Europe was born from the ashes of the Second World War, with a forced split into West and East, which culminated in the poignant metaphor of the 'Iron Curtain'. However, discussions of common features shared by the cultures of East Central Europe reach much deeper than the middle of the twentieth century. A group of postwar Western scholars would find distinctive traits of Eastern Europe back in the rise of nineteenth-century nationalism, seeing in their forms the dichotomy of the continent ('inherently' liberal Western nationalism and 'inherently' authoritarian Eastern model as theorized by Hans Kohn and his followers). More recently, historians such as Larry Wolff (1994) and Maria Todorova (1997) proved that the 'West' has been steadily constructing its constitutive 'other' in the East at least since the eighteenth century. Their works belong to the denunciatory wave which, after Edward Said's *Orientalism* discloses the Western tendency to negatively stereotype other cultures. With the advent of new postmodernist concepts of 'multiple modernities' (Eisenstadt 2002) or 'entangled modernities' (Arnason 2003), Eastern Europe is not seen as the constitutive 'other' for the West anymore. The latter concept encourages us to look for mutually formative links between them. It is believed that the experience of totalitarianism and the end of the Cold War were the most recent encounters in Europe's entangled modernity, especially assuming that fascism, together with Stalinism, signifies a watershed in modern thought as a whole. This follows Hannah Arendt's conclusions on totalitarianism as one of modernity's political possibilities (Stöckl 2000: 44).

Looking for the entanglements and intertwinements between the cultures, scholars remain sensitive towards important differences that arise from different historical experiences. These draw a strong distinction between the West and the East of Europe of the postwar era. Both the experience of totalitarianism and of the end of the Cold War, though shared by the European states, obviously ran differently in the two 'halves of the continent'. East Europeans were confronted with double totalitarianism and the long decades of socialist experience that followed.

This relatedness of the political experience is one of the reasons for thinking about Eastern Europe after 1945 as a coherent region. Stefan

Troebst's (2010a, b) understanding of East Central Europe follows the tradition of Oskar Halecki's *meso-regions*, or Klaus Zernack's concept of *Geschichtsregion*. These concepts serve as a framework for analysis of the regions sharing a significant number of common historical experiences that can be observed in the *longue durée*, such as in the Braudelian concept of the Mediterranean.[1]

Then again, despite the common experience of double totalitarianism and of the socialist decades, the states of the region lived divergently through the wartime occupations and differed in their response to communism. That is why perhaps the only way of conceiving of the East European region as a really coherent whole in historical terms must be through Michael G. Müller's (2010) concept of 'multiple geographies'. Within it we do not take spatial entities for granted; instead we reflect on them with reference to a specific issue. The term 'Eastern Europe' could then be perceived as a landscape with fluid, shifting borders. Using this regional concept as an analytical tool, hence adopting a transnational approach, can undoubtedly be beneficial to research – 'often what happened to one group is intelligible only in light of what had happened to another', to quote the words of Timothy Snyder (2010: XIX). He has himself defined an East European space of that kind. Under the empirical criteria he adopted, this space covers a part of Eastern Europe, stretching from the Baltic to the Black Sea, and from Berlin to Moscow, and was valid for a clearly defined time: 1933 to 1945. The 'bloodlands', as Snyder has called them, were singled out as the geographical space of common experience with the highest death toll among civilians. 'The bloodlands were no political territory, real or imagined; they were simply where Europe's most murderous regimes did their most murderous work' (ibid. XVIII). A similar approach has been used by Peter Gatrell and Nick Baron in their two books about the East European borderland entitled *Homelands* (2004) on the region of post-First World War independent states and *Warlands* (2009) on the region of population resettlements, or in Alexander Prusin's *The Lands Between* (2010) on the ethnic patchwork of Eastern Europeans facing various nationalizing processes.

Memory

The same chain of thought can be used for mapping an East European region of memory. In the words of Tony Judt (2005: 3), given their double totalitarian experience and compared with Western Europe, 'East Europeans have much more to remember – and to forget'. A common feature distinguishing the memory of the Soviet-controlled space from that of Western Europe was coined in number of well-turned phrases, like 'imposed collective amnesia' (Judt 2002: 168), 'organized forgetting', 'communicative silencing', 'fantasy reality' (Wydra 2010), or 'mnemonical hibernation' (Kwaśniewski 2002). The communist regimes suppressed inconvenient memories as a political control technique that created a schizophrenic situation of coexisting double memories – the official and unofficial ones.[2]

Besides the fifty years of 'fantasy realities', what has been common to East European societies is the experience of the 'liberation' of memory after 1989 and the subsequent twenty-year-long period of new challenges. That is to say, while civil society in Western Europe could start dealing with the past immediately after the Second World War, Eastern European societies had to wait for their chance and began 'peeling back the layers of ideological reinterpretations of their past(s) decades later' (Mälksoo 2009: 658).

The *annus mirabilis* 1989 released suppressed memories, but also often revealed unexpected discrepancies in what was remembered. Describing the way that the communist era ended, Karl Schlögel (2008a) had several reasons to doubt the all-encompassing effect of that year. Looking at the course of the Second World War it seems 'hardly surprising that there is nothing like a shared memory' of those events in East Central Europe, in the words of M.G. Müller (2010: 120). Additionally, long and diverse incubation periods for 1989 and myriad national versions of communism were among the reasons accounting for a variety of cultures of remembrance that emerged in East Central Europe after the end of communism. Stefan Troebst grouped those cultures into four categories: 1. with anticommunist consensus; 2. with fierce public debates on recent history; 3. where apathy and ambivalence dominate; and 4. where communism has not been de-legitimized.[3]

All that considered, an East European region of memory – similarly to other regions of memory – can be, once again, most accurately defined and redefined within the concept of 'multiple geographies'. In the context of 'multiple geographies', this chapter investigates whether it is possible to draw a mnemonic map of the Gulag in the regional perspective of East Central Europe. Is the Gulag something that unites or rather divides the memory of the region? Does the Gulag, as a *lieu de mémoire*, bind societies into a community of memory?

* * *

In Central Eastern Europe, Estonia, Latvia, Lithuania, Poland, Ukraine, Belarus, Hungary, Czech Republic, Slovakia, Romania and Germany were all touched by the experience of the Gulag. However, forced deportations did not affect all of them to the same extent. Proportionally, the most affected were the Baltic republics: it is estimated that 10 per cent of the entire adult population was deported or sent to labour camps.

Violated Memory 1945 to 1989

The memory of the Gulag has always been politicized to an extent that strongly disturbed the functioning of community of memory. In the first, and the longest, stage – the communist period – we can speak of a kind of structural 'state violence against memory'. The victims living in the Soviet bloc were deprived of the possibility of speaking, witnessing, even mourning; they could not commemorate their losses. There were hardly any subjects more under official taboo than the deportations to the Gulag (Kwiatkowski et al. 2010: 15; Paczkowski 2004). Furthermore, the memories of the Gulag inmates and their families were disarmed by state policies aiming at integration of those individuals into the system.[4]

At the same time, the accounts of Gulag survivors were collected and published upon emigration, most notably in Great Britain, Italy, France and the United States, putting the Gulag memory on a completely different path. Part of this literature reached oppositional circles in the authors' homelands, thus Siberia remained an encrypted motif of the oppositional literature and arts.[5] Yet even in the West, the memory of the Gulag fell prey to shifting political winds, which regulated the volume of writing being published (depending on the reception of communism in individual Western countries; publishing activity was also limited by reluctance towards bringing up the potential discourse of East European victims 'betrayed' by the West).

'Liberation' of Memory versus 'Failed' Historical Recovery Project

The decline of communism 'liberated' the memory of the Gulag from censorship and official 'taboo' status. The two streams of the Gulag memory river – the emigrational one and the untold stories at home – could finally join their courses and create one coherent narrative. The former deportees began to establish associations, and publishing on the Gulag, largely carried out by the late 1980s illegal underground press, intensified towards the early 1990s. As long as the memory of the Gulag served as incitement to resist and as a form of opposing the enforced silence, the memoirs of the deportees made popular reading. Outpourings of memoirs, diaries and testimonial literature, published in great quantities, lasted until the mid-1990s. Soon, however, the public interest waned (Sariusz-Skąpska 2002: 17–25; Avižienis 2010: 504) and such publications started to be perceived as little more than the works of scribblers of sentimental stories.

As regards the narrative and style, the trauma of past political violence against memory and the long postponement of testimony's cathartic effect have made much of the deportees' rhetoric confused and emotional. Nonetheless, the lack of public interest in the Siberian accounts cannot be explained merely by the mediocre style in which some of them were written. Memoirs could be published and research on the Gulag conducted without political impediments; still, most of these initiatives remained local, underfinanced, based on voluntary work and often limited to capable enthusiasts. Factual material prepared by the associations of deportees was printed in a small font on flimsy paper. More effective independent centres, such as KARTA in Poland with its Eastern Archive, conducted painstaking but financially ruinous empirical work, while their impact on the public memory discourse has remained at a relatively low level.

After the fall of communism, the states of the region demonstrated a rather lukewarm attitude towards commemorating the Gulag. There was no major state-run historical 'recovery' project, and hardly any public financial support or commemoration policies. Initiatives towards the expression of what was by then 'forbidden memory', such as the 'Day of the Gulag Deportee' in Poland (since 1993)[6], or the unveiling of statues to the Gulag victims, were attended by state authorities, without ever being initiated by these authorities or receiving much publicity. The deportees appealed to commemorate the victims, in order to testify to future generations about the criminality of the totalitarian regime; they called to reveal the 'truth' about one of the most important historical 'blank spots' to which the Soviet deportations belonged (Reiff 1989).

Notwithstanding the deportees' efforts, their calls received equally little backing from non-state actors, the prominent intellectual elite. There were unsynchronized attempts to address the hitherto untold past rather than the clear-cut symbolic inauguration of a new narrative.[7] Most probably, the low popularity of the Gulag memory had something to do with the symbolic exploitation of the theme of the Gulag by dissident movements prior to 1989. Afterwards the region was expected to witness the revival of an ethnocentric, xenophobic nationalism, the ultimate 'fruit of a dying totalitarianism, unravelling the pandemonium of nationalistic feuds' in disoriented East European societies (Michnik 1990: 202). According to a negative scenario, reawoken national sentiment fuelled by a sudden aspiration of freedom and dormant resentments would fill the postcommunist ideological vacuum.[8] Therefore, Western standards of building European unity on the rejection of nationalism as a force productive of 'serious evil' were quickly prescribed to the postcommunist space. Following the reshuffling of 'the good' and 'the bad', which took place soon after 1989 in Eastern Europe, nationalism was denounced as the new major danger, according to the dominant narrative. Polish sociologist Paweł Śpiewak has analyzed how in Poland, influential intellectuals originating in the dissident movement constructed the obtrusive Manichean discourse distinguishing between the proponents of nationalism and of Europeanness, between those dwelling on the past and those focusing on a better future (Śpiewak 2005: 91).

For the memory of the Gulag this new discursive setting of the early 1990s implied that a new type of taboo was associated with the topic of deportations, as suggested by the Lithuanian author Jūra Avižienis. She reflected on the non-issue status of the Siberian deportations in her country in the mid-1990s. Why is it – she asked referring to the words by Egidijus Alekasandravičius – that 'this remains a topic without controversy ... without discussion, doubt, or interpretation?' (Avižienis 2010: 45). The deportees' memoirs 'are widely thought to express an irredentist, ethnocentric historical consciousness fundamentally at odds with the demands of modern, multicultural nationhood' (Davoliūtė 2005: 51).

Both in state policies as well as on the level of intellectual discourse the term 'pragmatism' prevailed. The pragmatic understanding that the future economic development of these states would depend on neighbourly cooperation, including with Russia, has surpassed the need for imminent reconciliation with the past. The 'thick line' concept coined by the first non-communist Polish prime minister has come to symbolize orientation towards the future, but at the same time it meant a lack of catharsis in the public sphere (Olschowsky 2011). Perhaps this nipping of potential national(ist) perspectives in the bud was carried out without adequate sensitivity towards the differences in historical experience between Western and Eastern Europe, as in this part of Europe nationalism has only been experienced as a liberating force, whereas all evil was brought about by the 'twin totalitarianisms' (Auer 2010a, 2010b: 1166; Hackmann 2009: 169).

It is possible that at state and public levels this moderation of memory went too far and alienated the parts of societies that were looking out for help from the state and elites in coming to terms with the past. According to those striving to commemorate the violent past of their countries, the state institutions, education system, art, etc., did not grant sufficient attention to 'telling the truth', which was often discussed in the context of dismantling the communist legacies. This in turn pushed them to more radical actions. The previous suppression of memories, strengthened by (sometimes pristine) opposition to communist ideology, made many of those concerned with the Gulag memory turn to trust the ideas of nationalist movements. Thus previous anxieties present in the mainstream discourse were validated, which led to the stigmatization of that milieu and contributed even further to the public disaffection for Siberia.[9] Commemoration initiatives were often treated with suspicion and perceived as an unsophisticated political ploy of the conservatives, behind whom the deportees often rallied.

Regardless of political connotations, the Gulag as a place of memory has not been an easy issue to handle from the perspective of commemoration rituals. First of all, it refers to a non-clearly defined place: the faraway steppes of Siberia – endless, empty and dispersed. Secondly, since the experience was not unique to any of the nations in the region, it could not easily be turned into a distinct foundation myth, like Katyn, Holodomor or Goli Otok (a secret prison and labour camp in Yugoslavia). The potential that the memory of Siberia had for national identity-building has stumbled over the large number of other nationalities who suffered from the Gulag, even within societies themselves; e.g., of Polish citizens deported up to 1941, Jews, Ukrainians and Belarusians constituted almost a half (Grudzińska-Gross and Gross 2008: 7). Moreover, a number of reasons of a more psychological nature, described by Charles Maier (2002) in his distinction between 'hot' and 'cold' memory, explain why the memory of Stalinism, even in former socialist societies, remained somewhat 'cold'. In the case of Nazism not only collaboration, but also taking a bystander position burdened the conscience, causing a more universal sense of shame, whereas communism produced much less of a sense of guilt around complicity and normally spared the conscience of those who did not collaborate. Finally, ideological and psychological reasons for the 'cognitive eclipse' regarding the Gulag itself and leading to non-memory of Siberian prisons, particularly in the West, were analysed by the Polish-American literature scholar, Dariusz Tolczyk (1999, 2009).

The Emergence of an East European Community around the Memory of the Gulag?

For the reasons discussed above, the memory of the Gulag has not become a central element of postcommunist national identity-building in individual East European states. Neither has it become one at the regional level. In many countries in the region the associations of deportees spontaneously sprang up around 1989. Their work concentrated mostly on 'keeping the memory alive', preserving the memory of those who perished and thus preventing atrocities of that kind from ever happening again. The mission statements of these associations sound very similar between different countries. Also similar were their problems with attracting greater public interest in their initiatives. Although the narratives of these associations remained chiefly national, external non-governmental organizations made attempts towards cooperation in gathering sources and testimonies from deportees from different states of the region. Already in 1992, the programme was initiated under the significant name 'Common Place – Eastern Europe' at the Warsaw Week of Conscience. The meeting gathered deportees from Lithuania, Ukraine, Bulgaria, Czech Republic, Slovakia, Belarus, Russia and Poland (Mitzner 1994: 75). Although the project is still ongoing, it has no media coverage and very low visibility.

These grass-roots initiatives aiming at turning Eastern Europe into a 'common place' were not supported at the level of state memory policies. No instruments of common identity building such as international commemorations (e.g., of the Gulag victims) or common history textbooks were employed to this end as they did not correspond with the geopolitical vision of the states concerned. The reason was simply that after the fall of communism the attention of policymakers was directed principally towards the West. The West symbolized a positive project, a Europe to which Easterners yearned to belong. Public discourse was dominated by the conviction that the states of the region were historically Western, but had been 'kidnapped' and forced into an alien Eastern culture, as in the famous claim of Milan Kundera (1984). The 'return to Europe' has become the objective of the European East. Confronted with the magnetic and seductive appeal of the West, the concept of the East as a fundament upon which a common regional identity could be built had little chance and was rather a centrifugal force. In contrast to Western Europe there was no positive ideological frame in which the new Eastern identity could be defined. In this respect, the figure of the Gulag, looking backwards and being reminiscent of the weakness of the region, again, was not likely to become a 'memory figure' uniting the region.

In this context, we may speak of a disruptive influence of the image of the West on the creation of a common East European identity and memory. Moreover, whenever the idea of commonality between the states of the region came into sight, it referred to 'historical justice' expressed in their eventual joining with the West. Frequently this commonality of fate was, however, felt as a 'race to Europe', engendering rivalry and blocking regional cooperation. Alternatively, it implied their 'supremacy' over other states further to the East, rather than a sense of solidarity following the shared experience of nations once under Soviet domination (Sabatos 2011: 26). The 'East' as a label has had negative connotations deeply ingrained in the consciousness of the societies of the region, partly imposed on them by the longstanding orientalizing West European discourse. Over the first postcommunist decade, no positive project associated with the East emerged, which impeded the cultivation of the East European memory.

Brussels – A Crossroads and a Catalyst of East European Memories

This situation changed, however, in the following decade, which was connected to the emergence of new actors promoting the Gulag memory. This time the subject matter was taken up in Brussels, mainly by East European members of the European Parliament. Apart from numerous public hearings and conferences where the topic of the Gulag was discussed, the parliament hosted many exhibitions and commemoration events devoted to the deportations to Siberia, such as 'Birch Bark Letters from Siberia' in June 2011, or 'Your Past is Our Past' in May 2011, commemorating seventy years from the first mass deportations from the Baltic States. Most recent activities by MEPs are in the field of legal settlement for communist crimes, including establishing deportation as a crime against humanity.

This interest in the memory of Siberian deportations is part of the policy of dealing with the legacy of Soviet totalitarianism realized in the so-called 'Prague process' and under the auspices of subsequent Eastern European EU presidencies.[10] The most active people in that process include representatives from organizations renowned in the field of remembrance (memory institutes, museums, etc.) and members of the European Parliament (around fifty) mostly from Eastern Europe. Those MEPs belong to the interfactional Reconciliation of European Histories Group founded in the European Parliament in 2010. The group is chaired by the former Latvian European Commissioner, Sandra Kalniete, born in Tomsk to a family of Siberian deportees. It organizes regular public hearings in the Parliament on the subject of the memory of totalitarian regimes, which mostly gather deputies from the 'new Europe', among whom the most active are former dissidents: László Tőkés (Romania/ Hungary), Vytautas Landsbergis (Lithuania) and Tunne Kelam (Estonia).

The members of the Reconciliation Group say that in 2004, when eight Central and Eastern Europe countries entered the EU, the 'true history' of the Iron Curtain still had to be written. Similarly, in numerous declarations, meetings and statuses of new institutional bodies, the East European politicians, accompanied by non-governmental organizations, point to the deficiency of knowledge of the Stalinist crimes in the West and the need to fill in this painful and dangerous gap. In this rhetoric, they take up the previously neglected arguments used by the associations of Gulag deportees from the 1990s, who also expressed their duty to speak for the victims and to prevent such atrocities from happening again. The same claims pronounced by the new cluster of social actors – the MEPs and organizations promoting awareness about totalitarian crimes – have grown in prominence. They strongly believe in memory policy, especially in the ability of European institutions to make something be remembered. In their discourse, the common collective memory is a remedy for the nagging feeling of insecurity that East Europeans feel, despite their membership in the EU and NATO, as a Lithuanian speaker in Brussels stated (Stranga 2009: 71). They believe in the salutary effects of shared memory, which in their view creates solidarity between people. Using the Brussels parlance: the strive for the 'communitization' of East European memory aims at avoiding new potential fragmentations within the European community and at annihilating the old ones lasting to date (security through integration).[11] This is how the East European MEPs state their plea to include the memory of communism in the collective European memory.

This new way of approaching the communist past also affected the handling of the Gulag memory and was closely connected with the EU accession. Maria Mälksoo analyses the politics of 'becoming European', looking at the East Europeans' attempts to enlarge the mnemonic vision of the 'United Europe' by placing their 'subaltern pasts' in contest with the conventional Western European understanding of the Second World War (Mälksoo 2009: 653–655).[12] These attempts form a part of their quest to belong to the 'true Europe', as opposed to the 'Europe but not quite Europe' position they have endured for long decades. In this, Brussels also serves as a new imagined 'appeal court' for East European states, which have been turning to West European capitals seeking recognition of their claims since at least the nineteenth century (Requate and Wessel 2002). In the last decade, those states which at the beginning did not take part in the EU project have striven for recognition of their identity from the 'old' EU states. The latter acted here as a 'significant other' on which such claims could be projected (Closa 2011: 13). In the pursuit to merge their memory with the 'Western' European one, Eastern actors have imagined the existence of some kind of Western 'consensual memory'.

The claim for equal remembrance of their pasts has roots reaching back to the period prior to accession. As candidates for EU membership those states had to keep a low profile when reflecting on the historical origins of their political and economic retardation (e.g., the Yalta agreement). Moreover, a low input in the shaping of the Europe they were entering in 2004 could cause a partial backlash against the process of Europeanization.[13] In the field of history, 'the hegemonic model of memory by Western design'[14] (Wydra 2012: 127) left candidate states with little room for negotiating interpretations of the Second World War, which also meant they had to enter and operate on the West European level of handling the issue that, as described by Dan Diner, has become the European Union's 'founding act' – the Holocaust.[15]

The difficult process of national soul-searching for complicity in the Holocaust, though dilatory, had already been on its timid way to some countries in the region before these states entered the EU accession phase (e.g., Błoński 2008 [1987]). The strong emphasis on the recognition of the Holocaust, described by Tony Judt as a 'contemporary European entry ticket' (2005: 803), has undoubtedly accelerated this process of self-reflection. The simple schemes of victims versus perpetrators have been severely challenged, which strained the capabilities of East European societies to adopt a self-critical approach. At the same time, they were confronted with the debate about their responsibility for the post-Second World War expulsion of Germans, and this focus on German victimhood proved additionally irritating (Siddi 2012). While dealing with their own culpability, they have increasingly looked for and found comfort in emphasizing their own victim status, thus 're-exporting' the guilt. Hence the emphasis on the Nazi and communist crimes suffered by Eastern Europeans, which has been accompanied by a self-delusional conviction that they were committed almost completely outside the respective societies (Apor 2010: 237).

This tendency was growing in parallel in many societies of the region with similar conditions for memory evolution. Although postcommunist societies lacked consensus about how to evaluate the past, in each of them some actors began to emphasize their nation's victim status, but separately, because collective memory has been strongly nationalized. The first initiatives commemorating the communist crimes had a domestic origin, but a more coherent regional narrative seemed to have been forged only on the external ground – in Brussels. In the European institutions, the East European representatives had the opportunity to meet on a regular basis, establish a stable network and, confronted daily with colleagues from the 'old Europe', could more easily recognize what they had in common. The EU institutions acted here as a catalyst for the East European memory and identity, a crossroads of memories that has facilitated the emergence of a common East European narrative about the past. Still contested and rather divisive on a domestic ground, when exported at a European level the Eastern European postwar history has been recounted much more consistently. In the European Parliament it has been presented solely through the story of repression and resistance, which is supposed to bring a cohesive understanding to the Western public about the imposed and criminal nature of the communist system.

How has it all affected the memory of the Gulag? Recourse to the memory of the Siberian deportations appeared to be a handy instrument of defence against the unnerving currents of various West European memory politics which destabilized East European self-perception. References to Siberia were especially efficient at the transnational level. The Gulag – the experience of Stalinist labour camps, common to many states, with victims in the millions – has been assigned the role of a symbol of the Stalinist/communist crimes, a counterpart of the Holocaust and, as discussions have become increasingly dramatic and tempers frayed – its competitor.

Consequently, the Gulag issue has been increasingly 'hotting up' in the post-enlargement context (Zhurzhenko 2007). 'Gulag contra Shoah', 'Auschwitz versus Gulag', and 'The Holocaust-Gulag Competition' – are only some of the recent titles addressing this problem (Münch 2011; Troebst 2006; Shafir 2011; Leggewie 2010; Droit 2007). Memory of labour camps in distant Siberia was employed as a string to pull for historical interpretation to be exercised in the EU institutions. It has become an integral component of the common East European strivings to replace the demand 'Never again Auschwitz' with 'Never again totalitarianism' (Troebst 2012). It quickly turned into one of the chief *lieux de mémoire*, next to 'Yalta' and 'August 23rd', which seemed to be shared by a newly identified East European community as defined by MEPs. This became visible especially during heated debates in the European Parliament on declaring August 23rd (the date of the Nazi-Soviet Pact of 1939) a pan-European Day of Remembrance for the Victims of Totalitarian Regimes (Troebst 2012), as well as in recent attempts to ban the use of totalitarian symbols inside the European Parliament and further in all member states (swastika, red star, hammer and sickle). Many Eastern European deputies criticize 'the silent toleration for the communist symbols', which in their opinion continue violating the memory of millions of victims. These types of claims have caused a stir not only along a West-East line, but have also revived Left-Right rifts around the 'Holocaust as unique vs. Hitler and Stalin as equally evil' memory frames (Wæhrens 2011; Littoz-Monnet 2012). Next to the European Parliament – the EU institution that is the main battleground for memory – the struggle for symbolic condemnation of communist crimes takes place in the Council of Europe (resolutions), the Council of the European Union during Eastern European Presidencies (declarations) and in the European Commission, e.g., via 'questions for a written answer' (Closa 2010). In 2007 the Commission launched a programme called 'Active European Remembrance', offering funding for projects commemorating Nazi and Stalinist crimes. The programme was designed to endorse a common European memory, also by establishing networks, but was often faced with mutual miscomprehension between the delegates from Western and Eastern Europe. To overcome the problematic Nazism-Stalinism dichotomy, the programme was thematically expanded and its financial means significantly raised in the new framework 2014–2020 (Prutsch 2013).

While on the EU level the Eastern 'memory issues' raised controversy, national Western public spheres (with the exception of Germany)[16] evince rather limited interest in the East and continue their didactical approach vis-à-vis their new colleagues (Rostoks 2011: 196). Similarly, the influence of EU-level debates on the political and social discourses within national Eastern European contexts remains limited. However, the Brussels-rooted hotting up of the Gulag memory has undoubtedly coincided with growing visibility of Gulag commemorations in East European states. From the mid-2000s onwards, tributes to the victims have received new forms and have intensified. They are now more willingly supported by state authorities, and sometimes encouraged by EU funds, which has breathed new life into commemoration rituals. In some of the events it is possible to discern inspiration drawn from the culture of Holocaust remembrance. The commemorating initiatives are increasingly targeting teenagers at school age with the aim of 'help[ing] in their formation as a person'. The significance of Siberian deportations has grown, especially in the Baltic republics. For instance, as of 2006 Lithuanians began to organize a sort of recurrent, pilgrimage-style event: 'The Mission Siberia: Walking the Paths of our Grandparents', during which a selected group visits Gulag sites, tidies up abandoned graveyards of Lithuanian exiles and learns about the conditions experienced by prisoners and deportees (Tracevskis 2010). Every such 'Mission Siberia', supported by the EU-funded European Youth Forum, is thoroughly documented and publicized (films detailing the day-to-day events of the Siberian expedition are shown on Lithuanian TV).

Poles in turn organize an annual 'March of the Living Memory of Siberia' in Białystok, devoted to those 'who were deported to the inhumane land'. In 2011 the organizers succeeded in gathering around three hundred guests from the neighbouring states. In recent times the celebrations have been attended by high state officials and representatives of the Institute of National Remembrance. Similar memory institutes and newly created museums, which are springing up across the whole of Eastern Europe, are devoting increasingly more attention to the subject of the Gulag. Up until now, museums devoted to the Gulag alone tended to be in the form of 'virtual sites', i.e., designed and accessible online.[17] Recently small permanent exhibitions have been mushrooming in the countries of the region, e.g., in the form of 'heritage parks' (with replicas of Siberian huts and cattle cars in Riga and Vilnius or an authentic Siberian deportee house transported from Irkutsk to Polish Szymbark) and the extensive Museum of the Memory of Siberia, which is due to be created in Białystok using EU funds from the budget 2014–2020.

Moreover, in recent years it has been possible to witness another wave of intensified changes in the names of public spaces. More and more streets, avenues, parks, schools and roundabouts receive the name 'Deportees to Siberia'. Finally, the subject of the Gulag is very slowly making its way to the cinema. Giedre Beinoriūtė is the author of the successful Lithuanian *Grandpa and Grandma* (2007), a documentary telling a story about deportations in 1948. In Poland, apart from a series of documentary movies about Siberia that received low attention, the first big budget feature film, *Siberian Exile*, was released in 2013.[18] While the first Hollywood production on Siberia – *The Way Back* (2010), by Peter Weir – has made its way to the cinemas in the region, the recent critically acclaimed Russian movie *The Edge* (2007) by Alexei Uchitel, apart from being shown in film festivals, has not even been distributed in East European countries. Meanwhile, in Russia *The Edge* has sparked a debate about the absence of Gulag films from Russian cinema. Such films can be counted on the fingers of one hand, which is allegedly due to the fact that too many Russians have an indifferent attitude to the Stalinist past, and particularly to the Gulag.[19] The reasons why the Gulag as a subject is absent from Eastern European cinema have not yet been debated.

Conclusion

The junction of memories that occurred in European institutions stimulated a discourse of solidarity between the nations of the region and generated more transnational cooperation between them. The Gulag was assigned the status of a symbol of the Stalinist crimes, even though so far it has not played a particularly prominent role in individual Eastern European states (the degree varies). The Gulag is supposed to encapsulate a common experience of the region, which as a *lieu de mémoire* could be juxtaposed or placed next to the memory of the Holocaust endorsed by Western Europeans. This revival of the discourse on Siberia is beginning to reach back to the region itself and to slowly affect the way the memory of the deportations is being handled there. This transnational memory can be described as the solidarity of victims, awoken by the confrontation with the Western master narrative of regret.[20] In this new discursive frame, the notion of Eastern Europe seems to finally acquire some 'positive' agenda. On the map of memory it is more comfortable to have been a victim for the moral benefits it entails,[21] and Eastern Europe, if conceptualized properly, may guarantee desired whereabouts. In this sense, it is possible to observe a certain play with identity in the states of the region. Hitherto largely rejected 'Eastern Europeanness' is now becoming somewhat more attractive. On the one hand, a united Eastern Europe can achieve more at the EU level. On the other, the discourse of their common past can, of course, conflict with other East European efforts to create one united Europe with a shared memory. Hence, the two strands of memory politics implemented by East Europeans in Brussels in fact collide.

As the above collision is an ongoing process, it is better to leave the conclusion open and to cast some doubt on the gradual emergence of a transnational dimension of the East European memory presented here, because there is still at least one important element of ambivalence in this process. Many East European partner organizations most active in the field of common remembrance tend to represent fairly national perspectives. Some of the memory institutes and new museums lack critical reflection on the history of their respective nations. It is possible that these transnational networks established in Brussels and their European efforts serve to legitimize national policies at home. Regardless of whether they recognize themselves as a region, in many East European states the development of national memories connected with the Gulag followed a fairly similar path. Shortly after the initial interest in 'blank spots', dealing with the Stalinist past has ceased to be a priority in public spheres in the region. Now, the Gulag as a subject may be reimported into national public spheres through Brussels, in part in the form of a European stamp on a blank cheque with which remembrance organizations try to gain approval for their memory projects. This stamp may be a way of seeking acceptance for some national projects that otherwise would have been criticized for an exclusivist approach.

A valid question to ask here is to what extent the societies of the region internalize the 'solidarity of victims' formed in the European Parliament. What do they actually think about one another? Why do Lithuanians turn against Poles, or Hungarians launch a special policy for their minorities in Slovakia and Romania? Western Europeans have had more than sixty years to learn the benefits of integration. For East European countries, quite unsurprisingly, it does not yet seem obvious that integration in all spheres is attractive. Apart from the natural aversion towards centralizing projects, from which they liberated themselves only two decades ago (Habermas 2008: 102), they need to tackle the dormant memory of ethnic conflicts that took place on their territories. Perhaps Jörg Hackmann's optimistic statement that 'collective memories in Eastern Europe no longer form new emerging islands of nationalism which appear again under the melting ice of the Cold War' was premature.[22] Undoubtedly, the memory conflicts between the states of the region are still unresolved and overlap with the common memory which is being built from above, around the Gulag among others.

Only time will tell if the *Hochkonjunktur* for the memory of Siberian exiles persists and if it produces effects reaching beyond the controversies in Brussels and permeating national public spheres. As in the case of any delayed onset of public debates on memory, the Gulag deportees and their families, who have directly experienced traumatic events 'only have a chance to shape the national memory if they command the means to express their visions' (Kansteiner 2002: 188) and 'if their visions fit within a framework of contemporary interests' (Weissberg 1999: 15).

Notes

1. Stefan Troebst (2010a: 82) enumerates at least three times when East Central Europe was a region affected by similar spring tides of political change in the twentieth century: in 1918, when so far 'the lands between' transformed from imperial territories into nation states; in 1945, with Soviet communism turning its societies upside down; and in 1989 with its end (state socialism was replaced by regional blends of market economy and freedom of speech).
2. 'Not only are the different pasts in Eastern Europe loaded with catastrophes, killings, and violations of national dignity, but these facts were constantly manipulated by lies, thus creating fantasy realities and double memories' (Wydra 2010: 5).
3. Examples being: 1. Baltic States, 2. Hungary, Poland, 3. Bulgaria, Romania, 4. Belarus, Moldova (Troebst 2010b: 58).
4. In some countries the former deportees were presented with the benefits of joining the 'right-minded', e.g., Wojciech Jaruzelski was deported to Siberia in 1940, at the age of sixteen. During forced labour in the Karaganda coal mines he lost his father and, having experienced snow blindness, developed permanent damage to his eyes and back. His later career path led him to the position of the last communist head of state in Poland.
5. In Poland works by Gustaw Herling-Grudziński, Józef Czapski, Barbara Skarga, et al.
6. It is celebrated on the anniversary of the Soviet attack on Poland, 17th September, mostly in small towns.
7. Concerning the subject of forced deportations to the USSR, in Poland *Gazeta Wyborcza* began a series of articles in autumn 1991 opened by Krystyna Kersten's 'The Choice and the Borders'. The motto for the series were the words from Adam Mickiewicz's *Forefathers' Eve* describing the Siberian exile of his era: 'If I forget about them, let you my Lord forget about me'; nowadays the words are often quoted on the plaques commemorating the deportations.
8. That vacuum was supposed to be a result of a diagnosed lack of any ideological programme of the East Central European dissident movement. It just appealed to a set of basic human values without proposing any new ideas. That is why for J. Habermas 'the

most plausible explanation for the revolutions of 1989, was to see them as "catching up revolutions", revolutions which simply allowed the societies behind the former Iron Curtain to catch up with the rest of Europe in its never-ending march towards modernity' (quoted after Auer 2004: 2).
9. E.g., in Lithuania survivors of the deportations were involved with the extremely unpopular conservative nationalist party, Tevynes Sajunga (Avižienis 2005: 41).
10. Beginning with Slovenia in 2008 (when the public hearing on 'Crimes Committed by Totalitarian Regimes' was organized and followed by signing the 'Prague Declaration on European Conscience and Communism') and continued during the Polish 2011 presidency, when the European Day of Remembrance for the Victims of Totalitarian Regimes was celebrated for the first time. Furthermore, the 'Warsaw Declaration' was signed that day, which according to the Polish minister Krzysztof Kwiatkowski was a 'unanimous agreement of all EU member states' which needed to 'do absolutely everything to prevent any totalitarian regime from reviving in any country of the great European family'. The same year the Platform of European Memory and Conscience was founded in Prague.
11. E.g., the goals of the public hearing in the European Parliament 'What do Young Europeans Know about Totalitarianisms?' (29 March 2011) were defined as follows: to emphasize the importance of providing comprehensive information about the totalitarian past, as public discourse can lead to a better, deeper understanding of our shared history; to keep the memories of the millions of victims alive; to warn future generations of the dangers of totalitarianism; to promote a greater feeling of unity and understanding among Europeans.
12. These states are now all the more forcefully pushing for their 'remembrance right' to their own narrative of the events and aftermath of the Second World War. Polish and Baltic foreign policymakers have called for the 'Europeanization' of 'European' memories.
13. The European unification matrix had been developed by Western criteria. 'How would the Central and East Europeans adjust to a Europe that was defined without them?' was the question asked after the 1989 breakthrough by G. Shöpflin (1990: 16).
14. Apologetic, antifascist, focused on regret and acknowledgement of crimes.
15. Dan Diner (2000) uses the word *Gründungsereignisse*.
16. Germany is the Western country that needs to tackle both Nazi and Stalinist dictatorships that originate in specific historical disputes and controversies (Uhl 2009b: 64).
17. Apart from Russian museums: the Gulag Museum in Perm with online facilities (http://gulaghistory.org/nps/onlineexhibit/museum); designed by Memorial – the Virtual Museum of the Gulag (http://www.gulagmuseum.org/); French Sound Archives European Memories of the Gulag (http://museum.gulagmemories.eu); and an American virtual museum devoted to the history of the Gulag (http://www.thegulag.org).
18. In a small number of movies where the motif of Siberia appears, the Gulag has not been a main subject of the film, e.g., *Cynga* by Leszek Wosiewicz (1991).
19. Daniil Dondurei's opinion quoted after Norris 2011.
20. E.g., it is visible in the Polish 2009 resolution commemorating the Soviet aggression in Poland mentioning 'the hundreds of thousands of lives of the nations of the region which the Archipelago Gulag had claimed ... The Soviet crimes began with acts of violence which ended up in the tragedy of the Eastern Golgotha. Polish fate was shared with many other East Central European nations: Lithuania, Latvia, Estonia, Finland, Romania', dzieje.pl/node/1198 (accessed 15 October 2011).
21. 'Victimhood confers a right to complain, protest, and demand ... The greater the crime in the past, the more compelling the rights in the present – which are gained merely through membership in the wronged group' (Todorov 2003: 26).

22. Instead, he says 'What may be described as a common feature is the projection of history as a departure from a place to which no one ever wants to return – negative notions' (Hackmann 2009: 176).

Lidia Zessin-Jurek is an independent expert for the 'Europe for Citizens Programme' (2014–2020), European Commission, and postdoctoral junior fellow at the *Imre Kertész Kolleg*, Friedrich Schiller Universität Jena (2012–2013). She studied history in Łódź, and holds a PhD from the European University Institute, Florence. She is an author of *Polish Risorgimento* (Peter Lang, 2012) and currently works on the Eastern European remembrance of the Gulag.

Chapter 8

Two Concepts of Victimhood
Property Restitution in the Czech Republic and Poland after 1989

Stanisław Tyszka

After the fall of communism in Eastern Europe, new democratic governments had to confront the issue of what to do with the perpetrators of repression and human rights violations. They also had to decide how and to what extent to compensate the victims. Among the various instruments of postcommunist transitional justice implemented in the countries of the region, we can distinguish between retributive and reparatory measures. While de-communization and lustration were meant to exclude certain categories of functionaries of the communist regime from holding important positions in the democratic state, and thus included the naming of specific perpetrators other instruments, such as rehabilitation of political prisoners and restitution of nationalized property, were intended as a means of redressing injustices committed by the communist regime. These processes involved the naming of victims. The legal and administrative measures have taken different shapes in each country of the region, reflecting different historical legacies which have entered into the democratic transformation of each society.

The demise of communism created a certain ideological vacuum and the values fundamental for the organization of every society were redefined in the processes of political and economic transformation. The historical narratives promoted by communist propaganda and official historiography also suddenly lost their legitimacy. In the context of the adoption of the policies of transitional justice, the recent past of East European societies has become a subject of contentious and emotional debate. These debates involved many of the historical issues that had been previously censored or effaced and could not be publicly discussed. In these processes of coming to terms with the communist past, an important role was

---

Notes for this chapter begin on page 168.

played by the law, which served as a powerful instrument for (re)shaping collective memories.

1989 is often seen as a caesura in public memories in postcommunist societies: the fall of communist regimes is thought to have liberated public spheres, wherein previously 'frozen' memories could enter the public realm and shape national historical awareness; alternatively, the post-1989 era is presented as dominated by active politics of history run by national memory institutes and political agents. The case of property restitution draws a somewhat different image of the presence of the past in postcommunist societies: the processes of active forgetting run hand in hand with the uncovering of silenced pasts. The legal solutions employed in the process of property restitution, or lack of them, could both open the public realm for various memories of past injustices as well as close it, leaving particular pasts in oblivion, unworthy of compensation or remembering. In this chapter I will discuss the issue of property restitution and its relation to memory in the example of the Czech Republic and Poland in the context of postcommunist transformation.

Memory in the context of postcommunist property restitution may be seen as historical narratives, or particular visions of the past, that have been produced and presented in public debates by their different participants in order to support or oppose either restitution in general or particular restitution claims. These narratives have been intentional, in the sense that they have been directed at effective property restitution or against it, and therefore have been motivated, at least to some extent, by material interests. This does not exclude the fact that they have also been based on various symbolic interests, such as the need for commemoration, for recognition of past suffering and for symbolic compensation for past injustices. Sometimes the telling of a personal story may have been an aim in itself. Claims for restitution of property have been accompanied by specific narratives about past injustices, but by no means was it only representatives of the groups of expropriated owners who participated in the debates on restitution. Various advocates and opponents of restitution in general or of particular restitution claims also constructed historical narratives, basing them on concepts of justice and property rights that either justified or denied compensation for particular historical injustices.

The fundamental relation between property restitution and collective memory was noted by Dan Diner, who addressed the connection between the post-1989 property restitutions and the processes of collective memory in the introduction to *Restitution and Memory*, writing:

By restoring former private ownership rights, the social substratum inherent to the institution of property – and by covering a period far beyond the biological life span of the individual owner, the practice takes on a trans-generational dimension. As a result – re-privatization – not just privatization – re-invokes the trans-generational dimension of memory. By its very nature, restitution of private property acts as a means of remembrance, while the postwar nationalizations and socializations carried out by the communists in Central and Eastern Europe had had just the opposite effect: they functioned to neutralize memory. Not just memory about the legal rights of private property, bound to mere objects – no, this went far further, to encompass memory of times past, tethered to *longue-durée* prewar events as well as *court-durée* traumatic events during the war. (2007b: 15)

Thus, while the property revolutions carried out by the totalitarian regimes neutralized memories, postcommunist restitution of property has acted as a means of remembrance. However, Diner also claimed that memory and restitution were interconnected. Therefore, not only did restitution of property lead to the evocation of past memories, restitution could also be the result of recovered memories. These observations made by Diner on the connections between memory and restitution should be inscribed in a broader theoretical framework that would consider both the relations between memory and law in general, and memory and property rights in particular.

The father of collective memory studies, Maurice Halbwachs, in his last manuscript, *Collective Memory* (1980), provided such a broader perspective on the role of legal institutions in the formation of collective memories of groups, societies and nations. According to Halbwachs, law, by defining relations of domination and subordination within a society and between different groups, leaves its visible stamp on social space and thus shapes the collective memory of groups and society as a whole. This is, however, a dialectical relationship, because law also builds on collective memories for its legitimacy and the justification of the rights it provides. Therefore, collective memory must intervene to guarantee the rights which law invests (see Karstedt 2009). The connection between restitution and memory is therefore a consequence of a more fundamental relation between law and collective memories.

In the same study, Halbwachs also discussed the relation between memories and property rights. In the section titled 'The Legal Space and the Memory of Laws', Halbwachs wrote:

> An individual or several individuals acquire property rights only when their society grants the existence of a permanent relationship between them and an object itself. Such a convention does violence to reality, for individuals are constantly changing. Any principle invoked as a basis for property rights

gains value only if the collective memory steps in to guarantee its application. Suppose I were the first person to occupy or clear a certain piece of land, or that a certain possession is the result of my own labor. If we can't go back to the past and if there is a dispute about the original situation that could undermine my claims, how would I verify the original state of affairs unless a group preserved a remembrance of it? But the memory guaranteeing the permanence of such a situation is itself based on the permanence of space, or at least on the permanence of the attitude adopted by the group toward this part of space. (1980: 142)

Collective memory is viewed here as a fundamental factor in the legitimization of ownership rights. But Halbwachs also touched on the difficult question of the permanence of the relation between memories and property rights, which has been one of the most significant problems in post-1989 restitution debates. Furthermore, for Halbwachs, law was increasingly important as a mechanism to establish collective memories in modern societies. He saw legal institutions as powerful mechanisms capable of establishing and contributing to the collective conscience of a society.

In what follows, I shall first briefly present the history of expropriations in the two countries, starting with the Second World War. Then I will summarize the main arguments that appeared in public discourses in the Czech Republic and Poland regarding property restitution, and present legal solutions that were undertaken. Finally, comparing the different attitudes towards restitution of nationalized property in the two countries, I will refer to the general character of coming to terms with the communist pasts and memory cultures in the two countries.

Property Revolutions

The issue of property restitution in Central and Eastern Europe after the fall of communism is historically exceptional in its scale and complexity. The problem of restitution as such is not a completely novel phenomenon: important precedents can be found in post-Second World War restitutions or the restitutions after the French Revolution, but only communist regimes aimed at a total eradication of private ownership of the means of production, an ambition in which, to a large extent, they succeeded.[1] As a result of the scale of communist nationalization, the amount of property claimed by the former owners after the collapse of communism was also incomparably higher than in the cases mentioned above. The problem of postcommunist restitution was complicated still further by the fact that the history of property expropriations in the region was multi-layered.

The problem of property restitution was a direct result of the large-scale nationalizations and confiscations of property of various social and ethnic groups carried out by the communist regimes, but these property seizures frequently amounted to confiscations of properties that had previously been confiscated during the war. Thus, the issue of the property of the Jews and of other groups expropriated by the Nazis and the Soviets quickly appeared in the discussions on restitution. The far-reaching changes in the structure of property rights were also connected to postwar border changes and population transfers, which constituted yet another subject of discussions.

At least three waves of expropriations, or of 'property revolutions', to use Götz Aly's (2006) term (see also Goshler and Ther 2007: 5), can be distinguished as regards large-scale changes in property relations. The first wave of expropriations took place during the Second World War, under Nazi and Soviet occupation. These were related to population transfers, economic exploitation and genocide. In both countries, all property belonging to Jews was expropriated, while in Poland material persecution also affected a considerable part of the non-Jewish population. The second wave took place in the immediate postwar period as a result of border changes, forced population transfers and radical socio-economic reforms (land reforms and nationalization of large industry). These measures overlapped to a significant degree. For example, during the land reforms the property of those Germans who had been expelled was redistributed. Following the establishment of an absolute communist domination in both countries in 1948, state ownership was extended through the collectivization of agriculture and the nationalization of all remaining sectors of the economy, and as part of this process property confiscations were often used as an instrument of class struggle. These expropriations went further in Czechoslovakia, where very little was left in private ownership. In Poland, due to an unsuccessful policy of collectivization, agriculture remained mostly in private hands. Although the major revolutionary changes in the property relations in both countries occurred within a relatively short period of war and the immediate postwar period, during the following decades the communists continued to nationalize what had been left in private ownership and violated property rights on a routine basis. During the communist era, large-scale emigration from both countries also had an important impact on the distribution of property rights.

The interferences with property rights discussed above were sometimes only a prelude to, but often an integral part of more widespread policies of persecution or discrimination, motivated by various political, ideological or economic considerations. With regard to the situation of the Jewish population under Nazi occupation, interferences with property rights represented only one aspect of a general process of abusive, discriminatory and, ultimately, genocidal treatment. A common denominator of these various policies was that they usually aimed to deprive people not only of property rights but also of their personhood and dignity. They were employed in order to exclude certain categories of people from society.

After 1989 the series of nationalizations and confiscations of properties belonging to various ethnic and social groups and carried out by successive oppressive regimes resulted in a very complex legal situation with regard to ownership rights, including overlapping rights. There might, for example, be such a case that a particular property in Bohemia belonged to a Jew until the war, had then been taken over by a German, who was deported after the war and followed by Czech owner who, in turn, was evicted by the communist state. In such cases it was often difficult to establish the legal owner. Also, the variety of historical policies of expropriation and of the different motivations behind them sometimes disappeared from public view, since the specificity of the restitution debate to some extent required that these various historical injustices be categorized together. With regard to the politics of memory, this could pose a risk of relativization and, sometimes, threatened to blur important moral differences. While on the individual level the experience of expropriation and expulsion in different historical circumstances might have been comparable, on the level of historical narratives such associations often turned out to be problematic. This problem was especially striking when Jewish and German claims appeared simultaneously.

Postcommunist Restitution

What makes the comparison of the Polish and the Czech cases interesting is the fact that these countries, both examples of a successful postcommunist transformation, represent two extremes with regard to the processes of coming to terms with the past by legal means. As far as restitution legislation is concerned, the Czech Republic has implemented the largest restitution programme in Central and Eastern Europe, returning property both to individuals and to some legal entities, while Poland, despite numerous legislative attempts, has not to date adopted a general law on restitution to individual owners, and thus occupies the opposite end of the spectrum of postcommunist countries of the region, all of which have, in one way or another, compensated individual former owners.[2]

The question of how to deal with the claims of expropriated owners appeared immediately after the transitions of 1989 in the context of a necessary denationalization of the economy and reintroduction of private property rights. The basic question of whether to return property to its former owners at all turned out to be a complex problem, involving difficult economic, moral, political and legal dilemmas, each of which provoked similar debates in every country of the region. Restitution programmes have influenced the life of postcommunist societies on many levels, and the solution to the problem of nationalized property was of fundamental significance for the outcome of the processes of democratic and economic transformation.

From the economic point of view, the return of property to its former owners was only one of the possible means of privatization in the broad sense, i.e., of the transfer of state-owned assets into private hands. In the countries of the region, denationalization of property has generally taken the form of a combination of property restitution to its original owners or their heirs, lease or sale of enterprises, housing and agricultural land to domestic and foreign investors and the mass distribution of state assets to the general public. As a result of this the problem of defining the relation between restitution and other methods of privatization appeared. The question of which of these policies was given priority was important because rapid privatization limited the extent of possible natural restitution (restitution in kind) to the former owners. From the economic perspective, however, the most important factor was the effectiveness of the different modes of privatization and the ways in which they affected the speed of transformation to a market economy.

From the beginning, the processes of property transformation raised questions about morality and justice. One of these issues was that of responsibility for past wrongs. To what extent was the new democratic state responsible for injustices committed by the former regime? Was it right to ask current generations to pay for the injustices inflicted forty years earlier? Another issue regarded the connections between various historical injustices inflicted by the previous regimes, and the question of which of these deserved to be redressed. At this point various concepts of historical and social justice collided, entailing different understandings of private property rights.

On the political level, restitution was part of the struggle between various groups representing different interests, which was decisive for the pattern of distribution of property in the new democratic states. The groups of expropriated owners tried to influence parliaments and governments to implement appropriate property restitution legislation. Other influential interest groups, such as the new economic elite connected to the government or the old networks of members of the communist *nomenklatura* interested in maintaining social status and material wealth gained under the previous regime, were often fundamentally opposed to restitution, since they were favourably positioned to benefit from the privatization of state-owned assets.

Finally, the legal dilemmas of restitution were part of a broader problem of continuity with the legal order of communist regimes. A complete rejection of the previous legal order seemed impractical or even utopian, since it is likely that this would have resulted in complete legal chaos; the democratic governments thus adopted various concepts of legal continuity. This meant that an existing corpus of laws and regulations inherited from communist regimes has been gradually changed in view of new democratic principles. With regard to restitution, in order to return nationalized property to its former owners, new laws that would nullify the effects of communist nationalization acts had to be adopted. Restitution legislation therefore established a degree of legal discontinuity with the previous system. At the same time, the concept of legal continuity has itself created certain possibilities for claiming restitution directly in courts, especially when the previous regime violated its own laws during expropriation.

If restitution was accepted in principle, the design of a restitution programme has had to consider various aspects, such as the period of expropriation, the type of assets, the eligibility of claimants and the form of redress. The choice was essentially between natural restitution and some kind of monetary compensation. The former, usually preferred by the expropriated owners, was in some cases impossible, because the claimed properties had already been transferred to third parties. Restitution programmes have largely focused on real estate. This has been due to the fact that because of the difficulties in establishing the ownership titles, it was usually considered impossible to adopt general legislation providing for restitution of movables (with some exceptions, e.g., works of art). Certain assets, however, such as forests or national heritage sites, were often excluded from restitution. Finally, there were many technical difficulties regarding the ways of establishing the value of the returned assets or relating to the questions of investment and repair, on the one hand, and to lost profits, on the other.

The question of nationalized property triggered discussions between the proponents and opponents of restitution in which similar arguments were used by both sides in the two countries. The proponents supported restitution on moral grounds, as a means of redressing past injustices, on legal grounds, as a means of showing respect for private property, and, finally, on economic grounds, as a means to help provide the private ownership needed for a competitive market economy. They argued for the necessity of redressing property injustices to the extent that it was possible, stressing the necessity of respecting the right to property as one of the inalienable human rights and the foundation of the new socio-political order. Recalling the sanctity of ownership, they often repeated the popular slogan, 'What was stolen must be returned'. They also claimed that a return of property to the original owners was the easiest and most economically effective form of privatization, that it would quickly restore an entrepreneurial class and also limit the enfranchisement of the former communist *nomenklatura*, who, because of their material situation and connections, were in a particularly favourable position to benefit from privatization. The idea that the latter might benefit from privatization was regarded as deeply unjust, for not only did this deny compensation to the victims, it also rewarded those privileged under the previous regime.

The opponents of restitution argued that essentially everybody suffered under communism. Whereas some lost their property, others lost their lives, health or had opportunities denied to them. Redressing property injustices would constitute, in their view, unjustified preferential treatment of a particular group of victims of past injustices, and would lead to reconstruction of unjust precommunist patterns of property distribution. These opponents invoked arguments about social justice, saying that restitution would benefit only a small minority of the population at the expense of the majority or the poor, because it would reduce potential budget revenue if the state divested for restitution property that might otherwise be sold. Moreover, restitution would involve numerous legal disputes and as such it would mean a prolonged legal uncertainty. It would also slow down privatization of state property, while priority given to privatization would mean a faster transformation of property relations, which would increase the capacity of the economy to attract foreign investments, and in this way would benefit all citizens victimized by the communist regime.

The economic, legal and moral dilemmas were solved in both countries in quite different ways. The Czech Republic implemented a large and relatively comprehensive restitution programme. Basic restitution laws were adopted in 1990 and in 1991, therefore before the Czech and Slovak Federal Republic split into two countries in January 1993. At first restitution rights were given only to Czechoslovak citizens with permanent residence in the country and these concerned private property that had been nationalized between 25 February 1948 (the date of the communist takeover) and 1 January 1990. The Czech programme gave preference to restitution in kind, as opposed to financial compensation, which was subsidiary. Restitution was also given priority over privatization, thus an asset could be privatized only if there were no restitution demands from former owners. In Poland, despite numerous legislative attempts, to date a general law on restitution to individual owners has not been adopted.

Due to this lack, privatization was given priority and the assets claimed by former owners have often been transferred to third parties. Poland only returned property that prior to the Second World War had belonged to churches and religious communities. The first in a series of laws provided for the return of property to the Catholic Church and was passed in 1989, while the law returning property to Jewish communities was passed in 1997. As a result of a ruling by the European Court of Human Rights on an individual case, in 2005 a law was adopted to provide compensation to those who had left their property in the prewar Eastern provinces of Poland. Despite the lack of a general restitution programme for individual owners there are also some opportunities for claiming restitution of unlawfully nationalized private property on the basis of administrative law and procedures. These opportunities exist by virtue of the fact that the communist regime violated not only human rights but also its own nationalization laws. Therefore, if a former owner can prove that the seizures were made in violation of the laws, he or she can demand a nullification of the expropriation, the return of the property or, when this is not possible, financial compensation. This legal framework for restitution was thus based on the presumption of the legality of the existing legal order.

The general legal framework for restitution in both countries was to a large extent already defined at the beginning of the 1990s. In the Czech Republic it was defined by the restitution laws adopted in 1990 and 1991, and in Poland it was determined by the 'legislative silence' and a resulting creeping restitution. In both cases, the initial decisions regarding restitution had a crucial influence on the character of further restitution debates. The original decisions about restitution could be seen as expressing the dominant attitudes among democratizing societies, or at least their elites, towards the communist era, and as testifying either to the will towards radical condemnation and rejection of the communist legacy or to a preference for following a path of a more evolutionary transition from communism to democracy. With time also new restitution claims appeared, related to the violations of property rights that took place during the war and in the immediate postwar period. They were formulated, above all, by Jewish and German former owners. This 'archaeology of legal claims', to use Dan Diner's expression, has added new fuel to the debates on restitution in the post-1989 period. The discussions on restitution, which at the very beginning of the 1990s concentrated mainly on the question of whether to return property to the former owners at all, have gradually shifted their focus to the specific claims of various categories of former owners, such as: aristocracy, former middle-class, kulaks, Catholic Church, German expellees, émigrés and Jews. Providing for compensation of various kinds, particular legal solutions legitimized the right of particular groups to be remembered, while the lack of such solutions denied it.

In both countries, restitution debates on particular issues were framed by the existing legal schemes for restitution. In the Czech Republic, the post-1989 governments accepted the principle of restitution as a means for the alleviation of property injustices committed by the previous regimes. The adoption of this principle had an important impact on the further character of the Czech restitution discourse, and meant that whenever restitution claims appeared they became the subject of public discussion or were at least noticed by public opinion. In Poland, on the other hand, on a symbolic level the legislative silence with regard to restitution, which in practice constitutes a decision not to return property, gave a message that past property injustices do not need to be compensated for. Thus, the space for public debate on the past as determined by the state was symbolically closed for the stories of the expropriated. The lack of a restitution law meant that an egalitarian concept of victimhood was accepted. The latter denied distinctions between victims of various historical injustices and privileging some of them over others by means of compensation.

In the literature on the subject, restitution programmes in Eastern Europe are typically presented as a means of establishing a new postcommunist national identity. In *The Guilt of Nations* Elazar Barkan observed that 'by selecting deserving victims and undeserving victims, legislators and governments rewrote the national identity and favored one national story over another' (2000: 120). In Barkan's view, the privileging of particular groups of victims 'amounted to pursuing a specific policy of national identity that excluded other groups in order to create homogenous nations that did not recognize minorities' (ibid. 121). In a similar way, Shlomo Avineri noted that most of the former communist countries chose cut-off dates for restitution that coincided with the most ethnically pure moment in the country's history (1993: 35). These interpretations of postcommunist restitution are justified only to some extent and, as far as this comparison is concerned, rather with regard to the Czech restitution programme in its initial shape. Since they were mainly substantiated by the examples of exclusion of German and Jewish past minorities from restitution, the new postcommunist national identities – allegedly constructed through restitution – appeared as essentially nationalistic. These interpretations seem to be rooted in a rather simplistic model of the postcommunist transformation in which nationalism as an ideology has filled up the ideological vacuum created by the demise of communism. This approach seems to miss the essential characteristics of the postcommunist restitutions, namely that the shape of the restitution legislation was fundamentally related to the general character of coming to terms with the communist past in each country (as well as being influenced by various economic and legal considerations). The dynamics of restitution and memory were for the most part determined by the general processes of coming to terms with the communist past, and, therefore, memories of communism have influenced the processes of dealing with Second World War-related issues. Below, I highlight some important aspects of coming to terms with communism in both countries, to explain the relation between the various approaches to restitution in the Czech Republic and Poland and the two countries' different memory cultures after 1989.

Drawing Thick Lines under the Past and Concepts of Victimhood

The term 'a thick line' (Czech: *tlustá čára*, Polish: *gruba kreska*) has been a feature of both the Polish and Czech political discourses since 1989. This phrase has been related to the political and legal attempts to establish continuity or discontinuity with previous regimes. In the context of public processes of dealing with the past, this term can be viewed as a keyword for 'forgetting'. Below, I would like to underscore its significance within the broader processes of memory and forgetting after communism in both societies, considering a few aspects of these processes more or less remotely related to remembrance of past property revolutions.

In the Czech Republic, the term 'a thick line' came to be used frequently in politics with regard to Czech-German relations. It appeared in particular in the context of the negotiations leading to the Czech-German declaration of 1997, the objective of which for many Czech politicians was to draw that 'thick line' separating the past from the future in relations between the two countries. This clearly coincided with the fact that dealing with the past through restitution was meant to stretch back only to 1948, while the period 1945 to 1948 was not included in the scope of regulation. The consequence of this was the rejection of Sudeten German restitution claims. Therefore, in the context of restitution the thick line under the past was drawn at 25 February 1948.[3]

Considering the processes of dealing with the communist past in the Czech Republic since 1989 (or 1993, the dissolution of Czechoslovakia) in general, one should note that in this context anticommunism had a systemic character in the sense that it was legitimized by the state through the adoption of polices of de-communization, lustration, rehabilitation and restitution. Despite the relatively broad scope of these measures, Czech transitional justice has often been criticized for failing to inflict retribution for communist crimes. For example, the conservative Czech politician

Karel Ledvika (2009) wrote: 'The crimes of communism were separated from the present by a thick line, as a result of which the national memory absorbed the lesson that crime pays – and pays well – as long as the crimes are committed collectively and are sufficiently large'. Other critics of Czech postcommunist memory culture argued that anticommunist political rhetoric, as well as legal and administrative measures, did not coincide with a popular need to understand the implication of Czech people in the establishment and maintenance of the communist system. For example, the historian Muriel Blaive (2005) wrote about a lack of a true *reckoning with* Communism after 1989:

> To understand and to accept the past it would have been, and still is, necessary to study and to support with documentary evidence the way in which the Czech population either 'compromised itself with', or 'let itself be compromised by', or 'invested itself in', or 'purposely abstracted from resisting to' the communist regime. The only real way of dealing with the past was to strongly condemn the old regime and to draw a thick line between the present and the past, so as to not have to deal with it anymore.

Therefore, critics of the shortcomings of Czech transitional justice and the fact that the repudiation of communism in the Czech Republic was accompanied by a lack of broader discussions about the involvement of Czechs in the communist system, identified the 'thick line' separating the present from the past at 1989. Significantly, this criticism regarded the questions of responsibility or guilt for communist injustices. In contrast, the recognition of victims of communist injustices was better inscribed in the processes of public remembrance. Two examples illustrate how the rejection of nationalization and recognition of private property rights as the foundation of a new democratic regime reappeared in Czech politics.

In the Czech Republic, the 28th of October is a public holiday commemorating Czechoslovak independence of 1918. After February 1948, the communists had denominated it a Nationalization Day (*Den znárodnění*), a holiday meant to celebrate the decrees from October 1945 signed by President Benes to nationalize industrial and financial enterprises. After 1989 the holiday was given its previous meaning back. In a speech delivered on 28 October 2005 President Vaclav Klaus stated:

> We certainly do not see the long-term and permanent significance of October 28th, 1945, as of Nationalization Day, for we have been trying for the past sixteen years to overcome the adverse effects of the measures that were adopted then. Nationalization is remembered only by very few people as a positive event. Still, we should never forget it is a warning memento.[4]

A significant event in this context was the banning of the Communist Youth Organization in October 2006. In its manifesto the 'Union of Communist Youth' called for the revolutionary overthrow of the capitalist system and the nationalization of all private property. The Minister of Internal Affairs argued that such demands contravened the Republic's Charter of Fundamental Rights and Freedoms, and had the organization outlawed.[5] This case demonstrates that the dominating anticommunist discourse in the Czech Republic included the decisive repudiation of the concept of the abolition of private property as one of the main ideological pillars of the communist regime. The above examples are particularly revealing when considered in comparison to the remembrance of communism in Poland.

To a large extent the Polish public discourse since 1989 has been defined by a repudiation of the past and by ensuing political conflict about the memory of communism. Poland's first non-communist prime minister, Tadeusz Mazowiecki, declared in his opening statement to parliament on 24 August 1989: 'The government that I am forming bears no responsibility for the inherited debt. ... We draw a thick line under the past. We will answer only for what we have done to help Poland out of the current crisis.'[6] Mazowiecki has since repeatedly insisted that all he meant by this was that his government should be held responsible only for what it had done itself. Yet the phrase 'thick line' rapidly became proverbial and was understood to stand for such an approach to the communist past, in which the government was against policies meant to punish the communists for their wrongdoing. While this might be unfair considering the original context in which Mazowiecki first used the phrase, it was an apt characterization of the general attitude of his government. In this sense, however, the statement by Mazowiecki refusing responsibility for the communist past seems to capture even better the ensuing dominant approach to restitution of property in Poland. In comparison to lustration, restitution has been a much less discussed subject after 1989, so in this respect the repudiation of the past has been more discursively blunt. With regard to restitution in particular, the thick line under the past in Poland was drawn at 1989. The amnesia regarding the communist injustices imposed on society through the failure to adopt policies of transitional justice was justified by the liberal intellectual Marcin Król as follows:

> The controversy about these issues [the memory of the former communist system and the eventual consequences that should ensue from the crimes and injustices remembered] is a controversy that, regardless of its meaning, has an undemocratic nature because memory cannot be fully democratic and there is no question of justice or of equal treatment of all those who deserve to be

remembered. Therefore, in fact, and not for moral reasons, moderate forgetting is highly conducive to the building of a liberal-democratic society. (1996: 169)[7]

The key question remains: who is entitled to select who deserves to be remembered and who should become a subject of 'moderate forgetting'? In the debate on restitution the proposition that memory cannot be fully democratic translated into the argument that not all past injustices could be rectified. As a consequence, on the symbolic level, the Third Republic attempted to erase from national memory the fact that two or three generations earlier many properties had belonged to different owners from various social and ethnic groups. As there can be no total amnesia in social reality, however, the 'moderate forgetting' had to be about particular content of collective memories. In practice, this approach implied the relativization of the recent past. In terms of property relations it necessarily preserved a material and symbolic continuity with the communist regime. The historian Wojciech Roszkowski described the far-reaching moral implications of the failure in settling accounts with the communist past as follows:

> The mentality of contemporary Poles is consumed by indifferentism, the roots of which are in the communist era, and which outlived it as a result of relativization of the recent past. This relativization is the work of communists, who effectively blurred good and evil in social life, but also, and unfortunately, of some new political and intellectual elites, who have forsaken a full reckoning with the history of the Polish People's Republic or belittle the differences between the PRL and present Poland. (1996: 98)

With regard to property transformations, this relativization of the past resulted from the fact that after 1989 there was no symbolic repudiation of the abolition of private property as one of the ideological foundations of the communist regime.

The debates on the recent past have been, to a large extent, constitutive for the Polish political scene, contributing to fundamental political divisions. Until 2005, the main distinction run between the postcommunist and post-Solidarity forces, and since then the division within the post-Solidarity political forces has become prominent. After 2005, an important intellectual debate on the necessity of state-sponsored 'politics of history' (*polityka historyczna*) contributed to the new political division mentioned above. The philosopher and sociologist Zdzisław Krasnodębski defined the politics of history as follows:

> Memory and tradition are not in conflict with democracy, only with a particular understanding of democracy. In order to recognize the approach to the past as belonging to the essence of politics, it is necessary to transcend the conviction

that 'normal' politics is just a game of interests and compromises. One needs to acknowledge that politics also regards the question of collective identity and that values and identity cannot be reduced to interests. One could even say that full democracy presupposes a connection between generations, between the dead and the living and the unborn. (2003: 243)

This conservative perspective on the politics of history has to a large extent defined Polish politics of memory during the period 2005 to 2010. Questions appear regarding the content and form of this desirable national memory, in the sense that the politics of history has been perceived by right-wingers as the antithesis of 'moderate forgetting' promoted by the liberal intellectuals after 1989. In general, in the Polish politics of memory one should distinguish, on the one hand, the liberal deconstruction of the traditional narratives of heroism and victimhood, and, on the other hand, the conservative objection against the attempts to construe the nation as a community of shame and the emphasis on the promotion of positive historical images and on national pride. Paradoxically, the most significant success of the right-wing politics of history is the Warsaw Uprising Museum depicting the uprising in romantic-heroic rather than in tragic terms.

As it appears from the above quote, while considering the politics of history the representatives of the right tended to reject thinking in terms of interests as individualistic and in conflict with the communitarian spirit. This obviously excluded discussion on restitution, because restitution was precisely about particular interests and naturally remained in conflict with national egalitarianism. The problem of property restitution was therefore out of sync with political divisions and was easily pushed away from the mainstream public debate. Considering that the Catholic Church obtained compensation for its nationalized property, restitution has remained a prominent issue only for politically marginal forces. In consequence, nor could restitution contribute to any 'return to diversity' in the sense of a more pluralist public memory. The latter was to some extent promoted by liberals, but they were also in favour of separating the symbolic and material aspects of restitution and leaving the former mostly to historians or moralists of various sorts.

These broad tendencies in the post-1989 politics of memory translated into dominating notions of historical victimhood. A few examples of commemoration of the victims of past injustices in the public space in both countries offer a good illustration of the two distinct national memory cultures.

The Czech approach to the victims of historical injustices is well captured by the memorial to the victims of communism in Prague, which was unveiled on 22 May 2002, the first such memorial in the capital city. It consists of a series of statues commemorating the victims of the communist era between 1948 and 1989. Situated in the Lesser Town (Malá Strana) under Petřín hill, the memorial is the work of renowned sculptor Olbram Zoubek and architects Jan Kerel and Zdeněk Holzel, and was supported by the local council and Confederation of Political Prisoners. The line of imposing bronze statues descending a flight of stairs represents different phases of a human figure's destruction. At first one part of the body is missing, then another and another until the figure seems to totally disappear into the void. As an attempt to picture different degrees of victimization, it symbolizes how people were differently affected by communism. The bronze plaque under the memorial reads: 'The memorial to the victims of communism is dedicated to all victims, not only those who were jailed or executed but also those whose lives were ruined by totalitarian despotism'. There is also a strip that runs along the centre of the memorial, showing estimated numbers of those impacted by communism: 205,486 arrested; 170,938 forced into exile; 4,500 died in prison; 327 shot trying to escape; 248 executed. Thus the underlying idea behind the memorial is that various categories of victims of past injustices should be distinguished. This way all become subjects of public memory. This inclusive approach to the victims of historical injustices was also reflected in the programme of property restitution, which on a symbolic level additionally recognized the victims of communist property injustices.

Although there are several monuments dedicated to particular victims of communist repressions in Poland, the first memorial to commemorate the victims of communism in general was unveiled as late as 12 December 2009 in Łódź. Designed by Wojciech Gryniewicz, it depicts a Polish eagle rising proudly above a set of bars. It is dedicated to all those who died and suffered under communism from 1918 to 1989. Apart from its highly abstract form, one should note that it covers a period much longer than that of the Polish People's Republic (1944–1989), which necessarily dilutes its message. Furthermore, the memorial is situated in front of the building which, under the German occupation was the seat of the local Gestapo and then became a seat of the communist security services in 1945 to 1956. On a symbolic level, this location seems to communicate a message about the continuity between the Nazi and communist oppression, making it a memorial against totalitarianism in general.

Another memorial that reveals important characteristics of Polish memory culture was a temporary exhibition commemorating the victims of the Second World War. It was unveiled on the Piłsudski Square in the centre of Warsaw on the occasion of the seventieth anniversary of the outbreak of the Second World War. It was organized by a non-governmental organization, KARTA, with a contribution from the Foundation for Polish-German Reconciliation. The large-scale installation was entitled 'Each of 12 million people: Tribute to victims of both totalitarianisms'.[8] It consisted of several short biographies of wartime victims of both the Nazi and Soviet persecutions, representing different degrees of victimization and victims of different social and religious backgrounds. Despite the apparently inclusive character of the historical narrative constructed by this installation, what was more striking was the general message about the universal victimhood of citizens of prewar Poland. The relative significance attributed to both memorials seemed to reflect the fact that in the practices of public commemoration the memory of enormous suffering of Polish citizens during the Second World War overshadows the memories of the communist period and its victims. At the same time, it should be emphasized that the installation was ultimately an expression of the dominant egalitarian concept of victimhood, которое does not allow for differentiation between various categories of victims of past injustices.

Conclusion

In both national cases two conflicting memory discourses shaped the dynamics of restitution debates. On the one hand, there was the discourse of condemnation of communist crimes presupposing the principle of compensation for past wrongdoing, and, on the other hand, the discourse rejecting property restitution on the basis of the arguments of universal victimhood and on the impossibility of universal compensation. In each country a different narrative was legitimized by law. In the Czech case this came in the form of the adoption of restitution laws at the beginning of the 1990s and in Poland by legislative silence and far-reaching legal continuity with the communist legal order. These factors set a framework for further restitution debates with regard to particular restitution claims. It should be stressed that in spite of many political attempts to close the problem of restitution in both countries, it remains open, and it seems likely that it won't easily disappear. In *Closing the Books*, Jon Elster notes an interesting phenomenon regarding the issue of *biens nationaux* in France, the estates seized from the Church and noble émigrés during the Revolution and then only partly returned after the Restoration. It turns out that the heirs of the purchasers of these properties continued to be regarded by the local communities as illegitimate owners until well into the twentieth century (2004: 44). This example testifies to a surprisingly long persistence of memory in relation to property injustices, and might indicate that in the

Czech Republic and in Poland property restitution disputes are also likely to continue for the foreseeable future.

Notes

1. For historical precedents, see Elster 2004.
2. General restitution laws were adopted in the following countries: East Germany (1990), Croatia (1990), Lithuania (1991), Hungary (1991), Slovenia (1991), Bulgaria (1992), Latvia (1991), Estonia (1991), Romania (2001).
3. In the context of the Czech restitution discourse, the returning postulates of a so-called 'restitution full-stop' (*restituční tečka*), or political attempts to formally close the problem of restitutions with regard to restitution to the churches or in the case of restitution claims based on the land law, might be interpreted as a concept somewhat analogous to that of a 'thick line under the past'.
4. From the official website of the President of the Czech Republic: www.hrad.cz (accessed 17 September 2013).
5. P. Gabal, 'Ministerstvo vnitra rozpustilo mladé komunisty', Radio Prague, 19 October 2006, available at http://www.radio.cz.
6. Quoted after A. Smolar, 'Poland: Radicals in Power', *Eurozine*, available at http://www.eurozine.com/articles/2006-09-28-smolar-en.html.
7. Quoted after Z. Krasnodębski, 'In Darkest Jedwabne', February 2001, available at http://wiez.free.ngo.pl/jedwabne/article/27.html.
8. www.karta.org.pl/Aktualnosci/_Kazdy_z_12_milionow__Hold_ofiarom_obu_totali taryzmow_/132.

Stanisław Tyszka is assistant professor at the Institute of Social Prevention and Resocialization, Warsaw University. He studied law in Warsaw, and obtained his doctoral degree in history at the European University Institute in Florence, Italy. Since 2011 he has been active in Polish public debate as an expert on systemic deregulation. His publications in English and Polish include articles on property restitutions after 1945 and 1989 in the Czech Republic and Poland in the context of collective memory processes and political and social transformations. His research areas include: collective memories and transitional justice in Central and Eastern Europe, theory of law, sociology of law and systemic deregulation.

Chapter 9

SHARED MEMORY CULTURE?
Nationalizing the 'Great Patriotic War' in the Ukrainian-Russian Borderlands

Tatiana Zhurzhenko

Borders and borderlands, particularly in Eastern Europe, are ideal sites for studying memory cultures and commemorative politics. Historically, borderland territories have often been exposed to changing powers, to military and political expansion by the neighbours and to ethnic and religious conflicts. In most cases European borderlands are 'victim intensive' places, with their historical memories shaped by collective traumas, former hostilities and shared guilt. At the same time, they are places where different cultures coexist and enrich each other, creating 'hybrid' or 'creole' identities, sometimes seen as a challenge to the nation-building efforts of the political elites. Thus, borders and borderlands are not marginal places but central sites of power where the meaning of national identity is created and contested. The implementation of a new international border encourages the nationalization of collective memories and generates differences in a formerly shared memory culture, as has been exemplified by the events since 1991 in the post-Soviet borderlands.

This chapter addresses some aspects of memory politics in the Ukrainian-Russian borderlands using the example of the 'Great Patriotic War', the official Soviet narrative of the Second World War which has been transformed and adopted by the post-Soviet political elites in both Ukraine and Russia. Focusing on two neighbouring regions – Kharkiv (Ukraine) and Belgorod (RF) – it compares the new national (and regional) memory cultures while concurrently tracing the transformation of the common Soviet narrative of the 'Great Patriotic War' and its integration into a new transnational discourse of East Slavic unity. The fates of Kharkiv and Belgorod during the Second World War were closely connected: both cities were liberated by the Soviet Army in August 1943, in

---

Notes for this chapter begin on page 191.

the aftermath of the Kursk Battle. During the postwar decades they shared the official Soviet commemorative culture, including the state-sanctioned historical narrative, the pantheon of heroes and the memorial calendar. Today Kharkiv and Belgorod can serve as examples for studying the processes of pluralization and nationalization of memory cultures on both sides of the border.

The pluralization of memory cultures in the post-Soviet societies is a result of democratization, which opened the way for public representations of the past by different social groups and 'communities of memory': traditional (such as Soviet veterans, former Nazi KZ prisoners) as well as new ones (e.g., victims of Stalinist repressions, Holocaust survivors, former deportees). The nationalization of memory refers to the renarration of the 'Great Patriotic War' and the reinterpretation of its key events, symbols and 'historical lessons' in the process of the construction of new post-Soviet national identities. Unlike in Western Ukraine and in the Baltic states, in the Ukrainian-Russian borderlands this creeping nationalization of memory does not imply its radical de-Sovietization. Rather, we can speak about pragmatic policies of the regional authorities, which step by step replace 'archaic' Soviet symbols with national and religious ones, or rather integrate the former national narratives into new ones. At the same time, the myth of the 'Common Victory in the Great Patriotic War' remains an important symbolic resource used by various political actors on the national as well as regional level. In Ukrainian-Russian relations it serves for legitimizing post-Soviet integration projects and the 'strategic partnership' of both countries.

This chapter starts with introductory remarks on the memory of the Second World War in Ukraine and Russia, and continues with some brief comments on the specific political and cultural situation of the Ukrainian-Russian borderlands and on the political uses of memory in cross-border cooperation projects. As the next step, the new memory cultures in Kharkiv and Belgorod will be analysed and compared. This analysis is illustrated by two examples of new war memorials – the Prokhorovka Field in the Belgorod region and the Marshal Konev Height near Kharkiv. Both memorials were initiated by the local political elites after the disintegration of the Soviet Union. While representing new projects of national and regional identities supposedly free from Soviet ideology, they reflect the fragmented and ambivalent character of the new national narratives and demonstrate the tendency to political instrumentalization and reideologization of Second World War history.

The Memory of the Second World War in Ukraine and in Russia

The official Soviet narrative of the 'Great Patriotic War' was elaborated in the Brezhnev era (Dubin 2005). Not only did it provide the Soviet system with legitimacy but it also helped consolidate the collective identity of the 'Soviet people'. The myth of the 'Common Victory' played a special role in the relations between Moscow and Kyiv; it corresponded to the basic historical paradigm of East Slavic unity and helped to silence the counter-memory of the anti-Soviet Ukrainian nationalist resistance and its collaboration with the Nazis (cf. Grinevich 2005). As will be shown later, with the disintegration of the Soviet Union, 'Brezhnev's empire of memory'[1] did not collapse at once. Due to various geopolitical, cultural and historical reasons the political uses of the Second World War in post-Soviet Ukraine and Russia differ significantly.

Unlike in Russia, in Ukraine conflicting views on the Soviet past and alternative interpretations of the Second World War contribute to a profound political conflict which divides society. In this respect Ukraine is reminiscent of a country that has experienced civil war (Shevel 2011). On the national and regional level, the right to interpret the historical and geopolitical outcome of the Second World War has been openly claimed by the competing political forces. The reinterpretation of the Second World War and its role in Ukrainian history is directly linked to the 'postcolonial' search for national identity and the problem of geopolitical choice between Russia and the West. While during Leonid Kuchma's decade the official rhetoric referred to the Second World War as the 'Great Patriotic War of the Ukrainian people', the narrative preferred by former president Yushchenko presented the Ukrainian nation as a victim of two totalitarian regimes. According to Sofia Grachova (2008: 4), 'the new official historical narrative represented the war not so much as a glorious event, but rather as a terrible tragedy that struck the Ukrainian people in the absence of a national state'. At the same time, Yushchenko's symbolic politics, which aimed at the glorification of Ukrainian nationalism and at denouncing the Soviet regime as anti-Ukrainian, polarized the country. The Eastern Ukrainian regions (including Kharkiv), being the stronghold of the Party of Regions, became the main arena of memory wars during Yushchenko's presidency.

In Russia, some aspects of the Second World War also remain the subject of hot public debates (primary amongst them the role of Stalin). At the same time, a basic consensus exists among the political elites (shared by the Russian society at large) on the role of Russia in the Second World War and on the meaning of this event for national history. State managers, technocrats, nationalists and even liberals share the interpretation of the victory over the Nazis as the only achievement of Soviet history to survive the collapse of communism. There is, of course, a geopolitical dimension to this triumphalist narrative: the 'Great Victory over Fascism' became the Soviet Union's entry ticket to the club of world powers and legitimized its new global status and sphere of influence on the European continent. Like the USSR, post-Soviet Russia draws its geopolitical status from the historical outcomes of the Second World War. In its relations with the former Soviet republics (such as the Baltic states and Georgia), where war memory has become a subject of de-Sovietization and 'decolonization', Russia uses the symbolic capital of the 'Great Victory' for denouncing the pro-Western political elites as 'Nazi sympathizers'. The Soviet myth of the 'Great Patriotic War' remains basically unchallenged but at the same time has been integrated into the new narrative of Russian history; it serves as an instrument of national consolidation and patriotic education. The same policy can be observed in the Russian regions, as the example of Belgorod will demonstrate.

Politics of Memory in the Regions

Regional elites in Russia and in (Eastern) Ukraine use the myth of the 'Great Patriotic War' as a symbolic resource for a number of purposes. Firstly, for strengthening their dominant position and for legitimizing the political status quo in the region. As the war myth is deeply rooted in mass consciousness, no wonder that local authorities try to present themselves as heirs and guardians of the 'Great Victory', caring about Soviet veterans and protecting historical memory. Secondly, the history and memory of the war are used to induce local patriotism, seen by the regional authorities as an important pillar of social and political stability. Remnants of the Soviet ideological and educational institutions and new social initiatives (military-patriotic clubs, *poisk* movements, historical re-enactment groups) are usually directly controlled and even encouraged by the local authorities.Thirdly, memory politics is an instrument of regional branding; it is believed to improve the investment climate of a region and the chances of receiving funding for prestigious local projects from the central budget. True, the painful memory of the Second World War seems not to be the best choice for regional branding; however, the more the war becomes history the more the tragic past turns into cultural heritage. The Belgorod elites, for example, promote the brand of Prokhorovka as the 'Third Battlefield of Russia', along with the Kulikovo Field and Borodino.[2] In the case of Belgorod, such politics of memory are supposed to compensate for the lack of other symbolic resources and the relatively young age of the Belgorod oblast as an administrative unit (Reutov 2004). Unlike in Belgorod where the local context of the war memory was reshaped by the triumphant narrative of the Kursk Battle, in Kharkiv the war has been associated in collective memory with catastrophic defeats of the Red Army and strategic failures of Soviet military leadership. While such memory is not quite usable for regional branding, other local myths such as Kharkiv as 'First Capital'[3] proved more productive (cf. Kravchenko 2009, Zhurzhenko 2010). Therefore, history is not a 'limitless and plastic symbolic resource' (Appadurai cited in Yekelchyk 2004) that the regional elites can use on their own; this is even more true for the recent past.

Politics of memory in the regions cannot be reduced to the 'symbolic management' of the authorities. In a democratic society there are also political parties, NGOs, professional and cultural associations, academic institutions, local media and civic activists that pursue their own interests and shape regional memory cultures. Pluralism of memory depends on the level of political pluralism in the region, the strength of civil society, the independence of local media, the level of political competitiveness, the interest of the local authorities in history and their openness to public dialogue. The example of the Belgorod region demonstrates that the semi-authoritarian regime created by the local governor tends to monopolize and control public memory. The opposite example of Kharkiv proves that memory wars caused by the deep ideological split in Ukrainian society and by the fight between local interest groups, provide more space for pluralism of public memory but also lead to reideologization and political manipulation.

'Shared Memory' and the New Border

The new border between Ukraine and Russia contributes to the transformation and disintegration of the shared memory culture inherited from the Soviet era. National holidays and remembrance days differ on both sides of the border, Ukrainian and Russian school textbooks are based on different historical narratives, and national media in both countries often give opposite interpretations of the same historical events. The nationalization of the formerly shared memory culture brings, however, rather different outcomes in Kharkiv and Belgorod. Kharkiv, similarly to other regions of Eastern Ukraine, has undergone an ambivalent process of integration into the new Ukrainian nation, while the latter itself still remains in the political gravitational field of Russia (Zhurzhenko 2010).

In largely Russian-speaking Kharkiv, mixed and overlapping identities pose a challenge to the politics of Ukrainization and nationalization of the past, while from the perspective of the Ukrainian nationalists the city represents a stronghold of the pro-Russian forces. After 1991 local political and business elites used positive symbols of Russian imperial and Soviet modernization for constructing the new image of Kharkiv as a multicultural borderland city with a tolerant and liberal capitalist spirit (cf. Kravchenko 2009). At the same time, Kharkiv elites actively promoted the new regional brand of *Slobozhanshchyna* (Sloboda Ukraine), which goes back to the history of seventeenth-century Ukrainian-Cossack colonization of this territory. The invention of *Slobozanshchyna* reflected the search for Ukrainian roots of their regional identity, but at the same time it is often used as a symbol of a centuries-long peaceful Ukrainian-Russian coexistence (Zhurzhenko 2010). Characteristically, the first Ukrainian-Russian Euroregion initiated by Kharkiv and Belgorod in 2003 was given the name *Slobozhanshchyna*, while Kharkiv was declared the 'capital of the Ukrainian-Russian cooperation'.

Both Kharkiv and Belgorod were founded three-and-a-half centuries ago as military fortresses for protecting the Muscovite state against the Tatars, but were soon integrated into the Russian imperial, later Soviet heartland; today they are rediscovering their borderland identity. For Kharkiv the border is rather a contact zone, while Belgorod sees itself first of all as a stronghold of the Russian state, Russian identity and the Orthodox Church. In the last two decades Belgorod authorities succeeded in attracting state funding for various local projects (border and transport infrastructure, a new university) appealing to the new geopolitical status of the region. At the same time, the Soviet toponyms referring to the Ukrainian-Russian brotherhood survived in the Belgorod symbolic landscape. In 1954, on the occasion of the 300th anniversary of the Pereiaslav Treaty (a symbol of the Russian-Ukrainian 'reunification' in the Soviet historiography), a monument to the Ukrainian-Cossack Hetman Bogdan Khmelnytskyi was erected in the city.[4] While the monument was later removed for technical reasons, the main city avenue still bears the name of the Hetman. On the outskirts of Belgorod one can find an old oak that according to local legend was a witness to the meeting between Bogdan Khmelnytskyi and the ambassadors of the Russian Tsar. In the 1990s, Belgorod authorities inscribed these elements of the symbolic landscape into the new narrative of 'East Slavic unity'. The Assembly of the Slavic Peoples, cross-border business forums, and festivals of 'Slavic culture' were supposed to demonstrate the economic and cultural reintegration of the post-Soviet states, or at least of the Slavic core. Belgorod presented itself as a stronghold of East Slavic unity and a motor of Russia's cooperation with Ukraine and Belarus.

Figure 9.1 Orthodox chapel with the Bell of Unity in front of Peter and Paul Cathedral. Photo: T. Zhurzhenko.

The Prokhorovka war memorial (1995) near Belgorod was integrated into the new narrative of Slavic unity and became a mandatory site to be jointly visited by Russian, Ukrainian and Belarusian leaders. An Orthodox chapel with the 'Bell of Unity' was erected for the meeting of Putin,

Lukashenka and Kuchma in Prokhorovka in May 2000; it is decorated with the icons of three saints – the patrons of the three Slavic countries (Figure 9.1). Patriarch Alexy, who had initiated the meeting of the three presidents in Prokhorovka on the occasion of the fifty-fifth anniversary of the victory over Nazi Germany, stressed the issue of Slavic unity in his speech:

> Sons of the Russian, the Ukrainian and the Belorussian nations fought here heroically against the common enemy, protecting their common Motherland. Many of them gave their lives for our peaceful and free future. Nobody can separate their graves. In fight, in sacrifice, in victory they were together. They share military glory and we share the memory of their deeds ... Our best gift to their memory will be a strong union of the Ukrainians, the Russians and the Belorussians.[5]

In the mid-2000s Prokhorovka became a symbol of the 'East Slavic reunification', understood as the political, economic and cultural reintegration of the three former Soviet republics. Political elites interested in this project sought to inscribe the 'Great Victory' in the new discourse of pan-Slavism and Orthodox unity, adapting Soviet symbols, narratives and rituals. As a part of cross-border cooperation, mutual visits by Kharkiv and Belgorod Soviet veterans and their meetings in Prokhorovka were supported by the regional authorities. The memorial was also visited by student delegations from both cities, participants of business forums and academic conferences. These activities were significantly reduced after the Orange Revolution, but resumed from 2010. A special train organized on the occasion of the sixty-fifth anniversary of the 'Great Victory' brought Kharkiv Soviet veterans via Belgorod, Orel and Kursk to Moscow, and a new cross-border tourist route 'Battlefields of Slobozhanshchyna' was developed under the auspices of the Euroregion. Visiting Kharkiv in May 2011, the Patriarch of the Russian Orthodox Church Cyril paid tribute to the Memorial of Glory and warned against historical revisionism with regard to the Second World War.

Belgorod – City of Military Glory

In Belgorod, the politics of memory reflect the specific features of the local semi-authoritarian political regime, created by governor Evgeniy Savchenko during the two decades of his rule. A former communist and a representative of the agrarian lobby, he was one of the first governors to join the pro-Putin 'United Russia'. Savchenko managed to consolidate his power thanks to his ability to reach a compromise with all influential groups and to provide the Kremlin with satisfying electoral results. Political monopoly allows the governor to implement prestigious and expensive projects – such as the Prokhorovka tank battle memorial. The Belgorod authorities present themselves as 'caring' for the local population and have implemented various social programmes, from encouraging small farming to affordable housing and state support for young families. The Russian Orthodox Church is very influential in the region and cooperates closely with the regional authorities, particularly in such areas as education, ideology and historical memory. Conflicts among the regional elites are usually non-ideological and rarely have a public dimension. The only ideological opponent of the authorities represented in the regional and local councils is the Communist Party. One of the rare conflicts around historical memory occurred in 2004 and concerned the issue of urban toponyms: on the initiative of the new city mayor and with support of the Russian Orthodox Church, most central streets of Belgorod, which until then had had Soviet names, were renamed without any prior public discussion. The local communists publicly protested against the renaming, but without success. A similar conflict happened in 2009, when the local authorities decided to remove the Lenin monument from the central square in order to make space for the planned obelisk 'Belgorod – City of Military Glory'. In 2007, Belgorod was one of the first cities to receive the newly introduced honorary title 'City of Military Glory' from President Putin; it has become the 'light' version of the Soviet title 'Hero City' (Figure 9.2). However, the conflict about the Lenin statue did not endanger the local consensus on the Great Patriotic War; the communists only proposed to erect the new memorial on a different, but still central place.

In Soviet times, Belgorod, known as the 'City of the First Salute',[6] possessed several war memorials: the 'Mourning Mother' (1953) on the central square, the 'Monument to the Liberators of Belgorod' as well as various monuments and busts in the central Victory Park dedicated to famous Soviet army generals and heroes of the Soviet Union. One of the most important local sites of memory is the 'Memorial to the Heroes of the Kursk Battle' (including a war museum) situated 624 km up the Moscow-Simferopol highway. As late as 1987 a new museum: The Kursk Battle – Advance to Belgorod was opened in the centre of Belgorod. The museum is organized around an impressive monumental diorama (67 × 15 m), one of the biggest in the former Soviet Union, which represents the culmination of the Prokhorovka tank battle.

In a kind of path dependency, the post-Soviet Belgorod authorities chose the myth of the Great Patriotic War as their main symbolic resource. They have been successfully promoting such regional brands

FIGURE 9.2 'Belgorod – City of Military Glory', patriotic visual propaganda in the urban landscape. Photo: T. Zhurzhenko.

as 'Prokhorovka – The Third Battlefield of Russia' and 'Belgorod – City of Military Glory'. This heroic war narrative provided the ideological foundation for the regional programme 'Patriotic education of Belgorod citizens'. The local authorities managed to preserve various Soviet institutions of education and youth policy, replacing communist ideology with Orthodox religion, Russian nationalism and pan-Slavism. For example, the DOSAAF (Voluntary Society for Cooperation with the Army, Aviation and Fleet), a Soviet paramilitary association formerly used to prepare young people for military service, was transformed into a dense network of patriotic military clubs active in all districts of the Belgorod region. 'Cadet classes' were created in Belgorod schools with the purpose of teaching children sport, military skills and patriotic values, encouraging them to pursue a military or police career, with the local border police actively cooperating with Belgorod schools. In 2002, the General Vatutin Award[7] for the best achievements in patriotic education was endowed by the Belgorod authorities. In the last two decades the urban landscape was supplied with new war monuments and the 'Alley of Heroes of the Soviet Union' in Victory Park was supplemented by busts of the new Heroes of Russia.

Belgorod's second ideological pillar is the Orthodox Church. In 1995, a separate Belgorod and Stary Oskol Eparchy was established with the bishop Yoasaf (Yakim Gorlenko, 1705–1754), canonized in 1911, becoming the city's official patron. A huge statue of prince Vladimir (Ukr. Volodymyr), who had baptised the Kievan Rus, was erected in 1998 on the occasion of the so-called 'Millennium of Belgorod'. The fact that the 'millennium' was criticized by historians as a fake did not keep the regional authorities from officially celebrating it. In the context of the Ukrainian-Russian borderlands the monument to Prince Vladimir has an ambivalent meaning as it symbolizes East Slavic unity and at the same time presents the Russian response to the Ukrainian claims for the heritage of the Kievan Rus (Vendina 2010). In the 1990s, a theological college with a special focus on missionary activity was re-established in Belgorod after seven decades of Soviet rule. It presents itself as a stronghold of Orthodox belief and Russian identity at the western border. Ukraine is often seen in this context as a source of various 'spiritual threats' such as schism, expansion of Protestant sects and of Catholic influences. Belgorod was one of the first regions to introduce 'Orthodox culture' into school curricula; the local eparchy is a co-founder of several local newspapers and magazines. The dominant status of the Orthodox Church corresponds with the pan-Slavism and Russian nationalism popular among the local elites. This link can be found in the works of the local sculptor Viacheslav Klykov (1939–2006), former head of the nationalist Union of the Russian People (*Soiuz Russkogo Naroda*) and creator of several monuments in Belgorod (including the one to the Prince Vladimir). Klykov, who received full support from the local authorities, was one of the designers of the Prokhorovka memorial that inscribes the epic tank battle in the centuries-long history of Russian military glory.

The Prokhorovka Memorial – 'The Third Battlefield of Russia'

The impressive war memorial in Prokhorovka, where in summer 1943 the biggest tank battle of the Second World War took place, is not only one of the most prominent sites of memory in the region but it also has national status. The project was initiated by the local authorities and supported by President Yeltsyn; Nikolai Ryzhkov, the last Soviet prime minister and now a senator from Belgorod, became the official patron of the memorial. It was inaugurated in 1995 on the occasion of the fiftieth anniversary of the victory. The most important element of the memorial site is the Bell Tower, which stands fifty-two metres high and is made of white marble and crowned with a golden statue of Mary, mother of God (Figure 9.3).

FIGURE 9.3 The Bell Tower on the Prokhorovka battlefield. Photo: T. Zhurzhenko.

The four walls of the Bell Tower, which symbolize the four years of war, are covered with numerous illustrations of heroic fighting, suffering and triumph. Images well known from Soviet iconography such as the invasion of the fascist aggressors, the self-sacrificing work of women and children and the Victory parade on Red Square are presented here in a new aesthetic paradigm. Communist and Soviet images are virtually absent; instead, Orthodox symbols are widely used. Soviet soldiers and generals are depicted as heroes of Russian, rather than Soviet history. A row of Orthodox icons presents Russia's most important national saints and warriors, and a 'Holy Trinity' icon referring to Andrey Rublev symbolizes the unity of the army, the people and the Russian Orthodox Church. The figure of Marshal Georgiy Zhukov corresponds with the icon of Saint George killing the dragon (on St George's day, 6 May, the war 'actually ended', as a local tourist brochure informs). In recent years, public festivities for the occasion of Victory Day have started in Belgorod on Saint George's day with religious services.

This new symbolism corresponds with one of the most important tendencies in Russian politics of memory: the nationalization and confessionalization of war memory (Forest and Johnson 2002). The Great Patriotic War is the most recent episode in Russian history interpreted as a cyclic process, a sequence of foreign invasions and Russian military triumphs. This interpretation is reflected in the new brand 'Prokhorovka – the Third Battlefield of Russia'. In this way, the Prokhorovka battle appears as one of three crucial events in Russian history. To stress the continuity of Russian military glory, military units, dressed in costumes of the fourteenth and early nineteenth centuries, take part in the official ceremonies. On the occasion of the sixty-fifth anniversary of the Kursk Battle, monuments to three military leaders in Russian history – Dmitriy Donskoy, Mikhail Kutuzov and Georgiy Zhukov – were erected on the Prokhorovka field. The confessionalization of war memory reflects the claims of the Russian Orthodox Church for its share in the symbolic capital of the 'Great Victory'. Today the Church argues that it was 'only after Josef Stalin opened the churches and released the priests from prison, [that] the decisive turning point of the war became possible' (Mitrokhin 2004). In their turn, the army and the Russian authorities rely on the Church as far as patriotic education, restoration of traditional moral values and loyalty to the Russian state are concerned.

In addition to the Bell Tower, a new cathedral was constructed in Prokhorovka village. Named after Peter and Paul (the saint's day of the tank battle according to the Orthodox calendar), the church was built in so-called 'old Russian' style associated with the nationalism and patriotism of the late nineteenth century. The names of the Soviet soldiers, fallen

Figure 9.4 The 'Third Battlefield of Russia' Museum with tank monument. Photo: T. Zhurzhenko.

in the Prokhorovka battle, are engraved on the inner walls of the church. In this way, they all are retroactively included in the imagined community of Orthodox Russians, regardless of their ethnicity or creed. The public library named after Nikolay Ryzhkov, the orphan house and the rest home for Soviet veterans were constructed at the same site and symbolize the link between the generations and the 'care' by the local authorities for children and the elderly. It seems that the Prokhorovka Memorial is an open project: every anniversary serves the authorities as a pretext to demonstrate their faithfulness to the memory of the 'Great Patriotic War'. In May 2010, a new museum 'The Third Battlefield of Russia' was opened in Prokhorovka and consecrated by Patriarch Cyril (Figure 9.4). The exposition of the museum adds nothing new to the traditional canon of the Great Patriotic War memory; it is largely devoted to the details of the Prokhorovka battle, figures of Soviet generals and the everyday life of Soviet soldiers.

Kharkiv – a Plurality of Memories

Kharkiv was one of the important economic, cultural and academic centres of the Russian empire and later of the USSR, and therefore possesses diverse symbolic resources for constructing a local identity and regional branding. At the same time, the Russian imperial and Soviet past of Kharkiv makes it difficult to reinvent it as a Ukrainian city. According to Volodymyr Kravchenko (2009: 220), 'Kharkiv situated within Ukrainian-Russian contact zone, is a place of contested national narratives, historical mythologies, and political projects'. Along with the traditional political pluralism in Ukraine, this particular borderland situation of Kharkiv makes local memory culture more fragmented and diverse than in Belgorod. The same is true for memories of the Second World War.

The inhabitants of Kharkiv and Belgorod, separated only by seventy kilometres, had rather similar experiences during the war of severe military destruction, population losses and repression by the Nazi occupation regime. Both cities were captured by the Nazis in October 1941, briefly regained by the Soviets in February-March 1943 and reoccupied by the Nazis to be finally liberated in August 1943. But if Belgorod came to be associated with the success of the Kursk Battle and, in this way, with the heroic narrative of the Great Patriotic War, the memory of the war in Kharkiv has been more traumatic and much less triumphalist. In the history of the Second World War, Kharkiv is linked rather with Soviet military defeats, such as the failed Soviet counter-offensive in summer 1942. A big industrial centre and an important transport junction, Kharkiv was of high strategic importance for both sides, and as the biggest Soviet city ever captured by the German army, it has become a symbol of Hitler's military success. Probably due to these reasons, Kharkiv, unlike Belgorod, never received official honorary titles or military rewards during Soviet times. Another possible explanation was the collaboration with the Nazis by a part of the Ukrainian intelligentsia and local population.

Although an obligatory element of official Soviet memory culture, in Kharkiv the myth of the Great Patriotic War did not take a central place in the urban landscape. Neither of the two main Soviet war memorials are located in the city centre. One is the statue of the 'Soldier-Liberator', a gigantic figure of a Soviet soldier with a Kalashnikov in his raised hand, erected in 1981 in a new residential area (Figure 9.5). The second is 'The Memorial of Glory', constructed in 1977 in Sokolniki, a green zone on the northern margins of Kharkiv, which during the war became a site of mass graves of Nazi victims (mostly civilians and Soviet war prisoners). The symbolic centre of the memorial ensemble is a 'Mourning Mother' statue at the end of an alley with an eternal flame in front of the statue and a heartbeat coming from inside it. A bas-relief panorama behind the statue presents the canonical images of the 'Great Patriotic War', from mass mobilization in June 1941 to Victory Day. A wooden cross – an Orthodox symbol – was added to the memorial in the early 1990s. In Soviet times

FIGURE 9.5 The 'Soldier-Liberator' statue in Kharkiv. Photo: T. Zhurzhenko.

the 'Memorial of Glory' was the main site for official commemorative ceremonies, and also a place visited by tourists, official delegations and young couples after a marriage ceremony. The public functions of this memorial site have not changed much since then. While the statue of the 'Soldier-Liberator', placed in the middle of a residential area, serves as a site for public performances, concerts and open air festivities for veterans, children and local residents, the memorial in Sokolniki is a place for mourning and silent reflection.

Unlike in Belgorod, where the 'Great Patriotic War' was renarrated and integrated into the new paradigm of national history, in Kharkiv in the first post-Soviet decade the absence of a national consensus on the role of the Second World War in Ukrainian history prevented the ruling elites from new ambitious commemorative projects. Rather, some fragments of the Soviet narrative were appropriated for local purposes. Thus, 23 August, the 'Day of Liberation of Kharkiv from Nazi occupation', became the Day of Kharkiv, officially celebrated as a popular local holiday. In general, the main tendency in the region was the pluralization of collective memory. In the early 1990s a private Holocaust museum was created, the first in Ukraine, and some years later the new Holocaust memorial 'Drobitskyi Yar' was opened at the site of mass executions of the Kharkiv Jews (Figure 9.6). The memorial cemetery at the place of the mass murder of about 3,800 Polish prisoners of the Starobelsk camp committed by the NKVD during April and May 1940 was opened in 2000 by the prime ministers of Ukraine and Poland. Finally, the new narrative of the Holodomor (the Great Famine in 1932–1933) as a crime committed by

FIGURE 9.6 The Holocaust memorial 'Drobitskyi Yar'. Photo: T. Zhurzhenko.

the Soviet regime against the Ukrainian nation, while causing political conflicts and ideological polarization, took a prominent place in the public space of Kharkiv. Against this background the Soviet myth of the Great Patriotic War became just one of several coexisting memory cultures.

The pluralism of the local public memory corresponds with the political pluralism characteristic of Kharkiv, which has always been an arena of competition between different interest groups. While the 'party of power' was in control of local politics during the Kuchma decade, the Socialist Party, the Communists, Narodny Ruch and pro-Russian and Ukrainian nationalist groups also played a role in local politics. To the end of the 1990s Evhen Kushnarev, the former mayor and later head of Kuchma's presidential administration, managed to consolidate the regional elites. As a governor of Kharkiv from 2000 to 2004, he mobilized the administrative resources in support of Victor Yanukovych in the 2004 presidential elections; but the Orange Revolution split the local elites. The newly appointed governor Arsen Avakov, close to Yushchenko's family and a member of his 'Our Ukraine' party, implemented the new president's commemorative policy in the region. The most important project of the local 'Orange' camp was the construction of a Holodomor memorial and the official commemoration of the seventy-fifth anniversary of this event. However, the Party of Regions, which had won the 2006 local elections and achieved the majority in the city and oblast councils, opposed the commemorative initiatives of the governor. As a result, after the Orange Revolution Kharkiv became a site of severe conflict over the memory of the Soviet past. Unlike in Belgorod, in Kharkiv the memory of the Second World War was instrumentalized in partisan conflicts.

One strikingly characteristic example of such instrumentalization and reideologization of Second World War memory is the UPA (Ukrainian Insurgent Army) monument that was erected in the early 1990s on the initiative of Narodny Ruch. A granite stone of relatively small size in a corner of the Youth park (which is a former city cemetery), it remained practically unnoticed by the majority of local inhabitants, all the more as the UPA is marginal in the local collective memory. When this issue was politicized, however, after the Orange Revolution, the monument became the site of violent clashes between Ukrainian nationalists and pro-Russian organizations supported by the communists and Soviet veterans. The city council controlled by the Party of Regions decided to remove the monument, referring to the alleged lack of formal permission. This decision was opposed by Ukrainian nationalists and other political opponents of the Party of Regions; voluntary guards protected the memorial overnight to prevent its dismantling. To make the story even more absurd, in December 2007 the monument was kidnapped by members of the extremist pro-Russian

Eurasian Youth Organization. The stone was found and restored to its place, but remained in the centre of media attention in both Ukraine and Russia and continued to generate political conflicts. Kharkiv mayor Mikail Dobkin proposed to 'deport' it to Western Ukraine, promised to build instead a memorial to the victims of UPA violence and even offered asylum to the Tallinn Bronze Soldier. With such provocative manipulation of Second World War memory the mayor hoped to direct public attention from the real problems of local self-government and to stay in office despite the growing pressure of his political opponents. However, in 2009, in the wake of the European championship, some kind of 'non-aggression pact' was made between the Kharkiv elites, including a ceasefire in the local memory wars. One year later, with the victory of Viktor Yanukovych the Party of Regions consolidated its power in Kharkiv and marginalized the opposition, which since then has been unable to pursue alternative commemorative projects.

The Marshall Konev Height

It is worth comparing the Prokhorovka memorial with the new Marshal Konev Height war memorial, devoted to the liberation of Kharkiv in August 1943. Both are ambitious projects by the local elites, reflecting their search for a new national identity and their attempts at regional branding. The example of the Prokhorovka memorial, regularly visited by Kharkiv politicians on various occasions, provided a major source of inspiration for them. The idea of a memorial was lobbied by the Kharkiv Soviet veterans' organizations which were well informed about the more active commemorative politics of the Belgorod authorities. Kharkiv historians, stressing the key role of the city in the history of the Second World War argued that a new war museum was needed to fill blank spots in public memory.

Therefore, in the early 2000s Kharkiv authorities, not without the influence of their Russian neighbours, tried to restore and instrumentalize the Soviet triumphalist narrative of the 'liberation from fascist occupation'. The Marshal Konev Height memorial was constructed in Solonitsevka on the outskirts of Kharkiv, at the site where the headquarters of Marshal Konev, a Soviet army commander who directed the military operation, were located in August 1943. The project initiated by governor Kushnarev, one of the architects of the post-Soviet identity of Kharkiv, was officially opened in May 2005, Kushnarev himself having been dismissed as a result of the Orange Revolution. The new regional administration adopted the memorial, which was given national status by a decree of president Viktor

FIGURE 9.7 Victory Day 2010 on the Marshall Konev Height. Photo: T. Zhurzhenko.

Yushchenko in 2008. Apart from the renovated Soviet-era obelisk with a relief portrait of Marshal Konev (Figure 9.7), the memorial includes a new Orthodox Chapel dedicated to Ivan the Warrior, an open-air exhibition of Soviet military weapons and a small museum. Despite its official national status, the memorial remains in fact a regional site of memory and cannot equal the more ambitious Prokhorovka memorial (Figure 9.8). However, both memorials show some stylistic parallels, such as a combination of Orthodox symbols with Soviet monumental architecture, references to the Soviet narrative of the Great Patriotic War and the cult of Soviet military leaders.

The new Kharkiv memorial can be seen as an attempt by the local authorities to appropriate fragments of the Soviet myth and to use them as building blocks for a new regional identity. While the Prokhorovka memorial demonstrates a new interpretation of the 'Great Patriotic War' as a national struggle of the Russian Orthodox people against the foreign invasion, the Konev memorial can be hardly inscribed in the fragmented and controversial narrative of Ukrainian history and remains an enclave of Soviet war memory. The exhibition at the memorial's museum focuses on the military history of the Second World War in the region and presents the liberation of Kharkiv in summer 1943 as its highlight. Many museum objects on display, such as a reconstruction of the Soviet military headquarters and personal belongings of Soviet soldiers and commanders, are very similar to those in Belgorod museums.

FIGURE 9.8 Orthodox chapel on the Marshall Konev Height. Photo: T. Zhurzhenko.

At the same time, a closer look reveals some details pointing to the pluralism and ambivalence of the Kharkiv war memory. Despite the conceptual framework set by the museum's name – 'The Kharkiv region in the Great Patriotic War of 1941-1945' – it actually narrates the Second World War. The exhibition includes information on the Soviet occupation of Poland in September 1939 and on the tragic events of the Katyn massacre. Obviously, this aspect of Second World War history is difficult to ignore in a city that, together with Smolensk, has become a site of pilgrimage for Polish families and of official visits by Polish politicians. A monumental painting entitled *Katyn* presents the scene of the mass killing of the Polish officers. Small wonder that the Soviet veterans found this part of the exhibition disturbing and demanded it be removed. While continuing educational work aimed at children and Soviet veterans, the museum provides space for various commemorative projects, some of them having little in common with the traditional narrative of the 'Great Patriotic War'. For example, in 2008 the Museum of the Warsaw Uprising organized the exhibition 'The Poles in the Second World War' here, which impressed the local public and experts with its high technical level, and presented the history of the Second World War from a different, little-known perspective. Unlike the Prokhorovka museum, this is not a museum of one battle; the social history of war, everyday life under occupation, the Nazis repression of civilians and of course the Holocaust – all of these themes are addressed in the exposition. The story of the mass murder of the Kharkiv Jews in Drobitsky Yar, near the Kharkiv Tractor Plant, is presented in a special section of the museum.

Conclusion

The new post-Soviet commemorative cultures in Ukraine and Russia reflect the nationalization and pluralization of the 'Great Patriotic War' memory. However, while in Russia there is a basic consensus on the role of the war in national history, in Ukraine the divided collective memory contributes to regional pluralism and fuels ongoing political conflict. These differences are especially visible in the Ukrainian-Russian borderlands, which were an arena for severe fighting during the last war, and are exposed today to competing geopolitical influences. In this situation the memory of the Second World War has been instrumentalized by national as well as regional political actors for legitimizing competing geopolitical projects such as the European integration of Ukraine and the East Slavic reunification.

At the same time, the local elites concerned with electoral support, political stability and the image of the region have their own reasons for instrumentalizing the memory of the Second World War. As the comparison of Kharkiv and Belgorod demonstrates, it is not only the priorities of national commemorative politics, but also the character of the local political regime, the level of political pluralism and competition, the strength of civil society and the freedom of local media that influence local memory cultures. In Belgorod, under the conditions of the governor's semi-authoritarian regime, the de facto monopoly of the pro-Putin 'United Russia' party and the alliance of the local authorities with the Russian Orthodox Church, we can observe the reideologization of memory based on the nationalization and confessionalization of the Soviet narrative. In Kharkiv, which is an arena for competing interest groups, the memory of the Second World War has become the subject of open ideological conflicts and often of populist manipulations. While the Prokhorovka memorial in Belgorod presents the 'Great Patriotic War' as a fight for national liberation from foreign invasion, the Konev memorial in Kharkiv, at first glance an enclave of Soviet war memory, is in fact open to alternative interpretations of the Second World War.

Notes

1. A paraphrase of Serhy Yekelchyk's *Stalin's Empire of Memory* (2004).
2. The victory of Muscovy prince Dmitri over the Tatar forces in the Battle of Kulikovo (1380) has been presented by Russian historiography as the beginning of the liberation from the Golden Horde yoke. The Battle of Borodino (1812) was a pivotal point in Napoleon's invasion of Russia.
3. Kharkiv was the capital of Soviet Ukraine from 1920 until 1934.
4. Bohdan Khmelnytsky was the hetman of the Zaporozhian Cossack Hetmanate. In 1654, he concluded the Treaty of Pereiaslav with the Muscovite state which led to the eventual incorporation of Ukraine into the Russian Empire.
5. 'The Patriarch of Moscow and all the Rus' Alexi Two and the presidents of Russia, Ukraine and Belarus visited Belgorod and Prokhorovka', on *The Russian Orthodox Church. The Official Site of the Department for the External Church Relations*, www.mospat.ru/archive/nr005172.htm (accessed 17 May 2000).
6. In 1943, with the liberation of Belgorod, Kursk and Orel, the tradition of gun salutes in Moscow in honour of the Soviet army victories was established.
7. General Nikolai Vatutin, born on the territory of today's Belgorod *oblast'*, was a Soviet military commander during the Second World War. His army liberated Belgorod in August 1943. In February 1944, general Vatutin was ambushed and wounded by the UPA insurgents and died some weeks later.

Tatiana Zhurzhenko is research director of the 'Russia in Global Dialogue' programme at the Institute for Human Sciences (IWM) in Vienna, Austria, and lecturer at the Institute of Political Science, University of Vienna. She studied political economy and philosophy at V.N. Karazin Kharkiv National University (Ukraine) where she started her academic career before moving to Austria. Tatiana Zhurzhenko published widely on gender politics and feminism in Ukraine, on borders, borderland identities and memory politics in Eastern Europe. Her latest book is *Borderlands into Bordered Lands: Geopolitics of Identity in Post-Soviet Ukraine* (Stuttgart: Ibidem, 2010).

Chapter 10

HISTORY, POLITICS AND MEMORY (UKRAINE 1990S – 2000S)

Georgiy Kasianov

In this chapter the term 'historical politics' means the utilitarian use and misuse of history and 'historical memory' in ideological debates, legal and legislative practices, diplomatic conflicts, political promotion and in the imposition of certain visions of the past in the interests of politically active groups in power or groups in the struggle for redistribution of power. Historical politics in this sense is congruent to memory politics since it belongs predominantly to the domain of the 'collective memory'.

In this sense historical politics is not a new phenomenon; however, in the last three decades its manipulative effects and intensity have dramatically increased by rapid development and dissemination of informational and media technologies. It is also worth mentioning that radical geopolitical shifts in Europe, which have occurred from the end of the 1980s up until the first decade of the 2000s (the reunification of Germany, the collapse of communism in Europe, the demise of the Soviet Union and EU enlargement) have provoked a large-scale identity crisis both in an old Europe and in a postcommunist world. This crisis has also been exacerbated by a large-scale infusion of transnational cultural forms into traditional domains of national cultures. This in turn was a consequence of cultural globalization, which has provoked a conflict between traditional nationalism and cosmopolitan globalism.

Notes for this chapter begin on page 208.

Ambivalent Nationalization of History and Memory: 1990s to Early 2000s

One can argue that Ukraine was not an exception in terms of modes of action in the field of historical politics: it has shared the same scenario as other postcommunist Central and East European and Baltic countries in public representations of historical politics – from establishing specialized institutions (like the Institute of National Memory)[1] to the creation of ideologically overloaded sites of memory (the Holodomor memorial in Kyiv, Lontsky prison in Lviv),[2] from passing special legislation (law on Holodomor of 2006, 'memory laws' of 2015)[3] to setting up special bodies for investigation of the crimes of the totalitarian past (special groups of the Security Service in Ukraine functioned in 2008–2009, investigating communist regime crimes in 1932–1933).[4]

However, what makes the Ukrainian case particularly complicated both for pursuing historical political goals and for analysis is a multiplicity of challenges. Ukraine has faced a colossal challenge in the realm of identity-building related to its history and 'historical memory': it had to deal with the 'communist legacy' under the rule of former communists who turned themselves into nationalists. In this case Ukraine might be compared with some East European or Baltic countries like Slovakia, Lithuania or to a certain extend, Poland – at least in the 1990s.

However, in the field of national identity-building the difference was crucial. Ukrainian elites had to construct a modern Ukrainian identity based on cultural and historical self-identification of a 'titular' nation, while the collective identity of this titular group and of its cultural elite had been mostly tied to the values of traditional society and was deeply affected by postcolonial syndromes (in the absence of colonialism in the past). The task of cultural homogenization was challenged by internal regional divisions congruent to different historical and cultural legacies of the Russian/Soviet and Habsburg empires, the divisions often purposefully cultivated and manipulated by regional political elites. Additionally Ukraine had to separate its own history from historical space and time that was previously held in common with its neighbours, particularly with Russia.

This makes the 'Ukrainian case' an example of 'ambivalent' transformation in the field of commemoration, politics of memory/history and public debates over these issues. The political instrumentalization of 'historical memory' and 'history' itself (the last regularly presented by different actors as a 'past in the present') started in the final years of Soviet rule. Not surprisingly, political uses and abuses of 'historical memory' were modelled using Soviet examples. Anticommunism as a conventional set of public actions and ideological forms designed to discredit Soviet power in fact just reflected and repeated – or replaced – relevant ideological practices of communism. Moreover, nationalist historical symbolism, mythology and commemorative practices designed to create a certain form of counter-memory were tailored using the same psychological and cultural patterns, forms of action and standards of attitude.

Passion for 'true history', the rehabilitation of 'repressed memory' and the filling-in of 'blank spots' in history/memory professed by the anticommunist opposition in the late 1980s has led to the confusion of 'memory' and 'history'. Since the late 1980s 'memory' (collective, historical) has been presented as an integral, and in many cases, dominant part of 'history' – including history writing.

The process of the 'nationalization' of history launched in the same period was also perceived and presented by its agents as a process of 'national revival' – a very obvious reference to the metaphor that emerged in the course of construction of the nations in the second half of the nineteenth century. Reviving the nation meant reviving its 'collective national memory' (which was obviously suppressed by the communists). That in turn harks back to a revival of the 'true history' – contrary to the 'faked' communist version of the past. In a truly populist manner (which combined the cultural legacy of both Soviet and pre-Soviet times) the humanities (history in the front ranks) were mobilized for the 'recovery' of national memory/history, which together with revitalization of the Ukrainian language were considered major constituents of a nation-building (or rebuilding) agenda.

Since 1991 the humanities (mostly history, philosophy, literature studies and freshly invented *Ukrainoznavstvo*[5] have served as a tool for the legitimization of a newly born state (which in many instances was presented as a nation state with a millennial history) and as the titular nation's claims for a leading role in this state. As a result, an ethnocentric version of 'national history' was constructed and introduced at the levels of academe, school curricula and politics of memory; it remained however, infused with certain elements of Soviet historical symbolism. For instance, the Holodomor as a central symbol of Ukraine's victimhood was counterbalanced with the Great Patriotic War mythology,[6] while B. Khmelnytsky and T. Shevchenko, who were presented in the Soviet Ukrainian Pantheon as proponents of the Ukrainian people's liberation and fighters against national oppression, were then redressed as builders of the Ukrainian nation.

Concurrently a set of commemorative practices were introduced both at grass-roots and all-national levels – all aimed at the construction of a new culture of national commemoration, again a mixture of national and Soviet rituals, discourses and practices. For instance, the official annual commemoration of the 1932–1933 Great Famine (introduced in 1998) was followed in 2003 by official celebrations of the anniversaries of Volodymyr Shcherbytsky (former First Secretary of the Communist Party of Ukraine) and the Ukrainian Young Communist League. The Holodomor commemorations coexisted with the Great Patriotic War ceremonies, and when the Holodomor memorial was constructed in Kyiv it was purposefully located close to the Soviet-style 'Tomb of the Unknown Soldier' and the 'Memorial of a Great Patriotic War' – with an obvious hidden agenda: to counterbalance the Soviet symbols with a nationalist one.

Until 2005 concern with history in official policy was mainly a concession to a specific political conjuncture. On the one hand, introducing the canonical version of nationalized history into the curricula of schools and higher education institutions, which occurred in the 1990s, was supposed to promote the civic education of new citizens of a new country (Popson 2001; Janmaat 2002).[7] On the other hand, the supreme governing institutions concerned themselves with historical symbols and commemorative practices pro forma, just enough to meet the needs of the moment. Moreover, those in the highest (especially presidential) offices avoided radical declarations at all costs, except for instances when historical concerns were essential for their own legitimation (for example, refuting the view that those holding power at the time were successors to a 'criminal' communist *nomenklatura*) or for the ideological discreditation of political opponents (in the given instance, these were the communists, who were assigned the role of 'official opposition').

However, at the beginning of the twenty-first century Ukraine has faced serious problems with so-called 'divided memory/history'. The division has two major dimensions: regional, in terms of different historical and cultural legacies cherished in different regions, and ideological, in terms of different representations of the past by political agents as well as by media and scholars. Territorial patterns in some cases align with ideological ones, moreover they were heavily instrumentalized by politicians. Contested memories and conflicts in the past transferred to the present are a remarkable feature of recent Ukrainian history.

The years 2005 to 2014 saw a notable strengthening of the tendency toward acute confrontation on problems of historical policy, which became part of a broader political struggle.

Victor Yushchenko and the Politics of Ethnosymbolism

Almost immediately after the Orange Revolution, president Victor Yushchenko took a number of steps that infringed on a shaky consensus attained in the sphere of historical politics in the previous years. This was associated in part with the person of President Yushchenko and the presence among his associates of ideologically active members of the Ukrainian diaspora and radically-inclined representatives of the 'national-democratic' intelligentsia who were dissatisfied with the status of the 'titular' nation and the provisions for its cultural rights in independent Ukraine.[8]

Both the president himself and these elements of his entourage were convinced that the lack of a nationally oriented, systematic policy with regard to the humanities was the cause of the moral decline of Ukrainian society and its lack of moral and political unity. At the same time the preoccupation with problems of culture in general and history in particular, was dictated by a desire to exert moral and political pressure on political opponents: it can hardly be considered an accident that active concern with problems of historical memory and the onset of the discussion of such problems in society coincided with moments of acute internal political crisis (2007–2008).

From mid-2005, more systematic[9] and goal-oriented (but by no means always well-considered) policies took shape in the president's office with regard to the politics of history and memory. They were based on a strategy of ethnosymbolism characteristic of the standard cultural nationalism and romanticism of so-called 'non-historic' (stateless) peoples of the nineteenth century. The main element here was the revival or strengthening of the myth of the exclusive historical path of one's own nation, with particular stress on its heroism and suffering. To that end, two historical phenomena of the greatest significance were chosen – the Ukrainian Insurgent Army (UPA) as an example of the heroic pages of history, and the Holodomor as an example of a national tragedy on an extraordinary scale. Since both were presented in extremely exclusive form, as constituents of Ukrainian ethnic history alone (the UPA as representing the Ukrainian struggle for independence and the Holodomor as genocide of the Ukrainian people),[10] they aroused not only quite acute social and political discussion that rose to the level of international and interstate relations but also active counter-measures on the part of opponents.

In 2005, in connection with a 'round' anniversary of the end of the Second World War, a heated discussion broke out concerning the evaluation of that period of Ukrainian history in schoolbooks. The debate, initiated by organizations of Soviet veterans, was picked up by certain headliners from the Party of Regions who came out, like the veterans, against what they considered the inadequate elucidation of the role of the Organization of Ukrainian Nationalists and the Ukrainian Insurgent Army (OUN-UPA) in school textbooks, and against the replacement of the term 'Great Patriotic War' with the broader 'Second World War'. Those nostalgic for the Soviet past were also annoyed by the change in the conceptualization of the warring parties: in the official conception of history, Ukraine was figured as a victim in the clash of two totalitarian regimes, while in previous settings it was represented as part of a victorious Soviet family of peoples.

If for veterans this was in some measure a question of moral priority and an inability to overcome ideological stereotypes, then for the left-wing parties, above all the Communist Party of Ukraine (CPU) and its allies in the Party of Regions, it was a matter of presenting the political incumbents (presidential and governmental) as nationalists twisting history and dividing the country.

The controversy did not end with the traditional appeals and demands to the authorities to replace 'incorrect' textbooks with 'correct' ones: it came to physical skirmishes in the central squares of the national capital.[11] In the same year, 2005, there was a scandal in connection with the publication of a new textbook of Ukrainian history (for fifth grade). One of the texts approved by the Ministry of Education and Science for use in schools contained a chapter on the Orange Revolution written in the most apologetic manner.

In 2007 an unprecedented ideological and political campaign was undertaken to turn the famine of 1932–1933 (Holodomor) into the central mobilizing symbol of Ukrainian history – the symbol of the greatest human catastrophe of the twentieth century, surpassing the Holocaust and other instances of genocide (Kasianov 2012: 167–188). The Holodomor campaign not only introduced or imposed a number of commemorative actions (including the construction of a number of a new monuments and sites of memory)[12] (Gleinig, Kaminsky and Heidenreich 2008), all-national actions like 'Burn the candle' and the composition of an eighteen-volume National Book of Memory, but it also called for extermination of the symbols of the Soviet past, particularly those connected to the persons responsible for the Holodomor.

This campaign was also followed by a set of commemorative actions aimed at the intensification of an ethnic particularism of Ukrainian history.[13] Some of these initiatives brought up a particular context in relations with Russia, whose top leadership and diplomatic institutions were not sparing with very harsh comments, declarations and actions – in fact, Russia fell into diplomatic war with Ukraine from 2007 to 2010, and the controversies over the past were used as an excuse for putting political pressure on Yushchenko.[14]

Russia also took unprecedented measures at the level of international organizations (the European Parliament, UNESCO, the UN) intended to block Ukrainian diplomatic efforts to have the Holodomor recognized as an act of genocide against Ukrainians. The refusal of the President of the Russian Federation Dmitrii Medvedev to take part in the official ceremony marking the seventy-fifth anniversary of the famine of 1932–1933 (in November 2008) may be considered the peak of the conflict. The refusal was not conveyed through diplomatic channels but as demonstrative action: on 14 November 2008 Medvedev sent Yushchenko an open message. It is worth noting that less thunderous but no less effective counter-measures were taken by Israel against the promotion of the 'genocidal' version of the Holodomor in international organizations.[15]

This dispute between senior Russian and Ukrainian state authorities over the representation of the Holodomor was not the only zone of conflict to open up in historical policy in the early 2000s. No less excitement was aroused by the intention of Yushchenko and his parliamentary supporters to give UPA veterans equal rights to those of veterans of the Great Patriotic War, as well as concurrent official actions to turn the OUN and UPA into positive features of national mythology, a heroic page of the national history. Particular displeasure, accompanied by critical public statements on the part of leaders of the Russian Federation, was provoked by Yushchenko's decision to award the title of Hero of Ukraine[16] posthumously to the commander-in-chief of the UPA, Roman Shukhevych. Russia raised this question at the highest levels, including a resolution 'pushed through' at the UN in November 2008 condemning the glorification of Nazi collaborators.[17] As the curtain was falling on his presidency, Yushchenko awarded the title of Hero of Ukraine to another OUN leader, Stepan Bandera. This demonstrative action aroused protests not only from a considerable part of the population and politicians in Ukraine but also abroad: it was condemned by President Lech Kaczyński of Poland and by a number of Jewish organizations in Ukraine and elsewhere. On 25 February 2010 the European Parliament adopted a resolution expressing 'regret' with regard to Yushchenko's decree and affirming the hope that the new leadership would 'review those decisions and maintain its dedication to European values' (European Parliament 2010).

Within Ukraine the battles over the past for the sake of the present took on a physical dimension. The public controversy concerning the erection of a monument to Bandera[18] in Lviv in 2006–2007 (the Polish community of Lviv treating it as provocation) caused suspicions about plans to destroy the monument – the activists of right-wing nationalist group Svoboda (Liberty) then declared their plans to organize 24-hour guarding. By 2013 acts of vandalism against Bandera monuments (their total number reached thirty-seven in western regions) as well as against Soviet symbols and sites of memory had become routine. This includes defacing of monuments (Lenin and other Communist Party leaders of the past), spraying paints, posting derogatory signs and graffiti, desecration of memory sites (including Soviet-era monuments and Holocaust memorials), even physical destruction.[19]

The battle of the monuments in some cases reaches the most extreme forms. In May 2010, communists and an organization of veterans of the Soviet army placed a monument to Stalin in Zaporizhia, provoking sharp debate both at home and abroad. The human rights commissioner of the Council of Europe, Thomas Hammarberg, expressed 'regret' concerning the communists' intention to erect the monument. It was installed in a wing of the Zaporizhia oblast committee of the CPU: the local authorities forbade a public meeting to mark the unveiling, but it took place nevertheless in the guise of a meeting with a parliamentary deputy. In protest, representatives of the nationalist organization Svoboda organized a march to the municipal council, where communists pelted them with eggs. On 27 December 2010 a 'mobile detachment' of the All-Ukrainian Stepan Bandera Tryzub (Trident) Organization decapitated the monument with a power saw (*Newsru.ua* 2 October 2013). In a few days the chief's visage reappeared, but on the eve of 1 January 2011 the monument was blown up by members of the same organization (*Dzerkalo tyzhnia(novyny)* 1 April 2013). The Ministry of Internal Affairs registered thirty-seven acts of destruction or damaging of the 'objects of historical-cultural heritage' in 2011–2012 (*Dzerkalo tyzhnia (novyny)* 1 April 2013).

Cynical Pragmatism: Historical Politics under Yanukovich

The year 2010 saw Yushchenko's opponents, the Party of Regions, come into power. Viktor Yanukovych won the presidential elections of February 2010, and over several weeks after his victory, a parliamentary majority was formed that made it possible to adopt laws and establish a government obedient to the president. The Party of Regions itself never had a clear ideological platform, being a conglomerate of representatives of big business and associated bureaucratic elements, as well as local political elites. As the political struggle continued, becoming more acute after the Orange Revolution, a group appeared within the party that sought to develop an ideological orientation for that political force in order to define it more sharply.

The basic elements of that ideological platform were the status of the Russian language in Ukraine and, accordingly, the defense of the rights of the 'Russian-speaking population', as well as a 'struggle against nationalism', above all in the sphere of historical policy. Both elements were closely associated with the political struggle against Yushchenko and were part of the acute confrontation with him. They were used to create a repulsive image of Ukrainian nationalism and, accordingly, to discredit Yushchenko and the 'Orange' elements morally and politically. As something of a side effect of this struggle, ideological motifs became more prominent in the public actions of the Party of Regions.

The tactic remained basically the same as under Yushchenko[20]: the president himself spoke and acted in rather neutral fashion (except for asserting that the Holodomor was not genocide). Yanukovych returned to the line of conduct tested in Kuchma's time, which consisted of avoiding acutely ideological subjects and, when necessary, calling for pluralism of ideas. For Yanukovych, as for the technocrat Kuchma, questions of historical policy were of secondary importance,[21] and his approach to them was determined by *raison d'état*.

A mere two days after Yanukovych's inauguration (28 February 2010), headings pertaining to the Holodomor vanished from the president's official internet site. Subsequent reproaches from the opposition were brief in duration, as the corresponding pages were restored in abridged form (*Pam`yati zhertv Holodomoru 1932–1933 rokiv v Ukraini 2002–2006*). Yanukovych's next significant remark, made during the traditional commemoration ceremony at the grave of Taras Shevchenko in Kaniv on 9 March 2010, was that Ukrainian alone should be the official language in Ukraine.

Uncertainty lurked for some time over the annulment of Yushchenko's decrees on awarding the title of Hero of Ukraine to Shukhevych and Bandera (during the election campaign, Yanukovych had promised to review or annul the decrees). On 5 March 2010, during a joint press conference with Medvedev, Yanukovych said that by Victory Day he would 'make a decision' (*Interfax* 5 March 2010). In April 2010 the Donetsk regional administrative court declared that Yushchenko's decree awarding the title to Bandera was illegal and subject to annulment (on the grounds that Bandera had never been a citizen of Ukraine). The same procedure was followed with regard to Shukhevych on 21 April. (At almost the same time, the city councils of Ivano-Frankivsk, Lviv, Ternopil and Lutsk awarded honorary citizenship to Bandera and Shukhevych.)[22] Soon after Victory Day, Yanukovych did indeed make a decision, but not the one expected of him. On 14 May 2010, speaking at a meeting of the Civic Humanitarian Council attached to the office of the President of Ukraine, he said that it was necessary to attain mutual understanding with regard to historical figures who aroused public controversy and declared himself in favour of 'gradualism and delicacy' in resolving such problems (*Information Agency 'Unian'* 13 May 2010).

On 27 April 2010, speaking at a session of the Parliamentary Assembly of the Council of Europe in Strasbourg, Yanukovych asserted that 'declaring the Holodomor an act of genocide against one nation or another would be incorrect and unjust' (*Information Agency 'Unian'* 27 April 2010). He made this statement the day before the session was to consider a report on the famine of 1932–1933 and adopt a resolution concerning which Ukrainian participants in the session were waging a rearguard action against their Russian opponents in an effort to secure the use of the term 'genocide'. Yanukovych's declaration was agreeable to most delegations (especially that of Russia) but aroused the ire of Ukrainian parliamentarians representing the Ukrainian national-democratic opposition.

Unwillingness to characterize the Holodomor as genocide did not mean rejection of the ideological symbol. Over the past twenty years the Holodomor has become firmly established as one of the basic symbols of the constitutive Ukrainian historical myth. Commemorative practices associated with it have become habitual, and stereotypical notions and public representations of it have become part of constructed 'historical memory' and official ceremonies. The very word 'Holodomor' has entered the language of official documents, legislative acts and international relations.

Rejection of the 'genocidal' version of the Holodomor was an essential symbolic gesture for Yanukovych that eliminated tension in one aspect of relations with Russia. All other components of the corresponding historical myth and the ideological practices associated with it (as well as the very term 'Holodomor') remained untouched. A visit to the 'Memorial of Remembrance of Victims of Holodomors in Ukraine'[23] erected in Yushchenko's day has become a standard protocol item for visiting leaders of foreign countries, on a par with the laying of wreaths at the 'Eternal Flame' and the 'Monument to the Unknown Soldier' on the Avenue of Glory (a symbol of Soviet commemorative practices). In that sense, the visit to Kyiv on 17 May 2010 by President Dmitrii Medvedev of the Russian Federation was symbolically telling: he visited the 'Memorial of Remembrance of Victims of Holodomors in Ukraine', whose dedication he had demonstratively refused to attend two years earlier.

On 26 November 2010, the Day of Memory of victims of the Holodomor, an appeal was posted on the presidential website in which Yanukovych, calling the famine of 1932–1933 an 'Armageddon', came out against speculation with regard to the number of dead (having in mind the 'chase after numbers'), and called for speaking 'the truth and nothing but the truth' (President of Ukraine 2010a). On the following day, in the company of Prime Minister Nikolai Azarov, he took part in commemorative mourning at the 'Memorial of Remembrance of the Victims of Holodomors in Ukraine'. This ceremony has become a regular procedure.

Yanukovych's political declarations and ritual symbolic gestures were accompanied by a number of changes to infrastructure, the most significant of which was a change in the status of the Institute of National Memory. Under Yushchenko, the institute was granted the de facto status and powers of a state agency. In the course of an administrative reform announced as an 'optimization' of the state apparatus, the Institute of National Memory was abolished by Yanukovych's decree of 9 December 2010 (President of Ukraine 2010b) and re-established the same day, this time as a scholarly research institution attached to, and funded by the Cabinet of Ministers. Its functions remain quite murky – it has lost its significance as a suggested coordination centre of historical politics.

It may be said that Yanukovych has personally made a de facto return to the 'ambivalent' historical policy practised in Kuchma's time. That policy combines ethnosymbolism (to the extent required for the authorities' national legitimation) with elements of Soviet nostalgia (as a necessary gesture to that part of the citizenry attached to the corresponding collective experiences).

While Yanukovych himself plays the role of a president standing above the battle and 'uniting the nation', representatives of the Party of Regions' 'ideocracy' periodically create public disturbances with actions and declarations that on the one hand are hypothetically intended to overcome 'Yushchenko's legacy' and 'resist nationalism' and, on the other, to affirm something of their own ideological standard. That standard combines elements of Soviet nostalgia, a rhetoric of reunion (vis-à-vis Russia), and rather vague observations and slogans pertaining to 'internal unity' in Ukraine.

In some cases the actions of official agencies and certain significant figures of the new establishment take the form of demonstrative provocations. On 8 September 2010 officials of the Security Service of Ukraine (SBU) detained the director of the Lontsky Prison Memorial Museum (formerly a strict regime KGB prison and a Polish jail), Ruslan Zabily, on the pretext that he intended to provide secret information to certain third parties. Zabily's computer and electronic data devices were confiscated, he was interrogated (by his account) for fourteen hours and then released.

Subsequently the SBU undertook a criminal investigation, whose object became, for a week perhaps, the most popular figure on news programmes and political talk shows. The opposition immediately began a campaign against 'witch-hunting', a return to the 'times of the KGB', and the persecution of dissidents and 'independent historians'.[24] The former director of the SBU archives, Volodymyr Viatrovych, who had been dismissed immediately after Yanukovych's inauguration, even asserted that the 'Zabily case' was a 'Kremlin action' intended to wipe out the memory of the UPA

(*Glavred* 9 October 2010). More moderate explanations (which were not, however, voiced openly) came down to a banal attempt to divide property in central Lviv or to 'clean up' the composition of cadres in institutions subordinate to the SBU (the senior staff of the SBU archival service was of course replaced immediately after Yanukovych's accession to power). These explanations find some measure of corroboration in the fact that Yanukovych intervened in the situation as supreme arbiter: by his decree, the Memorial Museum was placed under the supervision of the Institute of National Memory, and the 'Zabily case' somehow blew over of its own accord.

No less resounding, but more consequential, were the actions of the Minister of Education and Science, Dmytro Tabachnyk, concerning the 'normalization' of the school curriculum in Ukrainian history and of the language situation in the education sector. As a member of the opposition during the 'Orange' period, Tabachnyk emerged as one of the most radical critics of Yushchenko's historical policy, distinguishing himself with very harsh comments about the president and his entourage, especially the 'Galicians'. The national-democratic intelligentsia and the opposition took Tabachnyk's appointment as minister of education and science to be an anti-Ukrainian measure. An 'anti-Tabachnyk campaign' developed in the Western Ukrainian oblasts, and opposition deputies submitted a bill to dismiss the minister, calling him 'virulently anti-Ukrainian' (*ukraïnozher*).

In a BBC interview given in April 2010, Tabachnyk said that Ukrainian history textbooks were written from an ethnocentric viewpoint: they should be revised and written from an anthropocentric viewpoint. In this connection, he made an indirect reference to the results of the activity of a working group of historians at the Institute of National Memory ('Tabachnik khochet sdelat' uchebniki po istorii 'gumannymi' 2010). In June 2010 he posted a programmatic article on the official site of the Party of Regions, repeating his thesis about an 'anthropocentric approach' to history in schools and declaring that 'the treatment of the history of the homeland and the world cannot vary with changes of presidents or ministers of education; it cannot and should not depend on the personal tastes, complexes, and phobias of any official'. This was promptly followed by a declaration of his personal treatment, wholly conditioned by politics, of the history of the Second World War and of such individuals as Stalin, Shukhevych and Bandera.

Further steps pertaining to the 'review of national history' had no particular resonance and developed according to the laws of bureaucratic hierarchy: some authors of textbooks received behind-the-scenes directives to make corrections. An image of the 'Orange' Independence Square disappeared from the cover of a textbook. In its text, the formula 'artificial [i.e., man-made] holodomor' was removed (the term 'Holodomor' remained); the description of UPA activity was abridged; a photo of Shukhevych was deleted; and the book ended with the year 2004. Material on the UPA was also abridged in another textbook, which said that the army fought against the Germans and the Bolsheviks (not a word about the Poles). According to the authors, they received directives by telephone from the ministry about correcting their textbooks: the directives came down to reducing anti-Russian motifs and abridging material on the UPA (Kapluk 2010).

It is worth noting some more radical public actions that go beyond official declarations on historical subjects, but which enjoy the de facto, behind-the-scenes sponsorship of elements of the Party of Regions that align with the communists on ideological questions. Their actions are usually directed towards those who are nostalgic for Soviet times and live by the stereotypes of Soviet propaganda. Such actions included, first and foremost, the erection of monuments to victims of the OUN-UPA in Luhansk, Simferopol and Odesa and in raion centres and villages of Luhansk and Sumy oblasts in 2010 ('Pamiatniki zhertvam OUN-UPA' 2010), as well as a highly tendentious exhibition entitled 'The Volhynian Slaughter: Polish and Jewish Victims of the OUN-UPA', which was displayed in Kyiv and major cities of Eastern and Southern Ukraine. Paradoxically, the exhibition repeated the actions of the Yushchenko period, copying the techniques and methods of representing the past that were used in the travelling exhibition 'Ukraine Remembers! The Holodomor of 1932–1933 – The Genocide of the Ukrainian People'.

Under Yanukovich historical politics in Ukraine has undergone an evolution from 'ideology' to overt and cynical political utilitarianism. Both components were always presented, however in recent years the balance was disrupted by major actors: historical politics was turned into the sole instrument of political spoiling, the major tool for 'spin doctors' in generating a smokescreen for 'bigger' issues. It is not coincidental that the hottest public battles over problems of the past in Ukraine always occur at the moments when possible social controversies over current economic, social and political issues become a matter of sharp political agenda.

Additionally, the permanent relevance and importance of interpretations of the past for the sake of the present proves the validity of one of the major arguments of this chapter: the Ukrainian identity-building project based on an antiquarian, ethnically exclusivist model of the nation seems to be incongruent with the realities of the beginning of the twenty-first century. In the 1990s this exclusivist project was relatively successful under the terms of 'restoration of historical rights of the titular nation'.

In the 2000s it contradicted the idea of civic homogeneity and citizenship based on the loyalty to civic nation (i.e., community of citizens loyal to common civic principles and foundations).

Maidan Revolution and After: Use and Abuse of History/Memory

Mass public protests, demonstrations and street fights from 24 November 2013 to 22 February 2014 resulted in the fall of Yanukovich, called the 'Maidan revolution' or 'revolution of dignity', and were followed by the intensive use of history by protesters as well as by opponents of a new Kyiv power in Crimea and Eastern Ukraine.

At Maidan references to the past and to certain historical myths have become visible at the moment of transition from peaceful protest to violent confrontation. For instance, self-defence at Maidan followed the self-naming and some forms of collective practices of Ukrainian Cossacks. The major units were called *sotnia* ('a hundred', i.e., a Cossack unit of one hundred fighters) and their commanders – *sotnyky*. The members of self-defence called each other *pobratymy* ('blood brothers') – an obvious reference to the Cossack legacy. Several units were formed by members of the contemporary Cossack movement; many used historical outfits: the Cossack hairstyle – *oseledets* have become extremely popular among protesters and youth. Maidan was covered with pictures and fictional portraits of Cossacks.

Some appeals to the past initially provoked disputes among protesters. The nationalist Svoboda party has actively used the slogan *Slava Ukraini – Heroiam slava!* ('Glory to Ukraine – Glory to Heroes!'), in fact a party greeting of the Organization of Ukrainian Nationalists – a right-wing organization from the 1930s with a disputable reputation.[25] However, in the course of events, particularly after the first fights between protesters and riot police and after the first victims, the slogan partly lost its historical address and became a slogan of Maidan and its supporters, with obvious appeal to contemporary Ukraine and contemporary heroes.

Since the fall of Yanukovich the territory of Maidan and its closest surroundings has established itself as a single memorial space, covered with a number of sites mostly dedicated to those who died in the conflict. Protesters have established a mourning ritual dedicated to the heroes of the 'Heavenly Hundred' – people who were killed during the revolution. In July 2014 the newly elected president of Ukraine, Petro Poroshenko, established a state award: an Order of Heroes of the Heavenly Hundred.

Meanwhile, previous iconoclastic extremes reached their height throughout Central and Southern Ukraine: in January and February the monuments to Lenin were almost simultaneously destroyed by the mobs led by right-wing activists in their dozens. The advancement of the Ukrainian army and paramilitary forces in Donbass was followed by the destruction of Lenin monuments. Following the events, supporters of the anti-Lenin campaign created a group on Facebook called *Leninopad* ('Lenin flurry').

The use and misuse of history after the Maidan revolution reached its most extreme forms in the annexation of Crimea and war in Donbass. The annexation of the peninsula was supported by arguments based on the 'restoration of historical justice' and references to the 'illegal nature' of the transfer of Crimea to the Ukrainian SSR. War in Donbass, sponsored and organizationally supported by Russia, also makes history and memory a valuable tool. The Ukrainian army are described as 'fascists' in the rhetoric of Putin and insurgents' propaganda, and active supporters of the separatists claim that they fight against fascism, with direct allusions to the 'Great Patriotic War' – the Soviet military myth – a central element of contemporary Russian state historical mythology and politics of memory.

The ideological ground for the separatist movement in Donbass is also found in the past. Vladimir Putin personally presented the concept of so-called *Novorossia* (New Russia) – referring to the imperial nineteenth-century name of the Southern Ukrainian lands.

Almost immediately Novorossia has been visualized and conceptualized, provoking debates and actions (including the formation of fake political parties and ideologically ambivalent, organizationally undetermined 'public movements' supported by rebels and terrorist groups from Eastern Ukraine). On 24 May 2014 self-proclaimed Luhansk and Donetsk 'people's republics' declared their unification into one single state – Novorossia.

Respectable academic arguments were mobilized to legalize this movement. Russian historians from official academic institutions have proclaimed their readiness to write a book on the history of Novorossia. The Director of the Institute of Russian History, National Academy of Sciences, has made a statement that 'Novorossia objectively exists as a historical and cultural phenomenon', and that this distinctive 'region possesses ethnographic, historical and cultural unity'.[26]

It would be a commonplace to say that the events of the Maidan revolution and war in Donbass in many aspects should be to a great extent considered as social outcomes of historical politics of the previous decades. State and intellectual elites have failed to elaborate flexible, comprehensive and integrative politics in the field, based on the principles of cultural inclusion and civic nationalism. As a result, different regions have cherished their own historical myths, stereotypes and prejudices. Forced 'nationalization' of history under Yushchenko based on exclusivist ethnosymbolic myths has helped to bring more cohesiveness within the Ukrainian-speaking community, but has turned a great portion of the population, particularly from the east of the country, into inhabitants of an ideological ghetto, oversupplied by Soviet-based historical myths. This narrow-minded historical policy was intensively used by Yushchenko's opponents within and outside the country to discredit him and his vision of 'Ukrainianism'. Ideological and historical clichés used by the Party of Regions and communists in the struggle for power against 'nationalists' were readily consumed by part of the population excluded from Yushchenko's historical project – the ground for separatism was duly prepared through political abuse of history, which pursued a different goal. Struggle for Kyiv was turned into struggle against Kyiv.

Notes

1. Comparable to the Institute of National Remembrance in Poland, and likewise institutions in the Czech Republic and Slovakia.
2. The same can be found in Poland (Museum of Warsaw Uprising), Estonia and Lithuania (museums of occupation or genocide), Hungary (House of Terror), Czech Republic (Museum of Communism).
3. The most obvious examples: legislation on 'denial' of Armenian genocide in France, and Holocaust denial legislation in several European countries, including an attempt to introduce an all-European legislation on Holocaust denial.
4. Parallels can be found in a commission to investigate crimes against humanity in Estonia or the Institute for the Investigation of Crimes of Communism in Romania (the latter, however, is closer to the institutional shape of the institutes of national memory).
5. Might be translated as 'Ukrainian studies' – a mix of ethnography, folk cultural studies, history and philology devoted exclusively to ethnic Ukrainians.
6. At the level of the school curriculum the Soviet term 'Great Patriotic War' together with its interpretative core was integrated into a broader term: Second World War.
7. Inevitably, a standard canon of populist-romanticist history was introduced – with the obvious excesses of an ethnically exclusivist vision of the past: the history of Ukraine as a history of ethnic Ukrainians where the 'other' was represented either as an eternal enemy (for instance Poles, in some cases Russians or Crimean Tatars) or as a part of historical background needed to highlight the mainstream theme: a millennial existence of the Ukrainian nation and its struggle for independence and an independent state.
8. To put the issue into a broader context: ethnic Ukrainians still predominate among socially, economically and culturally marginalized groups of the population (first of all among agrarian strata which are traditionally perceived as a basis of the Ukrainian

nation). Ukrainian language, being introduced as an official language of education and state bureaucracy, is insufficiently used in business, hi-tech and other most advanced spheres of society.

9. Including the erection of new memorial complexes and institutions. Among the latter, the most significant was the Institute of National Memory, established by Yushchenko's decree on 31 May 2006. The institute was established on the Polish model. Unlike its Polish counterpart, the Ukrainian Institute of National Memory did not obtain substantial financing. For some time it coordinated the work of state institutions with regard to compiling the *Book of Remembrance of the Holodomor*; its other functions were public education and scholarly research, but it proved unable to compete with existing research institutions. Moreover, some of its projects were clearly in contradiction with Yushchenko's historical policy: the work of a group of historians under the aegis of the institute aimed at carrying out a critical analysis of school courses and textbooks on Ukrainian history. They produced a concept of historical education that was clearly at odds with the ideology of Yushchenko's ethnosymbolism ('Kontseptsiia ta prohramy vykladannia istorïi v shkolakh (proekt)' 2009).

10. In the Ukrainian intellectual and, in a narrower sense, historiographical tradition up to the turn of the twentieth century, 'people' and 'nation' were identical concepts; the Ukrainian nation meant ethnic Ukrainians. The concept of a civic nation is usually conveyed by the term 'people of Ukraine'.

11. In 2005–2006, when the October anniversary of the formation of the UPA was again being commemorated, UPA veterans and their supporters gathered in the central square of the capital, as did veterans of the Great Patriotic War, 'stirred up' by leftists. Fisticuffs between them became something of a tradition. Since 2007 a practice of holding public events representing the hostile parties in different places was introduced.

12. The total number of those devoted to the Holodomor reached more than 4,000. List of major Holodomor memorial sites, including photos (348 entries).

13. The restoration of Hetman Ivan Mazepa's capital of Baturyn (Chernihiv oblast) and the tercentenary of the destruction of Baturyn by the troops of Aleksandr Menshikov (1708); the celebration of the 'Constitution of Pylyp Orlyk' (claimed to be a 'first constitution in Europe'); 'the jubilee' of the Battle of Konotop (1659) where united Cossack-Tatar troops crashed the Moscow army; the nineteeth anniversary of the Fight of Kruty (1918) – a heroic myth about a handful of youth fighting with superior forces of Bolsheviks; and the tercentenary of the Battle of Poltava (1709).

14. Simultaneously Russia fell into conflicts over history with other close neighbours: Poland, Lithuania, Latvia and Estonia.

15. Here, to all appearances, one may speak of a certain competition between two projects, the Holodomor and the Holocaust. The actions of the Ukrainian side, which clearly followed the example of the formation of rhetoric about and representations of the Holocaust, reveal an intention to 'surpass' their predecessors with regard to the principal indicator – the number of victims. This could not fail to prompt counteraction on the part of Israel and those who consider the Holocaust unique. It is worth noting that anti-Semitic motifs are not infrequently to be found in the rhetoric of the Holodomor, both on the part of known anti-Semitic organizations (such as the Interregional Academy of Personnel Management) and of state structures, especially in the form of the 'unobtrusive' but insistent repetition of the true full names of 'Holodomor organizers' – to take a random example, the list published by the SBU in 2009: the Ukrainian Jewish Committee (a non-governmental organization) has alarmed authorities about the fact that the list 'in fact puts ethnic responsibility for the tragedy of Holodomor on Jews and Latvians'.

16. The title and the chest decoration pertaining to it are basically copied from the title of Hero of the Soviet Union.
17. The draft of such a resolution was adopted by the UN General Assembly. The United States voted against it; all countries of the European Union, including Estonia and Latvia, abstained, as did Ukraine. The adoption of the draft resolution was prompted by the actions of Baltic authorities that, in Russia's opinion, condoned the 'rehabilitation' of the soldiers and officers of national Waffen SS military formations (the Latvian Legion and the 40th Estonian Division). The reference was, of course, to the UPA, Shukhevych and Bandera.
18. The first monument to Bandera was erected in his native village in Western Ukraine in 1990. It became an object of repeated vandalism and was even blown up.
19. For the monitoring of the acts of vandalism see here: http://www.istpravda.com.ua/tags/tag_вандалізм.
20. Yushchenko, for example, while president, never personally said that Russia should bear responsibility for the Holodomor, apologize to Ukraine, or pay compensation. In his entourage, however, especially in the presidential faction of parliament, there was no shortage of such statements, often quite radical ones.
21. By all accounts, Yanukovych generally dislikes 'subjects pertaining to the humanities' and quite often finds himself in embarrassing situations when required to address such questions. The best known 'pearls' of his public appearances are associated with just such subjects: it was from him that Ukraine learned of the poetess Anna Akhmetova (confusion of Akhmatova with the Ukrainian tycoon's surname Akhmetov) and of the Russian poet Anton Chekhov, while Western Ukrainians were flabbergasted to hear that they were the 'genocide of the nation' (Yanukovych meant *henofond*, 'gene pool').
22. According to a survey by the Reiting sociological group, 53 per cent of respondents supported the annulment of the decree, 28 per cent did not support it, and 19 per cent expressed no definite opinion. Every tenth resident of Western Ukraine surveyed was prepared to take part in protest actions against the annulment of Yushchenko's decree.
23. The official name.
24. Zabily was an active promoter of the version of national history that was in accord with Yushchenko's policy. Zabily was a de facto staff member of the SBU and an active participant in the declassification of SBU documents while Yushchenko was in power. The files confiscated from him may indeed have been officially restricted at the time, but in Yushchenko's day such documents (dealing mainly with the history of the OUN and the UPA) were openly accessible and printed in generally available publications.
25. The OUN, established in 1929 by Ukrainian émigré army officers and by Western Ukrainian nationalist revolutionaries, was the most active force in the physical struggle against Poles in Western Ukraine and against Poles, Soviets and Germans during the Second World War. For a major part of Western Ukrainians and the Ukrainian diaspora abroad the OUN (particularly the Stepan Bandera faction) represents heroic national myth. For their numerous opponents the OUN is responsible for the murder of dozens of thousands of Polish civilians in Vohlynia (1943), collaboration with the Nazis and participation in the Holocaust, partisan war against the Soviet Army and numerous killings of Soviet officials, including their families. The OUN legacy and related politics of memory remains among the most controversial aspects of the past, heavily used and misused by politicians and statesmen.
26. http://www.bbc.co.uk/russian/russia/2014/07/140716_russia_ukraine_history_paper.shtml?print=1.

Georgiy Kasianov is head of the Department of Contemporary History and Politics at the Institute of the History of Ukraine (National Academy of Sciences). Author, co-author and co-editor of fourteen books and collective volumes, including *A Laboratory of Transnational History: Ukraine and Recent Ukrainian Historiography* (CEU Press, 2009, co-edited with P. Ther), *Danse Macabre: The Great Famine of 1932–1933 in Politics, Mass Consciousness and Historiography* (Nash chas, 2010, in Ukrainian), *Ukraine – Russia. How History is Being Written. Dialogues, Lectures, Articles* (RGGU, 2011, in cooperation with A. Miller). His research interests include the history of East-Central Europe, politics of memory, history and theory and intellectual history. He teaches at the National University Kyiv Mohyla Academy and Berlin Free University.

Chapter 11

Walking Memory through City Space in Sevastopol, Crimea

Judy Brown

In today's information-rich societies, memory studies scholars are facing the question of how to gather relevant data that accurately reflect the processes in play in their regions of study. This question is all the more pertinent when it comes to highly contentious topics, for which the fiery rhetoric of warring political factions all too often sets the parameters of public discussion. As a Western researcher of memory in Sevastopol, I have to navigate through much cultural 'shouting' regarding this distinctive naval city in order to analyse the synergies between history, memory and city space.

Sevastopol is a fascinating site for this kind of study. First, it has a rich cultural and historical heritage from both imperial and Soviet times, and into the post-Soviet era, which has produced both convergent and competing sites and artefacts of memory. Secondly, the transfer of the peninsula in 1954 from the Russian SSR to the Ukrainian SSR led, after 1991, to a majority Russian-speaking region within independent Ukraine. Crimea's particularity is expressed in its Autonomous Republic status and has, at times, uneasy inter-ethnic relations, a state of affairs compounded by the return of the Crimean Tatars from Uzbek exile after 1989. Sevastopol has remained at the centre of analysis of geopolitical studies of Crimea, as Ukraine and Russia make various attempts to resolve the question of the Black Sea Fleet. The complexity of this situation is deepened by the fact that Sevastopol has a special status – the municipality is administratively independent of Crimea and answerable directly to Kyiv, which appoints Sevastopol's 'mayor'.[1]

Notes for this chapter begin on page 225.

In regional and national disputes of the post-independence era, arguments of right and legitimacy have very often been underpinned by appeals to historical memory. Most recently, the justification given for Russia's dramatic annexation of Crimea and Sevastopol in March 2014 was couched in terms of 'historical significance', 'common history' and 'an unwavering conviction ... passed down through the generations'.[2] The data in this chapter are taken from my fieldwork in Sevastopol in 2011 and 2012; the reader is therefore offered an intriguing snapshot of Sevastopol's commemorative culture in the years preceding annexation. It demonstrates some of the ways in which Sevastopol's local commemorative infrastructure, relying on dynamic grass-roots enthusiasm, serves to promote and maintain a Russian imperial identity for the inhabitants and their city which is, in a sense, suspended outside its historic empires.

Sevastopol's 'stuff' of memory is particularly potent, ranging from monuments and memorial sites (over two thousand in number), to literary and cinematic representations. These can feed a plethora of competing memory projects – pro-Russian, pro-Ukrainian, neo-Soviet – which concentrate within this city the wider memory processes taking place across large parts of Ukraine today. Meanwhile, part of what makes Sevastopol distinct is its dynamic local culture of memory performances, which range from the didactic and dramatic to the ceremonial and martial. In order to access some of these memory processes on the ground, I developed a methodological tool that I call 'walking memory'. This involves taking commercial and informal guided walking tours around the city in order to understand how Sevastopolians experience urban space with regard to memory and how they present their city's past to tourists and outsiders.

Theory of Walking Memory

My conceptual focus on 'place' takes as its starting point Lefebvre's insights as to how spaces are socially produced (1991), that is to say how they become *places* through social subjectivities, and the writings of Yi-Fu Tuan on establishing the meaning of spatial and social existence (1977). Tuan looks at how these meanings are established variously in different eras and cultures; this becomes more dynamic when it comes to remembrance, since multiple historicities are constructed in the present. Moving on to the urban context of spatiality, De Certeau proposes that cities are constituted as their inhabitants walk around the city (1984: 97). He posits walking as a 'place-making practice', whereby the subject creates places whilst himself 'lacking space' through movement. In Sevastopol for example, the varying cultural artefacts of the city embody a range of temporalities which city-dwellers encounter and to which they ascribe meaning as they move through urban space.

From this understanding of walking as a place-making practice, we can derive guided walking tours around a city as a methodological tool. Admittedly very different from strolling or Benjamin's figure of *le flâneur*, this highly specific walking practice, which in Sevastopol is very Soviet-inflected, provides access to cultural 'texts' about the city that can be used for the purpose of discourse analysis. Rather than viewing such tours as a straightforward production-consumption of cultural information, consideration of the discursive positioning of actors (both tour guides and tourists) allows for a nuanced understanding of the production of tourist sites and the practice of sightseeing (Urry 1990).

In developing this 'walking memory' methodology, I was inspired by Tanya Richardson's (2008: 139–166) ethnographic study of a local-history walking group in Odesa. However, my Sevastopol study differed in several important ways: I planned to gather data by taking commercial walking tours through the city, including some informal tours[3] from non-specialist informants, and in a range of languages.[4] I also included several of the very popular guided boat tours out into the bays, which give a view onto the city.

(Re)negotiating Urban Identities

Scholars of memory practice in post-socialist cities have examined the ways in which city authorities and heritage institutions engage in the construction of new urban identities. Young and Kaczmarek (2008) note that some municipal elites hark back to a 'Golden era' in an attempt to obscure the city's socialist past, as in the case of Łódź and Leipzig (Young and Kaczmarek 1999; Coles 2003; Munasinghe 2005); others highlight certain aspects of their city's socialist past to showcase anticommunist elements, such as the House of Terror in Budapest or the museums of occupation in the Baltic states (Rátz 2006; Velmet 2011). Meanwhile planning elites in other cities such as Moscow have included the socialist heritage in the modern urban landscape (Forest and Johnson 2002; Boym 2001). Although it is the municipal authorities that often set the heritage agenda, in some cases this new post-socialist vision is contested by the demand for 'communist heritage tourism' (Young and Light 2006). Transnational demands such as Jewish heritage tourism can also contribute to such contestation (Gruber 2002; Murzyn 2006).

Regarding this (re)negotiation of cultural heritage, Sevastopol's journey into post-socialism was marked predominately by continuity rather than rupture. Serhii Plokhy (2000) traces the formation of the myth of Sevastopol from a city of glory (drawing on the Greek origins of the area) to a 'city of Russian glory' from the nineteenth to the twentieth centuries. In turn Karl Qualls demonstrates how, during the postwar reconstruction of Sevastopol, and in negotiation with central planners in Moscow, local urban planners were able to 'agitate' to preserve the prewar and indeed imperial appearance of the city, contributing to its distinctly Russian face. He concludes that 'Sevastopol was able to avoid the abrupt [post-Soviet] transition because it had become local decades earlier' (2009a: 156). I argue that, in addition to these continuities in Sevastopol's urban mythology, the continuities in the structure and orientation of the local tourism industry from the Soviet into the post-Soviet era, as well as continuities in demand, contribute to the salience of local mythology of the 'city of Russian military glory'.

The Business of Memory

During the Soviet era, Sevastopol had a highly developed industry of state-run *ekskursii* (excursions) – short guided tours around the main historical sights, at the heart of which lay the aim of patriotic education.[5] About one million visitors came to Sevastopol annually as part of organized tour groups; at its height in the 1970s and 1980s, the city's Bureau for Travel and Excursions offered one hundred and fifty separate guided tours, with three hundred tour guides working each day.[6] My interviews with some of these tour guides demonstrate the gravity and zeal with which they approached their excursion work. They recounted in great detail the heroic deeds of Russian sailors during the first Defence of Sevastopol (1854–1855), and of Red Army soldiers during the second Defence of Sevastopol (1941–1942) up to the liberation of the city on 9 May 1944. Drawing a distinction from the conventional tourist industry in Western Europe, the tour guides in Sevastopol saw their role first and foremost as *instructing* rather than entertaining tourists or simply showing them around. Within this Soviet didactic tradition, the emphasis is on history as scientific truth (restricting room for interpretation or debate) and on associated patriotic or moral lessons (Omel'chenko 1991: 30–53; Noack 2006: 288–289).

After the collapse of the Soviet Union in 1991 and the opening up of Sevastopol in 1997,[7] the tourism industry transitioned to a free market model with numerous tourist firms in operation. However there are important ways in which the current picture has been shaped by the Soviet experience. In effect, the ten main tour operators (which largely developed out of the Soviet-era Bureau for Travel and Excursions) are able to maintain their monopoly over city tours by sharing clients to form excursion groups. This means there is little variation between excursions, with all tour guides having received the same professional training that was designed in the Soviet period. It is also unsurprising, given the scientific view of history within the Soviet tradition, that sharing clients is viewed as unproblematic since, as one tour guide put it, 'the history is the same'.[8] The Director of the Department for the Training of Tour Guides spoke about the importance of maintaining high standards for excursions and a unified approach to history, at a time when history is being 'rethought even at the state level' and when the idea of 'who was a hero' is being turned upside down.[9] This indicates another important contour of memory in Sevastopol: not only is history attributed truth value, but it is also constructed defensively against those who would 'rewrite' it. Here the director had in mind those state and educational reforms whereby the traditional Soviet version of history is rejected in favour of a national narrative for the history of Ukraine (Kasianov 2009).

There has been a strong continuity in the local tour-guiding machinery in Sevastopol, however the scale of excursion activity has contracted in the absence of state sponsorship.[10] One might wonder therefore how the tastes of a new generation of consumers are potentially shaping such excursion provision in Sevastopol today. Qualls asserts that that there has been a shift in Sevastopol in the post-Soviet era towards leisure-based tourism, with greater demand for entertainment and distraction rather than factual information and lived experience of visiting historical sights (2009b: 172). Although Qualls's observation (based on analysis of guidebooks and pamphlets) is consistent with the opening up of the city in 1997 and the transformation to a capitalist economy, I argue that the composition of tourists visiting Sevastopol will likely maintain the trend towards Soviet-style, information-rich sightseeing for a number of reasons.

Anecdotal evidence suggests that Russian-speakers from Ukraine and the Russian Federation make up the vast majority of visitors to Sevastopol annually. In the case of tourists coming from Russia we can witness the reverse phenomenon of 'diaspora tourism'; that is to say, citizens of Russia proper 'return' to visit an area stranded outside the Russian Federation when the borders of the former Soviet Union ebbed in 1991. Such 'returning' to a site of great historical significance for the country can have the quality of 'pilgrimage' which is noted in diaspora tourism (Coles and Timothy 2004). In the same way Russian-speakers from Ukraine visit Sevastopol as an important heritage site. As such, tourists into Sevastopol could perpetuate the tendency towards didactic tourism specifically via their consumer demands, which need not necessarily be leisure-driven.[11] Furthermore the interest of both local Sevastopolians and Russian-speaking tourists in these 'pilgrimage' heritage sites is reinforced by Russia's concept of her 'near abroad'[12] and the corresponding 'compatriots policy' (1999).[13] This policy employs a strong rhetoric of protecting Russian citizens abroad and, among other stipulations, requires Russia by law to provide support to cultural centres, libraries, archives, museums, theatres and other creative groups that are engaged in Russian heritage education activities. This places Sevastopol firmly on the map for Russia's heritage trail and in the context of a 'compatriots' discourse marked by strong feelings of loss and entitlement.

Considering the contraction of the tourist industry in Sevastopol – specifically the scale of provision of excursions – it is less productive to characterize such walking tours in the post-Soviet era as a commodification of memory. Although Sevastopol is not without its tourist kiosks selling naval paraphernalia and Hero City fridge magnets, it stands in contrast to cities with highly commercialized memory or nostalgia industries, such as the Jewish Quarter in Krakow or 'Criminal Past of the Old Town' tours in Odesa. In actual fact, Sevastopol already made a very successful 'commodity' of its memory in the Soviet era, both financially (with revenues comparable to those of an average industrial firm or a *kolkhoz*)[14] and in the form of patriotic education. Many of these forms enjoy strong continuity in the present day, but more within a system of cultural rather than economic capital. The head of the Department for the Training of Tour Guides notes that the tour firms make the large majority of their revenues through leading tours to elsewhere in Crimea, whilst local tour guiding in Sevastopol is no longer lucrative.[15]

Sevastopol's *ekskursionnyi* apparatus is located within a wider city framework for 'patriotic education', which also helps to reinforce the Russian perspective. One notable feature is the mobilization of the school system for commemorative activity. Each of Sevastopol's sixty-seven schools is affiliated with a veterans' association, whose chairman sits on the school board, oversees the school's 'museum of heroic-patriotic education' and organizes events with pupils and veterans for the intergenerational transmission of memory as a matter of urgent priority.[16] Commemorative activity reaches its apogee at the annual Victory Day celebrations on 9 May to mark the contribution of Sevastopol and the Soviet Union to the 'defeat of fascism in Europe'. In addition to mobilizing the city's population, Victory Day together with Navy Day (on the last Sunday in July) attracts thousands of visitors to Sevastopol to watch and take part in the festivities.

Walking Memory as a Foreigner

I must be cognizant of the fact that Sevastopol's tour guides, knowing a foreigner is in the group, may simplify their text, practise self-censorship on certain issues or tailor their talk to what they imagine might interest me (especially if they are aware that I am conducting doctoral research). On the other hand it is important for me to reflect on my role as 'tourist-researcher', maintaining the distinction between tourism and fieldwork and understanding the ways in which this shapes what I *hear* and record as significant. As Crang puts it succinctly, 'homo academicus might be uncomfortably closely related to that embarrassing relative turistas vulgaris' (2011: 205). I try to be self-reflexive of my professional formation as a Russian studies scholar who has spent more time in Russia than Ukraine. I have also worked in my town's heritage centre, and as both an English language and Russian language tour guide, thus have my own ideas about how tourist work does and should operate. This led to inevitable cultural clashes and misunderstandings; in my walking memory study in Sevastopol, the starkest East-West encounter came in the culture of tour guiding. This point was reinforced in conversation with the local tour guides and their insistent distinction between the European model of 'guides' [*gidy*] and the Russian 'excursion leaders' [*ekskursovody*]. They said that guides simply show people objects and places, whereas excursion leaders undertake the more complex task of showing historical objects, recounting the history in detail, then drawing out meaning and conveying a patriotic lesson for tourists. In this way excursion leaders are seen as a source of authority and thus also function as carriers of authorized memory. In fact I learned the hard way that it is not common to ask questions of tour guides, even less so during the excursion; one time I was cut off abruptly while asking a question and was pointedly ignored for the rest of the excursion. This episode illustrates the Soviet tradition of didactic tourism according to which the tour guide is a 'teacher' figure, to be respected and not questioned.[17]

Memory Processes in Sevastopol

During fieldwork in summer 2011 I went on four commercial tours of the city (two walking tours, two minibus tours) led by women in their fifties, three commercial boat tours led by men in their forties to fifties, two full informal tours (one woman in her twenties, one man in his fifties) and various small informal tours. The data revealed the dynamic maintenance of the myth of Sevastopol as a 'city of Russian military glory' and thus a strong local identity as well as resistance to identification as a Ukrainian city.

Production of Memory in City Space

The built environment of Sevastopol is very conducive to narrative accounts of the city's history; there are over two thousand monuments, many of which are in the city centre and visible simultaneously from various locations – Nakhimov Square, Primorskii Boulevard and the bays. Likewise place and street names shape narratives of cultural memory. As we pass a particular street, the guide explains the significance of Ushakov[18] to the fleet or Ivan Golubets[19] during the Great Patriotic War. Out of the abundance of signifiers, the tour guide will also select and prioritize what to focus on, allowing certain narratives to crystallize. Laced through the historical accounts was a strong master narrative of wartime devastation and the unlikely but monumental feat of postwar reconstruction. On the point of the built environment, I took note of the reverential tone with which all the tour guides spoke about their monuments such as the 'Monument to the Soldier and Sailor', the 'Monument to Nakhimov', or the 'Obelisk of Glory' as 'one of the most beautiful'. These prioritizing processes also allowed for a specific chronology; whereas guidebooks begin with the Greek site of Khersones, all the tour guides approached the chronology of Sevastopol by hanging the city's history off the 'two defences' (*dve oborony*) – the siege of Sevastopol (1854–1855) in the Crimean War, and the Nazi seige of the city (1941–1942) during the Great Patriotic War. This is a pervasive motif of Sevastopolian bravery and steadfastness through which each historical era is interpreted.

The tours conveyed well the interplay between the 'hardware' and 'software' of cultural memory (Etkind 2004: 39). Often the tour guide, when speaking about a particular building or monument, would invoke an associated literary text. Tour guide Svetlana[20] commented, for example, 'This is the building Lev Nikolaevich Tolstoy lived in while writing his Sevastopol Sketches'. Likewise while Nina was discussing the fate of the ships during the second Defence of Sevastopol, she made the allusion 'as the children's song goes, "their fates are somewhat similar to those of people"' (*sud'by ikh tozhe chem-to pokhozhi na sud'by lyudei*). When talking about the Greeks' first encounters with the local inhabitants of Crimea in the fifth century BC, Nina referenced a poem penned by Pushkin about Old Tavrida during his visit to Crimea in the 1820s. Such allusions fix the physical space firmly within the Russian cultural imaginary. As well as linking between texts, the tour guides also drew connections between different sites; mentioned in common association were the Panorama and Diorama museums, where the events of the first and second Defences of Sevastopol are depicted respectively, therein reinforcing the motif of the 'two defences'.

When not pointing out individual sites of memory, the tour guides made use of mental mapping to describe the urban geography of the city (central square, then three main streets connecting the four main squares around the central mound, and four municipal *raions* divided up by the bays). This mental mapping was also used to convey the past and present borders of the city: Svetlana pointed out that the mosque and Uprisers' Square (both important heritage sites for local Crimean Tatars) marked the borders of the historic city centre.

In addition to hanging their narrative off the built environment, the tour guides used city space to indicate absences and to encourage us to imagine other things. Svetlana and Margarita told us to picture Bol'shaia Morskaia Street with only the post office and Pokrovskii Cathedral still standing, following wartime destruction. Yurii was not content with imagination: he urged us to go on to the internet at home and look up aerial shots of the city in 1945 to see how it had been razed to the ground. As Alena led me through the city, she frequently stopped to tell me what a building used to be (the School of Boxing as a Karaim Temple, Dom Moskvy as Hotel Kist), or how it had been rebuilt, or what used to stand in a certain place. This corresponds to De Certeau's observation that people live in 'the presences of diverse absences' as 'demonstratives indicate the invisible identities of the visible' (1984: 108). In most of these cases the 'addition' or 'subversion' upheld the dominating narratives already identified of Sevastopol as an undefeatable city and a city of Russian military glory.

Cosmopolitan Memory and Internally Competitive Memory

Within the tour guiding narratives, emphasis was often put on continuities. Nina began her tour with the words 'we are now standing on Nakhimov Square – it was the biggest square of the city at its establishment and it remains the largest today'. Later on she said 'comedies and tragedies were performed at the theatre at Khersones then and they are performed there today'. Likewise emphasis was placed upon Russian nationhood; the same tour guide, when referring to the Bolsheviks' destruction of Vladimir Cathedral asserted, 'they did not realize they were meant to serve the fatherland [*otechestvo*] and not just the Soviet regime'. This device of continuity is a common narrative strategy of post-Soviet texts when faced with a strong degree of historical diversity (Zajda and Zajda 2003: 379). A recurring motif in conveying the continuity of self (whether Sevastopolian, Russian or both) was the image of 'enemies of Sevastopol' as an ahistorical constant.

The tour guides did not shy away from presenting (some of) the changes the city had gone through; all four professional city tour guides commented on the removal, replacement (by a bronze statue of Lenin) and restoration of the Nakhimov monument and also significant street name changes, most prominently Balaklava Street – Catherine Street – Lenin Street. However given that the bronze statue of Lenin now stands upon the central mound, I suggest that the different facets of the city's history that are commemorated in the built environment are performatively celebrated here in a way that emphasizes historical continuity over time. This serves to play down periods of rupture in the city's history as well as any sense of internal competition that would be augmented by the removal of seemingly incongruous monuments. I would likewise associate the recollection of Lenin Street as formerly 'Catherine Street' more with justifying the rehabilitation of Catherine II's image in Sevastopol in recent years (as took place similarly in Russia). A monument to Catherine II as 'founder' of the city of Sevastopol was erected on Lenin Street in June 2008; this was vociferously protested by local Ukrainians and Crimean Tatars who objected to Russia's attempts to establish her 'meta-territory' in Ukraine.[21]

There was generally a good exposition of the city's multi-ethnic past as the tour guides pointed out the Muslim, Jewish and Karaim graveyards, but this had the effect of positing such minorities as a remnant of history. Although there was scant reference to the Muslim inhabitants of the city, a distinct 'othering' was noticeable in Nina's remark – 'there is the mosque; I would like to visit it but, as a woman, I'm not allowed to'.

While it would arguably be possible to construe the reinsertion of history where no material traces of it are left as evidence of cosmopolitanism in cultural memory, in actual fact the majority of these cases during the tours serve to reinforce narratives of the 'city of Russian military glory'. An especially visually striking instance of this was when the tour guide would pointedly ignore or subvert symbols of memory in the city. In one episode, our tour minibus drove through the Gagarin region – an important administrative centre of the city, where there were a great many Ukrainian flags on display for Ukrainian Independence Day. Despite driving past a vast wave of yellow and blue, Svetlana offered the sole comment 'This is the Gagarin region. This is where cinema "Rossiia"[22] is located', which I interpreted as a clear discursive challenge to the memory project of displaying Ukrainian flags in the city.[23]

Local Sevastopolian Memory

The tour data reveal a very strong sense of local pride with the frequent use of referents such as 'our city' and 'our pride' and with reverent tributes to local heroes. Comparison of tour texts shows recurring motifs of Sevastopol and Sevastopolians as 'brave and steadfast', with the use of explicit military imagery in this characterization. Current-day performative memory also featured, as the tour guides cited Victory Day and Navy Day as 'our main and most beautiful holidays'. They similarly invoked the intergenerational transmission of memory by talking about how senior class pupils guard the eternal flame. Expressions such as 'our young people today know that …' are rhetorical devices that aim to establish a very strong sense of local identity, underpinned and sustained by the historical memory of the city.

Much of the pride of local cultural memory is associated with a sense of uniqueness. First, Sevastopol Bay is described as geographically unique[24] and according to Yurii is 'the second most convenient bay in the world with twenty-six inlets for hiding things'. Secondly, the city's architecture is considered unique due to the distinctive Inkerman white stone used in its construction, not to mention the incredible feat of reconstruction in the space of ten years after the war. When referring to the design of buildings, the theme of 'both Russian and unique' was apparent. Valerii pointed out that the church in the fraternal graveyard on the city's northern shore was 'Orthodox but very unusual … the only pyramid-shaped Orthodox church in the world'. Likewise Svetlana emphasized the fact that Vladimir Cathedral has stained glass windows, which is unusual for Orthodox design.

Thirdly, the uniqueness of the city is focused around the life of the fleet – the reason for the city's foundation and a unique part of Russian imperial history. Ivan highlighted the fact that Sevastopol is not only an historical site but also an 'operational military city'; within such a formulation, the current presence of the fleets in Sevastopol is seen to provide not only continuity with naval legacy but also animation of it. The naval identity of Sevastopol undoubtedly links in with the common notion of Sevastopolians as a militarized society in the face of threat; Svetlana invoked the fear of pirates coming into the Black Sea and Nina cited the presence of two navies as a reason to 'sleep soundly at night-time'. Notably, all tour guides referred to the Russian Orthodox Church's canonization of Admiral Ushakov as patron saint of the Russian Navy in 2000, which emphasizes Sevastopol's continued belonging to Russian spiritual as well as cultural space.

As well as invoking 'we' and 'our' to emphasize a shared past, the tour guides were also keen to present the everyday life of Sevastopolians by, for example, pointing out the suburbs and dormitory districts. Nina made sure we knew where the central market was located and encouraged us to 'go and see what we buy and sell, see what kind of bread we eat, see how we live'. Regarding the issue of local pride, it is necessary to add that informal tour guides proved more likely to be open about shortcomings of the city, which the conventional tourism culture of Sevastopol is unlikely to address. Alena spoke frankly about 'architectural mistakes' and problems of reconstruction; she also spoke with a degree of irony about the 'changing priorities' of the present in noting that the former ticket office of the Lunacharskii Theatre is now a currency exchange point.

Sevastopolian Memory in Wider Narratives of Ukrainian, European and Global Integration

The walking memory data suggest that Sevastopol resists characterization as a Ukrainian city. Very little reference is made to Ukrainian administration, except possibly by phrases such as 'our politicians'. In one such instance, Valerii told a story about two new buildings in Artillery Bay. He recounted, 'Yushchenko started to build them but he did so without permission, so construction ceased. Recently it started up again so we all understood that Yanukovych had bought them and was finishing it [*laughs*]'. A similar 'poking fun' at political elites was evident in Ivan's story about the Konstantin Battery which is painted white only on the inside of the bay – 'the last time they painted it white was to hoodwink a certain president who shall remain nameless [*smiles knowingly*]'.

The issue of Ukrainian status also surfaces when discussing the division of the Black Sea Fleet in 1997. Svetlana said 20 per cent of the fleet went to Ukraine, Yurii said it was 13 per cent and Nina pronounced the slightly more innocuous 'we now have two fleets and sleep soundly at night-time'.[25] The more generalized belittling of Ukrainian statehood is conveyed by the widespread use of the term *na Ukraine* rather than *v Ukraine* (although informants maintain this is about adhering to the conventions of Russian language).[26] On this point of local particularity and resistance, Svetlana related that this part of the world resisted integration into the Greek Empire during the days of Julius Caesar. She joked, 'So I guess not much has changed since those days', and got good laughs from her Russian audience.

The presentation of the city leant strongly towards its links with Russia. In addition to the pervasive 'two defences' motif from Russian imperial and Soviet times, all the tour guides reached back to the history of Kievan Rus' in discussing the great significance of Khersones as the site where Prince Vladimir was baptized into Christianity (AD 988). They also discussed the works of Pushkin from his tour of Crimea in the 1820s and Tolstoy's *Sevastopol Sketches* (1855), appealing to the Russian literary canon as an authoritative account of Crimean history. The tour guides also foregrounded Sevastopol's title of 'Hero City', which was awarded in 1945; membership of this prestigious network continues to bring considerable accolades and material benefits. The tour guides also highlighted the present-day links between Sevastopol and Russia; for example, Svetlana reminded us that Dom Moskvy[27] was a gift from the mayor of Moscow.

Regarding globalization trends, reference was made to the cruise liners that moor in Sevastopol Bay for a few days at a time; this draws attention to the city as an international tourist destination. Likewise Alena stressed that 'dancers from all over Ukraine come to dance in the Lunacharskii Theatre, they have the international *Zolotaia Ryba* festival there', which elevated Sevastopol as a world player on the cultural stage. When passing through Lazarev Square, Margarita pointed out on her tour that 'this used to be the trading centre of the city and still is, look we have a McDonald's now' which recognizes the local manifestation (and first on the Crimean peninsula) of the 'McDonaldization of society' (Ritzer 1993).

Perhaps the clearest indication of the global integration narrative was the observation by all the tour guides that Khersones was then close to being confirmed on UNESCO's list of world heritage sites. Locals view this as worthy recognition of the importance of this site and also as a mechanism for investing money into the site and the local economy. However, the negative side of globalization was also expressed in relation to the Khersones site specifically; Svetlana complained, 'Who is excavating here now? The Poles! The French! The Americans! They're making money from our land and we are little fools.' She objects to what she perceives to be the appropriation and commercialization of Sevastopol's heritage sites by international groups and away from the local population.

Conclusions

The walking memory methodology was designed to gain insight into local Sevastopolians' experience of urban space with regard to memory and their presentation of the city's past to tourists and outsiders. This mobile methodology aimed to capture a more dynamic and nuanced account of the relationship between urban space and memory than other more conventional methodologies such as discourse analysis of guidebooks, interviewing and media sources. In the case of Sevastopol, the research design could not be implemented exactly as planned due to structural restrictions (low variation between tours, no variation by language, low response from non-specialist informants) and had to be adapted to the local context. However the discovery of these structural restrictions shed light on the specificities of local memory culture and current-day memory practice.[28] By focusing ultimately on one subset of Sevastopolians – namely local professional tour guides – this study explored the city's distinctive, strong tradition of patriotic educational excursions. Substantial elements of this tradition have been preserved, on a smaller scale, up to the present day. The mechanisms of Soviet tourism culture, which had been developed as an authoritative vehicle for memory, and patriotic memory in particular, are continuing to operate (albeit with certain adaptations) amidst and in response to current post-Soviet identity projects.

First, its practitioners have a renewed impetus to pass on the 'truth' of history at a time when the past is being reconfigured on the national level in the context of independent Ukraine. Secondly, the tour guides are using practices of sightseeing and *excursion* tourism for maintenance of the city mythology and patriotic Russian subjects in the context of a lost empire. In this regard the excursion industry is also meeting the demand for heritage tourism from some Russians in Ukraine and the Russian Federation who make of Sevastopol a pilgrimage site. In both of these projects, the city's historic mythology lends the tour guides a militarized language for understanding and engaging in both defensiveness and brave steadfastness in the face of change.

Notes

1. Chairman of the Sevastopol City State Administration.
2. For example, see President Putin's Crimean Speech from 18 March 2014 ('Obrashchenie Prezidenta RF Putina (polnaia versiia)' 2014).
3. This involved asking local informants for a city tour.
4. Ultimately, however, it was not possible to vary tours by language. Although the tour firms advertised tours in different languages, what they meant was that clients could pay for a personal interpreter to accompany them on Russian tours. Access to French and English tour groups was not possible.
5. In the 1980s, Sevastopol won on three occasions the All-Union contest for best provision of excursions. Oral communication with the former Director of the Bureau for Travel and Excursions, from 29 May 2012.
6. Oral communication with current Head of Department for the Training of Tour Guides, from 29 May 2012.
7. Sevastopol was formerly a 'closed city', entry to which was strictly by permit.
8. Oral communication with Sevastopol tour guide, from August 2011.
9. Oral communication with former Director of the Bureau for Travel and Excursions, from 29 May 2012.
10. Ibid.

11. Worth noting is the fact that tourists most often do not spend long stretches of time in Sevastopol due to the continuing lack of facilities and broader leisure activities. Tourists prefer to base themselves on the sunny southern coast and just take a day-trip to Sevastopol to 'fulfil their duty' (ibid.).
12. The term 'near abroad' (*blizhnee zarubezh'e*) emerged in the early 1990s to refer to those newly independent countries which had been in the Soviet bloc. It is used by Russian politicians who assert that this zone should be in Russia's sphere of influence as it defends its interests there.
13. Federal law passed on 24 May 1999 'On the State Policy of the Russian Federation with regard to Compatriots Abroad'.
14. Oral communication with the former Director of the Bureau for Travel and Excursions, from 29 May 2012.
15. Oral communication with the current Head of Department for the Training of Tour Guides, from 29 May 2012.
16. Oral communication with the Deputy Chairman of the Sevastopol Committee of Veterans of War, from September 2011.
17. On this issue of authoritativeness of tour guides, it is perhaps also significant that when asked to give an informal tour of Sevastopol, my contacts and informants were reluctant to give excursions around the city and talk about its history, since they considered themselves 'unqualified' and 'not experts'.
18. Admiral Fyodor Ushakov (1745–1817) oversaw the construction of the naval base at Sevastopol. Ushakov was canonized as patron saint of the Russian Navy by the Russian Orthodox Church in 2000.
19. Sailor of the Black Sea Fleet and posthumously declared Hero of the Soviet Union, Ivan Golubets (1916–1942) died whilst bravely throwing bombs off a burning vessel to prevent a chain reaction of explosions, which would have killed many more men and ships.
20. All names have been changed.
21. Oral communication with protest leader, from 9 September 2011.
22. Russian for 'Russia'.
23. Flags are a sensitive issue in Sevastopol and a certain 'one-upmanship' is noticeable between pro-Russian and pro-Ukrainian symbols. Flags assert not just sovereignty and right, but engage in the memory project regarding which languages were historically spoken there and what 'nation' historically lived there. At the time of this fieldwork in summer 2011 there was a greater proportion of Ukrainian flags (both belonging to state institutions and private individuals) which would have required comment regarding the recent national holiday; silence displays an unwillingness to engage with perceived 'Ukrainization' and comments highlighting the Russianness of the city can be seen as resistant to such characterization.
24. Sevastopol Bay extends more than 7.5 km from the open sea in towards the Inkerman Monastery. In total there are more than thirty separate bays along Sevastopol's coast, which are all convenient, protected and non-freezing.
25. Following an equal division of the fleet, Russia bought out the majority of Ukraine's share so that Russia owns 81.7 per cent and Ukraine owns 18.3 per cent. See Sherr 1997: 48.
26. *Na Ukraine* is roughly equivalent to 'the Ukraine' in English, whereas *v Ukraine* is equivalent to 'Ukraine'. The former carries the connotation of a region, whereas the latter implies a sovereign state.
27. The Moscow Cultural Business Centre, *Dom Moskvy* is a subdivision of the Moscow city government based in Sevastopol. *Dom Moskvy* was opened in 2007 to facilitate

cooperation between Moscow's executive organs as well as organizations and enterprises, with a range of partners in Sevastopol. Its activities encompass the spheres of economics, science and technology, sports, culture and the arts.

28. However these data are insufficient on their own to fully convey the city's cultural memory, as they represent only the dominant narratives of the city as a 'city of Russian military glory' whilst accessing less effectively the minority voices and forces of resistance to the dominant myth-making.

Judy Brown completed her PhD in the Department of Slavonic Studies at the University of Cambridge, where she was part of the collaborative research project Memory at War (Principal Investigator: Prof. Alexander Etkind). Her doctoral dissertation is entitled 'Cultural Memory in Crimea: History, Memory and Place in Sevastopol'.

PART IV
Foci of Memories in Eastern Europe

Chapter 12

THE SECOND WORLD WAR IN THE MEMORY OF CONTEMPORARY POLISH SOCIETY

Piotr Tadeusz Kwiatkowski

The Second World War has been one of the central themes of public debates about the past in Poland since the collapse of communism. Political transformation and the cultural metamorphoses taking place in recent decades have been setting the boundaries of this discourse. The first of the developments in the field of culture, referred to as a 'memory boom' (Beiner 2008: 107–112; Berliner 2005: 197–211; Nora 2002b), is the growth – observed in countries in Europe and North America – of interest in history combined with the conviction that discussion about past experiences bears a practical significance, and is important for the functioning of today's societies. A second cultural phenomenon is the change in assessment of violence in social and political relationships (Korzeniewski 2006: 112–146; Olick 2007: 121–138). Conquest, the effective use of force with the goal of destroying or subjugating other societies, was for centuries considered praiseworthy, whilst being a victim was (particularly in the United States and Western Europe) perceived as a cause for shame and a reason for remaining silent about humiliations (Connerton 2008: 67–69). During the last decades of the twentieth century this way of thinking changed fundamentally, with innocent victims becoming positive heroes, and those using violence deserving condemnation.

The first theme in Polish public discussions is tied to the question of assessment of the nation's wartime experience in altered political, social and cultural conditions. In this context the argument over the past becomes entwined with politics, since different leanings present rival visions of what happened in Poland and Europe during the past century (Dudek 2008: 194–198; Janowski 2008: 235–240). The left wing avoids discussion of the past, as its representatives are opposed to radically unfavourable appraisals of the Polish People's Republic (PRL), and talk of a need for positive thinking about the past. When right-wing groups take power, the media, the scenarios for official commemoration ceremonies, and official educational projects highlight the activities of the Polish government in exile, operations by the Western Allies, actions of the Polish Armed Forces in the West, the Home Army and anticommunist groupings, as well as the crimes of communism, the main symbol for which has become Katyn. The process of the Red Army taking control of Polish territory in the years 1944–1945, called the 'liberation' during the PRL years, has since 1989 frequently been described as 'Soviet occupation', while the battles fought by the Polish Armed Forces in the East and the activities of left-wing groups are rarely mentioned in public discourse.

In the context of discussion about the nation's wartime experience, the Holocaust became an important theme in Poland as well as in other countries of the region (Steinlauf 2001: 143–162). The most controversial question in this current of public debate is an issue not dealt with in public during the years of communism, namely the issue of Polish society's joint responsibility for what happened on Polish territory during the war. Tough questions were posed publicly in the late 1980s (Błoński 2008 [1987]), while discussion regarding a book by Tomasz Gross published in the year 2000, entitled *Neighbors: The Destruction of the Jewish Community in Jedwabne, Poland*, about the murder of the Jewish population of Jedwabne by a group of the town's Polish inhabitants, spread to embrace the entire sphere of Polish-Jewish relations (Czyżewski 2008: 117–120; Jedlicki 2008: 39–42; Orla-Bukowska 2006: 196–199).

Another current is the debate linked to the processes of European integration (Wolff- Powęska 2005) and Poland's inclusion in international organizations. The past two decades have witnessed multifarious Polish-German disputes (Schmidtke 2005: 78–85), although in recent years the attention of the Polish media has been focused on the forced expulsion of Germans as a result of the Second World War. At the same time discussions have been underway regarding Poles' relations with the Russians and Ukrainians (Nijakowski 2006: 287–341; Zaszkilniak 2008: 33–34). Although calls for the need for reconciliation can be heard in official declarations from all sides, these discussions are very difficult and are proceeding in an atmosphere of tension, of reluctance to revise established patterns of interpretation, and a tendency to burden the other side with the entire responsibility for past decisions and actions.

The various themes in discussions taking place in Poland after the fall of communism and regarding international relations have two features in common: firstly, they aim towards a revision of established narratives regarding the Second World War that has been accepted for decades.

And secondly, such discussions are often practical in nature and apply to issues involving material compensation. A new interpretation of past events sometimes constitutes justification for claims in which somebody demands symbolic acts or concrete material goods as compensation for wrongs experienced in the past by themselves or their ancestors (Korzeniewski 2006: 99–111; Żakowski 2002: 33ff.).

The question arises as to what degree this public discourse about the war, actively involving society's intellectuals and opinion-forming circles, influences the vernacular collective memory: what is thought about the war, and how it is reacted to by people not dealing professionally with the past, its exploration, its analysis and evaluation or its artistic re-enactment. In past decades this issue has repeatedly been a subject of interest for researchers. References to the Second World War can be found in the findings of research studies aimed at achieving an overall diagnosis of collective memory in Polish society (Żukowski 1997: 65–76; Szacka 2006: 147–186; Kwiatkowski 2008: 220–308). Secondly, sociology papers were written that were dedicated to a multifaceted, in-depth analysis of the vernacular memory of selected events or developments related to the Second World War, for example the Holocaust (Engelking-Boni 1994; Kaźmierska 2008: 95–209), Auschwitz (Kucia 2005: 287–312), the land known as the *Kresy* (Borderlands), territory belonging to Poland up until 1939 (Kaźmierska 1999: 28–132), or the processes of determining social perceptions of the death camps (Wóycicka 2009: 13–31) and the status of war veterans (Wawrzyniak 2009: 19–48). A third current embraces public opinion surveys, usually regarding selected issues that are of importance to public debate and frequently controversial. Such surveys were conducted on the anniversaries of the outbreak of war (CBOS 2009; TNS 2009) and its end (CBOS 2005; TNS 2000), and in relation to important public discussions regarding the crimes in Katyn (CBOS 1988, 2008a), Jedwabne (CBOS 2001a, b; TNS 2000, 2002) and Volhynia (CBOS 2003; 2008b; TNS 2003), as well as relations with other nations (CBOS 2004; TNS 2006).

Thus numerous academic papers and research reports have emerged in recent years, significantly enriching knowledge on selected aspects of vernacular memory of the Second World War. Comprehensive and multifaceted identification of contemporary Poles' memories of the war was the goal of a project carried out in summer 2009 on behalf of the Museum of the Second World War (Museum/Pentor 2009) embracing qualitative research conducted using the focus group interview method and quantitative research (a survey), conducted using personal interviews among a nationwide representative sample of adult residents of Poland. In this chapter I discuss selected findings from these studies, focusing on four topics: 1. the scope of interest in the Second World War in contemporary

Polish society; 2. the presence of wartime experiences in family accounts; 3. the war as a significant experience for national identity; and 4. the impact of events from the years 1939–1945 on the formation of national stereotypes and the perception of international relations in the region and in Europe.

Are Poles Interested in the Second World War?

Are the disputes regarding the Second World War between politicians and historians, publicized by the media, of any concern to Poland's ordinary inhabitants, preoccupied with their everyday work and paying the costs of political transformation? Survey results suggest that the answer is in the affirmative:

- 16 per cent of respondents claimed to be extremely or very interested in the history of the period in question,
- 36 per cent of respondents described their level of interest in the history of the Second World War as moderate,
- almost half the respondents (48 per cent) claimed to be relatively uninterested in the history of the Second World War: 32 per cent said they were not very interested, and 16 per cent of the respondents claimed not to be interested at all in the events of 1939–1945.

The level of interest in the history of the Second World War varies by respondent age and level of education. A high percentage of declarations of being extremely or very interested was noted among respondents with higher education (30 per cent) and older people, aged 70 or above (39 per cent) and aged 60–69 (21 per cent).

Verbal accounts continue to be very important in the shaping of memory regarding the Second World War, especially stories passed down by family members, more often from direct witnesses (33 per cent) than by people with no personal experiences from this period (22 per cent). People also have knowledge of events that took place in the years 1939 to 1945 from accounts given by witnesses not belonging to their families (27 per cent), while some respondents (22 per cent) interested in the war said they read published memoires. However, as in other countries in our cultural region, the development of vernacular knowledge of the Second World War is more and more the result of mass media communication: television (Anderson 2001: 20; Vos 2001: 138–140) as well as the press and radio (64 per cent). Respondents also frequently mentioned feature films (61 per cent), probably watched by many on television. Usage of the above sources within the past year (prior to the date of the survey) was declared by almost two thirds of the respondents interested (at least to a small degree) in the Second World War.

When searching for information about the Second World War, relatively frequent use is made of popular science publications (35 per cent), academic papers (26 per cent) and high literature (23 per cent). On the other hand, the internet plays a relatively small role in shaping memory. However, the importance of this information medium is set to increase steadily; although in the entire sample of respondents interested in the war the internet was given as a source of information by almost one in four, in the youngest group (up to 29 years old) the internet was an answer given by 45 per cent, and by 28 per cent of those aged from 30 to 39.

The War in Family Accounts

I have already referred above to the momentous significance of verbal accounts in shaping knowledge of the Second World War in Polish society. The research studies discussed here indicate that the intensity of informal family accounts was still high in 2009. The vast majority of respondents (86 per cent) possess at least elementary knowledge of the wartime fortunes of their families (17 per cent claimed to know a great deal; 31 per cent knew a moderate amount; and 38 per cent didn't know much). Almost half the respondents claimed to have talked to others about the wartime fortunes of their family. However, it has to be added here that the frequency of this spontaneous communicative memory (Assmann 2006: 1–30; 2008: 64–71) is distinctly dwindling:

- 19 per cent said they talk about the war quite often (a few times a year or more),
- 28 per cent talk about the events of 1939–1945 once a year or less,
- 28 per cent do not have such conversations now, but used to talk about the war in the past.

This means that with the passage of time, as well as with the dwindling of generations remembering the years 1939–1945, there are ever fewer direct family accounts about the war: 'There are going to be less and less people who remember it. Generations are growing up who will never have the opportunity to talk on this subject' (Museum/Pentor 2009: discussion group, respondents aged 26–45, Warsaw).

An important factor stimulating collective memory at a vernacular level is the presence in Poland of material wartime memorabilia in the everyday lives of millions of people. Some such objects bear the status of official mementos, and knowledge of them is disseminated via the education system and channels of social communication (Traba 2003: 193–197). Others carry no official status, yet are spontaneously treated by small, local communities (for example neighbours residing in a tenement building, the residents of a street or housing estate) as traces of war. Private souvenirs also constitute such memorabilia – with one in five Polish families on average keeping such items. These are most often photographs and documents, from government offices, the military and personal sources.

Over half those with knowledge of the wartime fates of family members (approximately 45 per cent of all respondents) had encountered accounts about their family members' participation in the struggle against the occupying forces, in regular army units and in resistance movements. 27 per cent of all the respondents' families have recollections of loved ones who died or went missing without trace during the war; the respondents most often mentioned death in battle in regular armies, or death during guerrilla warfare, as well as in German prisons and concentration camps. Stories of other losses and forms of persecution are also passed down in families. Those knowing of the wartime fortunes of their families often know about abuses committed by the Germans:

- one in three respondents had heard of a family member being deported 'for work' – taken for forced labour,
- one in five knew accounts of homes being destroyed by Germans during wartime activities, of the plunder of personal property, or of forced displacement involving the need to move to a different place of living,
- one in seven knew of family members being taken to a German concentration camp or being thrown out of their homes.

The Russians, in turn, appear to be the most common perpetrators of theft of personal property, the destruction of homes during wartime activities, forced resettlement and the removal of property ownership rights. This issue also reappeared in the group discussions:

> In 1945, when the Russians liberated us from the Germans, they burned down that church, because Gdańsk practically suffered very little during the war, and only once they'd liberated us did they burn and destroy. (46–65, Gdańsk)

> When those Russians drove them further towards Germany, then near the western border the Russians began running the village, they checked out the pigsty and took the little pigs, the piglets, mother cooked there, into the forest in a kind of steamer where they cooked, they took ... and another comes, shoes,

I'll give new shoes for father, just pour some vodka, and father ... they had somewhere some moonshine, he gave him a quarter [250 ml bottle] of moonshine and he gave those shoes and went in his socks to the forest, where those piglets were. (46–60, Białystok)

The studies of family accounts also reveal two dimensions of wartime experience poorly highlighted in public discourse. The first issue is the role of women: at a time when many men were fighting, women carried the burdens of everyday life, of looking after the family, finding food and avoiding the dangers of victimization by the occupying forces or warfare.

Granny told it as a kind of experience. During the war, in Warsaw. She ... went to him [a German officer] and explained the problem to him, and it turned out that he was able to do something, and he saved granddad. (18–25, Warsaw)

The other matter is the regional differentiation in wartime experiences (Kochanowski 2010: 61–63) and the question as to what degree these local experiences affect to this day the formation of regional identities. The recollection of terror and resistance against the occupying forces has an important place in the accounts of those who lived through the war in the territory of the General Government (Central Poland). There are tales of arrests and martyrdom in concentration camps, of village pacification, and of displacement and round-ups in cities. Much space is taken up with stories of everyday life, of problems with supplies and food shortages. At the same time, recollections of resistance have survived in many families – of the activities of guerrilla units, of clandestine teaching and about the Warsaw Uprising:

My parents are from Warsaw ... I mean, my father, before the uprising, then he was rounded up as they say, and was taken to let's call it Eastern Germany, to work. My mother lived through the entire uprising. (46–65, Warsaw)

The Soviet occupation occupies a prominent position in the tales of those living in the Eastern lands of Poland (mostly belonging today to Ukraine, Belarus and Lithuania): the imposition of their communist system, intensive propaganda campaigns, resettling and arrests. There are also tragic recollections of tension between nations – and in particular the ruthlessness and cruelty of the Polish-Ukrainian conflict; one in ten of those knowing their family history had heard of wrongdoings experienced by their family members, inflicted by Ukrainians:

I'll tell you, such huge translocation took place during the war, because when the Germans entered and handed power over to the Russians the Poles began running away en masse, and really large numbers of Belarusians began arriving here, besides, when the Russians ran the place Białystok was adjoined to the Belarusian republic. (46–65, Białystok)

The first thing is they didn't just fight the Germans, they also fought members of the Ukrainian Insurgent Army [UPA] in this area. So it wasn't just a German front, but ... armed by the Germans: the first Ukrainian militia and UPA units. (26–45, Przemyśl)

Those who lived through the war in territory incorporated into the Third Reich (Western and Northern Poland) passed down stories of terror to their children and grandchildren, including of the total elimination of Polish institutions, the prohibition on usage of the Polish language, abductions for forced labour, but also about the relative stability of everyday life. The price for this stability was the need to declare German nationality and undergo compulsory service in the German army, and after the war, the status of enemy territory conquered and plundered by the Red Army:

That was the Reich. And those born here in Silesia, from their grandfather's grandfather, were treated like Germans ... at eighteen into the army. When the Russians entered, all those forced into the army, the Wermacht, were arrested and transported out. (46–65, Katowice)

Granny was really reluctant to talk about it ... that women's psychosis about the approaching Red Army proved paralysing. That it would be a cataclysm ... that always made an incredible impression on me. (46–65, Gdańsk)

In qualitative research conducted in 2003, in answer to a question about what aspects of the past are the subject of taboo, only a few people mentioned family secrets related to their private lives (Kwiatkowski 2008: 211–217). The majority of answers were about the silence regarding the participation by acquaintances and family members in historical events. That inclined us to ask respondents in 2009 about whether they personally had met people who had experienced a lot during the war but who didn't want to talk about it. Almost one in five respondents knew such people, and trauma was most often considered the reason for their silence about their wartime experiences. Other reasons given much less often were: modesty – these people not liking to talk about themselves; fear of persecution by the authorities; nobody willing to listen to their stories; and finally – because of having done something which today would be considered shameful. The main place trauma occupies as a reason for silence, and in consequence oblivion, commands one to notice its therapeutic role. Oblivion is essential for the abating of emotions – of pain, the hatred towards those causing it and the accompanying desire for revenge and retaliation.

Signs of Identity

The Second World War understood as a nationwide experience leads to today's Poles contemplating this period in various ways. On the one hand, it evokes three kinds of association:

- the traumatic experiences of ordinary people (15 per cent),
- genocide and martyrdom (15 per cent), concentration camps (11 per cent) and the extermination of the Jews (7 per cent),
- and also warfare (15 per cent), the Warsaw Uprising (10 per cent), and the heroism and bravery of Poles (8 per cent).

On the other hand, memory of the war is important for contemporary national identification. A great deal has been written on collective identity and the role played in its formation by the awareness of possessing a common past (Zawadzki 2003: 9–10; Bokszański 2005: 54–99). However, it is rarely noticed that the processes of creating collective identity are frequently accompanied by oblivion (Connerton 2008: 62), since the feeling of 'we', differing from all 'others', sets in motion the mechanisms of biased perception of 'one's own' as described by psychologists. What remains in the memory is what was good, while negative people and behaviours either fall into oblivion or become neutralized. The causes behind negative developments are sought in conditioning resulting from external situations, while what is positive is seen to have derived from the noble character of members of the community (Baumeister and Hastings 1997: 283–291). Manifestations of such mechanisms were visible in the findings of previous research into vernacular collective memory (Szacka 1983: 73–83; Szacka and Sawisz 1990: 18–38; Kwiatkowski 2008: 231–237). Results from a survey conducted in 2009 indicate that perception of Poles' behaviour during the war is also currently dominated by positive stereotypes. Respondents realize that those living in times of war strived above all to survive, and frequently traded on the black market, while at the same time they attribute them relatively often with behaviour assessed positively today: involvement in the fight against the occupying forces, the condemnation of collaboration, mutual solidarity and helping the Jews. On the other hand, collaboration, informing on others to the occupying forces, indifference towards the Holocaust and the denunciation of Jews, are considered to have been rare. Research results also show that:

- most respondents know of people (70 per cent) and events (73 per cent) from the time of war which they can feel proud of,

- significantly fewer respondents know of people (27 per cent) and events (17 per cent) which are cause for shame.

The canon of wartime heroes seems rather weakly established, with the respondents' answers being widely dispersed. Characters linked to the communist movement, promoted during the years of the Polish People's Republic, are absent or criticized today by respondents. On the other hand, characters cited spontaneously as symbols of positive values important to national identity are:

- Władysław Sikorski (22 per cent), General, Prime Minister of the Polish Government in Exile in London,
- Władysław Anders (15 per cent), General, commander of Polish Army units fighting with the Allied forces,
- Maksymilian Kolbe (7 per cent), a monk who gave his life for that of another prisoner at Auschwitz,
- Irena Sendlerowa (5 per cent), involved in saving Jewish children during the Second World War, Righteous among the Nations.

One may suppose that these characters have become symbols for four important collective experiences: the continuity of the Polish state, perseverance and success in armed struggle, martyrdom and active opposition to the Holocaust.

However, there is a distinct canon of events treated as reasons to be proud. The top places here are occupied by: the Warsaw Uprising of 1944 (34 per cent); the battles of September 1939 (31 per cent); the fighting by soldiers of the Polish Armed Forces as part of the Allied forces fighting in the West (16 per cent); and the activities of resistance movements (12 per cent). At the same time all wartime activities highlighted during the years of communism and used to legitimize this period, such as the battles of the Polish Army fighting together with the Red Army and their march on Berlin, as well as left-wing resistance activities, have passed into oblivion.

Research from 2009 confirms that Poles' attitude towards the balance of the Second World War is highly complex. Almost two thirds of the respondents recognized Poland as a victor of the Second World War, as follows:

- 31 per cent of respondents acknowledged Poland's unconditional victory,
- the same percentage of respondents felt that although the Poles emerged victorious from the Second World War, this was not a complete victory,
- 23 per cent of the respondents considered it difficult to recognize Poland as a victor in the conflict of 1939–1945,
- the remainder (15 per cent) held no opinion.

The year 1945 as a place of memory causes dispute in many countries (Troebst 2009: 4–8). If Poles position their country among the victors, this is above all because Poland belonged to the winning coalition (14 per cent) and regained its independence (9 per cent). In addition, respondents emphasized Poland's significant contribution to the victory in their arguments (5 per cent), as well as the perseverance of Poland's soldiers in the fighting (also 5 per cent) and their heroism (4 per cent).

A sense of defeat was linked mainly (according to 14 per cent of respondents) to the fact that after 1945 Poland did not regain its independence, but became dependent on the Soviet Union, as well as due to the introduction of the communist system (3 per cent). Attention was also frequently drawn to the significant material damages and loss of Poland's Eastern territories, which after the war were incorporated into the Soviet Union (12 per cent).

The second element in respondents' pessimistic assessment of the war was the conviction that Poland had no influence on the course of events, as the war was a clash between two totalitarian systems and the world's superpowers determined its outcome:

> We had no influence, that's what I think, that we were like puppets for that Russian delegation. Despite the fact that the Polish forces fought alongside the Russians, but the way we were treated by the Allies was just as bad. They abandoned us to our fate, and simply didn't consider us important. (46–60, Katowice)

However, opinions are split with regard to this issue. Some group discussion participants were of the opinion that Poland, thanks to its active stance, played an active role in historical events of the years 1939 to 1945:

> Poles are known for that mentality, they have that kind of determined character, that they don't give up ... a dozen or so Poles can fight against, I don't know, several dozen ... we fight to the last drop of blood. (26–45, Warsaw)

The findings of surveys conducted on a representative sample of the adult population even point to a certain tendency in contemporary society towards national megalomania: almost two thirds of the respondents ascribed Poland with having made a similar contribution to the course of events as that of France, Great Britain or the USA.

Memory of War and Poland's International Relations

The responsibility for the outbreak of the Second World War is placed above all with Germany. Almost 9 out of 10 respondents recognized this country as bearing the decisive responsibility for the outbreak of war, whilst 8 per cent considered the country's responsibility significant. The respondents also frequently felt that the Soviet Union was to blame for the conflict, although in this case the percentage of answers 'to a decisive degree' was 43 per cent, while 36 per cent answered 'to a significant degree'. It was also relatively common for respondents to place responsibility – to a decisive or significant degree – with the other signatories to the Tripartite Pact (Italy – 40 per cent, Japan – 36 per cent) and the Allies, including in particular Great Britain (28 per cent) and France (24 per cent) – powerful countries whose leaders (in the opinions of contemporary Poles) were too passive and submissive towards Germany, and thereby failed to prevent the outbreak of armed conflict.

Poles and Jews occupy the main places in the memory of the suffering and victims of the Second World War: the level of suffering of both peoples was described by the vast majority of respondents as very high or high (93 per cent – Poles; 92 per cent – Jews). Despite the Third Reich and the Soviet Union being held responsible for the outbreak of the conflict, the Poles of today often also perceive the citizens of these countries as victims of wartime suffering:

- according to 70 per cent of respondents, the scale of suffering (and victims) among the Russians was very high or high,
- 64 per cent of respondents thought this about the Germans.

When talking about their perception of the victims of the Second World War, the participants in the group discussions separated evil political systems and ideologies from the fates and behaviours of ordinary people, bearing the consequences of political decisions at no fault of their own. This was particularly evident in comments regarding the citizens of the Soviet Union:

> The Poles, Jews, Russians ... because it would be hard to mention the Germans, they started it, so nobody would dare to stand up for them. (46–65, Białystok)

> Where suffering among the Germans is concerned, that it's a shame above all about the civilians who died mainly during the bombardments. Sometimes the Americans and Brits went too far with that. (26–45, Katowice)

> But you have to remember that the Russian people suffered no less than the other nations of Eastern Europe, and maybe even more. (26–45, Warsaw)

At the same time it is quite rare for Poles to admit that the level of suffering could also have been high (or very high) for the Ukrainian people

(39 per cent). This may be due to memory of the brutal ethnic cleansing carried out from February 1943 to February 1944 by Ukrainian nationalists among the Polish population living in territory which, up until 1939, belonged to the Polish state. A certain role was also played by policy regarding history in the period of the Polish People's Republic, representing the suffering borne by the population of the Soviet Union; as a rule the citizens of the USSR tended to be talked about in general, omitting any mention of them belonging to specific nations.

Past experiences affect how Poles think about the contemporary world, because a frequent opinion is that events from the war period are detrimental to Poles' current relations with other nations, above all with Germany (64 per cent) and Russia (59 per cent). Opinions that the legacy of the Second World War also harms Poland's relations with Ukrainians were also voiced relatively often (34 per cent). On the other hand, the legacy of war was relatively rarely felt to have a positive impact on relations with other nations. A positive impact was perceived most often in contacts with representatives of Poland's Western Allies (the UK, France and the United States). The issue of the war's impact on current relations with the Jewish people is distinctly controversial:

- 28 per cent of the respondents expressed the view that the Second World War had a positive impact on today's relations with Jews,
- 14 per cent of the respondents were of the opposite opinion.

Such a result seems to be an effect of the simultaneous influence of two historical narratives. Of the first, decidedly prevalent and cemented over the decades, presenting the Polish people as one of few (or the only one) to help victims of the Holocaust showing absolute sacrifice while risking reprisals for themselves, and of the second – expanding since 1989 – in which the question is posed regarding Polish responsibility for the extermination of the Jews. Such controversy also came to light during the group discussions. Wartime recollections functioning at a vernacular memory level, especially among those living in Central and Eastern Poland, include vivid themes of the extermination of the Jews and diverse attitudes shown by Poles: some respondents had come across accounts of the Jews' situation being taken advantage of, of them being robbed, blackmailed and handed over to the occupying forces. At the same time there are stories in the respondents' accounts of help being given to the persecuted. Some discussions also saw the emergence of stereotypes in regard to citizens of Jewish descent as wealthy businessmen taking advantage of Poles, or as champions of communism, inclined to support Soviet authority.

Awareness of the diversity of behaviours and attitudes among representatives of the different nations during the war often coexisted with a certain distance towards national narratives emerging during the group discussions. The war, as recounted in family circles by participants and witnesses (still telling their accounts), was a gauge of one's humanity and character, and split people into good and evil. In extreme conditions it frequently turned out that those representing 'ours' behaved with indifference or even ruthlessly, while 'foreigners' displayed kindness and a desire to help. During the research, we recorded recollections of plunder by kinsmen, or acts of barbarism by soldiers of the allied Soviet Army, yet simultaneously the respondents told of stories heard about 'good Germans', about soldiers helping Polish civilians, or 'Bauers' [Germans] treating forced labourers with respect:

> I think you have good and bad people in every nation. And even in World War Two, some did not agree with Hitler's policies, and there were those who dropped out during the war itself and before it. (18–25, Warsaw)

Conclusion

The project carried out in 2009 is an example of empirical sociological research studies into collective memory conducted in Poland for decades but rarely executed in other countries. As such, we cannot compare the findings with results obtained in other countries in Europe. In addition, it would be difficult to talk about comparison over time; studies from the 1970s, though still interesting in certain respects, were carried out under political censorship. This allowed for the investigation of the 'consequences of Nazism' (Pawełczynska 1977: 5) while prohibiting the addressing of such themes as the Polish-Ukrainian conflict or wartime experiences involving Soviet totalitarianism. Bearing in mind this inability to make comparisons, it is still worth ultimately drawing a few conclusions. Firstly, the Second World War – despite having reached an end almost seventy years ago – continues to remain an important point of reference and subject of discussion for the societies involved in it, both in public debate and vernacular memory. This spontaneous communicative memory is distinctly weakening as the number of people who lived through the war dwindles, while knowledge of the period functions to an ever greater degree thanks to the mass media, and in the future the internet will gain in importance.

Secondly, collective memory preserves and passes on to successive generations a recollection of war as a time of unique, unprecedented suffering, but also frequently of heroism, often evoking a stronger emotional reaction than events closer to those living today. In Poland (and most probably also in other postcommunist countries) vernacular memory of the war acquired its current form largely after 1989, while the influences of a few decades of communist propaganda are almost invisible. The picture emerging from the research is one of a society proud of its wartime fortunes and achievements, including attitudes shown by civilians, particularly women – probably largely in keeping with historical reality. However, it also shows a society in which (as elsewhere in Europe) there is substantial resistance to the acceptance of information on painful and shameful facts.

Thirdly, Poles' complex and frequently bitter attitudes towards the overall balance of the war, plus their past experiences, influence how Poles think of the contemporary world. According to the respondents, wartime events are detrimental to Poles' current relations with other nations, above all with the Germans, Russians and Ukrainians. The issue of the war's impact on current relations with the Jewish people is highly controversial. Information passed down by witnesses in regard to people's behaviour during the war also frequently generates distance towards official national narratives. The war, as told in family circles by participants and witnesses, was a test of character, and in the extreme conditions of the period it was frequently the case that 'ours' behaved badly or with indifference, while 'foreigners' displayed kindness and a willingness to help.

Translated by Jonathan Weber

Piotr Tadeusz Kwiatkowski is managing director at TNS Polska and professor of Sociology at the Academy for Special Education (APS) in Warsaw. He is interested in collective memory research, public opinion research and social research methodology. Between 2002 and 2005 he participated in a research project at the Institute of Political Studies, Polish Academy of Sciences entitled 'Modern Polish Society and the Past', and in 2009 he led a research project 'World War II in the Memory of Present-day Polish Society' for the Museum of the Second World War. He is the author of *Pamięć zbiorowa społeczeństwa polskiego w okresie transformacji* (*Collective Memory of the Polish Society in the Period of Transformation*) (2008), and the co-author of *Między codziennością a wielką historią. II wojna światowa w pamięci zbiorowej społeczeństwa polskiego* (*Between the Everyday and Big History: The Second World War in the Collective Memory of Polish Society*) (2010).

Chapter 13

AUSCHWITZ AND KATYN IN POLITICAL BONDAGE
The Process of Shaping Memory in Communist Poland

Jacek Chrobaczyński and Piotr Trojański

West European and East European memories of the Second World War, including memories of the Nazi and Soviet occupations, as well as the postmemory of these events, represent two distinct perspectives, not just reflecting different historical experiences but also divergent paths of postwar processes of dealing with these events in social and public awareness. The end of the war provided an important context for these discrepancies. The year 1945 stands for the victory of the democratic world over totalitarianism and Nazi barbarity for the whole of Western Europe, including West Germany since the Weizsäcker speech in 1985, while for the east of the continent the end of the war meant the beginning of a new political and ideological dependence, which strongly exerted the memory of the societies living there. For decades, the Iron Curtain was a natural blockade that prevented the development of a common European memory. The asymmetry of memories has often been seen as disadvantageous for the East Europeans who do not see enough room and understanding in Europe for the particularities of their history – wartime and postwar. What is often presented as a conflict between the so-called Holocaust and Gulag memories (see the introduction to this volume by Pakier and Wawrzyniak) can be seen in a new light when viewed from a particular national perspective.

This chapter analyses and compares the trajectories of memory of two symbolic sites of crime committed by totalitarian regimes in twentieth-century Europe: the Polish public and social memories of Auschwitz, on the one hand, and of Katyn, on the other. Auschwitz is a global symbol of the German Nazi genocide of European Jewry. Katyn has recently become a transnational icon of Soviet war atrocities (Etkind et al. 2012). These two

---

Notes for this chapter begin on page 262.

memorial sites are still separated in European discourse on the Second World War, whereas in Poland they are directly interconnected as the most important war cemeteries, as well as mnemonic clues for grasping the nature of both Nazi and communist totalitarian systems.

In this chapter we are going to discuss the process of shaping the representations of Auschwitz and Katyn in communist Poland. Such a historical perspective also allows us to understand the state of memory of the Second World War in Poland today. The equation of the two totalitarian regimes is natural and obvious in East European countries, while often questioned in the western part of the continent, as the controversy following Sandra Kalniete's statement in 2004 showed. Also the recent popularity of Timothy Snyder's *Bloodlands* (2010) shows that juxtaposing Nazism and communism as the criminal regimes of twentieth-century European history is not that obvious either for historians or in public awareness, and may still be presented in terms of a novel historical interpretation.

By reflecting on the significance and symbolism of Auschwitz and Katyn in Polish social memories, and by analysing the process of formation of the postwar stories of both genocidal events, this chapter will attempt to shed a different light on the memory of these two dark chapters in European history, starting with the similarities of both criminal regimes, and following with instrumentalization of the memory of their victims from a national perspective, in particular that of postwar Poland.

Similarities and Differences, and the Symbolic Diversity

Auschwitz was a complex of German Nazi concentration camps and extermination camps. It was established in April 1940 in the area of the town of Oświęcim as a concentration camp for political prisoners – mainly the Poles. In the following years it was enlarged and became the main death camp for Jews from all over Europe. Today's estimations indicate that in Auschwitz between 1.1 and 1.5 million people perished, mainly Jews (960,000) (Piper 1992: 49). Other groups of victims included Poles, Sinti and Roma, as well as Soviet prisoners of war.

Katyn is one of the sites of mass murder of Polish army officers committed by the Soviets during the Second World War. Between the 3rd of April and the 12th of May 1940, by virtue of the decision of the highest authorities of the Soviet Union, 4,410 Polish officers, previously held in the prisoner of war camp in Kozielsk, were executed there. Today the name of this town, or rather the term 'Katyn crime' refers also to other sites of mass murder committed in 1940 in various parts of the Soviet Union, of over 21,500 Polish prisoners of war and political prisoners.

The victims of the Katyn massacre were officers of the Polish army (mainly reservists), policemen, soldiers of the Border Protection Corps, judges, prosecutors, political and social activists, aristocrats, landowners and factory owners. Contrary to the ethnic diversity of the victims of Auschwitz, they were mainly of Polish ethnicity and belonged to patriotic, social and intellectual elites, which, according to the plans of the Soviets, were to be destroyed in order to make the subordination of the occupied areas easier. It should be emphasized here that the German Nazis' plans were quite similar and at the same time they started eliminating Polish elites in the General Government. This strategy was being consistently carried out later, at KL Auschwitz (among other places), where in June 1940 the first transport of Polish prisoners arrived (from Tarnów). In total about 150,000 Polish political prisoners were deported to Auschwitz.

The convergence of goal, time and methods of the Soviets (Katyn operation) and the Germans (operation 'AB', establishing KL Auschwitz) pose a question of possible cooperation between NKVD and Gestapo (Materski 2000: 26–40). It is worth mentioning that according to some sources 'it was the exposure of the Katyn massacre by Nazi propaganda that made Himmler order mass cremation of the bodies in Auschwitz, Treblinka and other extermination sites' (Oświęcim 2009: 112–113). The German Nazis wanted to protect themselves against a similar exposure. Thus those events are interconnected not only at their origins but also at their tragic end.

Auschwitz and Katyn were therefore a function of both Nazism and communism, a function of politics and of the occupation practice of the Third Reich and the Soviet Union. The Nazis intended to eliminate a part of the Polish society; the Soviets above all to Sovietize it, but unyielding elements were to be eliminated as well. It is worth mentioning that in the case of the Third Reich it was racist factors, but in the case of the Soviet Union it was class factors that played a key practical role. Auschwitz and Katyn perfectly fitted those goals and were among the methods of achieving them (Chrobaczyński 1997: 133).[1]

Despite this kind of historical affinity, those places evoke different symbolisms. They differ not only in their meaning, but also in significance and in their range of influence. Auschwitz is known all over the world as a symbol of the worst evil that could possibly be done by men. The name of the camp itself became a specific cultural code, used for describing a collapse of culture, thought and interpersonal relations during the war. This occurred due to various factors, but above all the enormity of the crime committed in Auschwitz, ethnic diversity of the victims, size of the camp area and nature of the evidence of the crime that survived. The complicated history of the camp resulted in the variety of meanings that Auschwitz has for various nations and social groups, which – as Teresa Świebocka observes – 'depending on their paradigms, traditions and religions, each group has created its own Auschwitz, or its own metaphor of the camp and ways of commemorating it' (Białecka et al., 2010: 16; Kucia 2005: 229).

For Jews, who amounted to ninety per cent of its victims, Auschwitz has become a symbol of the Holocaust. For Poles it is a symbol of occupation, terror and the systematic extermination of the cultural, social and political elites of the nation, a symbol of resistance and slave labour. This place is of equal importance for the Sinti and Roma people, who just like the Jews (although on a smaller scale) were deported to the camp due to their ethnic origins. Auschwitz also has a symbolic meaning for other groups of victims, such as Soviet prisoners of war or Jehovah's Witnesses, who were deported there because of their beliefs.

In the case of Katyn there is no such symbolic diversity. Its symbolism is in principle of a local nature, virtually ethnically homogeneous, because it was initially the Poles who created its meanings. In the course of time, despite the fact that Katyn was not the site of the first, the only, nor of the biggest mass murder of Poles in the Soviet Union (e.g., in Kalinin over six thousand prisoners of war were murdered from the camp in Ostaszków), it became a symbol of martyrdom of the Polish nation in the East. Katyn is also a symbol of the political ruthlessness of the Soviets; an instrument of a long-lasting, dexterously organized and efficient political lie. Moreover, according to recent research Katyn gradually became the pivotal object of the public memory of Soviet crimes in the whole of Eastern Europe:

> Yet the 'cursed place' of Katyn and the 'terrible symbol' of Katyn are not congruent. The place is singular; the symbol is, in effect, plural, signifying a multitude of killing fields and burial sites. The majority of those killed in what has become known as 'Katyn' in fact perished in other places well beyond the Katyn forest in the Soviet Republics of Belarus, Russia, and Ukraine. The toponym associated with their murder, moreover, has become a referential touchstone and descriptive shorthand throughout Eastern Europe ... Today Katyn circulates with alacrity in public memory and in political discourse in Eastern Europe, fueling both solidarity and suspicion, fellowship and fear. (Etkind et al. 2012: 2)

The Beginnings of Forming Public Memory

The process of forming memory of both events began during the Second World War. The words 'Auschwitz' and 'Oświęcim' (the latter Polish name was then being used most commonly) often appeared in Polish underground press distributed in thousands of copies (Piper and Świebocka 2008: 239–245). They got into mass circulation, were transmitted by word of mouth as symbols of total danger. After round-ups, which were organized systematically in Warsaw and resulted in deportations to the camp, there was hardly anyone who did not share the news about their fellow inhabitants who got sent to Auschwitz. The news spread widely and confirmed the central place of the camp in both individual and collective memories. Hundreds of thousands of Poles knew at least one person who had been deported or who had lost his or her relatives there. It was of immense importance for forming an awareness of this place as the site of the martyrdom of the Polish nation (Kucia 2005: 232).

The case of Katyn was quite different. During the war it appeared in the collective consciousness only once – in 1943 – when the German army discovered the crime. Some bits of information had appeared before, but they were received with disbelief, so they did not carry much weight. There were many reasons why Polish society under the occupation had such a limited awareness of the Soviets' crime. Compared to Auschwitz, Katyn was a far more distant place, uncommon and sometimes even unbelievable, though equally painful and dramatic, particularly when being publicized by German propaganda. During the war Katyn was 'only' a scene of a war crime (mass execution), a particular moment in history.

Auschwitz was something more. It remained a concentration camp throughout the war period. It lasted, threatened and warned. It was an everyday present, tangible sign of mass genocide. The differences in attitude of Polish society to Auschwitz and Katyn were undoubtedly also a consequence of different attitudes towards the war enemies. Auschwitz and an image of a German Nazi have integrated all society in their right to hate and resist, whereas Katyn has polarized attitudes and divided society politically into those who believed in the guilt of the Germans (the communists) and those who doubted it (the anticommunists). Sometimes, quite contrary to the case of Auschwitz, it imposed – under the influence of external factors (e.g., Soviet propaganda) – silence. That is why Katyn caused a profound split in Polish society (which was not the case with Auschwitz and the German war criminals). Finally it became also a significant caesura in the political attitudes and choices of Poles, that has formed their consciousness for many years (Chrobaczyński 1997: 136; see also Chrobaczyński 2012).

From the very beginning the memory of the Katyn massacre was instrumentalized and became an instrument of untruth. It started with the concealing of the crime and ended with its distorting, manifested in deceitfully charging the Germans with it. As a result Katyn was used by the Soviets for breaking diplomatic relations with the Polish government in exile, accused of collaboration with the Germans to the detriment of the Soviet Union. In the face of the passivity of the Western Allies who feared the possible collapse of the anti-Nazi coalition, those actions proved to be diplomatically efficient and were among the many reasons that ultimately lead to the subordination of Poland to the Soviet Union at the end of war (Carlton 2000: 105). Before it happened though, the Nazi German authorities had also tried to play the Katyn card, suggesting that there were more bodies in the graves than they found in reality. This way they aimed at winning the favour of the Poles and turning them against the Soviets. This would paralyze the communists' actions in the hinterland and complicate the relations of the Polish government in exile with their Western Allies. Notwithstanding the intensity of their actions, the Nazi Germans did not manage to achieve their goals (Łysakowski 1990: 108–114).

Political Instrumentalization and Manipulation of Memory

After the war the ways of cultivating memory of Auschwitz and Katyn as well as of commemorating the victims were very different in both cases. The concealment and misrepresentation of the Katyn massacre by the communist authorities, at the same time as drawing attention to the Auschwitz crime, together with an instrumental treatment of its size resulted in the asymmetry of perception of those two events and consequently in a distortion of historical knowledge. Memory gaps and the lack of reliable historical knowledge about Auschwitz and Katyn have left their stamp for many years. The reinforcing myths led to the rivalry of memory, appreciation/depreciation of the victims, indifference and even exculpation of the murderers.

The Memory of Katyn

The 'Katyn lie' was a tacit part of the founding myth of the People's Republic of Poland (PRL), woven from the stories of Polish-Soviet friendship and the alleged patriotic intentions of the Polish communists. The disclosure of the truth about Katyn would destroy the political legitimacy of communist power in Poland and would pose the question of hidden motivations behind the 'liberation' of the country by the Red Army. That is why Polish communists followed Stalin in charging the Germans with murdering Polish officers in Katyn. They treated the Katyn crime instrumentally, suggesting that the Polish government in exile yielded to

German propaganda and became a voluntary and conscious instrument in Hitler's hands. Those claims by the Polish communists were 'based' on the outcomes of the investigation of the commission of Nikolay Burdenko established by the Soviets in January 1944, which concluded that it was the Germans who were responsible for the crime (Cienciala et al. 2007: 226–229; see also Lebiediewa 2008: 60–90). Polish communists publicizing Burdenko's report were trying to justify and evidence their own version of events. All this was being done under pressure from the Soviets, who wanted to control the memory of the Katyn case.

How much weight the Soviets attached to the Katyn massacre can be judged from the unsuccessful attempt to include it in the indictment against the Nazi war criminals during the Nuremberg trials (Kulesza 2010: 52–67). Katyn reappeared on the international arena in the early 1950s, when – following the motion of the Polish American Congress – the House of Representatives of US Congress instituted an investigation commission for the Katyn case. The results of its proceedings published in 1952 clearly indicated the Soviets were responsible for the crime.[2] It met with protests in Poland and the Soviet Union, followed by intensified propaganda actions. It was then that people began to get punished for telling the truth about Katyn.

The Katyn lie was maintained even after the thaw of 1956, though historian Piotr Łysakowski claims that there was a chance for the Kremlin to reveal the truth at this time. This was, however, squandered by a new party leader in Poland, Władysław Gomułka, who is said to have been afraid that it would compromise himself and lead to an increase in anti-Soviet attitudes (Łysakowski 2005: 89).

In the following years the Soviet Union continued their policy of concealing the truth about the Katyn massacre. For instance, the authorities hid information from the general public about the discovery in 1969 by Ukrainian children of mass graves of prisoners from the POW camp in Starobielsk, murdered in Piatikhatki near Kharkiv. Nor was it a coincidence as well, that near Katyn, at a place with a very similar name – Khatyn – a massive monument was erected commemorating civilians killed by the Nazis in Belarus. It seems that this village had been deliberately chosen because of the similarity of its name to Katyn, in order to misinform the Soviet society. As the Russian historian Natalia Lebiediewa (2000: 115) suggests, the intention was to link the crime to the Germans. This goal was achieved, as in Russia Khatyn is still a symbol of Nazi crimes against Soviet civilians. Over the years official celebrations have been organized there, commemorating victims of the Second World War, with the participation of foreign delegations and heads of state such as Richard Nixon, Fidel Castro and Jiang Zemin.

The first monument in Katyn was erected in 1978. It consisted of concrete steles with marble finials, on which were placed Polish and Russian inscriptions, which falsified history: 'To the victims of fascism – Polish officers shot by the Nazis in 1941'.

In the early 1970s there was silence about the Katyn case. Even mentioning the name 'Katyn' in public was forbidden. The communist authorities actively counteracted any attempts at dissemination of the truth about the Soviets' crime. Appropriate censorship restrictions were introduced, forbidding any attempts at charging the Soviets with the death of the Polish officers in the press, schoolbooks, scholarly papers or memoirs. In the mid-1970s for the first time the mention of Katyn was allowed in print, but Polish officers interned in the Soviet Union could not be characterized as prisoners of war. Any information about those murdered in Katyn had to be accompanied by the false date of the crime – after July 1941.

Summing up, for the Polish communists the truth about Katyn was one of the most troublesome themes and the source of recurrent breakdowns of the indoctrination machinery throughout the PRL period. The communist authorities – as the Polish historian Janusz Kurtyka rightly noticed – on the one hand:

> in defiance of the facts maintained the thesis of the German responsibility for the Katyn crime, and on the other hand, they never ventured to commemorate it officially as a Nazi crime. They did not intend to remember it nor organize falsifying celebrations, in spite of the fact, that numerous celebrations of this kind were being organized in connection with the German occupation. Quite the contrary, handbooks and officials' statements were to be silent about Katyn. The truth about the crime preserved in family stories and private talks became a hammer crushing the ideological hypocrisy of ubiquitous PRL propaganda – from the times of Bierut and Gomułka to the Jaruzelski's regime. (Kurtyka 2006: 177–178)

The Memory of Auschwitz

The memory of Auschwitz was formed in different ways and in different circumstances to the memory of Katyn. Contrary to the Katyn crime, it became a part of the official communist policy of commemoration of the Second World War, policy that became the authorities' main instrument in their political and ideological struggle. Through the many years of communist Poland it was a key element of communist propaganda (anti-German, anti-American, anti-Western), not only legitimizing their power, but also used for achieving short-term political goals. The falsification of the history of the camp emphasized the martyrdom of the Polish nation, and concealed the fact that it was Jews who constituted the majority of the victims. This was different in size and weight to falsifying the history of Katyn. Therefore one cannot describe the authorities' policy in this area as an 'Auschwitz lie' in the same way as the Katyn lie. One should rather describe it as an intentional and long-term instrumentalization of the memory of the victims of Auschwitz and the politicization of the significance of this crime. In any case, it resulted in the distortion of historical consciousness of Polish society, and was marked with peculiar rivalry in suffering, mainly between the Poles and the Jews (e.g., Huener 2003, Steinlauf 1996, Kucia 2005).

The State Museum Auschwitz-Birkenau was the key instrument in this policy. It was opened on the 14th of June 1947. The transformation of the camp into a memorial was a result of the convergence of spontaneous processes involving former prisoners, local inhabitants and local authorities, with the intentional actions of the government (Kapralski 2011: 528). To understand this it is instructive to look more closely at public debates and controversies concerning Auschwitz Museum that were part of this process of transformation. It will help us to see more clearly the factors that influenced the formation of the memory of victims of the former camp. From the very beginning of its existence the Auschwitz Museum became an arena of clashes of various visions and ideas of commemorating the victims. In the act of the Polish parliament instituting the museum it was decreed that 'the grounds of the former Nazi concentration camp in Oświęcim together with all the buildings and equipment located there shall be preserved for all time as a Monument to the Martyrdom of the Polish Nation and other Nations' (Lachendro 2007: 71). This paragraph determined the character of the place and the ways of commemorating the victims of Auschwitz for many years. Emphasizing the martyrdom of the Poles and other nations, together with diminishing the significance of the majority of victims, that is the Jews, became a standard followed for many years by the exhibitions and expositions that marginalized the extermination of the Jews. It should be emphasized however, that 'neither the Museum authorities, nor the Polish government ever openly denied that the vast majority of victims of Auschwitz were Jews. However this fact was not specifically highlighted … The Jews were treated as citizens … of countries under Nazi occupation' (Huener 2003: 29). This policy was a result of government directives that obliged the administration of the Museum to vigilance in order – as it was put – 'not to separate out ethnic issues and above all the Jewish issue; not to give an impression, that Auschwitz was a place of death almost exclusively of the Jews, but contrary, to emphasize that the enemy of the Jews was at the same time the enemy of the Poles and others' (Wóycicka 2009: 325). That is why in the publications on Auschwitz the Jewish themes were not frequent, whereas the Polish and international character of the camp was emphasized.

In the 1950s the communist authorities' policy concerning the museum changed. In June 1950 a 'lustration commission' came to Oświęcim instituted by the Central Committee of the Communist Party. Its report stated that 'the existing museum plan contains many errors that are politically wrong, non-Marxist suppositions distorting the historical truth. Nationalism emanates from virtually all the exhibits, captions and charts, and the German nation is being described as an immemorial enemy of the Slavic peoples' (ibid.). Particularly the Jewish exhibition in block 4 ('Extermination of the millions') was criticized as – as the commission put it – non-Marxist and nationalist. There was no 'class attitude' in the way it presented both Nazi policy and the position of the Polish nation. It was also a mistake – as it was put – to separate the martyrdom of the Jewish, Polish, Soviet and other prisoners (ibid.). The lustration resulted in the decision to reorganize the museum, which 'is not to be only the history of the past, but eternally up-to-date, in order to be an instrument with which the Polish United Workers' Party would be able to influence the society' (ibid. 369). 'Struggling for peace' was now to become the main theme of an exposition. It required substantial modification to a scenario of the exhibition, which now emphasized struggle against imperialism and indicated that genocide and concentration camps were its distinctive feature. Instead of the Germans, now the 'Anglo-American imperialists' were being presented as the major enemies of mankind and peace (ibid.). It is worth mentioning that the changes introduced at that time at the Auschwitz State Museum should be viewed in the broader international context, because they were directly connected with the world political situation. Auschwitz became a part of the political rivalry of the Western and Eastern powers during the Cold War (see also Wóycicka 2005; Huener 2003). On the one hand, in 1949 the Soviet Occupation Zone in Germany was transformed into the German Democratic Republic, which naturally led to revision of the attitudes of the Poles toward the Germans. On the other hand at the turn of the 1940s and 1950s in all Eastern Bloc countries one could observe a change in the authorities' attitude toward the Jews. It was caused by the anti-Zionist policy of the Soviet Union, which in fact was directed against the Jews, who in the meantime came to be considered agents of Western imperialism. The apogee of this policy fell in the early 1950s, when political trials against people of Jewish origin took place in the Soviet Union and Czechoslovakia.

That the first period in the history of the museum was then characterized (as Sławomir Kapralski, quoted above, has suggested) by the coexistence of three unequally emphasized narratives and symbols of remembrance linked to them, which in various patterns and hierarchies would appear throughout the rest of its history. The first narrative was a national vision of Auschwitz as a site of martyrdom of the Polish nation. The second, a vision of Auschwitz as a site of extermination of the Jews. And the third, an official ideological narrative, transforming Auschwitz into arena of political struggle and instrumentalizing the museum (Kapralski 2011). According to Jonathan Huener, in postwar Poland the synthesis of the narratives and symbolisms mentioned before made the grounds of the camp above all a place of politically-biased commemoration of Polish national tragedy and of the sufferings of others, represented by international symbolism. Commemoration of the extermination of the Jews was not a substantial function of the museum then, because it was not a key highlighted element (Huener 2003: 3).

The thaw that followed Stalin's death brought about fundamental changes in the museum. In 1955 a new main exhibition was composed. Its form was determined not only by political changes but also by the activities of the International Auschwitz Council established in 1952. Its members emphasized the international character of Auschwitz and suggested that the new exposition should reflect the differences in remembrance of various categories of victims, citizens of various countries. This policy found its manifestation in the unveiling of the 'International Monument to Victims of Nazism' in Birkenau in 1967 and in creating so-called 'national expositions', presenting histories of inhabitants of various countries deported to Auschwitz. Among them was a Jewish pavilion opened in April 1968, which was, however, closed soon after. Later it was made accessible only occasionally, almost exclusively for foreign visitors. After being widely criticized the Jewish pavilion was renewed and reopened in 1978 (see Young 1993; Długoborski and Trojański 2008; Trojański 2012).

In effect, during the 1950s and 1960s the presence of unambiguously political symbolism was diminishing, together with an increase in the role of international symbolism as well as that of the Polish national state. The latter began to dominate after 1967 – an effect of the anti-Semitic campaign by the communist government (Huener 2003: XVIII–XIX; Kucia 2005: 236–237).

In the 1970s the tendency prevailed to diminish the size and significance of extermination of the Jews in the KL Auschwitz. The numbers were manipulated and the ethnic origin of the victims was concealed – with a clear tendency to avoid any mention of the Jews. The prisoners were categorized according to national state criteria, which made it possible to claim that 'the Poles and Polish citizens of Jewish origin' constituted the majority of them (ibid. 275). This is how the victims of Auschwitz were internationalized and 'Polonized'. For the Poles, who – as the Polish sociologist Zdzisław Mach has noted – all had to visit Auschwitz at school age: it was one of the places of martyrdom of their fellow citizens killed by the Germans. This was a general tenor and the political function of the museum. Therefore,

> Jews were being mentioned ... in exposition as citizens of particular countries – including Poland – and not as a uniform ethnic category, as such condemned to death by the Nazis. The issue of martyrdom of the Jews was pushed aside, according to the interests of the communist authorities, for whom the important thing was to present a historical Polish-German conflict and not the tragedy of the Jews. (Mach 1995: 20–21)

Struggling for the Truth and Memory Transformations

Throughout the whole communist period, official stories of the Katyn massacre and Auschwitz death camp were confronted with other sources of information and consequently questioned by many individuals and various groups of Polish society. However, there was no symmetry in the attitude of the authorities to the people questioning the official versions of Auschwitz and Katyn, or in the attitude of society towards these events. Consequently, only actions aimed at discovering the truth about the Katyn massacre were prosecuted and punished by the security services (see Gasztold-Seń 2010), while demanding the true picture of Auschwitz was at most criticized. It seems that the different treatments of Katyn and Auschwitz by the communists resulted in various attitudes of Polish society towards them. We can assume that the Katyn massacre was particularly perceived because the vast majority of its victims were Polish, while the issue of Auschwitz was marginalized because neither the communist regime, nor the general public was interested in focusing on the fact that majority of its victims were Jews but not Poles. Thus we can say that Polish society generally accepted the official version of Auschwitz, whereas it demanded to know the truth about Katyn.

The asymmetry described above also influenced the way in which the Polish people struggled to reveal the true story of Auschwitz and Katyn. Similarly it was reflected in the transformation of memory regarding those events during the communist time. However, despite these differences in both cases, the important role in the process of restoring memory was played by the Catholic Church and Polish democratic opposition, although with different intensity in each case. Various groups and organizations competed in employing historical symbols, including Katyn and Auschwitz among others. They organized ceremonies and anniversaries, erected monuments and plaques as well as published books and pamphlets. We can undoubtedly say that thanks to their consistent approach the memory of Katyn, and also to some extent the truth about Auschwitz, survived the communist era.

From the very beginning the general answer to the Katyn lie spread by the communist authorities was social resistance, expressed mainly by cultivating the memory within the families of those killed. A major role in this was played by the Catholic Church, which, among others through celebrating masses and allowing plaques to be erected in the churches, helped to create an informal environment for the 'Katyn families'.

At the end of the 1970s the Katyn case was taken up by all the fractions of the democratic opposition. Their activities mainly aimed at preserving its memory. As noticed by Witold Wasilewski, a Polish historian who researched this issue:

> In the years 1978–1989 the opposition were conducting intensive struggle against the Katyn lie and undertaking actions to commemorate the victims of Soviet crimes, focusing on breaking the communist's monopoly on information. The context of organized activities of the opposition in this period was made of the efforts of many today anonymous people: the witnesses of history, teachers and all those who in their own environment passed information about Katyn. (Wasilewski 2009: 60)

In 1978 the Katyn Institute in Poland was established in Krakow, and for a year remained in hiding. Its activists focused mainly on translating foreign literature on Katyn, including reports by the US Congress commission and the British Ambassador accredited at the Polish government in exile, Sir Owen O'Maley. They also started publishing the *Katyn Bulletin* aimed at disseminating knowledge about the crime in Polish society.

Another significant initiative was the erection of the *Sanctuary of the Fallen and Murdered* in the East at the Powązki Cemetery in Warsaw. Among its founders was Reverend Stefan Niedzielak, the chaplain of the Katyn families, which after forty years of silence began to organize themselves at the parishes of the Roman Catholic Church and demand the truth. In 1981 at the Powązki Cemetery a Katyn cross was erected but it did not survive even one night, being destroyed by the secret police. The secret police tried to silence Rev. Niedzielak with threats and were probably involved in his death a few years later. Another tragic episode of the struggles for the truth about Katyn was the death of Walenty Badylak, who in 1980 burned himself at the Main Market Square in Krakow, protesting against the communist system and against concealing the truth about Katyn. At his body a metal plate was found with the inscription 'Katyn'.

Intense activities of Polish political milieus in exile substantially contributed to the process of disseminating the truth and preserving remembrance of Katyn, especially publishing activities. The publications were smuggled to Poland and distributed in the so-called 'second circulation'. The erection of monuments was another important area of activity of the Polish diaspora. For instance, the erection of a Katyn monument in London in 1978 had wide repercussions when the Soviet authorities tried to stop it. In spite of the diplomatic protests, this monument was erected, as well as a few others in various countries all over the world.

It was not until the 1980s, however, that a real breakthrough appeared with regard to society's awareness of Katyn. It was linked to the Solidarity movement, which created opportunities for social debate on the latest history of Poland, including Polish-Soviet relations during the Second World War. Numerous publications on Katyn published in the 'second circulation' were distributed all over the country. Though the official version did not change, those publications began to affect the collective consciousness. Some substantial changes appeared at the end of the 1980s in connection with *perestroika*. In 1987 in cooperation with the Soviet authorities a common Polish-Soviet commission was established consisting of historians from both communist parties to explore 'blank spots' in the history of their mutual relations, including the Katyn massacre. On the 13th of April 1990, during the Polish president, Wojciech Jaruzelski's, visit to Moscow, Mikhail Gorbachev handed over the documents concerning the Katyn crime from the Soviet archives, and for the first time admitted officially that the crime was committed by the NKVD. On the same day, in a statement from the government news agency TASS it was announced that it was 'Beria, Merkulov and their assistants',[3] who bore direct responsibility for the Katyn massacre – 'one of the grave crimes of Stalinism'.[4]

The fundamental changes in the perception of Auschwitz did not appear until the 1980s, when the Jewish symbolism of the camp came out. They were an outcome of the process of 'reconstruction' and 'retrieval of the remembrance of Jews' that started at the turn of the 1970s and 1980s (Steinlauf 1996). Just as in the case of Katyn, it was linked to the Solidarity movement, where activists demanded the truth about the latest history of Poland as well as liberating memory from the framework of the communist ideology.

The breakthrough appeared in the mid-1980s, after the premiere of *Shoah*, the documentary film by Claude Lanzman, and publication of Jan Błoński's essay, 'Biedni Polacy patrzą na getto' ('The Poor Poles look at the Ghetto', see Błoński 2008 [1987]). They evoked a heated debate on Polish-Jewish relations during the war, which meant placing the extermination of the Jews at the very heart of the public discourse. And even if it did not directly concern Auschwitz, it paved the way for discussion about its Jewish dimension, mentioned for the first time by John Paul II during his pilgrimage to Poland in 1979. Those words – as Michael Steinlauf emphasizes – were of critical significance for Polish remembrance of the Holocaust and for the process of introducing Jewish symbolism into Auschwitz (Steinlauf 2001: 114). There were also substantial conflicts concerning for instance the Carmelites' convent, and canonizations of Maksymilian Kolbe and Edyta Stein, who had been murdered in Auschwitz. Many Jews interpreted those actions, a perceived particularly the location of the convent in close vicinity of the former camp, as an attempt at Christianization of Auschwitz, and they evoked numerous protests. The conflict concerning the monastery reached its culmination in 1989. Thanks to the media, which reported it extensively, the public at large could learn for the first time about the Jewish symbolism of Auschwitz. The recognition that Auschwitz was a symbol of the Holocaust was later strengthened, among others, by the publication of the research of Franciszek Piper, a researcher working for the Auschwitz Museum, regarding the number of victims of Auschwitz (Piper 1991). The new evidence not only reduced the number of victims from 4 to 1.1–1.5 million people, but also – what is most important – indicated that the Jews constituted the vast majority of them.

To sum up, one can say, following Sławomir Kapralski, that in the 1980s a 'religious-patriotic' narrative was superimposed on the previously dominating narratives – the 'internationalist' and the 'communist-nationalist'. At the same time a revival of Jewish memory took place that had been tabooed for many years (Kapralski 2011: 538). It ultimately led to the domination of the Jewish symbolism of Auschwitz that began with the end of the conflict concerning the Carmelites' convent in 1993.

The Harvest of the Communist Policy of History

The end of the Second World War, which was the turning point in European history, completely changed the way Auschwitz and Katyn were perceived in Poland. During the war and occupation these two events were rather homogeneously treated by Polish society as symbols of the crimes committed against the Polish nation (for many people Auschwitz was equal to Katyn). The situation changed after the war when those events began to be an instrument of communist propaganda. Consequently they became an issue of dispute between the West and the East of the world, divided by the Iron Curtain. This political division resulted in reinforcement of the different narratives of those events.

In Poland after the war, Auschwitz, though not at once or without debate, remained a universal symbol of German Nazi crimes committed against Poles. While Katyn was embraced by the communist propaganda and strongly divided people in Poland and abroad in their opinions on who was responsible for this crime, the memory of Auschwitz was more homogeneous than the memory of the Katyn massacre. Consequently different versions of Auschwitz and Katyn became a part of the competing ideologies of the so-called Western and Eastern blocs.

From the very beginning both Auschwitz and (particularly) Katyn were instrumentalized and used for political purposes. They became instruments of a lie, at first by the occupants and later by others, including the Western Allies and Polish communists. The memory of both was put to the test and consequently distorted. The historical facts were falsified to various degrees up to the collapse of communism in Poland, and finally resulted in the acknowledgement of the victims of Auschwitz and depreciation of the victims of Katyn. This has been proved by the high position of Auschwitz (25 per cent) and relatively low position of Katyn (8 per cent) in a ranking of Second World War symbols in the public opinion polls.[5] The important place of Auschwitz in the consciousness of Poles today is causally connected, as the Polish sociologist Marek Kucia (2000) rightly observes, with the transmitting of the memories of war and occupation to the next generations, in which Auschwitz became a symbol of a 'camp' as such.

The reduced significance of Katyn in collective consciousness is above all caused by political factors. During the communist period telling the truth about Katyn was forbidden, and there was only one official, false version, imposed by the centrally controlled mass media, propaganda and school. Censorship constraints on any research regarding the Soviets' attitudes toward Poles resulted in historiography focused exclusively on the German occupant. The permanent emphasizing of the Nazi crimes was also fostered by a sense of the German threat (lack of a guarantee of the inviolability of Poland's Western borders) and a common belief that only close relations with the Soviet Union could protect Poland against the revenge of the Germans (Paczkowski 1999).

The collapse of communism has changed the perception of Auschwitz and Katyn in Poland and also in the whole former Eastern Bloc. The memory of both events was no longer blocked by the authorities. But it was impossible to make up quickly for the deficit accumulated over years – changes in collective consciousness need time and persistent action.

Conclusions

These considerations were only an attempt to identify the continuity and changes in the historical process of forming the memory of Auschwitz and the Katyn massacre; an effort to draw attention to the similarities and differences in perception of those two events. It was also an attempt to show what happens to memory when it is subject to total political and ideological manipulation, as it was in the cases of Auschwitz and Katyn. This has been done from the Polish perspective, which, however, can be seen as representative of Eastern Europe more broadly in regard to the presence of the Nazi and communist pasts in European memory. It is the authors' conviction that such a perspective should be part of the European historical consciousness.

As we tried to prove in our chapter, the memory of Katyn survived the communist period thanks to the consistent attitude of the Catholic Church and the democratic opposition, as well as many individuals who did not want to accept the communist vision of history. Similarly, the memory of the Jewish victims of Auschwitz that was instrumentalized during the communist time was finally restored after the political transformation of Poland. The resistance of Polish society against distortions of history became the foundation of one of the most important contemporary Polish narratives about the past.

The specific *iunctim* between Auschwitz and Katyn, as presented above, is to support our thesis of one totalitarianism with two different forms and colours: the German/Nazi and the Soviet/Stalinist one. And although this is still a controversial thesis, as proved the aforementioned debate on Timothy Snyder's *Bloodlands*, it is worth supporting by using the exemplification of the memories of Auschwitz and Katyn as they were shaped in postwar Poland.

Notes

1. The recent accounts of the Katyn massacre and KL Auschwitz in e.g., Paul 2010; Kalbarczyk 2010; Cienciala et al. 2007; Sanford 2005; Długoborski and Piper 2000; Gutman and Berenbaum 1998; Rees 2005.
2. Report no. 2505 '82nd Congress Concerning the Katyn Forest Massacre', US Government Printing Office, Washington 1952. See also: Sanford 2005: 141–143; Fischer 1999–2000.
3. TASS (the Soviet Government Press Agency) statement given on Friday, 13 April, 1990 at 14.30, *Zeszyty Katyńskie* no. 1 (1990), p. 196.
4. Ibid.
5. Opinion poll carried out by TNS OBOP, 7–10 January 2010, 'Auschwitz in Collective Consciousness of Poles in 2010'.

Jacek Chrobaczyński is a historian, head of the Chair of Modern Polish History in the Institute of History at the Pedagogical University of Krakow.

He specializes in twentieth-century Polish history, especially the Second World War, the German and Soviet occupations, and the history of Poland after 1945. He has written many books and nearly 150 articles, reviews and dissertations, published in Polish and other languages. His most recent book is *Dramatyczny rok 1943. Postawy i zachowania społeczeństwa polskiego w rozstrzygającym roku II wojny światowej* (Krakow, 2012).

Piotr Trojański is a historian, assistant professor in the Institute of History at the Pedagogical University of Krakow. He is also a lecturer at the Centre for Holocaust Studies at the Jagiellonian University, as well as an academic advisor for the International Centre for Education about Auschwitz and the Holocaust at the Auschwitz-Birkenau State Museum. He specializes in history didactics, especially Holocaust education and Second World War memory issues in Poland and abroad, as well as the history of the Jews in Poland during the interwar period.

Chapter 14

Germans in Eastern Europe as a Polish–German *Lieu de Mémoire*?
On the Asymmetry of Memories

Matthias Weber

Germans in Eastern Europe

German and Polish perspectives on the past continue to differ. Even seventy-five years since the outbreak of the Second World War, wounds inflicted have clearly not healed. Recently, this became obvious once again through discussions about the film *Generation War* (*Unsere Mütter, unsere Väter*): the Second German Television (*Zweites Deutsches Fernsehen – ZDF*) held the apolitical view that the three-part television mini-series, screened in March 2013, was an opportunity for the generation of those involved in the Second World War to open a dialogue with their children, grandchildren and great-grandchildren about the period. By stark contrast in Poland, the production attracted a massive amount of criticism in the media, and even from the government, with regard to the content of the mini-series. It was felt that the Polish partisans and the general civilian population were unilaterally portrayed as primitive and anti-Semitic, and that the film would seriously damage the reputation of the Polish Home Army. Public indignation reached a peak after the screening in Poland in June 2013 (with an audience of 3.7 million): accusations of attempting to spread the blame or to modify Germany's war guilt and responsibility for the Holocaust arose once again.[1]

The German film-makers, at the very least, could have demonstrated greater sensitivity; possibly they simply did not possess sufficient core knowledge about the crimes inflicted by the Germans in Poland during the Second World War, and about how keenly these are still remembered today within Polish society. And so, once again, the disparity in the sense of memory between Poland and Germany is clearly evident.

Notes for this chapter begin on page 281.

The atrocities of the Second World War, occupation, oppression and mass murder in the twentieth century were preceded by centuries of peaceful coexistence between the Germans and the Polish people, characterized by diverse cultural exchange, the sharing of knowledge and culture, but also by rivalries and conflicts. As a result, the Germans, Poles and members of other ethnic groups and of other states (among others, the Baltic states, the Czech Republic, Slovakia, Hungary, Romania, Slovenia, Serbia, Moldova, Russia) have achieved a common cultural heritage in art, literature and architecture. The flight and expulsion of the Germans from Eastern Europe at the end of and after the Second World War largely brought the presence of the Germans in Eastern Europe to an end. Furthermore, as a consequence of the Cold War in the postwar decades there was effectively no further academic cooperation in the area of dealing with the themes of shared past.

Initially, in the years following 1989, historical discourse about issues relating to these historical periods increased markedly in Germany and Poland, and between these two countries. This historical discourse acknowledged the centuries of living together, but also recognized the period of Nazi dictatorship and Nazi occupation, as well as the postwar flight and expulsion of Germans. However, the actual historical discourse in each country was based on quite different experiences, memories and scopes of knowledge. The themes and issues that structured the historical debates in each country, as well as the perspectives for effective common historical examination differed significantly. State and regional history in the areas of German-Polish interaction and contact as well as the German-Polish twentieth-century history were discussed in the academic field, the media and to some extent in politics, against a background of controversy. There was considerable disagreement about the continuation of ethnocentric points of view in the new regional-historical syntheses. In addition, the relationship between 'region' and 'nation' was raised, together with the question of whether regional history could represent an alternative to national history. Since 1991, activities of the Cultural Community 'Borussia', based in Olsztyn, Poland, with regard to former Eastern Prussia, or simply Warmia and Masuria (German: Ermland and Masuren) have taken a leading role. The concept of an 'open regionalism' followed research by Robert Traba, taking into account the multicultural and poly-ethnic relationships. The significance of Prussia for the history of Poland was firmly given centre stage with two major anniversaries – the celebration of the 300th jubilee of the Prussian coronation in 2001, and the 300th birthday of King Frederick II the Great in 2012 – and yet again, the stark reality of the ongoing, vastly different, perceptions of Prussia between Germany and Poland came to the surface (see Bömelburg 2003;

Hackmann 2011: 117f). The focus point of this historical discord continues to be the twentieth century: the Second World War, the occupation of Poland, the war crimes and crimes of occupation by the Germans, Polish forced-labourers in Germany, as well as the flight and expulsion of the Germans.

This chapter deals with both past and current German and Polish historical debate on the common past and experiences, and especially the history of conflict in the twentieth century. It argues for reconciliation and a mutual completion of historical analysis and views of history. It argues likewise for the contrasting approaches to become attuned to and supplement one another without seeking to standardize the consideration of historical issues. Perspectives of scholarly as well as of practical questions of memory are reflected.

The main questions are: Is it possible for the Germans' history in Eastern Europe to be remembered together by Poles and Germans, so that it becomes the two countries' common *lieu de mémoire*? What are the obstacles to this? How have the memories in Germany and Poland taken shape since 1989? The German memory of the prewar Eastern provinces, as well as memories of the Second World War sufferings inflicted on Poland, up to memories of the postwar expulsions of Germans from what are now Polish territories; all of these constitute an important context when discussing the German presence in the East in Polish and German active awareness.

* * *

Reflections provided here come from both the point of view of a scholar dealing with history and memory issues, as well as that of a practitioner of memory. Starting in 2005 the author of this chapter has been involved in the conception, content development and organizational establishment of the European Network of Remembrance and Solidarity, in collaboration with partners from Germany, Poland, Hungary, Slovakia, Czech Republic and Austria. The mission of this network is to document, research, promote and popularize the study of twentieth-century history and the way it is remembered. The fields of interest centre on times of dictatorial regimes, wars and resistance to oppression with particular emphasis on the victims. Within these, the National Socialist war of annihilation carried out within and against Poland as well as against other Central and East European countries is an important part of the activities. An empathetic approach towards the experiences of affected people is the trademark of the historical discussions fostered by this initiative.[2]

The other topic of this chapter is connected with the Federal Institute for Culture and History of Germans in Eastern Europe,[3] based in

North-Western Germany, which is run by the author. The institute places particular emphasis on history dating from the current day back to the Middle Ages, 'the centuries and generations in which Germans were taken for granted as a familiar part of Eastern Europe' (Schlögel 2008b). This is about the times when Germans, whether as a minority or majority group, lived and regularly interacted with other ethnic groups in regions such as Silesia (Schlesien, Śląsk), Pomerania (Pommern, Pomorze), East and West Prussia (Ost- und Westpreußen, Warmia i Mazury), Bohemia (Böhmen), Moravia (Mähren), in the Baltic region (Baltikum), Transylvania (Siebenbürgen) and Russia. It is the history of the former Eastern regions of Germany itself and beyond those boundaries of areas where Germans had established communities. In 1945, the Eastern regions of the German Reich became the Western and Northern regions of Poland. Königsberg, together with a part of Eastern Prussia, likewise became part of the Soviet Union, and they now form the *Oblast* Kaliningrad, the smallest oblast in the Russian Federation. Nowadays, the numerous national, cultural and religious identities of this area are often viewed within the context of an 'entangled history' (*histoire croisée*) (Werner and Zimmermann 2002, 2004).

In the post-1989 reunification years, Germany has had to catch up on these 'Eastern' aspects of its history. On the one hand, the Nazi period and the Second World War, with their harsh consequences, are once again strongly coming to the fore in public consciousness and in the media. On the other hand, since the opening and fall of the Berlin Wall, there has also been an increasing awareness of the earlier culture and history of these regions, where the ethnic, national, religious and linguistic diversity was originally manifestly more distinctive than is the case today. Karl Schlögel (2008b) has noted that the network of inter-relationships and contacts in Eastern Europe, which Germany itself once destroyed, is now finally being re-established to a certain extent. For a long time previously Germany's writing of history had been strongly aligned to a primarily Western European and transatlantic perspective. As a consequence, the need to catch up but also to revise the approach towards the history of Eastern Europe and the Germans living there was, and is, immense.

German and Polish Conflicting Historiographies and the Intensification of Discussion after 1989

Prior to 1989, historical viewpoints in Germany and Poland concerning the history and effect of the Germans in Eastern Europe were fundamentally organized and for the most part clearly differentiated from one another. At risk of over-simplifying the matter, the history of Silesia, Pomerania or Prussia were considered to be part of German history, with an emphasis on the cultural achievements of the Germans in the Middle Ages and the early modern period. 'Awkward' themes in twentieth-century history, especially the Nazi era, tended to be neglected and overlooked. Conversely, from the perspective of Polish historiography, it was not unusual to find a marked over-emphasis on the presence of Polish culture and language in the relevant areas over the course of the history of these regions (see Hackmann 2001; Weber 2006). In this way, the master narrative in both countries seemed to be resolved to a large extent. However in the 1990s, the often intense discussions dealt not so much with historical events *per se* as with the clash of historical, national and foreign narratives, i.e., the reinterpretation of widespread, traditionally accepted views of history. At the end of the Cold War and the opening of the borders, politics and the media stopped the monological writing and talking *about* one another. On the contrary, for the first time a direct and reciprocal discussion about the past was instigated, finally without the restrictions of state or political policy. It quickly became apparent how fundamentally the historical views differed between various European states, especially between Germany and Poland. Furthermore, memories and views of twentieth-century history, in particular of the two World Wars, Nazi atrocities and the Stalinist acts of injustice, deviated strongly from one another. As a consequence, central themes such as the Nazi genocide of European Jews, the Nazi German occupation of Poland, or the end of the Second World War, were each handled with very varying levels of priority and relative weight according to whether the historical analysis was undertaken in Germany, Poland or in the Russian Federation. In the Soviet Union, for example, the date 9 May 1945 was celebrated as 'Victory Day', and, as such, was the only public holiday that was accepted by each and every level of the Soviet population. In contrast, the debate in Germany continued well into the 1990s as to whether the end of the war should be seen as a catastrophic defeat or a day of liberation. Whereas for Poland, the year 1945 did not just represent and continue to stand for the end of the war, but also the transition from one foreign dictatorial sovereign to another.

In the period following 1989, various historical debates could be observed in Germany. In 1996, the American political scientist Daniel Goldhagen inaugurated a discussion in his book *Hitler's Willing Executioners* (1996a, 1996b) about the implication of normal German citizens in the Holocaust. Also in 1996 at Hamburg's Institute for Social Research, an exhibition about war crimes of the Wehrmacht bade farewell forever to the myth of the 'honourable, clean Wehrmacht' (König 2011: 58). Both discussions led to further emphasis on Germany's guilt and the country's responsibility for war crimes. Moreover, the historiography on Eastern Europe was being critically re-examined; older more traditionally aligned paradigms were being re-analysed and gradually eliminated. The British historian Michael Burleigh's 1988 book *Germany Turns Eastwards: A Study of Ostforschung in the Third Reich* is important in this context for initiating a critical analysis of the highly politicized so-called '*Ostforschung*' (research on the East) of the period since the Weimar Republic, and for numerous subsequent publications. Burleigh shows how the relations between the Nazi regime and contemporary scholarly experts in Eastern Europe eventually put an entire academic discipline on a path that led to biological racism and manipulation under the Nazis. He describes the collaboration of the academic profession, the growing links with state authorities and with the SS, even before the outbreak of the war and German expansion brought the 'Hour of the experts', and, finally, the aspects of the *Ostforschung* after 1945.

The turn of the millennium saw the unexpected emergence of a form of complementary historical discourse that dealt with the suffering, losses and hardships faced by the Germans during the Second World War. Initially, the focus was on the theme of the 'flight and expulsion of the Germans'. Although this topic had not been considered taboo beforehand, over the preceding decades it had generally been regarded as being of marginal importance. This discussion was set in motion by the Association of Expellees' plan to establish a Centre against Expulsions in Berlin, initiated in 2000. The increased focus in the 1990s on German victims of the Second World War also raised the issue of the Allied wartime bombardment of German cities, or the rape of German women by Red Army soldiers (see Friedrich 2002).

However, this came to be criticized as a trend towards 'victimization' and whitewashing of the German guilt (see Berger 2002), and led to controversial publicity in the media as well as heated debate between politicians and academics in Germany and Poland, and on a smaller scale between Germany and the Czech Republic. In the case of the Czech Republic, discussion centred on the continuation of the Beneš-Decrees from 1945. These decrees established the legal foundation leading to the forced migrations of Germans at the end of the war. Many groups, especially Expellee Associations have fought for years – as yet in vain – to have these decrees lifted (see Brandes 2010; Frommer 2001).

In Poland, critical voices started to make their concerns more public. It was feared that the new path of historic discourse in Germany could potentially lead to Poland being defamed as an expelling nation and thus as an offender, rather than a victim of the war. It comes then as no surprise that a sense of fear progressively increased that Germany wanted to present itself more and more as the victim and gradually less as the perpetrator of Second World War atrocities. Polish historian Paweł Machcewicz summarized this problematic issue in 2004:

> In Poland we speak openly about the darker sides of our history; we remember the suffering that Polish hands have inflicted on the citizens of other countries. However, in Germany the tendency is increasing to concentrate on their own suffering – often accompanied by unjust accusations towards other nations. Any responsibility for the outbreak of the Second World War and the criminal policy of occupation seems to fade into the shadows as the effective cause for what happened to the Germans at later times. (Machcewicz 2006: 118)

By association, the contrasting historical views also affected the organization of memorial heritage in the public domain through the establishment of new museums and memorials. In this process, questions were raised in particular with reference to how the German-Polish history of conflict in the twentieth century was affecting each country's individual perception of its historical national identity. Questions were also pursued intensively by the relevant 'other countries' in the face of increasing discourse across Europe at the time. It did not take long for these questions also to start to have an effect on national politics with regard to history. More and more, the discussion of history gained a political dimension and, at certain times, even gained in importance on the level of day-to-day politics (Pomian 2009; Rydel 2011). The dispute about history was fuelled by a private German organization called the Prussian Claims Society (Preußische Treuhand) which attempted to win back former German property in Poland through legal channels. Even though the German government did not support these activities, their existence alone led to a sense of instability in Poland and to antagonistic responses in the Polish media and political sphere. Because the Prussian Claims Society had close relations to some of the associations of expellees (*Landsmannschaften*), Poland's conservative news magazine *Wprost* published a scandalous composite photo depicting the President of the Expellees (who had specifically distanced herself from the Prussian Claims Society's demands) in a Nazi uniform riding on the back of the German Chancellor, with the commentary, 'The Germans owe the Polish people a billion dollars for the Second World War' (*Wprost* no. 38, 21 September 2003). In September 2004, the lower house of the Polish parliament, the Sejm, unanimously adopted a resolution with regard to 'Poland's right to war reparations from Germany, and Poland's rights in respect to the illegal demands against Poland and Poland's citizens put forward in Germany' (Lang 2004). The mayor of Warsaw at the time, Lech Kaczyński announced that even an amount in the realm of forty billion dollars would still be too little as compensation for the destruction of Warsaw during the Second World War.[4] These largely irrational, but nevertheless sensational, events contributed to the reality that far from losing its significance, history in fact confirmed its considerable importance for academic study and among the general public.

By 2010, many people in Poland felt deeply confronted by the course of political discussion when the president of the Federation of Expellees, claimed that it was, in fact, Poland who first mobilized their army in 1939, thereby implying that Hitler's attack on Poland was simply a response to Poland's mobilization. When this was combined with the highly emotional question of war guilt, leading German politicians found it necessary to intervene and reassure everyone involved that no one would or should ascribe blame to Poland with regard to the Second World War ('Steinbach hat Kriegsschuldfrage' 2010; Paterson 2010).

Repeatedly, however, the feeling was expressed that after the Germans' exemplary reappraisal of their own guilt with regard to the Jewish people, and following the Goldhagen debate where the Germans' role as perpetrators was once again discussed in depth, it was now reasonable to be able to turn with good conscience to Germany's own victims of war. The restriction of Germans to an 'eternally penitent role' might possibly finally be at an end (Ther 2006). The question of whether one ought ever to be allowed to 'forget' historical guilt arose notably in 1998, in the aftermath of the presentation of the Peace Prize of the German Book Trade to the writer Martin Walser at St Paul's Church, Frankfurt am Main. In his acceptance speech, Walser spoke about 'our historical burden, the never-ending shame', referring in particular to the Holocaust. As a result, a prolonged debate emerged about whether there would, in fact, ever be a time when a final line could be drawn under this issue (see Brumlik, Funke and Rensmann 2010).

During the Cold War, the historical perspective in the Federal Republic of Germany concentrating on Eastern Germany (*Ostdeutschland*), as well as any investigation covering topics such as the Nazi occupation of Poland, or the flight and expulsion of Germans, would have been easier because the different views were fixed, and there was no international or bilateral argument on the topic in the media or in the political sphere. Nevertheless, the times were not conducive to broadening the historical viewpoints about these regions so as to incorporate Polish social and academic perspectives. Accordingly, any recognition of guilt with regard to Poland was more challenging than such acknowledgement regarding Israel. Added to which are the perspectives of other national states in Eastern Europe. Put simply, if brutally, from many Germans' point of view, the reign of terror in Poland effectively represented just one facet of the terrible overall picture of the Nazi crimes in the East (Ther 2006).

In post-reunification Germany, the historical viewpoint in the former German Democratic Republic revealed itself to be fundamentally different from the historical perspective held in the old Federal Republic of Germany. In the GDR, the history of the Eastern provinces of the German Reich had been to a large extent blanked out or at best mentioned only selectively. The topic of German suffering during the last phase of the war was also avoided by the socialist politics of history. Resettlement, flight and the expulsion of Germans at the end of the Second World War remained taboo themes for historiographical research and for the media in the socialist bloc (Guth 2012: 55). GDR leaders painstakingly sought to avoid risk in any discussion of these questions, which could possibly lead to political tensions with the People's Republic of Poland, a socialist brother country. Consequently, in the years after 1989 there was a marked need for information on these topics and issues in the so-called 'new federal states'.

Poles have traditionally viewed their country as a victim nation (Hahn, Hein-Kircher, Kochanowska, 2008: 97ff) in light of such traumatic episodes as the partition of the Polish Commonwealth by Prussia, Austria and Russia at the end of the eighteenth century; the crushing of the insurrections and attempts to secure Polish independence in the nineteenth century; the double occupation by the German Reich and the Soviet Union during the Second World War; the Nazi terror; the tremendous victims during the Warsaw Uprising and ultimately the restricted sovereignty under Soviet domination after 1945. This view of the past from the perspective of the victim repeatedly came under scrutiny. However, since the 1980s and with greater impetus after 1989, discussion started to open up in the opposite direction. Self-critical debates about some Poles' behaviour towards Jews during the Second World War, and prewar Polish-Jewish relations, were started by historians and picked up in the media, involving broader circles of society. The new wave of reckoning with darker chapters in the national past included historical relations with other national groups as well (for example, Operation Vistula involving the forced resettlement of Ukrainian citizens in 1947), and the problem of the postwar expulsions of the Germans as well as the problematic issue of the camps in which the Germans were housed. In the process of this debate, the expulsion with all its associated side effects was documented and discussed, as well as being widely reappraised within the media (see also Kraft 2004). For the first time, Polish responsibility for the expulsions in general and their execution in particular was also made an issue. It was not only Poland's political and intellectual elite who dealt with this topic, but also larger parts of the general public. Particularly in those regions from which the Germans had been expelled, citizens began looking for traces of German cultural heritage and German traditions. Claudia Kraft stated that 'One may note, that during that time, people dealt more intensively with the fate of the East German expellees in Poland than in Germany itself' (Kraft 2004).[5] Yet these early discussions on the expulsions in Poland were scarcely picked up or even acknowledged in Germany – a neglect that triggered incomprehension in Poland. In addition to the discussions about expulsions and forced migrations, there was a further problematic issue to contend with when the American historian Jan Tomasz Gross published his book about the pogrom against the Jewish inhabitants of the small town of Jedwabne in North-Eastern Poland on July 1941 (Gross 2001). Attention started to turn to the concept of Poland's own responsibility for crimes in some cases.

Polish discourse then tentatively sought departure from the stereotyped victim-nation status. Just as Polish intellectuals had begun to assess the hitherto taboo problem of Polish guilt, in Germany debate steered to whether Germans might claim victim status even while acknowledging the country's responsibility for heinous war crimes. Simultaneously, there was a rediscovery in both countries of the centuries-old German-Polish cultural relationships in the Western Polish regions, formerly Prussia's Eastern provinces. Current inhabitants there have turned positive attention to the German history of 'their' region. German-Polish collaboration has intensified this process in encompassing nearly all historical and cultural-scientific areas, and has encouraged the development of new transnational research efforts and perspectives (using keywords such as 'area studies', *'Transfergeschichte'*, 'entangled history', *'histoire croisée'*, 'connected history' and 'the spatial turn') (see Werner and Zimmermann 2002). Thus the pursuit of regional historical research is at last transcending national limitations and has contributed to the development of an international discourse: in the domain of the history of Silesia, a first, comprehensive exchange of opinions took place in 1999 at the Sixteenth General Polish Historians Conference in Wrocław, when Polish and German historians were able to meet in a separate section and discuss 'Upheavals in the History of Silesia'. In this process, they were able to take up themes ranging from the Middle Ages through to the end of the Second World War (Ruchniewicz, Tyszkiewicz and Wrzesiński 2000). Further examples include the periodical *Śląska Republika Uczonych / Schlesische Gelehrtenrepublik / Slezská Vědecká Obec*, established in 2004, which is the first academic periodical to consider Silesia's history from the viewpoint of three nations: Polish, German and Czech (Fischer, Kerski, Röskau-Rydel, Ruchniewicz and Stekel 1992–2012). Pursuant to this trend, the late art historian Andrzej Tomaszewski, from Warsaw, initiated a working group of German and Polish art historians, along with a research colleague, Dethard von Winterfeld from Mainz. Together they shaped the concept of a 'common cultural heritage' of the formerly German, now Polish territories, to be explored jointly (Tomaszewski and von Winterfeld 2001; Omilanowska 2004–2012). A publication forum established in 1992, the *Inter Finitimos Yearbook of the History of German-Polish Relations* (*Inter Finitimos Jahrbuch zur deutsch-polnischen Beziehungsgeschichte*) has proved to be particularly innovative, as it informs readers about bilateral collaboration. With respect to research on the flight and expulsion of Germans, the four-volume German-Polish edition of primary sources, *Our Homeland Has Become a Strange Land* (*Unsere Heimat ist uns ein fremdes Land geworden... / Nasza ojczyzna stała się dla nas obcym państwem...*) forms the basis of the most significant progress (Borodziej and Lemberg 2000–2001). Through this type of scientific cooperation, similar efforts have become fashionable within German historical discourse during the first decade of the current millennium.

Academic Discourse Versus Popular Knowledge

Historical debates about the history of the Germans in Eastern Europe, about the history of German-Polish relations and the history of conflict in the twentieth century have now become a reality, rippling out from their instigators within the academic circle. In the first decade of the twenty-first century, against the background of the accession of Poland, the Czech Republic and further states to the EU (2004 and 2007), these topics also came to be more strongly represented in the general book market and in the mass media. Representative examples of this trend could include Günter Grass's (2002) novella *Crabwalk* (*Im Krebsgang*), which took up the theme of the expellees in a literary form. Alternately, there is the film *March of Millions* (*Die Flucht*) from 2007, dealing with events in Eastern Prussia in 1945, as well as numerous film and television documentaries covering topics from the German-Polish history. In Poland, the publishing company DEMART printed the atlas *Population Transfers, Expulsions, and Escapes 1939–1959* (*Wysiedlenia, wypędzenia i ucieczki 1939–1959*, 2008) in large numbers, which was soon translated into German and distributed on a massive scale through the Federal Agency for Civic Education (Bundeszentrale für politische Bildung). In 2010, Timothy Snyder's (2010) book *Bloodlands – Europe between Hitler and Stalin* was published, in which the struggles and suffering of the Polish people were impressively portrayed. Countless further examples could equally be listed. A considerable amount was done to popularize the history of the twentieth century.

Yet, public opinion research indicates that despite these groundbreaking efforts in academic study and in the media, we simply cannot assume that a collective knowledge among the general public about the past is actually developing within German society as a whole.

It would seem that in this day and age the over-used concept of 'collective memory' should actually be used with caution. In each case, we need to consider the question of which 'collective' it actually denotes. Does it refer to academic research and specialists, to particular political or social (interest) groups, or to the general public?

Two surveys may serve to illustrate these disparities. At the instigation of the House of the History of the Federal Republic of Germany (*Haus der Geschichte der Bundesrepublik Deutschland*) in Bonn, the Institute for Public Opinion Research in Allensbach carried out a survey that examined the topic 'Flight and expulsion from the point of view of the German, Polish and Czech populations'. The results were published in 2005 in German, Polish and in Czech (Petersen 2005). In 2011, the Foundation for German-Polish Cooperation (*Stiftung für Deutsch-Polnische Zusammenarbeit*) in Warsaw also published the results of a representative Allensbach survey that had been carried out in both Germany and Poland. This survey investigated the state of German-Polish relationships under the heading 'A big step in the direction of normality' (Fundacja Współpracy Polsko-Niemieckie Pojednanie 2011). The results can be summarized in the following ways.

Essentially, it becomes obvious through these surveys that the topic of historical German-Polish relationships does not actually constitute a genuine memorial heritage for German society as a whole. Typically, core knowledge within the German community about their neighbouring country continues to be, at best, modest and certainly full of gaping holes. In German schools it would seem that the history of Poland and Eastern Europe plays virtually no role at all. As an example, the 2005 survey revealed that when faced with a map of Europe without city names or marked areas, only 18 per cent of Germans could roughly identify the location of Silesia on the map. Even then, the concept of 'roughly identifying' allowed for a very generous margin of error. It would appear that barely one in ten Germans has even a basic historical, geographical or statistical knowledge about the topic of the 'Flight and expulsion of the Germans' at the end of the Second World War (Petersen 2005: 29–31). A similar picture arises with regard to knowledge of their neighbouring country's history. There is little knowledge in Germany about some of the key themes in Polish history. Concepts such as the Warsaw Uprising, the occupation of Poland during the Nazi era, or about the fact that Poland has suffered through two totalitarian regimes in the twentieth century alone remain for many a mystery. The comparative level of knowledge is even more meager among the younger generation. In Germany today, a mere 22 per cent of the population genuinely acknowledge any specific responsibility towards Poland as a result of the Second World War. What is worse, the younger the survey participants, the lower this percentage (Fundacja Współpracy... 2011: 47; see also Petersen 2005: 76).

When considering the typical knowledge base across the wider Polish society, surveys tend to come up with similar results on some aspects of this topic. The 2005 Allensbach Study revealed that overall knowledge among many Polish citizens about the history of modern Poland's Western and Northern regions and about the Germans who used to live there invariably tends to be relatively low. When given a list with the city names such as Warsaw, Łódź, Krakow, Wrocław (German: Breslau), Szczecin (German: Stettin) and Gdańsk (German: Danzig), only half of the Polish population were able to identify Gdańsk, Wrocław, and Szczecin as having been former German settlement areas. It is interesting to note that, even in the Northern and Western areas of Poland, those questions could not be answered with noticeably better accuracy than when asked among the general population (Petersen 2005: 76).

The 2011 survey confirmed that the memory of, and knowledge about, the Second World War continue to be far greater in Poland than in Germany. This includes awareness of the German war crimes in Poland and against the Polish people. Furthermore, this greater awareness is evident across all generations. The Polish historian Tomasz Szarota has repeatedly stated, in Poland:

> Events and individuals connected to the war are ubiquitous, whether on TV, on the radio, or in printed media. The theme remains an important element in literature and science, in film, theatre, and fine arts. Not to mention the fact that political elements constantly exploit it. Probably no other country marks anniversaries related to the events of the Second World War so often and so ceremoniously. (Quoted in Ruchniewicz 2007)

As a result, Polish society today assesses its relationship to Germany in a very different way to how the Germans view their relationship to Poland. Fifty-four per cent of all Polish people continue to hold the view that modern Germany still has a special duty with regard to Poland, which can be traced directly back to the crimes of the Second World War (see Fundacja Współpracy Polsko-Niemieckiej 2011: 48). In this respect, it is clear that there are few similarities between the two societies when it comes to how German and Polish citizens each remember their national and mutual history. However, we find quite a different picture when it comes to subject specialists and intellectuals: when taking into account specialists from both countries, whether German or Polish, there is a higher level of unanimity. Whenever the question is raised in historical discourse, over half of the specialists affirm their belief in such a sense of duty.

There is no doubt that Germans' interest in Poland and, equally, Polish people's interest in Germany is considerable. However, as far as society as a whole is concerned, this interest does not stem primarily from any sense of respect for the past or perception of a historical relationship between the two states. The decisive factor for the collective picture of their neighbour, for any sympathy or antipathy, is realistically the current day-to-day political developments of German-Polish relationships within Europe. In practical terms, this means news about economic collaboration, developments within the job market, successes in the sporting field, in academic research or in other aspects of society, as well as events in the cultural domain.

Exploitation of History

The past is inherently complex. Different peoples have different historical perspectives. Even if there is space for mutual interest, it may be combined with incomplete historical knowledge, constructed on contrasting, even contradictory, memories. As a result, history is once again proving to have an increasingly dangerous potential to be exploited for various purposes in social and political arguments. This happened repeatedly after 1989 and in quite different ways.

In the half-decade immediately after 1989, particularly after the signing of the Polish-German Treaty of Good Neighbourhood and Friendly Cooperation 1991, an intense and enthusiastic wave of reconciliation swept through both the German and the Polish peoples. In 1995, the Polish Foreign Minister, Władysław Bartoszewski, held an important speech in the German parliament, which was received very positively. He clearly and concisely addressed the difficult questions of German-Polish history, and at the conclusion called for consideration from the European perspective.[6] Reconciliation was expressed in a whole range of productions, gestures, get-together events and publications. This reconciled mood represented a general Europe-centred version of history that sometimes shut its eyes to the previously mentioned less comfortable sides of the relationships from the eighteenth to the twentieth century. Through this process of reconciliation, greater emphasis could be placed on common ground between the German and Polish peoples and on cultural exchange over the centuries. More often than not, this also seemed to serve a function of moral exoneration.

In 1994, the historian and political scientist Klaus Bachmann openly criticized this movement between Germany and Poland as 'reconciliation kitsch' (Hahn, Hein-Kircher and Kochanowska-Nieborak 2008). He argued that the mutual enthusiasm and the lack of serious bilateral discussion would result in future discord (Bachman 1994, after Jarząbek 2012: 37). It seems that after the initial euphoric phase, a subsequent chapter began in which the contrasting positions started to collide with one another. The suggestion from the Federation of Expellees in the year 2000 to build a Centre against Expulsions in Berlin brought this development starkly into focus. This plan instigated a bitter and controversial debate between Germany and Poland affecting both internal and foreign policy. Many Polish commentators thought the project represented an attempt to modify or minimize German guilt for Nazi crimes in Poland (Jarząbek 2012: 34) and the installing of a new historical discourse, where the victim and the killer are interchanged. In 2013, this critique was refined and broadened in a statement signed notably by Polish, German and Czech historians:

> there is the danger of de-contextualizing the past, thus breaking the causal relationship between the Nazi policies of radical nationalism and racial extermination on one hand and the flight and expulsion of ethnic Germans on the other hand. ... the danger of an ethnification of social conflicts, that is, the habit of interpreting political and social controversies in ethnic terms – and by that, in cementing the specific German völkisch ethno-nationalist tradition of viewing past, present and the future in ethnic terms. ('For a critical and enlightened debate...' 2003)

The coalition contract that was finalized between the governing parties in 2005 included the order to erect a 'visible representation' in Berlin, 'to remember the injustice of expulsions, and to outlaw expulsions forever'. The continuation of these discussions focused on the concept of this 'visible representation', which would ultimately be implemented by the German Federal Government in the form of a government foundation Flight, Expulsion, Reconciliation. Initially, Poland maintained its criticism of this project as well. Even though 'reconciliation' was embedded as a foundation goal in the wording of the law,[7] there were concerns that the Nazi period and the crimes of the Germans in Poland would not be appropriately represented, that the sufferings of the Germans would be overstated and that a 'rewriting' (Kittel 2012) of history might ultimately occur. After months of prolonged argument and negotiation, an initial period of active participation by a renowned Polish historian on the foundation's scientific advisory board was able to be achieved. Finally in 2012, a concept was adopted that was multi-perspective with regard to content.

This concept denoted the National Socialist expansion and extermination policies as the starting point for the expulsions, and was accepted both nationally and internationally.[8]

The historic questions about whether the twentieth century ought to be viewed as the 'century of expulsions' or the 'century of totalitarian dictatorships', as well as methodological questions about how 'the expulsions should be remembered in Europe' (Bingen, Borodziej and Troebst 2003; Naimark 2001) were each intensified through media attention on both the German and Polish sides. Sometimes stereotypes were invoked, that on the one hand focused on the continuous 'German push towards the East' and on the other hand on the hypersensitivity of the Polish people – both of which were thought to have disappeared long ago.

Differences of opinion in the area of processing history also affected other political fields, where time and again an exploitation of history occurred. In Poland, the perceived new threat caused by the changed German debate about history was frequently used as a political argument: it became a justification for opposing construction of the Russian-German gas pipeline in 2005 and it was easy to use as a political smear during various election campaigns. In the 2005 elections, it was even provocatively claimed that the grandfather of the sitting candidate, Donald Tusk, had served with the German Wehrmacht during the Second World War. Furthermore, the 2011 Polish election campaign saw the circulation of a picture depicting a militaristic German 'push toward the East' to reinforce the perceived threat from the expellee associations. It was easy to play on fear; some individuals even attributed an imperialistic policy to Germany compelling Germans to seek to win back the former German regions in the West and North of Poland. At the same time, however, the German mass media were equally quick to take up the image of the eternally dissatisfied Polish 'victim nation'[9] that just cannot let go of demands for war loss reparations.

Conclusions: Towards a Common Perspective

What consequences can reasonably be drawn from the outlined discussions in Germany and Poland? In dealing with the particularly complex history of German-Polish relations, special care and attention are needed, and simplifications and restrictions are to be avoided. In the recent political sphere, as well as in the European Union programme in support of culture, there has been a lot of consideration of potentially contentious issues such as the 'European memory culture', the 'common European understanding of history' and a 'European identity', and underpinning the considerations, the need to foster and develop these themes. In the light of the complexity of the past and the sensitivity of the outlined historical discourse, it is essential that we tread carefully when considering demands of this type, particularly when we are dealing with Eastern Europe, with the history of the Germans in this region and with problems of the German-Polish relationship in history. Attempts in the past to standardize the common view of history, for instance by totalitarian regimes, have already been discredited by communist regimes. Democratically based, pluralistic societies do not require standardized historical viewpoints. Realistically, these may not be achievable in any case, given the widely diverse experiences among people and the complexity of this particular subject.

And yet, the above very general, and in some cases simplified, analysis of historical discourse in Germany and Poland indicates that these neighbouring societies are seeking a better understanding of their diverse historical viewpoints. So realistically, what can actually be achieved? It would appear not only to be realistic but clearly desirable, that the 'national memories … gradually come into alignment', as indicated by Dan Diner (2002: 304). This means that the historical perspectives need to be reciprocally compared, and supplemented with the perspectives of the neighbour. Only then will these two countries be able to mutually enhance their all too frequently deficient historical viewpoints. One could even hope that there might yet be a breaking down of historical myths handed down over the ages.

What methods and instruments should be implemented to achieve these goals? The paradigm of *lieux de mémoire*, which has recently been tested in numerous Western and Eastern European contexts at national levels and beyond national borders, proved its value within a multinational historical discourse (Weber, Olschowsky, Petranský, Pók and Przewoźnik 2011; Kończal 2012). It is an appropriate method of looking at history, based on the assumption of a simultaneous analysis of both the historical events and the memory of these events, allowing for different national contexts, or in other words, 'divided' memories. In this way, the disparities of the remembrance become clear, and with this the possibility exists that any respective additions to the historical viewpoint can be undertaken. The research and publication project *German-Polish Places of Remembrance – Polsko-niemieckie miejsca pamięci*, conducted by the Centre for Historic Research, Berlin, of the Polish Academy of Sciences, is of central importance for the German-Polish history, and the project is dedicated to the research and mutual exchange of the cultures of remembrance for both these countries (Hahn and Traba 2012–2013). Through the approach adopted here, the concepts of history from the level of events alone through to the level of the narrative (or 'history of the second degree') will be gathered, so that it will be possible for individuals to achieve fundamental consensus.

The achievement of harmony within remembrance has long been sought and recognized within academic circles, but it is still important to broadcast it far and wide to the general public. This is particularly relevant for those times when the state of scientific argument has departed markedly from the general state of knowledge within society.

One instrument that seeks to reduce the disparity of memories not only between Germany and Poland, but across Europe, is the previously mentioned European Network of Remembrance and Solidarity. This project, supported by the governments of the participating states, is founded on an assumption of trying to include, as far as possible, all facets and themes of the history of the twentieth century without stipulating focal points that could lead to the neglect or masking of particular aspects. Because of its multilateral organization, conception and mode of operation, the network's work should be protected from the common problem of national perspectives in historical-political discourse, perspectives that can easily lead to disparities among views of history. The reconciliation of these asymmetries or disparities in remembrance cultures across European nations will continue to be a vital historical-political task, because there is nothing to indicate that the 'nation' is likely to lose its meaning as a primary point of reference for the remembrance communities in Europe in the foreseeable future (François 2013).

Notes

1. See ZDF-Mediathek: http://umuv.zdf.de/Unsere-M%C3%BCtter-unsere-V%C3%A4ter/Unsere-M%C3%BCtter-unsere-V%C3%A4ter-26223848.html; Documentation *Frankfurter Allgemeine Zeitung* http://www.faz.net/aktuell/feuilleton/medien/unsere-muetter-unsere-vaeter/; see also: *Gazeta Wyborcza*, 'Nasze matki, nasi ojcowie – skandal czy serial poruszający' http://wyborcza.pl/1,75968,14141962,_Nasze_matki__nasi_ojcowie____skandal_czy_serial_poruszajacy.html#ixzz2c7sHd300; and Steve Robson, 'Fury in Poland over German War Drama which Tries to Spread Blame for Holocaust', http://www.dailymail.co.uk/news/article-2300724/Fury-Poland-German-war-drama-tries-spread-blame-Holocaust.html.
2. See http://www.enrs.eu/en/about-us/ideas.html.
3. The Federal Institute for Culture and History of the Germans in Eastern Europe (German: *Bundesinstitut für Kultur und Geschichte der Deutschen im östlichen Europa*) was founded in Oldenburg in January 1989. On the basis of its academically independent documentation and supplementary research, the institute has the task of advising the

Government of the Federal Republic of Germany on questions related to the research, presentation and further development of culture and history of the Germans in Eastern Europe. The institute forms a part of the portfolio of the Federal Government Commissioner for Culture and Media: http://www.bkge.de/.
4. *Spiegel-Online* 22 September 2004: 'Umfrage: Polen erwarten von Deutschland Reparationszahlungen': http://www.spiegel.de/politik/ausland/umfrage-polen-erwar ten-von-deutschland-reparationszahlungen-a-319231.html.
5. Latest publication on the subject: Müller and Zielińska 2012; see also Borodziej 2003.
6. Speech of Władysław Bartoszewski in Deutscher Bundestag on 28 April 1995: http://www.bundestag.de/kulturundgeschichte/geschichte/gastredner/bartoszewski/rede_bartoszewski.html#bart.
7. Stiftung Flucht, Vertreibung, Versöhnung: http://www.sfvv.de; Documentation *Gazeta Wybocza*: http://info.wyborcza.pl/temat/wyborcza/fundacja+ucieczka+wyp%C4%99dze nie+pojednanie. The purpose of the foundation is 'to preserve, in the spirit of reconciliation, the memory and commemoration of flight and expulsion in the twentieth century in the historical context of World War Two, National Socialist expansionism and extermination policy, and their consequences'.
8. For the conceptual framework for the foundation Flight, Expulsion, Reconciliation and guidelines for the planned permanent exhibition, see: http://www.sfvv.de/sites/default/files/downloads/conceptual_framework_sfvv_2012.pdf.
9. Examples from the contributions of Urban 2005: 157–165, 175–179; see also 'Kaczyński Warns of Germany's Imperial Ambitions' 2011.

Matthias Weber is a historian and Germanist. Since 2005 he has served as the director of the Federal Institute for Culture and History of the Germans in Eastern Europe (BKGE) in Oldenburg and as the German Coordinator of the European Network Remembrance and Solidarity. He was awarded his habilitation in Contemporary and German Regional History by the University of Oldenburg. He has been an associate professor since 1999. His main areas of research are the history of Silesia, early modern history, the Habsburg monarchy and German regional history. He is a member of the Silesian Historical Commission and of the J.G. Herder Research Council, which supports historical research in the history and social and cultural history of Eastern Europe.

Chapter 15

REMEMBERING COLLECTIVIZATION IN BULGARIA

Yana Yancheva

The mnemonic consequences of land collectivization have not played a large part in memory studies in Eastern Europe, although they have affected a large part of the population of this rural region. The recent interpretations of collectivization show that on the one hand, together with 'dekulakization, it was one of the communist authority's important instruments for constant and total control over the peasants' property, behavior, everyday practices and beliefs, as well as a way of achieving ethnic and social homogeneity of the population in compound territories' (Baberowski and Doering-Manteuffel 2009; Browning and Siegelbaum 2009). In such a view, collectivization was part of the total process of cultural and social transformation of the villages, which Lynne Viola (1999: 3) defines as violence, and a blow which aimed to destroy the common norms and moral principles of the peasant culture. These conclusions refer to collectivization in Soviet Russia in the 1930s, but they concern also the later stages of Soviet-type collectivization in Eastern Europe. On the other hand, some authors describe it as a long process of negotiations and 'persuasion' rather than as one dictatorial act. Recently, Katherine Verdery and Gail Kligman (Verdery and Kligman 2011; Kligman and Verdery 2011) discussing the Romanian example reveal the authorities' ways of imposing policies, of manipulating the social context in villages and especially the party activists' technology of 'persuading' peasants to join the collectives only by their 'voluntary consent' as well as describing the peasants' resistance against collectivization, and their alternative 'technologies' of modifying the official power.

Using this historical background, the present study reconstructs the contemporary viewpoints of Bulgarian farmers on collectivization. Based on the comparative analysis of recollections of two different rural communities in Bulgaria – Mezdreya and Brestovitsa – the research reveals the participants' and witnesses' memory strategies, narratives and interpretations of the former clashes between the peasants and the authorities' agents, and the creation of the cooperative farms. The chapter reveals two different interpretations of collectivization in the respective villages. The first, as it is reflected in life stories from the village of Mezdreya, presents the process as a traumatizing historical situation and social change (Sztompka 1994, 2000: 452–458; Alexander 2003), which caused disorientation, dislocation of social strata and disruption of order. The other interpretation is predominant for the population from Brestovitsa, which sees collectivization as a revolutionary change, which successfully enabled economic and social development for the community. This chapter argues that collectivization has been remembered in different ways by the residents of the two villages, because of the different social, economic and political conditions under which it was carried out. The most important purpose and contribution of this research is to show that multiple and competitive groups' memories of the past exist simultaneously and collectivization in Bulgaria cannot be studied and evaluated in a one-sided fashion. The comparative analysis of competing versions and assessments of the process reveal that it is a realm of public memory, but not a realm of common memory.

The chapter is informed by the branch of Bulgarian ethnology that examines the issue of collectivization within the context of the overall everyday peasant culture and 'lived history' (Dobreva and Roth 1997; Dobreva 1994, 1997a, 1997b, 2000, 2003; Roth 1998, 2001; Wolf 2000, 2003; Petrov 2003), as well as by those authors who pay attention to various memory groups and agencies in contemporary Bulgaria (particularly see Luleva 2010 on the divided memory groups; Deyanova 2009; and Dobreva 1997a, 1997b on the strategies of remembering collectivization). More generally, the analysis is based on the theory of divided memories of different generational units and social groups (Mannheim 1952). They differ in their experiences, which generate dissimilar interpretations, assessments and collective memories of particular events or facts. As a result, a group can ignore or omit in its memory facts that are significant to another group. The memory groups are framed depending on the place of living and mainly on the local historical, political and ecological environment. Inside the communities, there are also different groups, whose positions are defined by their political affiliation, social status and local history.

The present study's methodology is based on the narrative biographical interview approach (Wengraf et al. 2002), because it provides an opportunity to trace relations between the personal experience of the event, the historical act and the variety of different contemporary viewpoints. The subjective reflection on a particular event, such as collectivization, within the larger frames of life story is bound up with the reflection on memory work and recollection – a major research hurdle of my work. In this way the study draws on ideas from the works of Maurice Halbwachs (1992), Barbara Misztal (2003) and Jeffrey K. Olick (2008) about memory as a current retrospective interpretation ('reproduction') of the past. The dynamics of memory approach (Misztal 2003: 67–77) considers memory to be an active process of constant renegotiation between official ideology and the alternative outlooks, between versions and present representations of the past based on the interests of certain groups to which the individual belongs, 'a fluid negotiation between the desires of the present and the legacies of the past' (Olick 2008: 159). The chapter takes into account the selective function of memory and its ability to portray events as markers of change. Memory is considered an active and cognitive function capable of extracting events from their historical context and transforming them into 'symbolic texts', which make it possible to understand the identities and changes in the community's public life.

The Villages: Historical Scenarios and Research Strategy

Collectivization in Bulgaria was carried out under local social and economic specificities with various scenarios of the process for different regions of the country, which is why comparative study is necessary. The villages Brestovitsa, in the Plovdiv region of central South Bulgaria and Mezdreya, in the Berkovitsa region of North-West Bulgaria, were chosen for field studies for several reasons. They represent two geographical and ecological categories that determined the primary territorial and economic disparities between the agricultural cooperatives in the country. The history of the two villages and collectivization reflects two different aspects of public and political struggle in the rural communities from that historical period.

Brestovitsa is a large village in the vicinity of Plovdiv (Bulgaria's second biggest city) – a location that gives a number of advantages and development opportunities (Gatev 2009). Its population has decreased in number in more recent times – from 5,500 persons in 1951 to 3,750 persons in 2007. The village is situated in the rich and fertile Thracian Valley and occupies 5,302 hectares (with arable land as large as 3,202 hectares). Due to its geographical location, the village had well-developed agriculture, more particularly viniculture and wine making which was exclusively market-oriented. Before the act of collectivization, the social

Figure 15.1 Map of Bulgaria.

structure of the population was no different from the general picture for the country in this period: about 20 per cent of households had very small pieces of land or no land at all, 50 per cent was the share of small farms with 1–3 hectares of land, 25 per cent of the village residents had middle-size farms of 3–5 hectares, and the percentage of large farm owners was very small.

Brestovitsa is an example of early and comparatively voluntary formation of agricultural cooperatives in 1948, which was due to the early spread of socialist ideas in the region and the communist youth organizations' strong impact on community life in the 1940s. In 1948, ninety-nine farmers, most of them owners of middle-size farms, consolidated their plots and formed the Labour-Cooperative Farm 'New Life'. From its very beginning, the cooperative developed intensively and offered a good living, so it attracted about a third of the private farmers even before the obligatory mass cooperation in 1951 (Regional State Archive, Plovdiv: F1038-1-5). Over the next few years, the cooperative farm developed with wide-ranging and high-profit production activities and started to influence the public agenda of village life.

In Brestovitsa today one can observe the restoration of agriculture to its previous position of a major economic activity for the local population, only this time in a private form. However, present-day agriculture cannot compare with the achievements of the past before collectivization. Most private farmers now continue the vine-growing and wine-making traditions, working in their restituted vineyards, but their produce is for their own households' needs. Those farmers who are trying to make a living out of viniculture expressed strong discontent with the contemporary economic situation in the country which, in their opinion, is characterized by monopoly and corruption: the agricultural producers' rights not being properly guaranteed, a lack of subsidies and overly complicated application procedures. These adverse circumstances have forced large numbers of local residents to give up on viniculture as their major means for subsistence despite the favourable ecological and geographical features of the region. Still Brestovitsa, in contrast to Mezdreya, has retained the vitality of its community.

Mezdreya offers an example of a different scenario. The village is located in the mountainous region of North-West Bulgaria. Over the years, its population has been steadily decreasing in number and has reached an almost depopulated state: from 888 inhabitants in 1943 to a meagre 264 inhabitants at present (The Mayor of Mezdreya and the Regional State Archive in Montana: 34K-1-264). It occupies 1,042 hectares, of which 751 hectares are arable land (the Municipal Agricultural Service in Berkovitsa). The social structure of the population before the act of collectivization was similar to that in Brestovitsa, despite the lesser degree of development. Before collectivization, the village of Mezdreya was characterized by considerable fragmentation of land and ineffective agricultural production, mostly oriented to meet the households' needs. The major and most profitable produce was strawberries, which were exported for the national and international market. The agricultural cooperative in Mezdreya was essentially a small one, with limited production and limited use of mechanized equipment, and its impact on the modernization of the village was insignificant.

In Mezdreya, collectivization was carried through in the period 1956 to 1958, the final stage of the process for the whole country. In April 1956 twenty-nine petty farmers (15 per cent of the village households, basically the Communist Party supporters) consolidated only 61 hectares of land. Under the pressure of the local party organization they established the Labour-Cooperative Farm 'Strawberry'. The ultimate mass cooperation was carried through in 1958, but it was met with serious resistance, tension and general disapproval by the rural population because of the private farmers' traditionally strong bond with their land and the popularity of the Bulgarian Agrarian National Union's political platform.

Nowadays the population of Mezdreya mostly consists of retired people. There are very few families of active working age who live there or who have retained close family relations or agricultural connections with the village. Landowners typically give up on agriculture and even on the restitution of their inherited property because of the geographical location of the village in the poorest and most underdeveloped region in Bulgaria and the European Union. The impossibility of setting up profitable agricultural enterprises is due to the further fragmentation of small pieces of property among the many heirs.

Between 2006 and 2008 I carried out biographical interviews with about forty people in each village. The range of my narrators encompassed mostly former cooperative members, contemporaries of collectivization, participants or opponents of the process and their descendants. Thus the age criterion was somewhat restrictive to people over fifty-five, but on the other hand, the interviewees were characterized with a variety of jobs, social status, political affiliations and degrees of involvement in agriculture and collectivization. Among the interviewees there were former cooperative workers, as well as lower or higher rank former cooperative managers, village municipal employees and other functionaries in the socialist service industry, teachers, medical workers, higher and middle-rank representatives of the nomenclature. Some interviewees did not associate their lives with cooperatives, but experienced the process of collectivization. Others were children during collectivization, but they have a concrete opinion about the process and the cooperatives. A section of the people who experienced the process were politically engaged with one or other political ideology, but there were also many who supported or renounced collectivization without specific policy positions.

In this research I have tried to reveal personally experienced history through the narratives, considering the impact of the communicative situation, to find out how a particular historical event (collectivization) is rationalized and interpreted by individual biographical memories. At first the interviewees were asked to retell their life story and family history (if possible). After that they were asked open questions concerning the autobiographical story, as well as for more detailed information about the implementation of collectivization in the village, their own participation and experience, descriptions of the participants in the process and their actions. In the third phase the narrators were asked to present their personal assessment of the process, of its impact and influence on the village development and specifically on their lives.

Getting in touch with narrators from Mezdreya was facilitated by the fact that it was the birthplace of my grandparents (deceased at that time), and I used their social network of relatives and acquaintances. I knew two of them, who introduced me to their neighbours, colleagues and other relatives. They also took me to their acquaintances and I was able to interview the majority of the villagers, who participated in and experienced collectivization. The situation was similar in Brestovitza, although I did not know anyone there before I began my research. I was initially introduced to a man who is famous in the village as the author of the village history and who had worked in the public sphere and in the municipality for many years. My landlady also happened to be a very popular and respected former cooperative worker. In the same way, I used both of their wide social networks to meet a bigger part of the representatives of the target group from the village.

Most of the people I met accepted interviews as an opportunity to express their opinion on collectivization. Some of them, who did not support collectivization and the socialist rule as a whole (predominantly people from Mezdreya), sought a rehabilitation of their actions and ideas, which were rejected and condemned in the socialist period. They needed to provide assessment of their life in harmony with the contemporary (often antisocialist) conventions. Others (mostly from Brestovitsa but not exclusively), initiators or supporters of collectivization, wanted to morally justify their previous ideas, beliefs and actions to the present domineering rightist concepts and the outlook of the next generations, who refuse to accept, or simply ignore them.

Usually the interviews lasted for one and a half or two hours, but some narrators were interviewed more than once depending on their significant role in the process, recollection ability or willingness to narrate. I conducted all the interviews myself, then transcribed and archived them at the Scientific Archive of the Institute of Ethnology and Folklore Studies with Ethnographic Museum at the Bulgarian Academy of Sciences, archival unit no. 682–III.

Mezdreya: Remembering Violence and Destruction

For the respondents from Mezdreya, where cooperative farming was met with resentment and even resistance by the local private farmers, the clash with the 'agitators' (collectivization propagandists) and the elaboration of their image is one of the most important aspects of the memory of collectivization. The groups of 'agitators' included Communist Party members, members of the already established cooperatives from neighbouring towns and villages, and local activists. It was their task to 'persuade' by all means the private farmers to join the labour-cooperative farm.

The physical clash between the farmers and the 'agitators' during the mass collectivization is expressed through the verbal opposition between the images of the two sides, where the latter are rationalized as agents of change. In the narratives of the contemporaries and their descendants, the private farmers are portrayed as strong personalities with concrete individual features who felt emotions, fear, attachment and who protected their families, home and property, suffering a loss and having their hopes broken. To put it another way, their image is human, and their behaviour towards the 'agitators' is the result of their personal (and human) motives.

In contrast, the 'agitators' are devoid of their human nature or individual character and are portrayed as a super-organism – a swarm, a crowd as T.Z.T. (female, born 1945) describes them, 'They came one morning. Very early, at dawn. So many of them! A swarm of ants! Some of them from Borovtsi, all sorts of them'. It is emphasized that their activity and behaviour were not driven by personal motives or needs, but rather by a party assignment. The demonic and disastrous nature of the 'agitators' in the narratives is strengthened by their comparison to pests and predators (they are not only called 'ants', but also 'wolves' and some narrators tell about farmers being chased with dogs), and by their multitude and image of 'strangers' which is always mentioned in the narrative. They were described as 'enormous men from the field', 'a thousand agitators', etc. This image is completed with the notion of their criminal and immoral nature. A number of interviewees name the propagandists 'a gang' or 'robbers', and a lot of stories are told about violence, beatings, humiliation and the pointing of guns. In the narrative reflection of the conflict the peasants take on the image of victims because they are the ones who are chased, 'hunted' and beaten.

The clash between the private farmers from Mezdreya and the propagandists is the other significant realm of memory work, which represents collectivization as traumatic experience in the life of this rural community (Yancheva 2012). The narratives themselves induce the notion of this clash being perceived as a state of war. Some respondents mention prolonged sieges of private houses, isolation, pursuit and beatings, presence of the police, the army, dogs, the use of weapons, violence against women and the elderly. Others explicitly name all of this 'a war' or 'a revolution'. For example, Z.A.F. (male, 1930–2007) tells: 'There was a war going on. Twenty days of beatings inside the houses. And breaking of doors. And nobody dared to go out, even to the pub. … And you can't see a soul in the square, not a soul in the streets either. Everyone locked themselves in and barred the doors.'; 'They broke down people's doors and smashed windows, they did all sorts of things … They got inside the houses and the children screamed, and the women screamed, too, and … it was really a war going on here.'

The female narrators present the most expressive and emotional descriptions of that clash because they often had to meet and stop the activists at home while their husbands were trying to escape. T.G.N. (female, born 1938) relates that her father-in-law had left earlier to avoid signing up for cooperative membership. The activists followed her husband and shot at him. She remembers that she was pregnant at the time and everything happened while a brass band was playing in front of the house. L.G. (female, born 1922) had a similar experience. Beginning her story with 'My god! They're gonna finish us!' she remembers that the activists surrounded the house, smashed the door and found her husband hiding in the attic. They tried to kill him, but L.G. and her mother-in-law managed to push him outside. At the same time her father-in-law escaped from the village and hid in the nearby forest, but the activists let the army dogs hunt for him and so they caught him. N.A.Al. (female, 1937–2009) also mentions that one of the propagandists 'wanted to shoot me down through the window that morning. They had given him a pistol. ... And I was rocking my baby daughter in a rocker ... He pointed the gun to shoot me. Well, what could I do, I grabbed the child and ran off.'

The attitudes of the population of Mezdreya to collectivization are expressed in a straightforward way in the interviews. The outlooks of the respondents (witnesses, actual sufferers or their descendants) share several common trends.

Firstly, the mass imposition and set-up of labour-cooperative farms is seen as a horrifying event that evoked fear of the system and of the authorities (Yancheva 2012). The memory of collectively experienced trauma is considered fundamental for the formation of collective identity of certain generations or for the whole local community, because memory and the ability to reconstruct the past are deeply linked to the present sense of personal identity (Alexander 2003).

Another very important trend is that the interviewees deny the official socialist narrative of collectivization as a voluntary process implemented willingly and enthusiastically by the whole rural population. To counter this, the interviewees stake a claim for the authenticity of their own version of the story, according to which the process was carried out against the private farmers' will and by means of pressure and humiliation.

Collectivization is frequently evaluated as an act of robbery of private property performed by the local party and government elites. For example, T.Z.T. (female, born 1945) said, 'They stole everything. They took the money. They seized people's property. They destroyed and unfenced the plots of land.'; 'They took the land, they took it all. They took the cows and the ploughs. Well, they robbed everything down there ... the ploughs, the rakes ... And they put it all down there in the cooperative.'

Obviously, the process was not experienced as an input of private capital into the cooperative farm, but rather as its expropriation by the labour-cooperative farm. Some respondents even go further by making a parallel between collectivization and 'nationalization', which also supports the tendency described.

The attitude of the peasants to collectivization is unequivocally stated and can be summed up with a quote by L.G. (female, born 1922), 'We don't like the labour-cooperative farm. Who would give away their land for free!' The implication that the land had been taken away forcibly goes to show that the interviewee does not accept the official ideological version of this act being a change in the form of management (from private to collective ownership) and use of the land. The interviewees' frequent attempts to distance themselves from the society of cooperative members demonstrate how they viewed the labour-cooperative farm as a creation and 'sphere of dominance' of party activists who dealt with it as if it was theirs, and not collective property, as it was claimed in the propaganda documents. The statement by M. (female, born 1925) – 'And we enrolled to go to work in the cooperative ... We enrolled as workers there' – shows that peasants viewed themselves as wage-workers, not as members of the labour-cooperative farms.

A common trend in the opinions of people in Mezdreya is the rendering of collectivization in the image of disintegration, an ending, a complete destruction from which there is no recovery: 'they carried away everything', 'they liquidated our property and left the land barren'; 'they took it all ... and it was the end'; 'you're broke', 'it was over'; 'they destroyed so much you can't even speak it all'. The process of cooperation is evaluated as an 'end' – the end of their lives, the end of their high productivity, the end of the patriarchal idyll and the end of the village.

The reason for the negative attitudes towards collectivization of the peasants from Mezdreya is the unanimously shared opinion that it promised rapid progress for the village and its population, which never became a reality. On the contrary, it detached the younger generations from the land and farming, thus leading to the gradual depopulation of the community. The few people in Mezdreya whose assessment of collectivization is positive are those who were once involved in the Communist Party policy and ideology. According to them, it was a successful process that achieved the promised modernization in the form of machine-operated agriculture, development of various branches and farms, 'abundant' crops, a calm life with a sense of security for the rural population, work satisfaction, improved quality of life due to the mass construction of modern homes and development of the village infrastructure. However, most private farmers and their descendants disagree with this opinion.

Brestovitsa:
Remembering the Approval for Collectivization

The way collectivization is seen and evaluated by the population of Brestovitsa is contrary to the way it was narrated by the people from Mezdreya. Thus, in the interviews from Brestovitsa there are very few examples of negative attitudes towards the process of collectivization during the time of its implementation or in the present. The cooperative documents show that it was founded after the Regional Communist Party Committee's order. However, the local people's memories are dominated by two compatible ideas about the implementation of collectivization: one is ideological and the other economic. They are both explained in the light of general approval for collectivization and are developed into three complementary versions of how it was carried out.

The first version is that of the ex-Communist Party activists, functionaries and ideological supporters whose careers were not involved with agriculture – they witnessed, but did not participate directly in the process. They portray collectivization in the manner of communist ideology's rhetoric as a general people's initiative and the result of their great enthusiasm; they also underscore the leading role of the Communist Party as the initiator for the set-up of the local labour-cooperative farm. The stories told by this category of interviewees aimed to defend the idealized image of collectivization, which they truly believe in. Because of that, they deliberately or involuntarily softened any possible interpretation of events that could suggest public tension or unrest.

I.Y. (female, born 1928) is a typical representative of the ex-party activists in the village. She remembers:

> And so, at the end of 1947, and throughout 1948, 1949 and the beginning of 1950 this group of enthusiasts were lucky in their farming enterprise and earned a lot of money for their work. They were able to buy a few tractors and other machines and they started to cultivate the land which had actually been theirs earlier, but the plots had been scattered here and there, and now the Communist Party consolidated it all. As far as I can recall, we were compensated for our plot of land that joined the cooperative with another plot. There were quite a few protests, but in Brestovitsa there weren't any serious conflicts.

On the matter of mass cooperation the narrator said:

> In 1951, they had this music playing in the village square, and there were slogans on lamp posts which read 'Mass collectivization'. And then things started to turn unpleasant. I came home and started to push my grandfather to join the cooperative. I told him, 'You must join the labour-cooperative farm! You can't

stay out of it! You will ruin my future!' That's how I understood things back then.

In their memories of collectivization, the ex-party functionaries place the stress upon the clash of generations and 'the victory of the young people and the progressive spirit'; they tell ardently and with satisfaction about their achievements when they were young and active participants in the Communist Party youth organizations. These include, for example, the implementation of various 'progressive' ideas such as the youth volunteer movement, cooperation of land, set-up of youth dance groups and theatre companies, organization of sports events and even gender equality. Being influenced by their ideological convictions, they view the cooperators as a monolith, a mass of individuals who think and act as one, or distinguish between the cooperative members on the basis of age, i.e., between the young and 'progressive' members, bearers of socialist spirit, and the old members who are attached to traditional norms and private property interests.

The second viewpoint expressed in the interviews is that of the initiators and establishers of the labour-cooperative farm who later participated in its management. They were mainly adepts of the socialist ideology and communist activists and had been involved in antifascist activity ('our men, the communists'), and according to their narratives, were not simply fulfilling a party assignment; rather, they genuinely believed in the advantages that cooperative farms had to offer. They, too, portray collectivization as a voluntary process, but they believe it was the result of their own initiative, enthusiasm and organizational skills. This category of interviewees also views the cooperators as one organism; however, they distinguish between 'we – the managers' and 'they – the workers'. For them, the main realms of memory are the setting up of the cooperative, and the reminiscences of cooperative life and production activities, which are sometimes rendered as acts of heroism. Most of the narratives tell about productive competition, festivities, celebration of successes and abundant crops, etc.

The third perspective is that of the non-communist establishers and the cooperative workers who also describe cooperation of land as a voluntary act, but not motivated by ideological reasons. They point out the pragmatic economic reasons that motivated most of the private farmers, as the cooperative farm provided its members with satisfactory income and ensured employment for the petty farmers whose land was not enough to earn subsistence. For example, B.S.P. (female, born 1920) remembered, 'And in the autumn they paid us a thousand levs wages. It was very good money. So, the next year other people wanted to join, too, and that's how we got mass cooperation'. This group of interviewees identify as the initiators of the labour-cooperative farm, 'the more eminent' and wealthy people ('the more eminent in the village', 'The big farmers with a lot of land', 'a dozen rich farmers', 'those who had a lot of land ... became supervisors'), people of authority and experience in the village community. So they were aware of the existence of social stratification in the cooperative farm on the basis of two categories: 'the eminent', i.e., those involved in management, and 'the poor', i.e., the apolitical workers with whom they identify themselves.

All three groups of interviewees point out the fact that they were convinced about the success and advantages of the labour-cooperative farm from its very beginning, and that they still hold this opinion nowadays. Many of them make clear that they were willing to join the cooperative farm as soon as it was formed but they had to wait for a year or two until they could persuade their parents. The (slighter or greater) confrontation with their parents when they asked for a share of the family land with which to become cooperative members is the main realm of memory for these informants. They often describe how difficult it was for the old owners to part with their land. The narratives show that in Brestovitsa, the labour-cooperative farm attracted mostly the younger generation, who saw in it a chance for higher and more secure income and improvement of labour conditions and quality of life.

The memories of collectivization in Brestovitsa often underscore the enthusiasm with which the cooperative farm was founded. A few informants, however, give an account of a certain tension, which was due to the fact that the larger part of Brestovitsa's population joined the cooperation during its mass phase. In people's recollections there is some memory of pressure being put on private farmers who did not want to enter the cooperative. These were some larger landowners, a few supporters of the Bulgarian Agrarian National Union and some representatives of the older generation. The narratives often mention some acts of public defaming of these farmers – they were declared *kulaks* and their doors and walls were inscribed with the label '*Kulak* – enemy of the people'. However, in contrast to Mezdreya, in Brestovitsa nobody hinted at the use of physical violence against the resisting farmers, or at intense conflicts; psychological pressure was all that was mentioned. For this reason, the image of the 'agitators' and the clash with them does not hold such an important place in the memory of collectivization in Brestovitsa as in Mezdreya.

So the way that socialist agricultural collectivization has been remembered in Mezdreya and Brestovitsa presents dissimilar memories of two local communities, based on their different experiences of the process. Besides the differences in recollecting the establishment of the cooperative farms, the populations of both villages share some common realms of memory: how private farmers were manipulated through disadvantageous compensations for the private land given to the cooperative, increased delivery for the obligatory state supply system, insecurity for their children's future opportunities for education and employment, public greetings on the loudspeakers for everyone who joined the cooperative and public defaming for those who did not join it.

The two villages differ as well in terms of their population's attitude to collectivization. In contrast to Mezdreya, where the official version of the voluntary mass cooperation was renounced not only by those who suffered from it, but also by the supporters of the socialist regime and collectivization, most of Brestovitsa's middle-aged inhabitants (not only the retired ones) expressed their approval of it and the need to rehabilitate it and prove its positive impact on the village's development and people's lives. The current situation in Bulgaria with the anticommunist discourse that denounces collectivization and the reverse process of reprivatization come into conflict with the personal memories and attitudes of the ex-cooperators from Brestovitsa, making them feel the need to justify their past beliefs, decisions, actions and lives. Although the claims about the 'general enthusiasm' for cooperation in Brestovitsa are highly exaggerated, one cannot deny the fact that the process there was carried out with the approval and voluntary participation of the larger part of the population, as most interviewees asserted. That is why the scenarios for implementation of collectivization and mass cooperation in the two villages differ substantially. All respondents, even the opponents of collectivization, testify that in Brestovitsa there were no fierce conflicts like those in Mezdreya.

Another point of difference between the two villages is the attitude of their communities towards the functioning and management of their labour-cooperative farms. In Brestovitsa, joining the farm was considered mostly like the start of a new job, whereas in Mezdreya it was perceived as the deprivation of private property. Respectively, for many of the first members of the cooperative farm in Brestovitsa, their work on it was by far a better prospect than their small private farms or working as hired hands.

Most of the population of Mezdreya hold exactly the opposite position. They deny the effectiveness of collectivization and the local cooperative farm, pointing out the negative impact of the process which, for them, failed to achieve its goals. Among the most frequently mentioned reasons for the failure is the fact that collectivization resulted in a poor and unproductive cooperative that was unable to provide its members with satisfactory income or to favourably influence the economic and cultural development of the community. Moreover, the respondents blame collectivization for the village's depopulation, and most of all, for the younger generations' detachment from the land and farming.

The informers from Mezdreya demonstrated a critical and negative attitude to the labour-cooperative farm as an institution. It is seen as a place where the cooperative members were exploited by the managing body and the Communist Party functionaries. Most of the interviewees completely denied the collective factor in the management of the farm because their rights as cooperative members and collective owners were always ignored by the managing body. The villagers share the opinion that local agriculture was ruined as a result of collectivization, and mostly because of the corrupt practices developed by the managing elites; the constructive and modernizing role of the cooperative farm is usually denied.

Conclusion

This research has shown how the biographical approach makes it possible to study the memory of socialist collectivization decades after the actual implementation of the process. Through the comparative analysis of recollections from two different rural communities and regions in Bulgaria, the present chapter shows the existence of opposing interpretations and divided memories of the implementation of collectivization, based on differences in the way it was taken, experienced and remembered by the communities. In contemporary public discourse there is no agreement on the public value of collectivization and its consequences. Numerous individual and group counter-memories are engaged in mutually opposing their moral and political assessments about the past and in a heated argument, each one defending its own 'versions' and 'scenarios' of the actual development of collectivization.

The research on the selective function of memory enables us to understand people's perceptions of the event and of the deep transformations caused in their personal and communal lives. The collective memory transforms the historical event into political myths ('reproductions') that act as magnifying lenses through which group members perceive and reflect on the past, present and future. Through memory, collectivization is 'read' as a 'symbolic text', which both describes the event as a traumatic experience, which destroyed people's lives, or as a process of development, and as a creative common act of the villagers.

So the narratives of collectivization in Brestovitsa and Mezdreya offer a vivid illustration of the competition and dispute between the different versions – on one hand, there is the story of the enthusiasm shown by the first cooperative members and the voluntary character of cooperation; on the other hand, there is the narration of the pressure and violence against the rural population committed by the authority's agents during the mass phase of cooperation. As a result of these conflicting memories, the historical event in the focus of our attention can be classified as an active (even if not a dominant) realm of work of individual, family and public memory, but not as a realm of common memory and agreement, which means that past traumas have not yet been overcome.

The analysis of interviews reveals that all the narrators' attitudes to collectivization combine the nostalgic perspective with the present-day retrospective viewpoint which is influenced by the current circumstances. However, the research has also demonstrated that collectivization in Bulgaria cannot be viewed as an unequivocal process. It was a turning point in the country's development, a source of cultural crisis and trauma which was experienced, remembered and retold in a different way by the two village communities and by the different social groups within them.

Yana Yancheva is a senior assistant professor at the Institute of Ethnology and Folklore Studies with Ethnographic Museum at the Bulgarian Academy of Sciences. Her main interests are the ethnology of socialism and post-socialism, collective memory, everyday life, youth (sub)cultures and cultural heritage. Her dissertation focuses on the collective memory of agricultural collectivization and the everyday aspects of cooperative life. Other projects relate to the Bulgarian Bessarabians' recollections on the Soviet collectivization in Moldova and Ukraine, and a study on the development and identification of a local rock community.

Chapter 16

USES AND MISUSES OF MEMORY
Dealing with the Communist Past in Postcommunist Bulgaria and Romania

Claudia-Florentina Dobre

Immediately after the fall of the Iron Curtain, 'memory' became the key notion for approaching the communist past. The 'rediscovered memory' of East Europe (Brossat et al.1990) became the subject of numerous articles and books. Scholars analysed the collective/individual/national/historical memory of communism from different angles: nostalgia versus amnesia (Troebst and Brunnbauer 2006; Todorova and Gille 2010), mediums of remembering or 'genres of representation' (Todorova 2010), public monuments of the communist era (Losonczy 1999; Ladd 2002; Combe, Dufrêne and Robin 2009), communism as a *lieu de mémoire* (Znepolski 2004) and public policies on memorializing communism (Esbenshade 1995; Verdery 1999; Maurel and Mayer 2008). A few scholars have focused on the de-communization process and its legal and political ramifications (Welsh 1996; Huyse 1995).

This chapter deals with two case studies of de-communization in Eastern Europe. Focusing on Bulgaria and Romania and their struggle in coming to terms with their communist past, the chapter endeavours to show how collective memory is used and misused during the de-communization process. Rather than being a means of alleviating the communist trauma, memory was more often the subject of appropriation, manipulation, distortion and reconstruction.

There are solid grounds for studying the Bulgarian and Romanian postcommunist transitions in conjunction with each other. Both countries belong to the Eastern Orthodox world, had similar agrarian economies during (and even after) the interwar period and experienced a similar type of communism (Stalinization was followed by nationalism-communism, no revolutions or important dissident movements). Most importantly, in

---

Notes for this chapter begin on page 313.

both countries the transitional period after 1989 witnessed the continued presence of former communists in public life. Bulgaria and Romania faced the same hurdles in creating a functional constitutional democracy; their road to a democratic state and market economy was driven by the communist past and its avatars.

By the same token, the differences between the two countries cannot be ignored. Bulgaria had a more balanced society during the interwar period, and was traditionally closer to Moscow than Romania. Bulgarian civil society began to take shape before communism's collapse, whereas in Romania only a handful of people had the courage to openly oppose Ceausescu's regime. Lastly, Romania's transition was less dominated by the struggle around communist symbols and legacy than Bulgaria's.

My approach in this chapter focuses on the role played by 'political order' in shaping the postcommunist memorial landscape (Verdery 1999). Following Iskra Baeva and Evghenia Kalinova (2010), I am interested in how political parties distorted or manipulated memory in their efforts to gain political legitimization and/or to stay in power. In particular, the present chapter aims to contribute to scholarship in the field of postcommunist studies by comparing the state of public memory of communism in Bulgaria and Romania in the last twenty-five years. The analysis of the public memorial policies regarding the communist regime evinces both similarities and differences in the process of forging an official memory of communism in Bulgaria and Romania. The chapter also traces the influence of EU institutions on this process. Notwithstanding European and national efforts to manufacture a 'black memory' of communism, individual recollections range from grey to 'pink' to the 'red' stage of communist nostalgia.

The present study of public discourses, historiography and mass media is part of a larger work in progress.[1] It aims to contribute to the nuanced understanding of the postcommunist period in two former communist countries. The public memory of communism in both countries is like a palimpsest; therefore each new study can make its contribution to the nuanced understanding of this historical period and to the ongoing process of societal transformation from communism to democracy.

Collective Memory, Public Memory

Understanding postcommunist societies requires an understanding of the way they deal with their recent past. The traumas caused by communist regimes were not limited to the individuals who were the direct target of persecution and repression, but affected the whole society as fear, dissimulation, manipulation and repression were constant features of the communist system. The 'working through' process (*le travail de deuil*) via public displays of memories (individual and/or collective) could play an important role in healing individuals and societies.

Memory is an individual faculty, and societies can be said to remember only 'insofar as their institutions and rituals organize, shape, even inspire their constituents' memories' (Young 1993: xi). This inspiration finds its sources in the present since we always interpret the past through the lens of the present (Halbwachs 1925). This means that our memory focuses on some aspects of the past according to 'memorial regimes',[2] which select and organize the different collective memories while striving to accommodate conflicting remembrances in order to create public consensus about the past.

The collective memory unifies a group 'through time and over space by providing a narrative frame' (Eyerman 2004: 161). This narrative frame can travel in space and time and gives individuals, groups or communities the opportunity to bond with their past and to envisage their future. When a selected collective memory dominates the public space it plays an important part in shaping collective identity and in surpassing the cultural trauma through commemorations, rituals and cultural artefacts displayed in public spaces, such as memorials, museums and artistic installations. This selected collective memory informs the normative memorial framework and the memorial representations of public actors, who in turn are themselves fashioned by these memorial representations and norms (Michel 2010: 12–17).[3]

Anticommunism, Amnesia and Pink Nostalgia in Romania

After the fall of Ceausescu's regime and the bloody events of December 1989, power was seized by neo-communists; second-rank economic, social and political elites created by the communist system. Legitimized by the May 1990 general elections, the neo-communists managed to stay in power until 1996. Their public discourse promoted a complete break with communism by condemning Ceausescu and his wife to death, outlawing the Communist Party, and dismantling all the former regime's symbols. Converted to capitalism, the neo-communists were adamant about forgetting the recent past. Ion Iliescu, the first postcommunist president of Romania and the iconic figure of the neo-communist elite, stated that any debate on communism was unnecessary as the regime was already condemned by *History*. He argued that people should forget the past and invited reconciliation in order to rebuild the country.

The neo-communist position and later the anticommunist ideology were supported by the Romanian Orthodox Church, which never questioned its position during communism. Furthermore, the 'political order' guaranteed the Orthodox Church total silence regarding priests' collaboration with the political police (the notorious *Securitate*). Only a handful of archbishops and priests publicly recognized their collaboration with the communist regime. The majority of priest informants were protected by the law regarding the opening of the archives of the Romanian political police. Actually, public access to the *Securitate* files was used rather to validate a myth of collective culpability than to instigate the de-communization of the Romanian public space. The purging of the secret police's archives of those files pertaining to the neo-communists (perpetrated during the first months of postcommunism), together with the fabrication of false *Securitate* collaborator files to discredit political opponents, created the impression that a great number of Romanians had been informants to the political police. Moreover, many of the self-styled anticommunists were discovered to have been informants to and collaborators with *Securitate*. None of the pre-eminent neo-communist leaders were found guilty of collaboration with the former political police.

In the first postcommunist decade, lustration was not an option in Romania even if civil society was murmuring about demands to this end as early as March 1990. The 'Proclamation of Timisoara' asked for drastic restrictions of the right to run for public office in the case of members of the former *nomenklatura*, the political police, the communist-era police (*Militia*), and the national army. It was only two decades later, in 2010, that the lower chamber of the Romanian parliament voted in favour of this measure. Subsequently adopted by the upper chamber as well, the law was nevertheless struck down as unconstitutional by the Constitutional Court. In 2012, a different lustration law was adopted by the Romanian parliament only to meet with the same fate from the Constitutional Court.

The neo-communists legitimated themselves through the events of December 1989,[4] which they called a 'revolution'. The participants of the 'revolution' were called revolutionaries and they were entitled to all sorts of privileges like receiving state properties, free passes on public transportation and positive discrimination when applying for a job in public offices. Furthermore, a monument was erected in the memory of those who died during the 'revolution' and a celebration day was instituted in 2002.

Another perspective on the public memory of communism was promoted by intellectuals from the political right (the self-styled 'democrats' or 'anticommunists'), who denounced communism as a foreign regime imposed by the Soviet Union on the Romanian nation after the Allied powers 'betrayed' Romania during the peace negotiations at the end of the Second World War. This discourse emphasizes the uniqueness of Romanian communism by pointing to the brutality of repression and the chilling efficiency of the political police. Drawing on testimonies of former political prisoners as evidence, it depicts the Romanian concentration camp experience as extreme even by the standards of totalitarian regimes, and argues that the repression left deep scars and thus discouraged people from rebelling against the communist state.[5] In spite of this harsh repression, a few people did decide to fight communism. The armed resistance in the mountains became a myth during the postcommunist period.[6]

These two ideas, the overwhelming communist repression and the genuine anticommunist resistance, elaborated by the 'democratic' elite, eventually became the official discourse concerning the communist regime. They were imposed as the mainstream paradigm through constant promotion in the public space and the political arena by the former political detainees association (AFDPR),[7] by private foundations like the Memoria Cultural Foundation,[8] and by the 'Memorial to the Victims of Communism and to the Anticommunist Resistance in Sighetul Marmației' (known as the 'Sighet Memorial' – *Memorialul Sighet*). This last enterprise played an important role in disseminating the perspective of the political right on communism and political persecutions. This leading role was recognized by the president himself in his official condemnation of the former regime.

In 1992, Ana Blandiana, a well-known poet and dissident of the last years of Ceausescu's regime, designed a 'Memory Centre' dedicated to the memory of victims of communism. This project became the Sighet Memorial, recognized in 1996 as a 'centre of national interest' by the 'democrat' government. According to law 95 of 1997, this type of enterprise was entitled to financial support from the state. The Sighet Memorial includes an International Centre that keeps written, oral and visual archives pertaining to the communist repression and anticommunist resistance, and a museum. Under the aegis of the Council of Europe, the Sighet Memorial organizes numerous activities related to the memory of political persecution, including conferences and exhibitions. It also collects testimonies, publishes books and has founded 'Memory Schools' for students.[9]

Opened to the public in 1997, the Sighet museum is located in the northern part of Romania, away from the capital Bucharest (it is close to the border with Ukraine). The choice of the site was dictated, on the one hand, by the political situation of the country at the beginning of the 1990s, with the neo-communists in power, and on the other hand, by the history of Sighet itself, the site of a penitentiary in which the communists put into practice the extermination of the former democratic elite. The founders of the Sighet Memorial considered themselves as the inheritors of the interwar democratic elite (Dobre 2007: 181–85).

Challenged in the beginning by the neo-communists, this perspective became consensual among public actors, especially after the opposition forces won the general election in 1996. Although they lost the 2000 general election in favour of the neo-communists, their anticommunist discourse remained dominant in the public space. This public consensus led to former political prisoners' rehabilitation, the creation and dissemination of new myths of general victimization and culpability,[10] and eventually to the condemnation of the communist regime in December 2006.[11]

The public anticommunist discourse has never enjoyed a consensus among ordinary people. Periodic surveys revealed that around fifty percent of Romanians have rather a good image of communism;[12] a kind of nostalgia for a more secure, egalitarian and organized past in contrast to the uncertain, inequitable and disorganized present.

Furthermore, at the beginning of the 2000s, the public memory of communism, which depicted the former regime as 'criminal' and the Romanians both as victims and perpetrators, was challenge by a new generation of artists, scholars and political leaders who gained influential positions in the cultural, political and social fields. They started to promote an ironic memory of communism in the public space through a series of books, films, theatrical comedies and artistic installations.

I call this trend the 'pink' memory of communism, after a book of memories published by a few young artists, writers and scholars, under the title, *The Pink Book of Communism* (Decuble 2004). The book is a collection of personal memories about childhood and adolescence during the communist regime, in which auto-irony and 'golden age' nostalgia dominate the narrative.

In a country that has never seriously debated the communist past, *The Pink Book* succeeded in creating controversy. The authors were accused of trying to fabricate a 'good image' of communism. Furthermore, the book was perceived as a response to Stephane Courtois' *Black Book of Communism*, which had already been translated into Romanian with an addendum on Romanian communism. The sense was that *The Pink Book* was meant to diminish the communist crimes described in the *Black Book*.

This 'pink memory' trend culminated in an artistic project called 'Project 1990'. In March 1990, three months after the fall of communism, Lenin's statue in Bucharest was dismantled and stored.[13] The pedestal remained empty until 2010, when an artist succeeded in convincing the mayor of Bucharest to let her use the pedestal for a series of artistic installations.

The first one was a huge statue of Lenin made from pearl barley and fruit drops. It was inaugurated in January 2010. In the following years, nineteen other installations occupied Lenin's pedestal. The irony promoted by this artistic project was intended to increase awareness about Romania's recent past and to help heal the communist trauma. By questioning the way Romanian society remembers its communist past, the project called upon people to revise their beliefs about the former regime and its heritage. The project also aimed to provoke a civic response to the challenges and moral dilemmas of the postcommunist years.[14]

Conflicted Memories and the Bulgarian Public Space

In Bulgaria, in the first postcommunist decade, dealing with the communist past was very much part of the broader political, social and cultural struggles. This process was mainly shaped by the communist regime's internal transformations, the continuity in power of the former communists converted to 'humane socialism', the attachment of the population to the former regime, and the opposition's capacity to organize and promote an anticommunist discourse. Dealing with the communist past was a key component of political legitimization and delegitimization (Frison-Roche 2005). Furthermore, the politicians seemed to be the main actors of the liaison between the memory of the past and the representations of the past (Znepolski 2001: 82).

In the second half of 1989, the Bulgarian Communist Party (BCP) witnessed the formation of various factions that tried to reform the party in order to stay in power. On 10 November 1989, a few communist leaders orchestrated a *coup d'état* that succeeded in deposing General Secretary and head of state Todor Zhivkov. Subsequently, his regime was blamed for the economic difficulties of the country and for the outrageous public policies targeting the Turkish minority.[15] The abuses committed in 1944 when the communist regime was installed were also condemned. The coup, orchestrated from inside, was called a 'socialist renewal', meant to solve Bulgaria's economic problems. Dialogue, discussion and national consensus were the key terms used in the new communist official discourses (Melone 1994: 259).

The emerging democratic opposition, which took to the streets in the autumn of 1989 to manifest their rejection of the communist regime, coalesced in December 1989 and formed the Union of Democratic Forces (UFD).[16] The UFD took part in the Round-Table Talks initiated by the new communist government, with reforms as the key point on the agenda. But while the communists were prepared to deal only with economic measures, the UFD's representatives also demanded political reforms. While the opposition wanted to change the system, the BCP leaders simply militated for 'humane and democratic socialism', a pluralistic civil society and 'a strong democratic state' (Giatzidis 2002: 56).

The discussions advanced slowly for a few months, under the pressure of UFD public rallies. On 12 March 1990, three statements were issued proclaiming the end of the communist party's monopoly in political, social, cultural and religious life and instituting a short transitional period to becoming a democratic regime, with free elections to be held in June 1990. On 30 March 1990, an agreement on constitutional reform was also reached by the participants of the Talks (Melone 1994: 258). Meanwhile, the Communist Party changed its name to 'Bulgarian Socialist Party', proclaiming that anticommunism threatened the process of transition to democracy and the success of economic and political reforms. Better organized, more experienced in dealing with the challenges of governing the country and posing as a reformist party, the BSP won the elections held on 10–17 June 1990.

The opposition forces protested against the outcome of the election as early as June 1990. The focus point of their rallies was Georgi Dimitrov's mausoleum erected in the centre of Sofia, next to the former royal palace.[17] In the following months, in the heart of the Bulgarian capital, a 'City of Truth' was organized by students, artists and members of the opposition (Gradev 1992: 77). Three thousand people camped alongside Dimitrov's mausoleum protesting against communism and asking that Dimitrov's body, embalmed and on display in the mausoleum, be interred. The campers also demanded that the red star on the Communist Party House be removed. After a month of protesting, on the 18th of July, Dimitrov's body was removed from the mausoleum and buried. The next day, the people of Sofia gathered in front of the empty building and organized a 'waste-feast' (Gradev 1992: 77): portraits of communist leaders, books and other objects recalling communism were hurled at the mausoleum wall and afterwards burned. The 'waste-feast' functioned as an act of public exorcism.

The government also had to deal with the now empty building. A commission of architects was established to this end (Vukov and Toncheva 2006: 128). The older generation and Dimitrov's partisans wanted to transform the mausoleum into a memorial for all the victims of *all* forms of totalitarianism (the words communism or socialism were not to be used in conjunction with the project) or relocate it in a peripheral area that was meant to host a 'statue park'. The younger generation of architects wanted to partially destroy it and effectively turn it into a ruin – like the world that it stood for – or transform it into a market place or even a disco bar.

A group of intellectuals even proposed to transform it into a museum of communism. These discussions illustrate the different approaches to dealing with the communist past (Dobre 2012: 117–166).

None of these solutions were accepted. The government decided that the mausoleum should be used as the entrance to the National Art Museum (Gradev 1992: 85). It functioned as such for a few more years until 21 August 1999, when the anticommunist government of Ivan Kostov started to dismantle the building. This was a great endeavour, since the mausoleum was difficult to demolish. Three attempts were made to pull it down and in the end it took longer to demolish than it took to build (it was built in five days following Dimitrov's unexpected death in Moscow, in July 1949).

During the first postcommunist decade, the Bulgarian Socialist Party defended the material heritage as well as some of the practices and the public rhetoric of the former regime.[18] It opposed Bulgaria's accession to NATO as well as the International Monetary Fund's interventions in Bulgarian politics. The socialists also opposed the dismantling of the statues commemorating the Soviet army, the demolition of Dimitrov's mausoleum, the condemnation of communism, the opening of the former secret police archives and the adoption of a lustration law. Furthermore, every year on 9 September, leaders of the BSP commemorated the anniversary of the Socialist Revolution in the Liberty Park of Sofia, leaving flowers at the Fraternal Hill, *Bratskatamogila* (Vagabond 39–40: 54).

The Bulgarian Socialist Party represented the perfect political enemy for the UFD, which promoted a pro-Western, pro-European, anticommunist discourse.[19] Lacking the experience of governing the country as well as a coherent, pragmatic programme of reforms, the UFD concentrated in the beginning on the communist past and its heritage. After the loss of the June 1990 elections, the UFD asked for a retroactive judicial retribution. The strong position of the UFD within the judicial system eventually led to the opening of four political trials: of TeodorZhivkov and his associates; of 'the revival process' and its policies that had targeted the Turkish minority; of those blamed for the accumulation of Bulgarian foreign debt; and of those considered responsible for Bulgaria's 'economic catastrophe' (Baeva and Kalinova 2010: 66). In spite of the UFD's expectations, these trials did not succeed in condemning the communist regime and branding it as criminal (Baeva and Kalinova 2010: 71).

After winning the general election in October 1991, the UFD was so obsessed with the former regime that it focused more on decommunization and restitution than on political and economic reform (Giatzidis 2002: 67). A restitution law aiming to achieve 'historical justice' was proposed in February 1992. In December 1992, a very restrictive lustration law was adopted by parliament. Named the 'Panev law' after its initiator, the lustration law was upheld by the Constitution Court in February 1993. A year later the socialist government passed an 'anti-Panev law', meant to repeal the lustration legislation. Finally, in 1998, a milder lustration law was voted in by parliament but vetoed by the UFD-backed president, PetarStoyanov.[20] In 2000, another attempt to condemn communism was eventually successful. The UFD won the elections and enjoyed a solid majority in parliament. The path to condemning communism was opened. On March 2000, Georgi Panev proposed a law that proclaimed the communist regime 'illegal and criminal'. After some debate, parliament adopted the law in April 2000 (Deyanova 2008: 198). This law, which declared Bulgarian communism illegal, put an end to a decade of struggle over the communist past.

The unveiling of the State Security files (*DurjavnaSigurnost*, hereafter DS) represented another battlefield for the two parties, the BSP and the UFD. In 1997, a law to open the DS archives to the public was voted on by parliament. Along the lines of lustration laws, the legislation restricted the right of former informants and collaborators to run for public office. The law was instrumentalized during the electoral campaign, with candidates in the general elections denounced as former informants; however, the law did not fully come into force for several years. It was only after the intervention of a few members of the European Parliament that access to the DS archives became operational. The study of the DS files revealed the great involvement of the new postcommunist elite in the structures of the communist system (Dermendzhieva 2009).

During the first postcommunist decade, in Bulgaria as well as in Romania, the dissemination of the memory of communist repression was more a matter of private action than an official programme. Non-governmental organizations and private research centres were devoted to archiving, studying and disseminating the memory of repression in Bulgaria.

During the forty-five years of communism, no fewer than eighty-six permanent or temporary labour camps were built all over Bulgaria. Two of them are known as the epitome of terror: Belene – on the Persin Island on the Danube – and Lovech. The camp of Lovech functioned almost throughout the entire communist period. After the 'enemies of people' were released, the camp was used in the late 1980s to detain the Turkish minority leaders.[21]

Immediately after the fall of communism, a monument was erected near the camp of Lovech in order to honour the victims of the communist repression. The inauguration ceremony was used to communicate symbolically the idea of reconciliation, promoted by the reform-minded communists represented at the ceremony by the president of Bulgaria at the time, PetarMladenov, and Prime Minister Andrey Lukanov – both pre-eminent leaders of BCP (later BSP). At the same time, the director of the camp was put on trial for crimes committed in the camp under his supervision. Despite its initial appropriation by the BCP/BSP, the place preserved its anticommunist aura and has been seen and used as a site of anticommunist rituals and commemorations.

Although the memory of those who died in the camp of Belene is honored on that very spot every year on 9 September, it took no fewer than twenty years after the fall of communism until an exhibition introduced the 'labour educational community' (Baeva and Stefan Troebst 2007: 77) – as it was called by the communists – to a larger audience, in November 2009. The exhibition was the initiative of the Institute for the Study of the Recent Past, a private well-established research institution devoted to the study of the communist period.

The Bulgarian communist past was not a matter for political parties alone; it also played an important role in shaping postcommunist public opinion as well. The dismantling of the monuments of the Soviet Soldier and the fate of Dimitrov's mausoleum sparked debates, rallies and human chains surrounding the threatened monuments. The controversies reached the Constitutional Court, a real arbiter of the transition and an active actor in the public space (Sconfelder 2005: 61–92), which issued decisions on the demolition of monuments and the de-communization laws, as well as on the schism of the Orthodox Church.

The 'political order' played an important part in the way the Bulgarian Orthodox Church dealt with its past. The de-communization of the church was the pretext for the internal schism of the Bulgarian Orthodox church. After UFD came to power, in 1992, the patriarch Maksim was accused of being a close collaborator of Teodor Zhivkov; his election as patriarch was declared void and against the rules of the church by a state commissioner (the president of the communist-created Commission for Religious Affairs). Three leading metropolitans of Stara Zagora, Nevrokop and Vratsa supported this statement and denounced Maksim's election as patriarch in 1971 as illegitimate. A Provisional Synod was established, backed by a few priests interested in reforming the Church. The Provisional Synod, or the Blue Synod, was supported by UFD while the patriarch Maksim and his Red Synod was endorsed by the BSP (Dimitrov 2001: 51). After the election of Pimen as patriarch by the Blue Synod in 1996, the schism became so serious that the ecumenical patriarch of Constantinople tried to conciliate the Bulgarian Church (Broun 2002: 388). He did not enjoy great success as the Bulgarian Church was divided into many rival groups. In 2002 the Confessions Act voted by the government of Simeon II made patriarch

Maksim the legitimate patriarch of the Bulgarian Orthodox Church while attempting to put an end to the internal division of the Church. The Act allowed the state to interfere (even by force) in the Church affairs. The election of a new patriarch in 2008 invited reconciliation and unity within the church.

The Confessions Act symbolically put an end to a decade of struggles over the public memory of communism in Bulgaria. The communist/ anticommunist division of society, of civil and political groups, of acts and symbols became obsolete. Celebrating communist victims was the new memorial programme, and a beneficiary of European policies' inputs.

Communist Repression as National Patrimony

International interventions and the European political context added a new dimension to the ways in which Romania and Bulgaria dealt with their communist past. On 25 January 2006, the Council of Europe adopted 'Resolution 1481', which condemned communist regimes' abuses. Inspired by a Bulgarian, Latchezar Toshev, the first draft of the resolution being drawn during a meeting of the former Bulgarian political detainees, the final resolution had no immediate impact in Bulgaria, as the communist regime there had already been condemned (Deyanova 2008: 195). In Romania, surprisingly enough, it held the promise of a positive outcome. The President of Romania, Traian Băsescu,[22] instituted a Presidential Commission aimed at 'studying the communist dictatorship in Romania'. The Commission's report was presented to the Romanian parliament by the president on 18 December 2006. Based on this report, the president proclaimed communism as 'criminal and illegitimate'.

After the official condemnation of the Romanian communist regime, public space was invaded by interventions condemning communism and celebrating the anticommunist resistance. Textbooks dealing with the communist regime focused more on presenting the repressive nature of the regime than on introducing pupils to this period of time. Movies and memoirs kept on flourishing whilst an Institute for the Study of Communist Crimes was created under the direct supervision of the government.

Nevertheless, the official condemnation of the Romanian communist regime did not mean a condemnation of those perpetrating the 'crimes'.[23] No criminal has been yet condemned and no measures were taken to revoke the privileges of the agents of the former political police.[24] Furthermore, one could argue that declaring the communist regime illegitimate rendered all the laws, decrees and public acts issued by this regime illegal and without legal force.

In Bulgaria during the first postcommunist decade, the celebration of the victims of communism was part of the political struggle. Monuments and/or commemorative plaques were established according to the political orientation of the regional/local authorities. Besides the monument in Lovech, memorial plaques were settled in Sofia, Varna and Sliven. Only in 1999 was a memorial to the victims of communism erected in the square of the National Palace of Culture in Sofia. The memorial includes a marble wall on which are engraved the names of 7,526 people who were killed in the wake of 9 September 1944, and a chapel dedicated to 'all the Bulgarian martyrs' (Baeva and Troebst 2007: 78). The chapel and the wall are part of the commemoration ceremonies of 1 February, which celebrate the events of 1 February 1945, when 147 people, most of them abusively accused of fascism, were judged by the People's Tribunal and condemned to death. Beginning with 2011, 1 February has become the official day of Gratitude and Homage to the Victims of the Communist Regime.

Although the remembrance of communist repression was turned into a public policy after 2010, it still does not enjoy a wide consensus among Bulgarian public actors. The BSP never celebrated 1 February and made public its rejection of the International Black Ribbon Day.[25] Furthermore, the ordinary people evaluate the former regime in a seemingly positive way. A survey from 2004 shows that 32 percent of people interviewed considered the communist period as 'years of achievement' and 10 percent viewed them as 'successful years' (Baeva and Kalinova 2010: 89).

If the political, ethnic and religious persecutions have drawn public attention in Bulgaria after 2010, the resistance movement of *Goryani* is still not publicized widely. This armed resistance movement started soon after 9 September 1944. Known as *Goryani* ('those from the forest', in Bulgarian), the anticommunist fighters were helped initially by exiled Bulgarians and by the Americans. They spread all over the country and attracted peasants, officers and opposition leaders into the movement. The movement was dismantled in the late 1950s. More than 1,000 *Goryani* people were killed by the communist authorities (Crimes Committed by the Communist Regime in Bulgaria 2010).

In both countries, the commemoration of the victims of communism became public policy only after a number of resolutions condemning 'the crimes of totalitarian regimes' were adopted by European institutions. The aforementioned 'Resolution 1481' of the Council of Europe, the 'Prague Declaration on European Conscience and Communism' (June 2008) and the European Parliament 'Resolution on European Conscience and Totalitarianism' (April 2009) provided the impetus for the two countries to officially celebrate the victims of communist repression. Whereas in Romania no public actor has taken a stand against European memorial policies, in Bulgaria the former communists rejected them outright.

Conclusions

The comparison between Bulgaria and Romania evinces the contours of two particular ways of dealing with the communist past. In postcommunist Romania, communism was demonized and rejected by all actors of the public space. Communist symbols like statues and memorials were destroyed or reused and reinterpreted to fit the new paradigm. Conversely, anticommunist endeavours were put on display and heavily promoted through mass media. Furthermore, even the former communists began to rewrite and reinterpret their lives in order to present themselves as opponents of the extreme communism put into practice by the Ceausescu family. In postcommunist Bulgaria, the communist regime became a political frontier and a means of legitimization for political factions. On the one hand the Communist Party, converted into the Socialist Party, went on promoting the communist ideology and symbols but on the other, the united opposition forces fashioned themselves on the basis of anticommunist ideology.

After a decade of struggles to impose a politically-biased public memory of communism, the public space of the two countries became saturated with both anticommunism and active oblivion as well as humane communism. In Romania, an ironic memory of communism has emerged in the public space. In Bulgaria, the public space finally accommodates both communist and anti-communist memory. A park of communist statues and monuments was organized in Sofia almost at the same time as a commemoration day for the victims of the communist regime was established.

Furthermore, both countries aligned themselves with European memorial policies. In Romania, European policies were not questioned as such but were simply implemented in a half-hearted way. By contrast, faithful to their ideological commitments, the Bulgarian former communists chose to ignore the European demands. Ordinary people of both countries are in general ignorant about European memorial policies, a situation that can be partly attributed to European institutions' failure to communicate effectively.[26]

Even if at the institutional level one might talk of a 'saturated memory of communism' (Horvath 2008: 271), for many ordinary people remembering communism is a *milieu de mémoire*. People recall communism, with its positive and negative aspects, and it is this fact that has hindered the process of oblivion initiated by the official condemnations of the regime, including its relegation to museums and memorials.

Notes

1. My inquiry into the collective and public memory of communism in Bulgaria and Romania started in 2009 as part of a comparative project on communist traces in the public space. The analysis of public memory was combined with qualitative research on personal memories, based on focus groups comprising three age cohorts: 18–20, 35–40, 55–60. The findings of this research were published in Dobre 2012: 117–166.
2. By 'memorial regime' I understand a matrix of perceptions and representations of the past, which defines at a certain time the structures of public memory (Michel 2010: 12–17).
3. This official collective memory can be called 'public memory' (Michel 2010: 12–17).
4. On 16–17 December 1989 people from Timisoara started a revolt against communism. This was repressed by the *Securitate* (Secret Political Police) and the army. The news of Timisoara protests spread throughout the country and on 21 December 1989 a large manifestation against Ceausescu began in Bucharest. On 22 December, forced by the revolts of the people in Bucharest, Ceausescu and his wife fled the capital and sought refuge in the country. They were arrested by the army after a few hours. On 25 December, Christmas day, Ceausescu and his wife were put on trial and sentenced to death by an adhoc tribunal.
5. This discourse is put forward, e.g., in the weekly *Revista22*, on the website of the Sighet Memorial, and in the documentary series, the *Memorial of Sorrow* on public television.
6. The anticommunist fighters were small in number, a group encompassed from 4 to 20 members, they comprised around 10,000 persons in all of Romania, and even if there was a plan to fight against communism, a general resistance movement could not be organized even if it seems that the United States promised to help the resistance fighters. Supplies, guns and even soldiers were parachuted into the mountains, but only for a short period of time. The majority of the resistance fighters were killed or imprisoned by the authorities.
7. Soon after the fall of Ceausescu on 22 December 1989, the former political detainees created a national association called The Association of the Former Political Prisoners of Romania (*AsociațiaFoștilorDeținuțiPolitici din România* – AFDPR). It militated for the public rehabilitation of the political detainees and anticommunist fighters and the recognition of their merits.
8. The Memoria Cultural Foundation was created in 1991 as a non-governmental organization meant to promote human rights and civic values and to transmit the memory of political persecutions perpetrated by the communist regime in Romania.
9. The 'Memory Schools' are a type of summer school meant to familiarize students with the political persecutions of the communist regime.
10. The public discourse of the neo-communists emphasized that the whole Romanian nation was guilty of accepting communism and of adapting to the regime. But they also accepted the right wing's discourse of victimization, and argued that Romania was a victim of history and geopolitics.

11. In April 2006, Traian Basescu, president of Romania between 2004 and 2014, who had been brought to power by a centre-right coalition, decreed the creation of a commission intended to study communist crimes in Romania. After six months, the commission presented its report in more than six hundred pages. The report presented communism as a repressive regime which persecuted Romanians and destroyed the country's traditions, laws and former elite.
12. The 2006 Open Society Foundation survey shows that twelve percent of the population found communism a good idea that had been well applied, while forty-one percent considered that communism was a good idea but had been put into practice in the wrong way. Open Society Foundation, 'The Actual Perception of Communism': http://www.osf.ro (accessed December 2012). A 2011 survey by the Institute for the Investigation of Communist Crimes and the Memory of the Romanian Exile (IICCMER) shows that forty-three percent of respondents considered communism a good idea but wrongly applied, while eighteen percent viewed it as a good idea, well applied. IICCMER and CSOP, 'Atitudinii si opinii despre regimul communist din Romania. Sondaj de opinie publica' (Attitudes and Opinions about Communist Regime in Romania: Public Survey), 23 May 2011: http://www.iiccr.ro/(accessed February 2013).
13. All communist statues and symbols were removed from public spaces in the first months of 1990.
14. The installations addressed not only the memory of communism, but also some aspects of Romanian postcommunism like economic emigration, the nouveau rich and the crisis of values. For instance, in 2010, the pedestal featured a group of artists, 'Romanian Piano Trio' consisting of three young and well-known performers, Alexandru Tomescu, Răzvan Suma and Horia Mihail, who played for fifteen minutes. In 2012, an installation called *Hydra* was meant to draw attention to the invisible heritage of the communist regime. In 2013, a statue called *A4* stood for the excessive bureaucracy that characterizes both communist and postcommunist societies. The project ended in April 2014.
15. The new leaders even tried to create a heroic image by recounting the danger they had to face by opposing Zhivkov. Cf. Traikov Boris and Tomov Toma cited by Baeva and Kalinova 2010: 58.
16. The Union of Democratic Forces (UDF) is a coalition of anticommunist parties and movements. The UFD were also known as the 'blues' due to the colour of their political signs. The BSP were known as the reds.
17. Georgi Dimitrov Mikhaylov was born in Kovachevtsi on 18 June 1882 as the first of eight children to working-class parents. He studied to become a composer and got involved in political activism. Dimitrov joined the Bulgarian Social Democratic Workers' Party in 1902, and in 1903 followed Dimitar Blagoev and his faction as it formed the Social Democratic Labour Party of Bulgaria. This party became the Bulgarian Communist Party in 1919, when it affiliated to Bolshevism and the Comintern. Following a revolutionary uprising he was sentenced to death but fled to the Soviet Union. In 1933 he was arrested in Berlin for complicity in setting the Reichstag on fire. He was released after negotiations between the Soviet Union and Germany. He became General Secretary of Comintern in 1934, remaining in office until the organization's dissolution in 1943. In 1944, he returned to Bulgaria and became prime minister in 1946. He remained a Stalinist until his death on 2 July 1949.
18. The Bulgarian Socialist Party (BSP) stayed in power until 13th of October 1991 when The Union of Democratic Forces (UFD) won the general election. After a short period of UFD governance (October 1991 – October 1992), BSP return to power and eventually won the election in 1994. They governed the country for three more years until April 1997. On 19

April 1997, Ivan Kostov, the leader of UFD, became prime minister. UFD stayed in power until 2001.
19. BSP changed its profile only in 2000 when the party adopted a more Western European approach. In 2003, the party was admitted into the Socialist International (Ragaru 2005: 5).
20. He was the president of Bulgaria between 1997 and 2002, backed by the Union of Democratic Forces.
21. Between 1984 and 1989, 1,200 Bulgarian Turks were imprisoned there. Apud, *Crimes Committed by the Communist Regime in Bulgaria*. Country Report conference 'Crimes of the Communist Regimes', 24–26 February 2010, Prague. Online document at http://www.ustrcr.cz/data/pdf/konference/zlociny-komunismu/COUNTRY%20REPORT%20BULGARIA.pdf (accessed 20 October 2013).
22. He acknowledged that he found the inspiration to create this commission in 'Resolution 1481' of the Council of Europe.
23. Only in 2009 did a law (221/2009) create the possibility of financial compensation for those condemned for political reasons. The compensation was to be demanded in court. After a few significant trials in which the courts granted high compensations to pre-eminent former political detainees, the government set a fixed amount for compensation, irrespective of how long one had been imprisoned. Meanwhile, the categories of people who could receive compensation were also restricted to those condemned for other reasons than that referring to the guilt of endangering the state (i.e., the communist state), which greatly reduced the number of those entitled to ask for compensation.
24. In 2013, a list of thirty-one former directors and political officers of communist political prisons was presented to mass media by the former director of IICCMER and actual counsellor of president Klaus Johannis. Two trials were opened against the former director of Ramnicu-Sarat prison and against the former chief of Periprava labour camp, who are accused of crimes against humanity. In August 2013, the prime minister, a descendant the neo-communist elite, decided to revoke the pensions of former torturers who were awaiting trial.
25. 23 August was designated by the European Parliament in 2009 as the 'European Day of Remembrance for the victims of all totalitarian and authoritarian regimes, to be commemorated with dignity and impartiality'.
26. In Bulgaria, for instance, a poll conducted among young Bulgarians showed that 40 per cent of respondents had never heard of Belene or other prisons and death camps, 42 per cent of young people did not know that Stalin and Hitler were dictators, and 88 per cent had never heard of the Molotov-Ribbentrop Pact: http://www.novinite.com/articles/153780/Bulgarian+Youth+Mostly+Ignorant+about+Communist+Regime#sthash.xmj4K7ET.dpuf (accessed October 2013).

Claudia-Florentina Dobre is the editor-in-chief of Memoria magazine and an associate researcher at the Centre Régional Francophone de Recherches Avancées en Sciences Sociales. She completed her PhD on 'Former Political Detainees' Testimonies on Communism and Political Persecutions' at Laval University, Québec. She researches the memory of communism: museums, monuments and daily life. Her recent publications include: *Un pays derrière les barbelés. Brève histoire de la répression* *communiste en Roumanie* (Fundatia Culturala Memoria, Bucharest, 2014); 'Visual Discourses on the Recent Past: Communism in the Romanian Post-communist Cinema', *Sensus Historiae*, 4 (2014): 91–104; and 'Repression and Resistance: Women Remembering their Daily Life in Romanian Communist Prisons', *Martor,* 17 (2012): 39–50.

Bibliography

Adriansen, I. and M. Schartl (eds). 2006. *Erindringsstedernordogsydforgrænsen = Erinnerungsorte nördlich und südlich der Grenze*, trans. Tilo KrauseSchleswig: Museum Sønderjylland Sønderborg Slot, Kulturstiftung des Kreises Schleswig-Flensburg.
Aleksiejewicz, S. 2010. *Wojna nie ma w sobie nic z kobiety*. Warsaw: Wyd. Czarne.
Alexander, J.C. 2003. 'Cultural Trauma and Collective Identity', in *The Meanings of Social Life: A Cultural Sociology*. New York: Oxford University Press, 85–108.
Allport, G. 1954. *The Nature of Prejudice*. Reading, MA: Addison-Wesley.
Aly, G. 2006. 'Logik des Grauens', *Die Zeit*, 1 June 2006.
Anderson, S. 2001. 'History TV and Popular Memory', in *Television Histories: Shaping Collective Memory in the Media Age*, G.R. Edgerton and P.C. Rollins Lexington (eds). Kentucky: The University Press of Kentucky, 19–36.
Ankersmit, F. 2001. 'The Sublime Dissociation of the Past: or How to Be(come) What One Is No Longer', *History and Theory* 40(3): 295–323.
Apor, P. 2010. 'Eurocommunism: Commemorating Communism in Contemporary Eastern Europe', in *A European Memory? Contested Histories and Politics of Remembrance*, M. Pakier and B. Stråth (eds). New York: Berghahn Books.
Applebaum, A. 2003. *Gulag: A History of the Soviet Camps*. London: Allen Lane.
Arnason, J.P. 2003. 'Entangled Communisms: Imperial Revolutions in Russia and China', *European Journal of Social Theory* 6.3: 307–325.
Asséo, H. 2005. 'L'avènement politique des Roms (Tsiganes) et le génocide: La construction mémorielle en Allemagne et en France', *Le Temps des Médias* 2(5).
Assmann, A. 2006. *Der lange Schatten der Vergangenheit. Erinnerungskultur und Geschichtspolitik*. Munich: C.H. Beck Verlag.
——. 2007. 'Europe: A Community of Memory? Twentieth Annual Lecture of the GHI, November 16, 2006', *German Historical Institute Bulletin* 40, spring: 11–26.

———. 2010. 'The Holocaust – A Global Memory? Extensions and Limits of a New Memory Community', in *Memory in a Global Age: Discourses, Practices and Trajectories*, A. Assmann and S. Conrad (eds). Palgrave: New York.

———. 2011. 'To Remember or to Forget: Which Way out of a Shared History of Violence?', in *Memory and Political Change*, A. Assmann and L. Shortt (eds). Palgrave: New York.

———. 2012. *Auf dem Weg zu einer europäischen Gedächtniskultur?* Vienna: Picus Verlag.

———. 2013. 'Europe's Divided Memory', in *Memory and Theory in Eastern Europe*, U. Blacker, A. Etkind and J. Fedor (eds). Basingstoke-New York: Palgrave Macmillan, 25–42.

Assmann, A. and U. Frevert. 1999. *Geschichtsvergessenheit, Geschichtsversessenheit. Vom Umgang mit deutschen Vergangenheiten nach 1945*. Stuttgart: Deutsche Verlags-Anstalt.

Assmann, A. and L. Shortt. 2012. 'Memory and Political Change: Introduction', in *Memory and Political Change*, A. Assmann and L. Shortt (eds). Basingstoke-New York: Palgrave Macmillan, 1–16.

Assmann, J. 2006. *Religion and Cultural Memory: Ten Studies*. Stanford, California: Stanford University Press.

———. 2008. *Pamięć kulturowa. Pismo, zapamiętywanie i polityczna tożsamość w cywilizacjach starożytnych*, trans. Anna Kryczyńska-Pham. Warsaw: Wydawnictwa Uniwersytetu Warszawskiego.

Audigier, F. 2003. 'Les lieux de mémoire: un concept, son invention, sa mise en œuvre et sa réception', in *Mémoires et lieux de mémoire en Lorraine*, P. Martin (ed.). Sarreguemines: Pierron, 29–43.

Auer, S. 2004. 'The Revolutions of 1989 Revisited', *Eurozine*. Retrieved March 2010 from http://www.eurozine.com/articles/2004–06–14-auer-en.html.

———. 2010a. '"New Europe": Between Cosmopolitan Dreams and Nationalist Nightmares', *Journal of Common Market Studies* 48.5: 1163–1184.

———. 2010b. 'Contesting the Origins of European Liberty: The EU Narrative of Franco-German Reconciliation and the Eclipse of 1989', *Eurozine*. Retrieved November 2010 from http://www.eurozine.com/articles/2010-09-10-auer-en.html.

Augé, M. 2009. *Formy zapomnienia*, trans. Anna Turczyn. Krakow: Towarzystwo Autorów i Wydawców Prac Naukowych 'Universitas'.

Avineri, S. 1993. 'Forum on Restitution', *East European Constitutional Review* 2(3) summer: 30–40.

———. 2010. 'Israel Is the Opposite of Fascist', *Haaretz*, 15 November 2010. Retrieved 15 November 2010 from http://www.haaretz.com/print-edition/opinion/israel-is-the-opposite-of-fascist-1.324727

Avižienis, J. 2005. 'Mediated and Unmediated Access to the Past: Assessing the Memoir as Literary Genre', *The Journal of Baltic Studies* 36(1): 39–50.

———. 2010. 'Performing Identity: Lithuanian Memoirs of Siberian Deportation and Exile', in *History of the Literary Cultures of East-Central Europe: Junctures and Disjunctures in the 19th and 20th Centuries, vol. IV Types and Stereotypes*, M. Cornis-Pope and J. Neubauer (eds). Amsterdam/Philadelphia: Benjamins.

Baar, H. van. 2011. *The European Roma: Minority Representation, Memory and the Limits of Transnational Governmentality*. Amsterdam: Universiteit van Amsterdam.
Baberowski, J. and A. Doering-Manteuffel. 2009. 'The Quest for Order and the Pursuit of Terror', in *Beyond Totalitarianism: Stalinism and Nazism Compared*, M. Geyer and S. Fitzpatrick (eds). Cambridge: Cambridge University Press, 180–227.
Bachmann, K. 1994. 'Marnowane szanse dialogu', *Rzeczpospolita*, 22 November.
Baeva, I. and E. Kalinova. 2010. 'Bulgarian Transition and the Memory of the Socialist Past', in *Remembering Communism: Genres of Representations*, M. Todorova (ed.). New York: Social Science Research Council.
Baeva, I. and S. Troebst (eds). 2007. *Vademecum: Contemporary History of Bulgaria*. Sofia, Berlin: Stiftung Aufarbeitung der SED-Diktatur [u.a.].
Barkan, E. 2000. *The Guilt of Nations: Restitution and Negotiating Historical Injustices*. Baltimore: Johns Hopkins University Press.
Baron, N. and P. Gatrell (eds). 2004. *Homelands: War, Population and Statehood in Eastern Europe and Russia, 1918–1924*. London: Anthem Press.
——— (eds). 2009. *Warlands: Population Resettlement and State Reconstruction in the Soviet-East European Borderlands, 1945–50*. New York: Palgrave Macmillan.
Bartosz, A. 2010. *Małopolski Szlak Martyrologii Romów*. Tarnów: Muzeum Okręgowe w Tarnowie.
Bartov, O. and E.D. Weitz (eds). 2013. *Shatterzone of Empires: Coexistence and Violence in the German, Habsburg, Russian, and Ottoman Borderlands*. Bloomington: Indiana University Press.
Bauer, Y. 1978. *The Holocaust in Historical Perspective*. Seattle: University of Washington Press.
———. 2001. *Rethinking the Holocaust*. New Haven, London: Yale University Press.
Bauman, Z. 1991. *Modernity and Ambivalence*. Ithaca, NY: Cornell University Press.
———. 1992. *Mortality, Immortality and Other Life Strategies*. Cambridge: Polity Press.
Baumeister, R.F. and S. Hastings. 1997. 'How Groups Flatter and Deceive Themselves', in *Collective Memory of Political Events: Social Psychological Perspectives*, J.W. Pennebaker, D. Páez and B. Rimé (eds). Mahwah, New Jersey: Lawrence Erlbaum Publisher, 277–293.
Bednarek, S. 2010. 'Jeśli nie miejsca pamięci, to co? O badaniach pamięci', *Kultura Współczesna* 1(63): 100–109.
Beiner, G. 2008. 'In Anticipation of a Post-Memory Boom Syndrome', *Cultural Analysis* 7: 107–112.
Belton, B.A. 2005. *Questioning Gypsy Identity: Ethnic Narratives in Britain and America*. Walnut Creek, CA: Altamira Press.
Benedict, R. 2005 (1946). *The Chrysanthemum and the Sword: Patterns of Japanese Culture*. Boston-New York: Houghton Mifflin.
Berger, S. 2002. *The Search for Normality: National Identity and Historical Consciousness in Germany since 1800*. Berghahn Books.
Berliner, D.C. 2005. 'The Abuses of Memory: Reflections on the Memory Boom in Anthropology', *Anthropological Quarterly* 78(1): 197–211.

Bernhard, M. and J. Kubik (eds). 2014. *Twenty Years after Communism: The Politics of Memory and Commemoration*. Oxford University Press.
Bessonov, N. 2010. *Tsiganskaya tragediya 1941–1945. Fakty, dokumenty, vospominaniya, Vol. 2. Vooruzhonnyi otpor*. Saint Petersburg: Shatra.
Bezwińska, J., and D. Czech (eds). 2009. *Oświęcim w oczach SS*. Oświęcim: Panstwowe Muzeum Auschwitz-Birkenau.
Białecka, A., K.Oleksy, F. Regard and P. Trojański (eds). 2010. *European Pack for Visiting Auschwitz-Birkenau Memorial and Museum – Guidelines for Teachers and Educators*. Strasbourg.
Bilewicz, M. 2011. 'Społeczna pamięć Holokaustu i Auschwitz wśród licealistów: wokół projektu badawczego: "Trudnego Pytania"', in P. Trojański (ed.), *Auschwitz i Holokaust. Dylematy i wyzwania polskiej edukacji*. Oświęcim: Państwowe Muzeum Auschwitz-Birkenau.
Bilewicz, M. and M. Winiewski. 2014. 'The Emergence of Antisemitism in Times of Rapid Social Change: Survey Results from Poland', in *Antisemitism in an Era of Transition: Genealogies and Impact in Post-Communist Poland and Hungary*, F. Guesnet and G. Jones (eds). London: Peter Lang, 187–214.
Bilewicz, M. and M. Witkowska, 'Czy prawda nas wyzwoli? Przełamywanie oporu psychologicznego w przyjmowaniu wiedzy o Holocauście', unpublished article.
Bingen, D., W. Borodziej and S. Troebst (eds). 2003. *Vertreibungen europäisch erinnern? Historische Erfahrungen – Vergangenheitspolitik – Zukunftskonzeptionen*. Veröffentlichungen des Deutschen Polen-Instituts 18 Wiesbaden.
Bingen, D. 2005. 'Die deutsch-polnischen Beziehungen nach 1945', *Aus Politik und Zeitgeschichte* 5/6: 9–17.
Blacker, U. and A. Etkind. 2013. 'Introduction', in *Memory and Theory in Eastern Europe*, U. Blacker, A. Etkind and J. Fedor (eds). Basingstoke-New York: Palgrave Macmillan, 1–24.
Blaive, M. 2005. 'The Czechs and their Communism, Past and Present', in D. Gard, I. Main, M. Oliver and J. Wood (eds), *Inquiries into Past and Present: IWM Junior Visiting Fellows' Conferences* vol. 17, Vienna. Retrieved from http://www.iwm.at/publications/5-junior-visiting-fellows-conferences/muriel-blaive/
Blaive, M., C. Gerbel and T. Lindenberger (eds). 2011. *Clashes in European Memory: The Case of Communist Repression and the Holocaust*. Innsbruck, Vienna, Bolzano: Studien Verlag.
Błoński, J. 2008 [1987]. 'Biedni Polacy patrzą na getto'. Krakow: Wydawnictwo Literackie, 11–33.
Boer, P. den, H. Duchhardt, G. Kreis and W. Schmale (eds). 2011–2012. *Europäische Erinnerungsorte* vol. 1–3. Munich: Oldenbourg.
Boer, P. den. 2008. 'Loci memoriae – Lieux de mémoire', in *Cultural Memory Studies: An International and Interdisciplinary Handbook*, A. Erll and A. Nünning (eds). Berlin: de Gruyter, 19–25.
Bogumił, Z., J. Wawrzyniak, T. Buchen, C. Ganzer and M. Senina. 2015. *The Enemy on Display: The Second World War in Eastern European Museums*. Oxford and New York : Berghahn Books.

Boia, L. 1987. *L'exploration imaginaire de l'espace*. Paris: Editions La Découverte.
——. 1998. *Pour une histoire de l'imaginaire*. Paris: Les Belles Lettres.
——. 2001. *History and Myth in Romanian Consciousness*, trans. J.C. Brown. Budapest: Central European University Press.
Bokszański, Z. 2005. *Tożsamości zbiorowe*. Warsaw: Wydawnictwo Naukowe PWN.
Bömelburg, H.-J. 2003. 'Historia regionalna w dialogu polsko-niemieckim – granice zagrożenia i szanse dla dwunarodowego podejścia', *Studia Śląskie* 63: 123–139.
Bonnard, P. and M. Meckl. 2007. 'La gestion du double passé nazi et soviétique en Lettonie. Impasses et dépassements de la concurrence entre mémoires du Goulag et d'Auschwitz', in *L'Europe et ses passes douloureux*, G. Mink and L. Neumayer (eds). Paris: La Découverte.
Borodziej, W. 2003. 'Flucht, Vertreibung, Zwangsaussiedlung', in *Deutsche und Polen: Geschichte, Kultur, Politik*, A. Lawaty and H. Orłowski (eds). Munich, 88–95.
Borodziej, W. and H. Lemberg (eds). 2000–2001. *'Unsere Heimat ist uns ein fremdes Land geworden ...' Die Deutschen östlich von Oder und Neiße 1945–1950. Dokumente aus polnischen Archiven* (Quellen zur Geschichte und Landeskunde Ostmitteleuropas, Bde. 1–4 Marburg); Polish edition: *'Nasza ojczyzna stała się dla nas obcym państwem ...' Niemcy w Polsce 1945–1950. Wybór dokumentów*, 4 volumes. Warsaw.
Bourdieu, P. 1984. *Distinction: A Social Critique of the Judgment of Taste*, trans. R. Nice. Cambridge, MA: Harvard University Press.
Boyer, P. and J.V. Werstch (eds). 2009. *Memory in Mind and Culture*. Cambridge: Cambridge University Press.
Boym, S. 2001. *The Future of Nostalgia*. New York: Basic Books.
Brandes, D. 2010. 'Dekrete des tschechoslowakischen Präsidenten', in *Lexikon der Vertreibungen. Deportation, Zwangsaussiedlung und ethnische Säuberung im Europa des 20. Jahrhunderts*, D. Brandes, H. Sundhausen and S. Troebst (eds). Cologne, Weimar, Vienna: Böhlau, 112–114.
Brix, E., E. Bruckmüller and H. Stekl (eds). 2004–2005. *Memoria Austriae*, 3 vol. Vienna: Verlag für Geschichte und Politik.
Brossat, A., S. Combe, J.-Y. Potel and J.-C Szurek (eds). 1990. *A l'Est, la mémoire retrouvée*. Paris: La Découverte.
Broun, J. 2002. 'The Schism in the Bulgarian Orthodox Church, Part 3: Under the Second Union of Democratic Forces Government, 1997–2001', *Religion, State & Society* 30(4): 365–394.
Browning, C.R. and L.H. Siegelbaum. 2009. 'Frameworks for Social Engineering', in *Beyond Totalitarianism: Stalinism and Nazism Compared*, M. Geyer and S. Fitzpatrick (eds). Cambridge: Cambridge University Press, 228–265.
Brumlik, M., H. Funke and L. Rensmann. 2010. *Umkämpftes Vergessen. Walser-Debatte, Holocaust-Mahnmal und neuere deutsche Geschichtspolitik*. Schriftenreihe Politik und Kultur am Fachbereich Politische Wissenschaft der Freien Universität Berlin.

Burleigh, M. 1988. *Germany Turns Eastwards: A Study of Ostforschung in the Third Reich*. Cambridge: Cambridge University Press.
Buschmann, A. 1994. *Kaiser und Reich. Verfassungsgeschichte des Heiligen Römischen Reiches Deutscher Nation vom Beginn des 12. Jahrhunderts bis zum Jahre 1806 in Dokumenten*. Baden-Baden: Nomos Verlagsgesellschaft.
Buzalka, J. 2007. *Nation and Religion: The Politics of Commemorations in South-East Poland*. Berlin: Lit Verlag.
Calhoun, C. 2004. 'The Democratic Integration of Europe: Interests, Identity, and the Public Sphere'. Retrieved 20 May 2012 from http://www.eurozine.com/articles/2004-06-21-calhoun-en.htmlaccess
Carlton, D. 2000. *Churchill and the Soviet Union*. Manchester University Press.
CBOS. 1988. *Opinia publiczna o zbrodni w Katyniu*, report from research study 'Historia i teraźniejszość' conducted between 07.11.1987 and 28.12.1987, compiled by P. Kwiatkowski.
———. 2001a. *Polacy wobec zbrodni w Jedwabnem – przemiany społecznej świadomości*, report from research study 'Aktualne problemy i wydarzenia' conducted 03.08.2001–06.08.2001, compiled by B. Wciórka.
———. 2001b. *Polacy wobec zbrodni w Jedwabnem. Przemiany społecznej świadomości*, report from research conducted in April 2007 and the study 'Aktualne problemy i wydarzenia' conducted 03.08.2001–06.08.2001, compiled by B. Wciórka.
———. 2003. *Rocznica zbrodni na Wołyniu – pamięć i pojednanie*, report from the research study 'Aktualne problemy i wydarzenia', conducted 04.07.2003–07.07.2003, compiled by M. Strzeszewski.
———. 2004. *Opinie o stosunkach polsko-niemieckich repatriacjach wojennych*, report from the research study 'Aktualne problemy i wydarzenia', conducted 01.10.2004–04.10.2004, compiled by B. Roguska.
———. 2005. *Czy Polska wygrała wojnę?*, report from the research study 'Aktualne problemy i wydarzenia', conducted 01.04.2005–02.04.2005 and 09.04.2005–10.04.2005, compiled by M. Strzeszewski.
———. 2008a. *Pamięć o zbrodni katyńskiej i ocena jej znaczenia dla stosunków polsko-rosyjskich*, report from the research study 'Aktualne problemy i wydarzenia', conducted 10.04.2008–11.04.2008, compiled by K. Pankowski.
———. 2008b. *Wołyń 1943*, report from the research study 'Aktualne problemy i wydarzenia', conducted 06.06.2008–09.06.2008, compiled by K. Makaruk.
———. 2009. *Siedemdziesiąt lat od wybuchu II wojny światowej*, report from the research study 'Aktualne problemy i wydarzenia', conducted on 06.08.2009–12.08.2009, compiled by M. Strzeszewski.
Cesarani, D. and E.J. Sundquist (eds). 2012. *After the Holocaust: Challenging the Myth of Silence*. New York: Routledge.
Chałasiński, J. 1968. *Kultura i naród*. Warsaw: Książka i Wiedza.
Chrobaczyński, J. 1997. 'Oświęcim i Katyń w świetle postaw społeczeństwa polskiego 1940–1944. Zarys problematyki', *Rocznik Naukowo-Dydaktyczny WSP w Krakowie 'Prace Historyczne'* XVIII, vol. 181.
———. 2012. *Dramatyczny rok 1943. Postawy i zachowania społeczeństwa polskiego w rozstrzygającym roku II wojny światowej*. Rzeszów.

Churchill, R.S. (ed.). 1948. *The Sinews of Peace: Post-War Speeches by Winston S. Churchill*. London: Cassell and Company.
Cienciala, A.M., N.S. Lebedeva and W. Materski (eds). 2007. *Katyn: A Crime Without Punishment*, Annals of Communism Series. New Haven and London: Yale University Press.
Closa, C. 2010. 'Negotiating the Past: Claims for Recognition and Policies of Memory in the EU', *Instituto de Políticas y Bienes Públicos (IPP) Working Paper*, no. 8.
Cohen, S.J. 1999. *Politics Without a Past: The Absence of History in Postcommunist Nationalism*. Durham and London: Duke University Press.
Coles, T. and D.J. Timothy. 2004. *Tourism, Diasporas and Space*. London: Routledge.
Coles, T. 2003. 'Urban Tourism, Place Promotion and Economic Restructuring: The Case of Post-socialist Leipzig', *Tourism Geographies* 5: 190–219.
Collini, S. 1994. 'À la recherche de l'Angleterre perdue', *Le Débat* 78: 4–17.
Čolović, I. 2002. *The Politics of Symbols in Serbia*. London: C. Hurst & Co. Publishers.
Combe, S., T. Dufrêne and R. Robin (eds). 2009. *Berlin, l'effacement des traces: 1989–2009*. FAGE éditions.
Connerton, P. 2008. 'Seven Types of Forgetting', *Memory Studies* 1(1): 59–71.
Conway, B. 2010. 'New Direction in the Sociology of Collective Memory and Commemoration', *Sociology Compass* 7: 4, 442–453.
Conway, M.A. and C.W. Pleydell-Pearce. 2000. 'The Construction of Autobiographical Memories in the Self-Memory System', *Psychological Review* 107: 261–288.
Cornelißen, C., R. Holec and J. Pesek (eds). 2005. *Diktatur-Krieg-Vertreibung Erinnerungskulturen in Tschechien, der Slowakei und Deutschland seit 1945*. Essen: Klatext Verlag.
Crang, M. 2011. 'Tourist: Moving Places, Becoming Tourist, Becoming Ethnographer', in *Geographies of Mobilities: Practices, Spaces, Subjects*, T. Cresswell and P. Merriman (eds). Farnham: Ashgate.
Cresswell, T. and P. Merriman. 2011. *Geographies of Mobilities: Practices, Spaces, Subjects*. Surrey: Ashgate.
'Crimes Committed by the Communist Regime in Bulgaria'. 2010. Report from the conference 'Crimes of the Communist Regimes', 24–26 February 2010, Prague. Retrieved October 2013 from http://www.ustrcr.cz/data/pdf/konference/zlocinykomunismu/COUNTRY%20REPORT%20BULGARIA.pdf
Csáky, M. 2003. 'Geschichte und Gedächtnis. Erinnerung und Erinnerungsstrategien im narrativen historischen Verfahren. Das Beispiel Zentraleuropas', in *Klio ohne Fesseln? Historiographie im östlichen Europa nach dem Zusammenbruch des Kommunismus*, Ivanišević Osthefte 16. Vienna: Peter Lang, 61–80.
———. 2004. 'Die Mehrdeutigkeit von Gedächtnis und Erinnerung', in *Erinnern und Verarbeiten: Zur Schweiz in den Jahren 1933–1945*, G. Kreis (ed.). Basel: Schwabe, 7–30.

Cubitt, G. 2007. *History and Memory*. Manchester and New York: Manchester University Press.
Czapliński, P. 2012. 'Erinnerungspalimpseste. Über den Band "Parallelen" der Reihe "Deutsch-polnische Erinnerungsorte"', trans. M. Krzoska. *Dialog. Das deutsch-polnische Magazin* 101: 29–33.
Czyżewski, M., A. Piotrowski and A. Rokuszewska-Pawełek (eds). 1997. *Biografia i tożsamość narodowa*. Uniwersytet Łódzki, Katedra Socjologii Kultury.
Czyżewski, M. 2008. 'Debata na temat Jedwabnego oraz spór o "politykę historyczną" z punktu widzenia analizy dyskursu publicznego', in *Pamięć i polityka historyczna. Doświadczenia Polski i jej sąsiadów*, S.M. Nowinowski, J. Pomorski and R. Stobiecki (eds). Łódź: Instytut Pamięci Narodowej, 117–140.
Davies, N. 1981. *God's Playground. A History of Poland. Vol. 1: The Origins to 1795; Vol. 2: 1795 to the Present*. Oxford: Oxford University Press.
———. 1997. 'Polish National Mythologies', in *Myths and Nationhood*, G. Hosking and G. Schöpflin (eds). London: C. Hurst & Co. Publishers.
———. 2000. *Heart of Europe: The Past in Poland's Present*. Oxford: Oxford University Press.
Davoliūtė, V. 2005. 'Deportee Memoirs and Lithuanian History: The Double Testimony of Dalia Grinkevičiūtė', *The Journal of Baltic Studies* 36(1): 51–68.
De Certeau, M. 1984. *The Practice of Everyday Life*, trans. S. Rendall. London: University of California Press.
Decuble, G.H. (ed.). 2004. *Cartea roz a comunismului*, vol. 1. Iași: Editura Versus.
Delanty, G. and P. O'Mahony. 2002. *Nationalism and Social Theory: Modernity and the Recalcitrance of the Nation*. London: SAGE.
Dermendzhieva, M. 2009. 'Darzhavna Sigurnost (The State Security) and its place in the new security services', paper delivered at the international conference 'Sfârșitul regimurilor comuniste. Cauze, desfășurare și consecințe', 25–27 June, Sambata de Sus, Romania.
Deyanova, L. 2008. 'Des condamnations locales du communisme à la condamnation internationale de janvier 2006', in *Expériences et mémoires: Partager en français la diversité du monde*, B. Jewsiewicki and E. Nimis (eds). Paris: L'Harmattan.
———. 2009. *Ochertaniya na malchanieto. Istoricheska sotsiologiya na kolektivnata pamet*. Sofia: Critique & Humanism Publishing House.
Dimitrov, V. 2001. *Bulgaria: The Uneven Transition*. Routledge: London and New York.
Diner, D. 2000. 'Haider und der Schutzreflex Europas', *Die Welt*, 26 February.
———. 2002. 'Gedächtnis und Restitution', in *Verbrechen Erinnern. Die Auseinandersetzung mit Holocaust und Völkermord*, V. Knigge and N. Frei (eds). Munich, 299–305.
———. 2007a. *Gegenläufige Gedächtnisse: Über Geltung und Wirkung des Holocaust*, Toldot 7. Göttingen: Vandenhoeck & Ruprecht.
———. 2007b. 'Memory and Restitution: World War II as a Foundational Event in a Uniting Europe', in *Restitution and Memory: Material Restoration in*

Europe, D. Diner and G. Wunberg (eds). Oxford and New York: Berghahn Books.
Diner, H.R. 2009, 2010. *We Remember with Reverence and Love: American Jews and the Myth of Silence after the Holocaust, 1945–1962*. New York: NYU Press.
Długoborski, W. and F. Piper (eds). 2000. *Auschwitz, 1940–1945: Central Issues in the History of the Camp*, 5 vols. Oświęcim.
Długoborski, W. and P. Trojański. 2008. 'Facing the Holocaust in Poland: The History and the Present', in *Les Européens et la Shoah*, R. Dray-Bensousan (ed.). Marseille.
Dobre, C.-F. 2006. 'Looking for Specificity: The Anticommunist Resistance as an Element of a New Romanian Identity', in *Obywatelstwo i tożsamość w społeczenstwach zróźnicowanych kulturowo i na pograniczach*, vol. 1, M. Bieńkowska-Ptasznik, K. Krzysztofek and A. Sadowski (eds). Białystok: Instytut Socjologii–Uniwersytet Białystok Press.
———. 2007. 'Une mise en scène de la mémoire: le musée de Sighet', in *Inscenizacje pamięci*, I. Skórzynska, C. Lavrence and C. Pépin (eds). Poznań: Wydawnictwo Poznańskie.
———. 2012. 'Les traces du communisme. Mémoire et oubli dans l'espace public à Sofia et Bucarest. Le cas exemplaire de six monuments et leur destin', in *Da poznaem komunizma*, I. Znepolski (ed.). Institute for the Study of the Recent Past, Ciela Publishers, 117–166.
Dobreva, D. and K. Roth (eds). 1997. 'Seloto mezhdu promyanata i traditsiyata', in *Bălgarski Folklor* 23, no. 3–4.
Dobreva, D. 1994. 'Zhiteyski razkazi i identichnost. Po zapiski ot s. Raduil, Samokovsko', *Bălgarski Folklor* 20, no. 5: 57–69.
———. 1997a. 'Trudova deynost v kolektiva. Ofitsialna norma i deystvitelno povedenie v edno planinsko selo prez 50-te godin', *Bălgarski Folklor* 23, no. 3–4: 71–103.
———. 1997b. 'Razkazi za sotsialisticheskoto selo. Kam slovesnoto ovladyavane na minaloto i nastoyashteto', *Bălgarski Folklor* no. 5–6: 4–27.
———. 2000. 'Vremevi ritmi i upotreba na vremeto v trudovoto vsekidnevie na sotsialisticheskoto selo. Primerat na edno planinsko selo', *Bălgarska Etnologiya* 26, no 4: 17–33.
———. 2003. 'Da postroish sobstven dom. Za upotrebata na sotsialnite mrezhi v sotsialisticheskoto selo', in *Sotsializmăt: Realnost i ilyuzii*, R. Ivanova, A. Luleva and R. Popov (eds). Sofia: EIM – BAN, 63–75.
Domańska, E. 2006. *Historie niekonwencjonalne. Refleksja o przeszłości w nowej humanistyce*. Poznań: Wydawnictwo Poznańskie.
———. 2012. *Historia egzystencjalna. Krytyczne studium narratywizmu i humanistyki zaangażowanej*. Warsaw: PWN.
Donskis, L. 2009. 'The Inflation of Genocide', *European Voice*, 24 July. Retrieved 23 August 2009 from http://www.europeanvoice.com/article/2009/07/the-inflation-of-genocide/65613.aspx
Doyle, N.J. 2011. 'Rediscovering Political Sovereignty: The Rebirth of French Political Philosophy', in *Routledge International Handbook of Contemoprary Social*

and Political Theory, G. Delanty and S.P. Turner (eds). London and New York: Routledge.

Droit, E. 2007. 'Le Goulag contre la Shoah. Mémoires officielles et cultures mémorielles dans l'Europe élargie', *Vingtième Siècle Revue d'histoire* 94: 101–120.

Dubin, B. 2005. 'Goldene Zeiten des Krieges: Erinnerung als Sehnsucht nach der Breznev-Ära', *Osteuropa*, no. 4–6: 219–233.

Dudek, A. 2008. 'Spory o polską politykę historyczną po 1989 roku', in *Pamięć i polityka historyczna. Doświadczenia Polski i jej sąsiadów*, S.M. Nowinowski, J. Pomorski and R. Stobiecki (eds). Łódź: Instytut Pamięci Narodowej, 193–200.

'Duma i wstyd Polaków – sondaż'. 2004. *Gazeta Wyborcza*, 17 September 2004. Retrieved 22 September 2004 from http://serwisy.gazeta.pl/kraj/2029020,34317,2289803.html

Eisenstadt, S.N. (ed.). 2002. *Multiple modernities*. New Brunswick: Transaction Publishers.

Elster, J. 2004. *Closing the Books: Transitional Justice in Historical Perspective*. Cambridge University Press.

Engelking-Boni, B. 1994. *Zagłada i pamięć*. Warsaw: Instytut Filozofii Socjologii.

Erll, A. and A. Nünning (eds). 2010. *A Companion to Cultural Memory Studies*. New York: de Gruyter.

Erll, A. 2011. *Memory in Culture*. London: Palgrave Macmillan.

Esbenshade, R.S. 1995. 'Remembering to Forget: Memory, History, National Identity in Postwar East-Central Europe', *Representations* no. 49, winter. Special issue: 'Identifying Histories: Eastern Europe Before and After 1989': 72–96.

Etkind, A. 2004. 'Hard and Soft in Cultural Memory: Political Mourning in Russia and Germany', *Grey Room* 16: 36–59.

Etkind, A., R. Finnin, U. Blacker, J. Fedor, S. Lewis, M. Malksöo and M. Mroz. 2012. *Remembering Katyn*. Cambridge: Polity Press.

European Parliament. 2010. *Resolution on the Situation in Ukraine RC-B7-0116/2010*. Retrieved 2 October 2013 from http://www.Europarl.europa.eu

Eyerman, R. 2004. 'The Past in the Present: Culture and the Transmission of Memory', *Acta Sociologica* 47(2): 159–169.

Fabian, J. 1983. *Time and the Other: How Anthropology Makes Its Object*. New York: Columbia.

Filipkowski, P. 2012. 'The Recent Development in "Collective Memory" Research in Poland', *Acta Poloniae Historica* 106: 33–59.

Fincham, B., M. McGuinness and L. Murray (eds). 2010. *Mobile Methodologies*. Basingstoke: Palgrave Macmillan.

Fischer, B.B. 1999–2000. 'The Katyn Controversy: Stalin's Killing Field', *Studies in Intelligence. Journal of the American Intelligence Professional*, Winter 1999–2000. Retrieved 3 August 2001 from https://www.cia.gov/library/center-for-the-study-of-intelligence/kent-csi/vol43no3/pdf/v43i3a06p.pdf.

Fischer, P., B. Kerski, I. Röskau-Rydel, K. Ruchniewicz and S. Stekel (eds). 1992–2012. *Inter Finitimos – Jahrbuch zur deutsch-polnischen Beziehungsgeschichte*, Heft 1–10.

'For a critical and enlightened debate about the past', 10 August 2003, http://www.vertreibungszentrum.de/
Forest, B. and J. Johnson. 2002. 'Unravelling the Threads of History: Soviet-Era Monuments and Post-Soviet National Identity in Moscow', *Annals of the Association of American Geographers* 92(3): 524–557.
Foucault, M. 1991. 'Panopticism', in *The Foucault Reader*, P. Rabinow (ed.). London: Penguin Books.
François, E. and H. Schulze (eds). 2001. *Deutsche Erinnerungsorte*. Munich: Beck.
François, E. and T. Serrier. 2012. *Lieux de mémoire européens*. Paris: La documentation Française.
François, E. 2001. 'Eine Geschichte der deutschen Erinnerungsorte: Warum? Wie?', in *Gedenken im Zwiespalt: Konfliktlinien europäischen Erinnerns*, A. Escudier (ed.), *Genshagener Gespräche* 4, trans. Erik Kurzweil. Göttingen: Wallstein, 77–89.
———. 2005. 'Pierre Nora und die "Lieux de mémoire"', in *Erinnerungsorte Frankreichs*, Pierre Nora, 8th edn. Munich: Beck, 7–14.
———. 2013. 'Geschichtspolitik und Erinnerungskultur in Europa heute', in *Geschichtspolitik in Europa seit 1989. Deutschland, Frankreich und Polen im internationalen Vergleich*. Moderne Europäische Geschichte 3 eds. E. François, K. Kończal, R. Traba and S. Troebst. Göttingen: Wallstein, 541–558.
François, E., K. Kończal, R. Traba and S. Troebst (eds). 2013. *Geschichtspolitik in Europa seit 1989. Deutschland, Frankreich und Polen im internationalen Vergleich*. Göttingen: Wallstein.
Frevert, U. 2005. 'Europeanizing Germany's Twentieth Century', *History and Memory* 17, 1/2, 87–116.
Friedländer, S. 1993. *Memory, History, and the Extermination of the Jews of Europe*. Bloomington: Indiana University Press.
———. 1994. 'Trauma, Memory and Transference', in *Holocaust Remembrance: The Shapes of Memory*, G.H. Hartman (ed.). Oxford, UK and Cambridge, USA: Blackwell.
Friedrich, J. 2002. *Der Brand. Deutschland im Bombenkrieg 1940–1945*. Munich: Propyläen.
Frison-Roche, F. 2005. *La situation politique en Bulgarie à la veille de son entrée dans l'Union européenne*. Retrieved November 2012 from http://www.diploweb.com/forum/frison0511.htm
Frommer, B. 2001. 'To Prosecute or to Expel? Czechoslovak Retribution and the "Transfer" of the Sudeten Germans', *Redrawing Nations: Ethnic cleansing in East-Central Europe 1944–1948*, P. Ther and A. Siljak (eds). Lanham, MD: Rowman and Littlefield, 221–240.
Fundacja Współpracy Polsko-Niemieckiej / Stiftung für Deutsch-Polnische Zusammenarbeit. 2011. *Ein großer Schritt in Richtung Normalität: Der Stand der deutsch-polnischen Beziehungen. Ergebnisse repräsentativer Bevölkerungsumfragen in Deutschland und Polen*. Institut für Demoskopie: Allensbach.
Furedi, F. 2011. *On Tolerance: A Defence of Moral Independence*. London and New York: Continuum.

Ganzenmüller, J. 2005. *Das belagerte Leningrad 1941–1944. Die Stadt in den Strategien von Angreifern und Verteidigern*. Paderborn: Verlag Ferdinand Schöningh.
Gasztold-Seń, P. 2010. 'Siła przeciw prawdzie. Represje aparatu bezpieczeństwa PRL wobec osób kwestionujących oficjalną wersję Zbrodni Katyńskiej', in *Zbrodnia Katyńska w kręgu prawdy i kłamstwa*, S. Kalbarczyk (ed.). Warsaw: Instytut Pamięci Narodowej.
Gatev, Y. 2009. *Brestovitsa ot drevnostta do dnes*. Plovdiv: MAKROS.
Gensburger, S. and M.-C. Lavabre (eds). 2012. 'D'une "mémoire" européenne à l'européanisation de la "mémoire"', *Politique Européenne* 37.
Giatzidis, E. 2002. *An Introduction to Postcommunist Bulgaria: Political, Economic and Social Transformation*. Manchester and New York: Manchester University Press.
Giesen, B. 2004. *Triumph and Trauma*. Boulder: Paradigm Publishers.
Glaser, B. and A. Strauss. 1964. 'Awareness Context and Social Interaction', *American Sociological Review* 29(5): 669–679.
———. 1967. *Discovery of Grounded Theory: Strategies for Qualitative Research*. Chicago: Aldine.
Gleinig, R., A. Kaminsky and R. Heidenreich. 2008. *Erinnerungsorte an den Holodomor 1932/33 in der Ukraine*. Leipzig: Leipzig University Press.
Gluza, Z. 1997. 'Pozory obrachunku', in *Ofiary czy współwinni. Nazizm i sowietyzm w świadomości historycznej*. Warsaw: Volumen, 31–42.
Goldhagen, D. 1996a. *Hitler's Willing Executioners*, New York: Alfred Knopf.
———. 1996b. *Hitlers willige Vollstrecker*, transl. K. Kochmann. Berlin: Wolf Jobst Siedler Verlag.
Gołębiewska, I., 'Between Memory and History – Cultural Memory in Polish School History Books in the Years 1945–2011. Analysis of Historical Events: January the 17th, 1945 in Warsaw, The Katyń Massacre of 1940, The Warsaw Uprising of 1944', unpublished manuscript.
Goshler, C. and P. Ther. 2007. 'A History without Boundaries', in *Robbery and Restitution*, M. Dean, C. Goshler and P. Ther (eds). Oxford and New York: Berghahn Books.
Górny, M., H. Hahn, K. Kończal and R. Traba. 2012. 'Polish-German Realms of Memory: A New Paradigm?' *Acta Poloniae Historica* 106: 155–167.
Grabski, A.F. 1983. *Perspektywy przeszłości: studia i szkice historiograficzne*. Lublin: Wydawnictwo Lubelskie.
———. 1985. *Kształty historii*. Łódź: Wydawnictwo Łódzkie.
Grachova, S. 2008. 'Unknown Victims: Ethnic-based Violence of the World War II Era in Ukrainian Politics of History after 2004', paper presented at the Fourth Annual Danyliw Research Seminar in Contemporary Ukrainian Studies, University of Ottawa, October 23–25.
Gradev, V. 1992. 'Le mausolée de Dimitrov', *Communications* 55. Retrieved from http://www.persee.fr/web/revues/home/prescript/article/comm_0588-8018_1992_num_55_1_1836
Grass, G. 2002. *Im Krebsgang*. Göttingen: Steidl Verlag.

Grinevich, V. 2005. '"Raskolotaia pamiat": Vtoraia mirovaia voina v istoricheskom soznanii ukrainskogo obshchestva', in *Pamiat' o voine 60 let spustia: Rossiia, Germaniia, Evropa*, M. Gabowitsch (ed.). Moscow: NLO.

Gross, J.T. 1988. *Revolution from Abroad: The Soviet Conquest of Poland's Western Ukraine and Western Belorussia*. Princeton: Princeton University Press.

———. 2000. *Sąsiedzi. Historia zagłady żydowskiego miasteczka*. Sejny: Pogranicze.

———. 2001. *Neighbors: The Destruction of the Jewish Community in Jedwabne, Poland*. Princeton: Princeton University Press.

———. 2006. *Fear: Anti-Semitism in Poland after Auschwitz: An Essay in Historical Interpretation*. Princeton University Press.

———. 2012. *Golden Harvest*. New York: Oxford University Press.

Gruber, R.E. 2002. *Virtually Jewish: Reinventing Jewish Culture in Europe*. Berkeley and Los Angeles, University of California Press.

———. 2009. 'Beyond Virtually Jewish: Balancing the Real, the Surreal and Real Imaginary Places', in *Reclaiming Memory: Urban Regeneration in the Historic Jewish Quarters of Central European Cities*, M. Murzyn-Kupisz and J. Purchla (eds). Krakow, International Cultural Centre, 63–79.

Grudzińska-Gross, I. and J.T. Gross (eds). 2008. *'W czterdziestym nas Matko na Sibir zesłali...' Polska a Rosja 1939–1942*. Krakow: Znak.

Guth, S. 2012. 'History by Decree? The Commission of Historians of the German Democratic Republic and the People's Republic of Poland 1956–1990', in *Germany, Poland, and Postmemorial Relations: In Search of a Livable Past*, K. Kopp and J. Niżyńska (eds). Europe in Transition: The NYU European Studies Series, 43–63.

Gutman, Y. and Y. Berenbaum (eds). 1998. *Anatomy of the Auschwitz Death Camp*. Indiana University Press.

Gyáni, G. 2006. 'Memory and Discourse on the 1956 Hungarian Revolution', in *Europe-Asia Studies* 588: 1199–1208.

Habermas, J. 2008. *Ach, Europa. Kleine politische Schriften XI*. Frankfurt: Suhrkamp.

Hackmann, J. 2001. 'Deutschlands Osten – Polens Westen als Problem der Geschichtsschreibung', in *Deutschlands Osten-Polens Westen. Vergleichende Studien zur geschichtlichen Landeskunde*, M. Weber (ed.) Mitteleuropa-Osteuropa. Oldenburger Beiträge zur Kultur und Geschichte Ostmitteleuropas 2: Frankfurt/Main, 209–235.

———. 2008. 'Collective Memories in the Baltic Sea Region and Beyond: National – Transnational – European?', in *Journal of Baltic Studies* 394. Special issue 'Contested and Shared Places of Memory: History and Politics in North Eastern Europe', M. Lehti and J. Hackmann (eds), 381–391.

———. 2009. 'From National Victims to Transnational Bystanders? The Changing Commemoration of World War II in Central and Eastern Europe', *Constellations* 16(1): 167–181.

———. 2011. 'Landes- und regionalgeschichtliche Konzeptionen im deutsch-polnischen Kontext: Stolpersteine oder Wege zu einer postnationalen Historiografie', in *Historie – Jahrbuch des Zentrums für historische Forschung der Polnischen Akademie der Wissenschaften* 5, 2011/12.

Hahn, H.H. and R. Traba (eds). 2012–2013. *Deutsch-Polnische Erinnerungsorte*, vol. 1–2: 'Geteilt, Gemeinsam', vol. 3: 'Parallelen', vol. 4: 'Reflexionen', vol. 5: 'Erinnerung auf Polnisch'. Paderborn: Ferdinand Schöningh.

Hahn, H.H., H. Hein-Kircher and A. Kochanowska-Nieborak (eds). 2008. *Erinnerungskultur und Versöhnungskitsch*, Tagungen zur Ostmitteleuropa-Forschung, vol. 26. Marburg: Herder-Institut Verlag.

Halbwachs, M. 1925. *Les cadres sociaux de la mémoire*. Paris: Presses Universitaires de France.

———. 1941. *La topographie légendaire des Évangiles en Terre Sainte. Etude de mémoire collective*. Paris: Presses universitaires de France.

———. 1950. *La mémoire collective*. Paris: Presses universitaires de France.

———. 1980. *The Collective Memory*. New York: Harper and Row.

———. 1992. *On Collective Memory*, ed. and trans. L.A. Coser. Chicago: University of Chicago Press.

———. 2008. *Społeczne ramy pamięci*, trans. Marcin Król. Warszawa: Wydawnictwo Naukowe PWN [first edition 1969].

Halecki, O. 1950. *The Limits and Divisions of European History*. London and New York: Sheet and Ward.

———. 1980. *Borderlands of Western Civilization: A History of East Central Europe*, 2nd ed., A.L. Simon (ed.). Safety Harbor, FL: Simon Publications.

Hałub, M. and A. Mańko-Matysiak (eds). 2004–2012. *Śląska Republika Uczonych / Schlesische Gelehrtenrepublik / Slezská Vědecká Obec*, vol. 1–5, Wrocław.

Hancock, I. 1991. 'Gypsy History in Germany and Neighboring Lands: A Chronology Leading to the Holocaust and Beyond', in *The Gypsies of Eastern Europe*, D. Crowe and J. Kolsti (eds). Armonk, New York and London: M.E. Sharpe, Inc.

———. 2001. 'Responses to the Porrajmos: The Romani Holocaust', in *Is the Holocaust Unique? Perspectives on Comparative Genocide*. A.S. Rosenbaum (ed.). Boulder: Westview Press.

Hansen, P. 2000. '"European Citizenship", or Where Neoliberalism Meets Ethnoculturalism: Analyzing the European Union's Citizenship Discourse', *European Societies* 2(2): 39–66.

———. 2002. 'European Integration, European Identity and the Colonial Connection', *European Journal of Social Theory* 5(4): 483–498.

———. 2009. 'Post-national Europe – Without Cosmopolitan Guarantees', *RACE and CLASS*, 50(4): 20–37.

Hartmann, G. 1993. 'A Surfeit of Memory? Reflections on History, Melancholy and Denial', *History and Memory* 5(2): 147–150.

Hayashi, T. (ed.). 2003. *The Construction and Deconstruction of National Histories in Slavic Eurasia*. Sapporo: Slavic Research Center.

Hazan, P. 2007. 'Das neue Mantra der Gerechtigkeit', *Überblick. Deutsche Zeitschrift für Entwicklungspolitik*. Retrieved September 2013 from http://www.der-ueberblick.de/ueberblick.archiv/one.ueberblick.article/ueberblick28e0.html?entry=page. 200701.010

Henningsen, B., H. Kliemann-Geisinger and S. Troebst (eds). 2009. *Transnationale Erinnerungsorte: nord- und südeuropäische Perspektiven*, Baltic Sea region 10. Berlin: Berliner Wiss.-Verlag.
Heuss, H. 1988. 'Anti-Gypsyism Research: The Creation of a New Field of Study', in *Scholarship and the Gypsy Struggle: Commitment in Romani Studies*, T. Acton (ed.). Hatfield: University of Hertfordshire Press.
———. 1997. 'German Policies of Gypsy Persecution 1870–1945', in *The Gypsies During the Second World War*, vol. 1: *From 'Race Science' to the Camps*, K. Fings, H. Heuss and F. Sparing (eds). Hatfield: Gypsy Research Centre & University of Hertfordshire Press.
Himka, J.P., and Michlic, J.B. 2013. *Bringing the Dark Past to Light: The Memory of the Holocaust in Postcommunist Europe*. Lincoln: Nebraska University Press.
Hirsch, M. 1997. *Family Frames: Photography, Narrative, and Postmemory*. Cambridge, MA: Harvard University Press.
Hirsch, M. 1999. 'Projected Memory: Holocaust Photographs in Personal and Public Fantasy', in *Acts of Memory: Cultural Recall in the Present*, M. Bal, J. Crewe and L. Spitzer (eds). Hanover: University Press of New England, 3–23.
Hirszowicz, M. and E. Neyman. 2007. 'The Social Framing of Non-Memory', *International Journal of Sociology* 37(1): 74–88.
Hlavičková, Z. 2007. 'Wedged Between National and Trans-National History: Slovak Historiography in the 1990s', in *Narratives Unbound: Historical Studies in Post-Communist Eastern Europe*, S. Antohi, B. Trencsényi and P. Apor (eds). Budapest: CEU Press, 249–310.
Hobsbawm, E.J. 1991. *Nations and Nationalism since 1780: Programme, Myth, Reality*, 2nd ed. Cambridge: Cambridge University Press.
Hofer, T. 1994. *Hungarians between 'East' and 'West': Three Essays on National Myths and Symbols*. Budapest: Museum of Ethnography.
Hoffman, E. 2004. *After Such Knowledge: A Meditation on the Aftermath of the Holocaust*. London: Vintage.
Horvath, Z.K. 2008. 'Pour une économie symbolique du travail de mémoire: sites, survivants et politiques de reconnaissance en Hongrie 1989–2005', in *Expériences et mémoire, Partager en français la diversité du monde*. Paris: l'Harmattan, 260–274.
Hövermann, A., B. Küpper and A. Zick. 2011. *Intolerance, Prejudice and Discrimination: A European Report*. Berlin: Nora Langenbacher Friedrich-Ebert-Stiftung.
Hudemann, R. (ed.). 2002. *Stätten grenzüberschreitender Erinnerung: Spuren der Vernetzung des Saar-Lor-Lux-Raumes im 19. und 20. Jahrhundert = Lieux de la mémoire transfrontalière*, with the assistance of M. Hahn, G. Krebs, and J. Großmann http://www.memotransfront.uni-saarland.de/
Huener, J. 2003. *Auschwitz, Poland and the Politics of Commemoration, 1945–1975*. Athens: Ohio University Press.
Hughes, G. 2009. *Political Correctness: A History of Semantics and Culture*. Oxford: Wiley-Blackwell.

Husserl, E. 1965. *Phenomenology and the Crisis of Philosophy*. New York: Harper Torchbooks.
Huyse, L. 1995. 'Justice after Transition: On the Choices Successor Elites Make in Dealing with the Past', *Law and Social Inquiry* 20(1): 51–78.
Ingendaay, P. 2008. 'Der Bürgerkrieg ist immer noch nicht vorbei', *FAZ* no. 276, November, 25, 40.
Jahn, P. 2007. '27 Millionen', *Die Zeit*, no. 25, June, 14.
Janion, M. 1990. *Życie pośmiertne Konrada Wallenroda*. Warsaw: Państwowy Instytut Wydawniczy.
———. 1998. *Płacz generała: Eseje o wojnie*. Warsaw: Wydawnictwo Sic!
———. 2006. *Niesamowita Słowiańszczyzna: fantazmaty literatury*. Krakow: Wydawnictwo Literackie.
Janmaat, J.G. 2002. 'Identity Construction and Education: The History of Ukraine in Soviet and Post-Soviet Schoolbooks', in *Nation-Building and National Security in Ukraine*, T. Kuzio and P.D. Aniery (eds). Westport: Praeger.
Janowski, M. 2008. 'Polityka Historyczna. Między edukacją a propagandą', in *Pamięć i polityka historyczna. Doświadczenia Polski i jej sąsiadów*, S.M. Nowinowski, J. Pomorski and R. Stobiecki (eds). Łódź: Instytut Pamięci Narodowej, 229–246.
Jarausch, K.H. 2010. 'Nightmares or Daydreams? A Postscript on the Europeanisation of Memories', in *A European Memory? Contested Histories and Politcs of Remembrance*, M. Pakier and B. Stråth (eds). Oxford and New York: Berghahn Books, 309–320.
Jarausch, K.H. and T. Lindenberger. 2007a. 'Contours of a Critical History of Contemporary Europe: A Transnational Agenda', in *Conflicted Memories: Europeanizing Contemporary Histories*. K.H. Jarausch and T. Lindenberger (eds). New York and Oxford: Berghahn Books.
——— (eds). 2007b. *Conflicted Memories: Europeanizing Contemporary Histories*. New York and Oxford: Berghahn Books.
Jarząbek, W. 2012. 'Shadows of Memory in Polish-German Relations 1989–2005', in *Germany, Poland, and Post Memorial Relations: In Search of a Livable Past*, K. Kopp and J. Niżyńska (eds). Europe in Transition: The NYU European Studies Series, 25–42.
Jasiewicz, K. 2002. *'Pierwsi po diable'. Elity sowieckie w okupowanej Polsce, 1939–1941*. Warsaw, Oficyna Rytm.
———. 2010a. 'Recepta na prawdziwy antysemityzm', interview with, by P. Zychowicz, *Rzeczpospolita*, 30–31 January.
———. 2010b. *Rzeczywistość sowiecka 1939–1941 w świadectwach polskich Żydów*. Warsaw: Instytut Studiów Politycznych PAN.
Jaskułowski, K. 2010. 'Western (civic) versus Eastern (ethnic) Nationalism: The Origins and Critique of the Dichotomy', *Polish Sociological Review* 171(3): 289–303.
Jedlicki, J. 1988. *Jakiej cywilizacji Polacy potrzebują. Studia z dziejów idei i wyobraźni XIX wieku*. Warsaw: Państwowe Wydawnictwo Naukowe.

———. 1999. *A Suburb of Europe: Nineteenth-century Polish Approaches to Western Civilization*, trans. A. Doyle and B. Petrowska. Budapest: Central European University Press.
———. 2005. 'East-European Historical Request en route to an Integrated Europe', in *Collective Memory and European Identity*, K. Eder and W. Spohn (eds). Aldershot: Ashgate, 37–48.
———. 2008. Problem winy i odpowiedzialności. In *Wokół strachu. Dyskusja o książce Jana T. Grossa*, M. Gądek (ed.). Krakow: Wydawnictwo Znak, 32–44.
Jelin, E. 2003. *State Repression and the Labors of Memory*. Minneapolis: University of Minnesota Press.
———. 2010. 'The Past in the Present: Memories of State Violence in Contemporary Latin America', in *Memory in a Global Age: Discourses, Practices, Trajectories*, A. Assmann and S. Conrad (eds). Hampshire: Palgrave, 61–78.
Joas, H. 2009. *Gewalt und Menschenwürde. Wie aus Erfahrungen Rechte werden. Konstanzer Kulturwissenschaftliches Kolloquium, Diskussionsbeiträge* N.F. 5. Retrieved 8 July 2013 from http://www.exc16.de/cms/uploads/media/Kolloquium-Joas-Diskussionsbeitraege-NF-5.pdf
Judt, T. 1992. 'The Past Is Another Country: Myth and Memory in Postwar Europe', *Daedalus* 121, no. 4, 83–11.
———. 2002. 'The Past is Another Country: Myth and Memory in Postwar Europe', in *Memory and Power in Post-War Europe: Studies in the Presence of the Past*, J.-W. Müller (ed.). Cambridge: Cambridge University Press, 157–183.
———. 2005. *Postwar: A History of Europe since 1945*. New York: Penguin Books.
'Kaczynski Warns of Germany's "Imperial" Ambitions'. 2011. http://www.spiegel.de/international/europe/polish-opposition-leader-kaczynski-warns-of-germany-s-imperial-ambitions-a-790034.html.
Kaelble, H. 2006. 'Europäische Geschichte aus westeuropäischer Sicht', in *Transnationale Geschichte. Themen, Tendenzen und Theorien. Jürgen Kocka zum 65. Geburtstag*, G. Budde, S. Conrad and O. Janz (eds). Göttingen: Vandenhoeck & Ruprecht,105–116.
Kalbarczyk, S. (ed.). 2010. *Zbrodnia Katyńska. W kręgu prawdy i kłamstwa*. Warsaw: Instytut Pamięci Narodowej.
Kansteiner, W., R.N. Lebow and C. Fogu (eds). 2006. *The Politics of Memory in Postwar Europe*. Durham and London: Duke University Press.
Kansteiner, W. 2002. 'Finding Meaning in Memory: a Methodological Critique of Collective Memory Studies', *History and Theory* 41, 179–197.
Kapluk, K. 2010. 'Perepysana istoriia Ukraïny. Versiia epokhy Dmytra Tabachnyka', *Ukrainska Pravda* 26 August. Retrieved 2 October 2013 from http://www.pravda.com.ua/articles/2010/08/26/5332444/
Kapralski, S. 2010. 'Memories as Bridges, Memories as Trenches. Poland's Memories of "The Other" since 1989: From Myth to Remembrance to Politics', in *New Europe: Growth to Limits?* S. Eliaeson and N. Georgieva (eds). Oxford: The Bardwell Press.
———. 2011. 'Od milczenia do "trudnej pamięci". Państwowe Muzeum Auschwitz-Birkenau i jego rola w dyskursie publicznym', in *Następstwa*

zagłady Żydów. Polska 1944–2010, F. Tych and M. Adamczyk-Garbowska (eds). Lublin: Wydawnictwo Uniwersytetu Marii Curie-Skłodowskiej and Jewish Historical Institute in Warsaw.

———. 2012. *Naród z popiołów. Pamięć zagłady a tożsamość Romów*. Warsaw: Scholar.

Karlsson, K.-G. 2010. 'The Uses of History and the Third Wave of Europeanisation', in *A European Memory? Contested Histories and Politics of Remembrance*, M. Pakier and B. Stråth (eds). New York and Oxford: Berghahn Books.

Karstedt, S. 2009. 'The Legacy of Maurice Halbwachs', in *Legal Institutions and Collective Memories*, S. Karstedt (ed.). Oxford: Hart Publishing, 1–27.

Kasianov, H. 2012. 'Holodomor and the Politics of Memory in Ukraine after Independence', in *Holodomor and Gorta Mor: Histories, Memories and Representations of Famine in Ukraine and Ireland*, C. Noack, L. Janssen and V. Comerford (eds). Anthem Press, 167–188.

Kasianov, G. 2009. 'Nationalized History: Past Continuous, Present Perfect, Future…', in *A Laboratory of Transnational History: Ukraine and Recent Ukrainian Historiography*, G. Kasianov and P. Ther (eds). Budapest: Central European University Press.

Kaźmierska, K. 1999. *Doświadczenia wojenne Polaków a kształtowanie tożsamości etnicznej. Analiza narracji kresowych*. Warsaw: IFiS PAN.

———. 2000. 'Polish-German Relationships in Narratives on the Experiences of World War II from Poland's Eastern Border Region', in *Biographies and the Division of Europe: Experience, Action and Change on the 'Eastern Side'*, R. Breckner, D. Kalekin-Fishman and I. Miethe (eds). Opladen: Leske + Budrich, 217–232.

———. 2008. *Biografia i pamięć. Na przykładzie pokoleniowego doświadczenia ocalonych z Zagłady*. Krakow: Zakład Wydawniczy Nomos.

———. 2010. 'Biographieforschung in Polen', *BIOS, Zeitschrift fur Biographieforschung, Oral History und Lebensverlaufsanalysen*, no. 1, 153–163.

———. 2012. *Biography and Memory: The Generational Experience of the Shoah Survivors*. Boston: Academic Studies Press.

Kenney, P. 2002. *A Carnival of Revolution: Central Europe, 1989*. Princeton: Princeton University Press.

Kenrick, D. 2006. 'Resistance', in *The Gypsies during the Second World War*, vol. 3, 'The Final Chapter', D. Kenrick (ed.). Hatfield: University of Hertfordshire Press.

Kiliánová, G. 2005. *Identita a pamäť. Devín / Theben / Devény ako pamätné miesto*. Bratislava: Ústav etnológie SAV.

———. 2006. 'Poznámky k recenzentským posudkom', in *Etnologické rozpravy* XIII2, 267–269.

———. 2011. *Identität und Gedächtnis in der Slowakei. Devín als Erinnerungsort*. Frankfurt am Main: Peter Lang.

Kilias, J. 2013. 'Is There any Sociological Tradition of Social Memory Research? The Polish and Czech Case', *Polish Sociological Review* 183(3): 297–316.

Kiss, C. 2009. 'Transitional Justice: The Re-Construction of Post-Communist Memory', in *The Burden of Remembering: Recollections and Representations of the 20th Century*, E. Koresaar, K. Kuutma and E. Lauk (eds). Helsinki: Finnish Literature Society.

Kittel, M. 2012. 'Czy Niemcy rzeczywiście chcą napisać inną historię. Zadania i cele berlińskiej fundacji "Ucieczka, Wypędzenie, Pojednanie"', in *Transgraniczność w perspektiwie socjologicznej. Migracje przymusowe w Europie*, H.-P. Müller and M. Zielińska (eds). Lubuskie Towarzystwo Naukowe: Zielona Góra, 335–344.

Kizwalter, T. 1999. *O nowoczesności narodu: Przypadek Polski*. Warsaw: Semper.

Kligman, G. and K. Verdery. 2011. *Peasants under Siege: The Collectivization of Romanian Agriculture, 1949–1962*. Princeton: Princeton University Press.

Kłoskowska A. 1996. *Kultury narodowe u korzeni*. Warsaw: PWN.

———. 2001. *National Cultures at the Grass-root Level*. Budapest and New York: Central European University Press.

Knesebeck, J. von dem. 2011. *The Roma Struggle for Compensation in Post-War Germany*. Hatfield: University of Herfordshire Press.

Knigge, V. and N. Frei. 2002. 'Einleitung', in *Verbrechen Erinnern. Die Auseinandersetzung mit Holocaust und Völkermord*, V. Knigge and N. Frei (eds). Munich: Beck.

Kochanowski, J. 2010. *Oblicza okupacji*, 'Polityka' no. 32739, 61–63.

Kohli, M. 2000. 'The Battlegrounds of European Identity', *European Societies* 2(2): 113–137.

Kohn, H. 1955. *Nationalism: Its Meaning and History*. Princeton: D. Van Nostrand Company.

König, H. 2011. 'Politische und zeithistorische Debatten zur Weltkriegserinnerung im wiedervereinigten Deutschland', in *Erinnern an den Zweiten Weltkrieg. Mahnmale und Museen in Mittel- und Osteuropa*, S. Troebst and J. Wolf (eds). Schriften des Europäischen Netzwerks Erinnerung und Solidarität, vol. 2, 57–64.

'Kontseptsiia ta prohramy vykladannia istoriï v shkolakhproekt'. 2009. Retrieved 2 October 2013 from http://www.memory.gov.ua/ua/publication/content/1461.htm

Kończal, K. and J. Wawrzyniak. 2011. 'Polskie badania pamięcioznawcze: tradycje, koncepcje, (nie)ciągłości', *Kultura i Społeczeństwo* 45: 4, 11–63.

———. 2012. 'Erinnerungsforschung in Polen: Traditionen, Konzepte, (Dis)Kontinuitäten', *Osteuropa* no. 5, trans. P.O. Loew, 19–46.

Kończal, K. 2012. '*Les Lieux de Mémoire*/Realms of Memory: The Unparalleled Career of a Research Concept', *Acta Poloniae Historica* 106: 5–30.

Kopeček, M. (ed.). 2008a. *Past in the Making: Historical Revisionism in Central Europe after 1989*. Budapest and New York: Central European University Press.

———. 2008b. 'In Search of "National Memory": The Politics of History, Nostalgia and the Historiography of Communism in the Czech Republic and East Central Europe', in *Past in the Making: Historical Revisionism in Central Europe after 1989*, M. Kopeček (ed.). Budapest: Central European University Press, 75–95.

Koresaar, E., K. Kuutma and E. Lauk. 2009. 'The Twentieth Century as a Realm of Memory', in *The Burden of Remembering: Recollections & Representations of the 20th Century*, E. Koresaar, K. Kuutma and E. Lauk (eds). Helsinki: Finnish Literature Society, 9–36.

Korzeniewski, B. 2006. *Polityczne rytuały pokuty w perspektywie zagadnienia autonomii jednostki*. Poznań: Wydawnictwo Poznańskie.

Kraft, C. 2004. 'Debates on the Expulsion of Germans in Poland since 1945'. Retrieved from http://library.fes.de/library/netzquelle/zwangsmigration/en-46pl.html#top.

Krasnodębski, Z. 2003. *Demokracja peryferii*. Gdańsk: Słowo/obraz terytoria.

Kravchenko, V. 2009. 'Kharkiv: A Borderland City', in *Cities after the Fall of Communism: Reshaping Cultural Landscapes and European Identity*, J. Czaplicka, N. Gelazis and B.A. Ruble (eds). Washington, DC: Woodrow Wilson Center Press; Baltimore: Johns Hopkins University Press, 219–253.

Kreis, G. 2008/2009. 'Pierre Nora besser verstehen – und kritisieren', *Historie. Jahrbuch des Zentrums für Historische Forschung Berlin der Polnischen Akademie der Wissenschaften* 2, 103–117.

Król, M. 1996. *Liberalizm strachu czy liberalizm odwagi*. Warsaw and Krakow: Znak, Fundacja im. Stefana Batorego.

Kucia, M. 2000. 'Wiedza niepełna i często fałszywa. KL Auschwitz w świadomości społecznej Polaków, A. D. 2000', *Rzeczpospolita* no. 22, 27 Jan. 2000.

——. 2005. *Auschwitz jako fakt społeczny*. Krakow: Towarzystwo Autorów i Wydawców Prac Naukowych Universitas.

Kula, M. 2010. *Mimo wszystko bliżej Paryża niż Moskwy: Książka o Francji, PRL i o nas, historykach*. Warsaw: Wydawnictwa Uniwersytetu Warszawskiego.

Kulesza, W. 2010. 'Zbrodnia Katyńska jako akt ludobójstwa (geneza pojęcia)', in *Zbrodnia Katyńska. W kręgu prawdy i kłamstwa*. Warsaw, 52–67.

Kundera, M. 1984. 'The Tragedy of Central Europe', *New York Review of Books* no. 31, 7 April: 33–38.

Kurhajcová, A. 2012. 'Historical Memory Research in Slovakia', *Acta Poloniae Historica* 106: 77–98.

Kuromiya, H. 2007. *The Voices of the Dead: Stalin's Great Terror in the 1930s*. New Haven and London: Yale University Press.

Kurtyka, J. 2006. 'Katyń – zbrodnia symbol ludobójstwa', *Zeszyty Katyńskie* no. 21.

Kwaśniewski, A. 2002. *Letter of the President of Poland to Participants of Academic Conference on Operation 'Vistula'*, Warsaw, 18 April. Retrieved from http://lemko.org/gazeta/ubolewa.html.

Kwiatkowski, P.T., L.M. Nijakowski, B. Szacka and A. Szpociński. 2010. *Między codziennością a wielką historią. Druga wojna światowa w pamięci zbiorowej społeczeństwa polskiego*. Gdańsk-Warsaw: Museum of the Second World War & Wydawnictwo Naukowe Scholar.

Kwiatkowski, P.T. 2008. *Pamięć zbiorowa społeczeństwa polskiego w okresie transformacji*. Warsaw: Wydawnictwo Naukowe Scholar.

Kwiek, G.D. 2010. 'Afterword: Rom, Roma, Romani, Kale, Gypsies, Travellers, and Sinti… Pick a Name and Stick with It, Already', in *All Change! Romani Studies through Romani Eyes*, D. Le Bas and T. Acton (eds). Hatfield: University of Hertfordshire Press.
Kymlicka, W. 2001. *Politics in the Vernacular: Nationalism, Multiculturalism, and Citizenship*. Oxford: Oxford University Press.
Lachendro, J. 2007. *Zburzyć i zaorać…? Idea założenia Państwowego Muzeum Auschwitz-Birkenau w świetle prasy polskiej w latach 1945–1948*. Oświęcim.
Laczó, F. and M. Zombory. 2012. 'Between Transnational Embeddedness and Relative Isolation: The Moderate Rise of Memory Studies in Hungary', *Acta Poloniae Historica*, 106: 99–125.
Ladd, B. 2002. 'East Berlin Political Monuments in the Late German Democratic Republic: Finding a place for Marx and Engels', *Journal of Contemporary History*, no. 37, 1 January: 91–104.
Laitin, D.D. 1998. *Identity in Formation: The Russian-Speaking Populations in the New Abroad*. New York: Cornell University Press.
Landsberg, A. 2004. *Prosthetic Memory: The Transformation of American Remembrance in the Age of Mass Culture*. Cambridge, MA: Harvard University Press.
Lang, K.-O. 2004. 'Pragmatic Cooperation Instead of a Strategic Partnership: The Current Status and Perspective for German-Polish Relations', *Comments* 32, German Institute for International and Security Affairs. Retrieved from http://www.swp-berlin.org/fileadmin/contents/products/comments/comments2004_32_lng_ks.pdf
Le Bas, D. 2010. 'The Possible Implications of Diasporic Consciousness for Romani Identity', in *All Change! Romani Studies Through Romani Eyes*, D. Le Bas and T. Acton (eds). Hatfield: University of Hertfordshire Press.
Ledvinka, K. 2009. 'Dvacet let poté', *Konzervativní Listy*, 7 November.
Le Goff, J. 2007. *Historia i pamięć. Communicare. Historia i kultura*, trans. A. Gronowska. Warsaw: Wydawnictwo Uniwersytetu Warszawskiego.
Le Rider, J., M. Csáky and M. Sommer (eds). 2002. *Transnationale Gedächtnisorte in Zentraleuropa. Gedächtnis – Erinnerung – Identität*. Innsbruck: Studien-Verlag.
Lebiediewa, N. 2000. '60 lat fałszowania i zatajania zbrodni katyńskiej', *Zeszyty Katyńskie* no. 12, 97–121.
———. 2008. 'Komisja specjalna i jej przewodniczący Burdenko', *Zeszyty Katyńskie* no. 23, 56–101.
Lebow, R.N. 2008. 'The Future of Memory', *Annals of the American Academy of Political and Social Science* 617: 25–41.
Lefebvre, H. 1991. *The Production of Space*, trans. N. Donaldson-Smith. Oxford: Blackwell.
Leggewie, C. and A. Lang. 2011. *Der Kampf um die europäische Erinnerung. Ein Schlachtfeld wird besichtigt*. Munich: C.H. Beck Verlag.
Leggewie, C. 2009. 'Battlefield Europe: Transnational memory and European identity', *Eurozine*. Retrieved May 2010 from http://www.eurozine.com/articles/2009-04-28-leggewie-en.html

———. 2010. 'Seven Circles of European Memory', *Eurozine*, 20 December. Retrieved 3 May 2013 from http://www.eurozine.com/articles/2010-12-20-leggewie-en.html

———. 2011. 'Seven Circles of European Memory', in *Cultural Memories: The Geographical Point of View*, P. Meusburger (ed.). Dordrecht-Heidelberg: Springer.

Lehrer, E. 2007. 'Bearing False Witness: Vicarious Jewish Identity and the Politics of Affinity', in *Imaginary Neighbors: Mediating Polish-Jewish Relations after the Holocaust*, D. Glowacka and J. Zylinska (eds). Lincoln: University of Nebraska Press, 84–109.

———. 2012. 'Relocating Auschwitz: Affective Relations in the Jewish-German-Polish Troika', in *Germany, Poland and the Postmemorial Relations: In Search of a Livable Past*, K. Kopp and J. Nizynska (eds). New York: Palgrave Macmillan.

Lejeune, P. 2001. *Wariacje na temat pewnego paktu. O autobiografii*. Krakow: Universitas.

Lemon, A. 2000. *Between Two Fires: Gypsy Performance and Romani Memory from Pushkin to Postsocialism*. Durham: Duke University Press.

Lepsius, M.R. 1989. 'Das Erbe des Nationalsozialismus und die politische Kultur der Nachfolgestaaten des "Großdeutschen Reiches"', in *Kultur und Gesellschaft*, M. Haller, H.J. Hoffman Nowotny and W. Zapf (eds). Frankfurt /M. and New York: Campus Verlag, 247–264.

Lessing, D. 2004. *Time Bites*. London: Fourth Estate.

Levy, D. and N. Sznaider. 2002. 'Memory Unbound: The Holocaust and the Formation of Cosmopolitan Memory', *European Journal of Social Theory* 5(1): 87–106.

———. 2005, 2006. *The Holocaust and Memory in the Global Age*, trans. A. Oksiloff. Philadelphia: Temple University Press.

Lewy, G. 2000. *The Nazi Persecution of the Gypsies*. Oxford: Oxford University Press.

Lewicka, M. 2011. 'Historical Ethnic Bias in Collective Memory of Places: Cognitive or Motivational?' in *Perspectives on Thinking, Judging & Decision-Making*, W. Brun, G. Keren, G. Kirkebøen and H. Montgomery (eds). Oslo: Universitetsforlaget, 262–273.

———. 2012. *Psychologia miejsca*. Warsaw: Wydawnictwo Naukowe Scholar.

Linz, J. and A. Stepan. 1996. *Problems of Democratic Transition and Consolidation: Southern Europe, South America, and Post-Communist Europe*. Baltimore: Johns Hopkins University Press.

Lipták, L. 1995a. 'Pamätníky a pamäť povstania roku 1944 na Slovensku', *Historický časopis* 2, 350–367.

———. 1995b. 'Slovakia: History and Historiography', in *A Guide to Historiography in Slovakia*, E. Mannová and D.P. Daniel (eds). Bratislava: Historický ústav SAV, 8–25.

———. 2002. *Changes of Changes: Society and Politics in Slovakia in the 20th Century*, trans. M.C. Styan and S. Miklošová. Bratislava: Historický ústav SAV.

Lisicki, P. 2012. 'Centrum Polskiego Życia', *Uważam Rze Historia*, 3 July.

Littoz-Monnet, A. 2012. 'The EU Politics of Remembrance: Can Europeans Remember Together?', *West European Politics* no. 35/5, 1182–1202.
Losonczy, A.-M. 1999. 'Le patrimoine de l'oubli. Le "parc-musée des Statues" de Budapest', *Ethnologie française*, no. 29/3, 445–452.
Lotman, Y.L. 1990. *Universe of the Mind: A Semiotic Theory of Culture*, trans. A. Shukman. Bloomington: Indiana University Press.
Lübbe, H. 2007. *Vom Parteigenossen zum Bundesbürger. Über beschwiegene und historisierte Vergangenheiten*. Paderborn: Wilhelm Fink Verlag.
Luleva, A. 2009. 'Politiki na pamet v postsotsialisticheska Bălgariya – dva primera', in *Societies – Transformations – Cultures*, R. Ivanova, A. Luleva, I. Petrova and S. Yaneva (eds). Sofia: EIM –BAS, 21–35.
———. 2010. 'Politics of Memory in Post-socialist Bulgaria', *Ethnoscripts. Analysen und Informationen aus dem Institut für Ethnologie der Universität Hamburg* 12(1), 77–93.
———. 2013. *Bălgarskiyat dvadeceti vek. Kolektivna pamet i natsionalna identichnost*. Sofia: Gutenberg Publishing House, 48–69.
Łysakowski, P. 1990. 'Katyń – problemy i zagadki', *Zeszyty Katyńskie* no. 1.
———. 2005. 'Kłamstwo katyńskie', *Biuletyn IPN* no. 5/6.
Mach, Z. 1995. 'Czym jest Auschwitz dla Polaków?', in *Representations of Auschwitz*, Y. Doosry (ed.). Oświęcim.
Machcewicz, P. 2006. 'Statement from March 11, 2004', in *Vertreibungsdiskurs und europäische Erinnerungskultur. Deutsch-polnische Initiativen zur Institutionalisierung – eine Dokumentation*, S. Troebst (ed.). Publication of the Deutsch-Polnischen Gesellschaft Bundesverband e.V., Band 11: Osnabrück.
Macura, V. 1998. *Český sen*. Praha: Nakl. Lidové Noviny.
———. 2010. *The Mystifications of A Nation: The 'Potato Bug' and Other Essays on Czech Culture*, trans. H. Píchová. Madison: University of Wisconsin Press.
Maier, C. 1993. 'Whose Mitteleuropa? Central Europe between Memory and Obsolescence', in *Austria in the New Europe*, G. Bischof and A. Pelinka (eds). New Brunswick and London: Transaction, 8–18.
———. 2002. 'Hot Memory/Cold Memory: The Political Half-Life of Fascism and Communism', *Transit – Europäische Revue* no. 22. Retrieved October 2010 from http://www.project-syndicate.org/commentary/maier2/English
———. 2003. 'Overcoming the Past? Narrative and Negotiation, Remembering and Reparation...' in *Politics and the Past: On Repairing Historical Injustices*, J. Torpey (ed.). Lanham, MD: Rowman & Littlefield Publishers.
Makuch, J. 2008. Interview with, by M. Waligórska, 'Fiddler as a Fig Leaf: The Politicisation of Klezmer in Poland', in *Osteuropa: Impulses for Europe. Tradition and Modernity in East European Jewry*, M. Sapper, V. Weichsel and A. Lipphardt (eds). Berlin: Osteuropa, 227–238.
Mälksoo, M. 2009. 'The Memory Politics of Becoming European: The East European Subalterns and the Collective Memory of Europe', *European Journal of International Relations* no. 15, 4 December, 653–680.
Małczyński, J. 2009. 'Drzewa jako "żywe pomniki" w Muzeum-Miejscu Pamięci Bełżcu', *Teksty Drugie* 1–2, 208–214.

Mamul, N. 2009a. 'Fragmented Collective Memory and Negative Belarusian Identity', in *Ethnicity, Belonging and Biography: Ethnographical and Biographical Perspectives*, G. Rosenthal and A. Bogner (eds). Berlin: LIT Verlag, 145–160.

———. 2009b. 'Narrative Templates of Post-Soviet Identity in Belarus', *Polish Sociological Review* 165(1): 229–249.

Mannheim, K. 1952. *Essays on Sociology of Knowledge*. New York: Oxford University Press.

Margalit, A. 2002. *The Ethics of Memory*. Cambridge, MA: Harvard University Press.

Margalit, G. 1999. 'The Representation of the Nazi Persecution of the Gypsies in German Discourse after 1945', *German History* 17(2).

———. 2000. 'The Uniqueness of the Nazi Persecution of the Gypsies', *Romani Studies* 5, vol. 10, no. 2.

Mark, J. 2010. *The Unfinished Revolution: Making Sense of the Communist Past in Central-Eastern Europe*. New Haven and London: Yale University Press.

Marszałek, M. and S. Sasse (eds). 2010. *Geopoetiken: Geographische Entwürfe in den mittel- und osteuropäischen Literaturen*. Berlin: Kulturverlag Kadmos.

Martin, T. 2001. *The Affirmative Action Empire: Nations and Nationalism in the Soviet Union, 1932–1939*. Ithaca: Cornell UP.

Marushiakova, E. and Popov, V. 2006. 'Holocaust and the Gypsies: The Reconstruction of the Historical Memory and Creation of New National Mythology', in *Beyond Camps and Forced Labour: Current International Research on Survivors of Nazi Persecution*, J.-D. Steinert, I. Weber-Newth (eds), vol. 2. Osnabrück: Secolo.

Materski, W. 2000. 'Katyń – motywy i przebieg zbrodni (pytania, wątpliwości)', *Zeszyty Katyńskie* no. 12.

Maurel, M.-C. and F. Mayer. 2008. *L'Europe et ses représentations du passé, Les tourments de la mémoire*. Paris: L'Harmattan.

Max, F. 1946. 'Le sort des Tsiganes dans les prisons et les camps de concentration de l'Allemagne Hitlérienne', *Journal of the Gypsy Lore Society* 3rd series 25(1/2): 24–34.

Mayer, F. 2003. *Les Tchèques et leur communisme*. Paris: EHESS.

Meier, C. 1987. *Vierzig Jahre nach Auschwitz: Deutsche Geschichtserinnerungen heute*. Munich: C.H. Beck.

———. 2010. *Das Gebot zu vergessen und die Unabweisbarkeit des Erinnerns. Vom öffentlichen Umgang mit schlimmer Vergangenheit*. Munich: Beck.

Melone, A.P. 1994. 'Bulgaria's National Roundtable Talks and the Politics of Accommodation', *International Political Science Review* 15(3), July.

Mencwel, A. 2006. *Wyobraźnia antropologiczna. Próby i studia*. Warsaw: WUW.

Michel, J. 2010. *Gouverner les mémoires. Les politiques mémorielles en France*. Paris: PUF.

Michlic, J.B. 2007. 'The Soviet Occupation of Poland, 1939–1941 and the Stereotype of the Anti-Polish and Pro-Soviet Jew', *Jewish Social Studies* 13(3).

Michnik, A. 1990. 'Pułapka nacjonalizmu', *Gazeta Wyborcza*, 10 Feb.

―――. 2011. 'A European Russia or a Russian Europe', *Baltic Worlds* vol. IV, no. 1, March: 4–6.
Middleton, D. and S.D. Brown. 2011. 'Memory and Space in the Work of Maurice Halbwachs', in *Cultural Memories: The Geographical Point of View*, P. Meusburger, M. Heffernan and E. Wunder (eds). Dordrecht, Heildelberg, London, New York: Springer, 29–49.
Mikšíček, P., M. Spurný, O. Matějka and S. Zetsch (eds). 2004. *Zmizelé Sudety / Das verschwundene Sudetenland*, 3rd edn. Domažlice: Nakladatelství Českého lesa.
Miller, A. and M. Lipman (eds). 2012. *Istocheskaia politika v XXI veke*. Moskva: Novoe Literaturne Obozreniie.
Mink, G. and L. Neumayer. 2007. *L'Europe et ses passés douloureux*. Paris: La Découverte.
―――(eds). 2013. *History, Memory and Politics in Central and Eastern Europe: Memory Games*. Basingstoke and New York: Palgrave Macmillan.
Misztal, B.A. 2003. *Theories of Social Remembering*. Maidenhead and Philadelphia: Open University Press.
―――. 2010. 'Collective Memory in a Global Age: Learning How and What to Remember', *Current Sociology* 58(1): 24–44.
Mitrokhin, N. 2004. *Russkaia pravoslavnaia tserkov': sovremennoe sostoianie i aktual'nye problem*. Moscow: NLO.
Mitzner, P. 1994. 'Wspólne miejsce – Europa Wschodnia', *Zeszyty Historyczne*, no. 107, 75.
Morawska, E. 2000. 'Intended and Unintended Consequences of Forced Migrations: A Neglected Aspect of East Europe's Twentieth Century', *International Migration Review* 34.4: 1049–1087.
Mouffe, C. 1999. 'Deliberate Democracy or Agonistic Pluralism', *Social Research* 66.3: 745–758.
Müller, H.-P. and M. Zielińska (eds). 2012. *Transgraniczność w perspektiwie socjologicznej. Migracje przymusowe w Europie*. Lubuskie Towarzystwo Naukowe – Seria Monograficzna Tom VIII: Zielona Góra.
Müller, J.-W. (ed.). 2002. *Memory and Power in Post-War Europe*. Cambridge: Cambridge University Press.
―――. 2010. 'On "European Memory": Some Conceptual and Normative Remarks', in *A European Memory? Contested Histories and Politics of Remembrance*, M. Pakier and B. Stråth (eds). New York and Oxford: Berghahn Books, 25–37.
Müller, M.G. 2010. 'Where and When Was East Central Europe?' in *Domains and Divisions of European History*, J.P. Arnason and N. Doyle (eds). Liverpool: Liverpool University Press.
Munasinghe, H. 2005. 'The Politics of the Past: Constructing a National Identity through Heritage Conservation', *International Journal of Heritage Studies* 11: 251–60.
Münch, F. 2011. 'The Crusades of Civil Religion – "Holocaust versus GULag" and the Competition of Negative Founding Myths of Europe', in *Images and Myths*

of Europe: The Western and the Eastern Perspectives, B. Di Biasio, B. Michalski and L. Segreto (eds). Torun: Marszalek.

Murzyn, M. 2006. 'New Interpretations and Commercialization of Heritage in Krakow after 1989', in *Practical Aspects of Cultural Heritage – Presentation, Revaluation, Development*, Sebastian Schroder-Esch (ed.). Weimar: Bauhau-Universitat, 2006, 167–188.

Museum/Pentor. 2009. The Project *Druga wojna światowa w pamięci współczesnego społeczeństwa polskiego [World War II in the memory of contemporary Polish society]* carried out for the Museum of the Second World War by Pentor Research International. http://www.muzeum1939.pl.

Naimark, N. 2001. *Fires of Hatred: Ethnic Cleansing in Twentieth-Century Europe*. Cambridge MA: Harvard University Press.

———. 2010. *Stalin's Genocides*. Princeton: Princeton University Press.

Neumann, B. and A. Nünning. 2012. 'Travelling Concepts as a Model for the Study of Culture', in *Travelling Concepts for the Study of Culture*, B. Neumann and A. Nünning (eds), Concepts for the Study of Culture 2. Boston: De Gruyter, 1–22.

Nijakowski, L.M. 2006. *Domeny symboliczne. Konflikty narodowe i etniczne w wymiarze symbolicznym*. Warsaw: Wydawnictwo Naukowe Scholar.

Noack, C. 2006. 'Coping with the Tourist: Planned and "Wild" Mass Tourism on the Soviet Black Sea Coast', in *Turizm: The Russian and East European Tourist Under Capitalism and Socialism*, A. Gorsuch and D. Koenker (eds). London: Cornell University Press.

Nora P. (ed.). 1984–1992. *Les Lieux de mémoire* (1984–1992), 3. vols. Paris: Galimard.

Nora, P. 1989. 'Between Memory and History: *Les Lieux de Mémoire*', *Representations* 26, Memory and Counter-Memory, special issue. trans. M. Roudebush, 7–25.

———. 1996a. 'General Introduction: Between Memory and History', in *Realms of Memory: Rethinking the French Past*, P. Nora (ed.). New York: Columbia University Press.

———. 1996b. 'Mezi pamětí a historií: problematika míst', *Antologie francouzských společenských věd: Město, Cahiers du CEFRES* 10, special issue, F. Mayer, A. Bensa, and V. Hubinger (eds), 40–63.

———. 1998. 'Pokolennie kak mesto pamyati', trans. G. Dashevskiĭ, *Novoe literaturnoe obozrenie* 30, 48–72.

———. 1999a. 'Emlékezet és történelem között. A helyek problematikája', trans. Z.K. Horváth, *Aetas* 143: 142–157.

———. 1999b. *Franciya-pamyat*, trans. D. Khapaeva. Sankt Peterburg: Sankt Peterburgskiĭ gosudarstvennyĭ universitet.

———. 2001a. 'Czas pamięci', trans. W. Długski, *Res Publica Nowa* 7(153)/XV: 37–43.

———. 2001b. 'Naţiunea – sălaş al memoriei?', trans. M. Ispas, *Luceafrul* 20, 23 May, 23.

———. 2002a. 'Excedentul de memorie', trans. M. Vazaca, *Lettre internationale* 41/42: 123–126.

―――. 2002b. 'Reasons For the Current Upsurge in Memory', *Transit* 22. Retrieved from http://www.eurozine.com/ articles/2002-04-19-nora-en.html
―――. 2002c. 'Epoka upamiętniania', in *Rewanż pamięci*, J. Żakowski (ed.). Warsaw: Sic!
―――. 2004a. 'Întronarea mondială a istoriei', trans. M. Luca, *Observator cultural* 5238, September 9–11: 14–20.
―――(ed.). 2004b. *Mesta na pamet i konstruirane na nastoyashcheto*, trans. V. Genova et al. Sofia: Dom na naukite za choveka i obshchestvoto.
―――. 2007a. 'Czy Europa istnieje?', trans. K. Kończal, *Gazeta Wyborcza* 11–12 August.
―――. 2007b. 'Pasaulinė atminties viešpatija', in *Europos kultūros profiliai: atmintis, tapatumas, religija*, A. Samalavičius and L. Kanopkienė (eds). Vilnius: Kultūros barai, 9–24.
―――. 2008. 'Wolność dla historii', trans. J. Kurska, *Gazeta Wyborcza* 24 Oct.
―――. 2009. 'Między pamięcią a historią: Les Lieux de Mémoire', *Tytuł roboczy: Archiwum (Muzeum Sztuki Współczesnej w Łodzi)* 2, trans. P. Mościcki, 4–12.
―――. 2011. 'Między pamięcią a historią: les lieux de mémoire', trans. M. Borowski and M. Sugiera, *Didaskalia* 105: 20–27.
Norris, S. 2011. 'Wanted: A Good Gulag Film', *Russia: Beyond Headlines*. Retrieved March 2011 from http://rbth.ru/articles/2011/02/14/a_good_gulag_film_12455.html
Novick, P. 2001. *The Holocaust and Collective Memory: The American Experience*. London: Bloomsbury.
Novitch, M. 1968. *Le Génocide des Tziganes sous le Régime Nazi*. Paris: La Comité pour l'Erection du Monument des Tziganes Assassinés à Auschwitz.
Nowak, A. 2009a. 'Istoriia kak prestupleniie', *Ab Imperio* no. 3, 122–138.
―――. 2009b. 'Istoryk na poli bytvy za pamat', *Ukraina Moderna* 15, no. 4, 95–102.
―――(ed.). 2010. *Imperial Victims/Empires as Victims: 44 Views*. Warsaw: Instytut Pamięci Narodowej.
Nowinowski, S.M., J. Pomorski and R. Stobiecki. 2008. *Pamięć i polityka historyczna. Doświadczenia Polski i jej sąsiadów*. Łódź: Instytut Pamieci Narodowej.
'Obrashchenie Prezidenta RF Putina (polnaia versiia)', *Pervyi Kanal*, 18 March 2014. Retrieved 29 June 2014 from http://www. 1tv.ru/news/social/254389
Olick, J.K. 1999. 'Genre Memories and Memory Genres: A Dialogical Analysis of May 8, 1945 Commemorations in the Federal Republic of Germany', *American Sociological Review* 64(3), 381–402.
―――(ed.). 2003. *States of Memory: Continuities, Conflicts, and Transformation in National Retrospection*. Durham, NC: Duke University Press.
―――. 2007. *The Politics of Regret: On Collective Memory and Historical Responsibility*. New York and London: Routledge.
―――. 2008. 'From Collective Memory to the Sociology of Mnemonic Practices and Products', in *Cultural Memory Studies. An International and Interdisciplinary Handbook*, A. Erll and A. Nünning (eds). Berlin and New York: De Gruyter GmbH & Co, 151–161.

Olick, J.K., V. Vinitzky-Seroussi and D. Levy (eds). 2011. *The Collective Memory Reader*. Oxford: Oxford University Press.
Olšáková, D. 2012. 'From Legacy and Tradition to Lieux de Mémoire', *Acta Poloniae Historica* 106: 59–76.
Olschowsky, B. 2011. 'Czy pamięć w XX wieku łączy? Europejska Sieć Pamięć i Solidarność a rysy w krajobrazie pamięci starego kontynentu', *Remembrance and Solidarity Studies*. Retrieved October 2011 from http://www.enrs.eu/pl/artykuły/253
Omel'chenko, V. 1991. *Ekskursionnoe Obshchenie. Poznanie. Vospitanie. Otdykh*. Moscow: Nauka.
Omilanowska, M. (ed.). 2004–2012. *Das Gemeinsame Kulturerbe / Wspólne dziedzictwo*, vol. I – vol. VIII. Warsaw: Instytut Sztuki PAN.
Orla-Bukowska, A. 2006. 'New Threads on an Old Loom: National Memory and Social Identity in Postwar and Post-Communist Poland', in *The Politics of Memory in Postwar Europe*, R.N. Lebow, W. Kansteiner and C. Fogu (eds). Durham and London: Duke University Press.
Ossowski, S. 1967. *Przemiany wzorów we współczesnej ideologii narodowej. Dzieła*, vol. 3. Warsaw: PWN.
———. 1984. *O ojczyźnie i narodzie*. Warsaw: PWN.
Outhwaite, W. and L. Ray. 2005. *Social Theory and Postcommunism*. Malden, MA; Oxford, UK; Carlton, Australia: Blackwell.
Oz, A. 1998. 'Israelis und Araber: Der Heilungsprozeß', in *Trialog der Kulturen im Zeitalter der Globalisierung, Sinclair-Haus Gespräche, 11. Gespräch 5.–8. Dezember*. Bad Homburg v.d.Höhe: Herbert Quandt-Stiftung, 82–89.
Paczkowski, A. 1999. 'Nazizm i komunizm w pamięci i świadomości Polaków. Doświadczenie egzystencjalne', *Rzeczpospolita* no. 207, 4–5 IX 1999/349.
———. 2004. 'Nazism and Communism in the Polish Experience and Memory', in *Stalinism and Nazism: History and Memory Compared*, H. Rousso and R.J. Golsan (eds). Lincoln: Nebraska University Press.
Pakier, M. and B. Stråth (eds). 2010. *A European Memory? Contested Histories and Politics of Remembrance*, Studies in Contemporary European History. Oxford and New York: Berghahn Books.
Pakier, M. 2013. *The Construction of European Holocaust Memory: German and Polish Cinema after 1989*. Frankfurt a.M.: Peter Lang.
'Pam`yati zhertv Holodomoru 1932–1933 rokiv v Ukraini 2002–2006'. Retrieved 2 October 2013 from http://www.president.gov.ua/content/golodomor_75.html
'Pamiatniki zhertvam OUN-UPA'. 2010. Retrieved 2 October 2013 from http://dragonmoonbird.livejournal.com/759184.html
Paterson, T. 2010. 'Merkel Ally Quits after Claiming Nazis Didn't Start War', *The Independent*, 11 September 2010.
Paul, A. 2010. *Katyń: Stalin's Massacre and the Triumph of Truth*. Northern Illinois University Press: DeKalb.
Pawełczyńska, A. 1977. *Żywa historia – pamięć i ocena lat okupacji*. Warsaw: Ośrodek Badania Opinii Publicznej i Studiów Programowych.

Petersen, T. 2005. *Flucht und Vertreibung aus Sicht der deutschen, polnischen und tschechischen Bevölkerung /Ucieczka i wypędzenia w oczach ludności niemieckiej, polskiej i czeskiej*. Bon: Haus der Geschichte der Bundesrepublik Deutschland.

Petrov, P. 2003. 'Sotsialisticheskite trudovi praznitsi i rituali – kontseptsia i potreblenie', in *Sotsializmăt: Realnost i ilyuzii*, R. Ivanova, A. Luleva and R. Popov (eds). Sofia: EIM-BAN, 133–149.

Pine, F., D. Kaneff and H. Haukanes. 2004. 'Introduction. Memory, Politics and Religion: A Perspective on Europe', in: *Memory, Politics and Religion: The Past Meets the Present in Europe*, F. Pine, D. Kaneff and H. Haukanes (eds). Munster: Lit Verlag.

Pinto, D. 1996. 'Pięćdziesiąt lat po Zagładzie: konieczność budowania nowej pamięci polsko-żydowskiej', in *Pamięć żydowska, pamięć polska*. Krakow: Instytut Francuski w Krakowie and C&D International Editors.

Piper, F. 1991. 'Estimating the Number of Deportees to and Victims of the Auschwitz-Birkenau Camp', *Yad Vashem Studies* vol. XXI.

———. 1992. *Auschwitz: How Many Perished Jews, Poles, Gypsies…* Krakow: Poligrafia ITS.

Piper, F., T. Świebocka. 2008. *Auschwitz. Nazistowski obóz śmierci*. Oświęcim.

Pleskot, P. 2010. *Intelektualni sąsiedzi: Kontakty polskich historyków z francuskim środowiskiem 'Annales' w latach 1945–1989*. Warsaw: Instytut Pamięci Narodowej.

Plokhy, S. 2000. 'The City of Glory: Sevastopol in Russian Historical Mythology', *Journal of Contemporary History* 35(3): 369–383.

Pocock, J.G.A. 2005. *The Discovery of Islands: Essays in British History*. Cambridge: Cambridge University Press, 259–310.

Podol's'kyi, A. 2008. 'A Reluctant Look Back: Jewry and the Holocaust in Ukraine', in *Osteuropa: Impulses for Europe. Tradition and Modernity in East European Jewry*, M. Sapper, V. Weichsel and A. Lipphardt (eds). Berlin: Osteuropa.

Pomian, K. 2009. *European Identity: Historical Fact and Political Problem*. Retrieved from http://www.eurozine.com/articles/2009-08-24-pomian-en.html

Pomorski, J. 2008. 'Ucieczka od historii jako element poprawności politycznej', in *Pamięć i polityka historyczna. Doświadczenia Polski i jej sąsiadów*, S. Nowinowski, J. Pomorski and R. Stobiecki (eds). Łódź: Instytut Pamięci Narodowej.

Popson, N. 2001. 'The Ukrainian History Textbooks: Introducing Children to the "Ukrainian Nation"', *Nationalities Papers* 29(2): 325–350.

Portnov, A. 2009. '"Western Categories" in the Ukrainian Post-Soviet Historiography – Language Changes in the "Age of Translations"', in *East-Central Europe in European History: Themes & Debates*, J. Kłoczowski and H. Łaszkiewicz (eds). Lublin: Instytut Europy Środkowo-Wschodniej, 435–458.

President of Ukraine. 2010a. *President's Address to Ukrainian Nation on Holodomor Victims' Memory Day*. Retrieved 2 October 2013 from http://www.president.gov.ua/news/18809.html

———. 2010b. 'Decree no. 1085/2010 "Pro optymizatsiiu systemy tsentral'nykh orhaniv vykonavchoï vlady"'. Retrieved 2 October 2013 from http://www.president.gov.ua/documents/12584.html

Prusin, A.V. 2010. *The Lands Between: Conflict in the East European Borderlands, 1870–1992*. Oxford: Oxford University Press.

Prutsch, M. 2013. 'European Historical Memory: Policies, Challenges and Perspectives' *European Parliament's Study Note*. Retrieved 1 May 2014 from http://www.europarl.europa.eu/RegData/etudes/note/join/2013/513977/IPOL-CULT_NT%282013%29513977_EN.pdf

Qualls, K.D. 2009a. *From Ruins to Reconstruction: Urban Identity in Soviet Sevatopol After World War II*. London: Cornell University Press.

———. 2009b. 'Travelling Today through Sevastopol's Past: Postcommunist Continuity in a "Ukrainian" Cityscape', in *Cities after the Fall of Communism: Reshaping Cultural Landscapes and European Identity*, N. Gelazis, J. Czaplicka and B.A. Ruble (eds). Washington D.C.: Woodrow Wilson Centre Press.

Radstone, S. and B. Schwarz (eds). 2010. *Memory: Histories, Theories, Debates*. New York: Fordham University Press.

Ragaru, N. 2005. 'Bulgarie: des éléctions législatives indécises', *Centre d'études et de recherches internationales*. 5 October. Retrieved from http://www.ceri-sciences-po.org

Ramet, S.P. 2014. *Religion and Politics in Post-socialist Central and Southeastern Europe. Challenges since 1989*. London: Palgrave Macmillan.

Raphaël, F. and G. Herberich-Marx (eds). 1991. *Mémoire plurielle de l'Alsace: Grandeurs et servitudes d'un pays des marges*. Strasbourg: Soc. Savante d'Alsace et des Régions de l'Est.

Rátz, T. 2006. 'Interpretation in the House of Terror, Budapest', in *Cultural Tourism in a Changing World: Politics, Participation and (Re)presentation*, M.K. Smith and M. Robinson (eds). Clevedon: Channel View Publications.

Reading, A.M. 2012. 'The European Roma: An Unsettled Right to Memory', in *Public Memory, Public Media, and the Politics of Justice*, P. Lee and P.N. Thomas (eds). Houndmills and Basingstoke: Palgrave Macmillan.

Rees, L. 2005. *Auschwitz: The Nazis & the Final Solution*. Random House.

Reiff, R. 1989. 'Wyciąg z protokółu zebrania wyborczego Związku Sybiraków'. Retrieved September 2010 from http://zwiazeksybirakow.strefa.pl/Rok%201989A.htm

Reiter, J. 2005. 'Divided Memory in United Europe', *Frankfurter Allgemeine Zeitung*, 7 May.

Report No. 2505. 82nd Congress Concerning the Katyn Forest Massacre. 1952. US Government Printing Office Washington.

Requate, J. and M. Schulze Wessel (eds). 2002. *Europäische Öffentlichkeit: transnationale Kommunikation seit dem 18. Jahrhundert*. Frankfurt: Campus.

Reutov, E. 2004. 'Politicheskie mify Belgorodchiny', in *Sotsionavtika: internet-zhurnal sotsial'nykh diskurs-issledovanii*. Retrieved 30 June 2014 from http://socionavtika.narod.ru/Staty/diegesis/belmif.htm

Rév, I. 2005. *Retroactive Justice: Prehistory of Post-Communism*. Stanford: Stanford University Press.
Richardson, T. 2008. *Kaleidoscopic Odessa: History and Place in Contemporary Ukraine*. London: University of Toronto Press.
Ricoeur, P. 1995. 'Pamięć – zapomnienie – historia', in *Tożsamość w czasach zmiany*, K. Michalski (ed.). Krakow: Znak.
———. 2004. *Memory, History, Forgetting*. Chicago and London: Chicago University Press.
———. 2006. 'Pamięć, historia, zapomnienie', *Horyzonty nowoczesności* 54, trans. J. Margański. Krakow: Towarzystwo Autorów i Wydawców Prac Naukowych Universitas.
Rioux, J.-P. 2006. *La France perd la mémoire: comment un pays démissionne de son histoire*. Paris: Perrin.
Ritzer, G. 1993. *The McDonaldization of Society*. Thousand Oaks, California: Pine Forge Press.
Robins, K. 1996. 'Interrupting Identities: Turkey/Europe', in *Questions of Cultural Identity*, S. Hall and P. du Gay (eds). London: Sage.
Rokuszewska-Pawełek, A. 2002. *Chaos i przymus. Trajektorie wojenne Polaków – analiza biograficzna*. Łódź: Wyd. Uniwersytetu Łódzkiego.
Rosenfeld, G.D. 2009. 'A Looming Crash or a Soft Landing? Forecasting the Future of the Memory Industry', *Journal of Modern History* 81(1): 142–146.
Roskies, D.G. 1984. *Against the Apocalypse: Responses to Catastrophe in Modern Jewish Culture*. Cambridge: Harvard University Press.
Rostoks, T. 2011. 'Debating 20th Century History in Europe: The European Parliament and the Parliamentary Assembly of the Council of Europe Compared', in *The Geopolitics of History in Latvian-Russian Relations*, N. Muižnieks (ed.). Rīga: University of Latvia Academic Press.
Roszkowski, W. 1996. 'Wczoraj i dziś', in *Spór o PRL*, M. Fik, A. Friszke and M. Kula (eds). Krakow: Znak.
Roth, K. 1998. 'Praktiki i strategii za ovladyavane na vsekidnevieto v edno selo v sotsialisticheska Bǎlgariya', *Sotsiologicheski problemi* no. 3–4, 224–237.
———. 2001. '"Narodna kultura" – (sotsialisticheska) "vsekidnevna kultura": edin nezhelan nauchen prevod?', *Bǎlgarska Etnologiya* no. 3, 5–18.
Rothberg, M. 2009. *Multidirectional Memory: Remembering the Holocaust in the Age of Decolonization*. Stanford: Stanford University Press.
Rousso, H. 2007. 'History of Memory, Policies of the Past: What For?' in *Conflicted Memories: Europeanizing Contemporary Histories*, K.H. Jarausch and T. Lindenberger (eds). New York and Oxford: Berghahn Books, 23–56.
Ruchniewicz, K. 2007. 'The Memory of World War II in Poland', http://www.eurozine.com/articles/2007-09-05-ruchniewicz-en.html#footNoteNUM1.
Ruchniewicz, K., J. Tyszkiewicz and W. Wrzesiński (eds). 2000. *XVI Powszechny Zjazd Historyków Polskich*, Sekcja 1: Przełomy w dziejach Śląska Toruń. 111–359.
Rüsen, J. 1993. *Konfigurationen des Historismus. Studien zur deutschen Wissenschaftskultur*. Frankfurt am Main: Suhrkamp.

Rybicka, E. 2008. 'Miejsce, pamięć, literatura – w perspektywie geopoetyki', *Teksty Drugie* 1–2, 19–31.
Rydel, J. 2011. *Polityka historyczna w Republice Federalniej Niemiec. Zaszłości, idee, praktyka*, Prace Monograficzne no. 599. Krakow: Uniwersytet Pedagogiczny im. Komisji Edukacji Narodowej.
Sabatos, C. 2011. 'Shifting Contexts: The Boundaries of Milan Kundera's Central Europe', in *Contexts, Subtexts and Pretexts: Literary Translation in Eastern Europe and Russia*, B.J. Baer (ed.). Amsterdam: Benjamins.
Said, E.D. 2000. 'Invention, Memory, and Place', *Critical Inquiry* vol. 26, winter, 175–192.
Samuel, R. (ed.). 1989. *Patriotism: The Making and Unmaking of British National Identity*, vol. 1: *History and Politics*, vol. 2: *Minorities and Outsiders*, vol. 3: *National Fictions*. London: Routledge.
Samuels, S. 2013. 'Holocaust Memory as a Fig Leaf for Modern Hate', *The Times of Israel*, 24 January 2013. Retrieved 8 February 2013 from blogs.timesofisrael.com/memory-as-a-fig-leaf-for-contemporary-hate/
Sanford, G. 2005. *Katyn and The Soviet Massacre Of 1940: Truth, Justice And Memory*. Routledge, Chapman & Hall.
Sariusz-Skąpska, I. 2002. *Polscy świadkowie Gułagu*. Krakow: Universitas.
Saryusz-Wolska, M. 2010. *Spotkanie miejsca z czasem: Studia o pamięci i miastach*. Warsaw: Wydawnictwo Uniwersytetu Warszawskiego.
Sasse, G. 2007. *The Crimea Question: Identity, Transition, and Conflict*. Cambridge, MA: Harvard University Press.
Schlögel, K. 2008a. 'Orte und Schichten der Erinnerung. Annäherungen an das östliche Europa', *Osteuropa* no. 58, June, 13–25.
———. 2008b. *Places and Strata of Memory: Approaches to Eastern Europe*. Retrieved from http://www.eurozine.com/articles/2008-12-19-schlogel-en.html
Schmidtke, O. 2005. 'Re-modelling the Boundaries in the New Europe: Historical Memories and Contemporary Identities in German-Polish Relations', in *Collective Memory and European Identity: The Effects of Integration and Enlargement*, K. Eder and W. Spohn (eds). Aldershot Hunts and Burlington, VT: Ashgate Publishing, 69–86.
Schüle, C. 2003. 'The Dead are Coming Home', *Die Zeit*, May 22.
Schwan, G. 1997. *Politik und Schuld. Die zerstörerische Macht des Schweigens*. Frankfurt am Main: Fischer Taschenbuch.
Schwartz, B. 1991. 'Social Change and Collective Memory: The Democratization of George Washington', *American Sociological Review* 56(2): 221–236.
Sconfelder, B. 2005. 'Judicial Independence in Bulgaria: A Tale of Splendour and Misery', *Europe-Asia Studies*, 57, 1 January 2005, 61–92.
Semprún, J. 2005. 'Nobody Will Be Able Any More To Say: This Is How It Was!' *Die Zeit*, April 14.
Serejski, M.H. 1965. *Przeszłość a teraźniejszość; szkice i studia historiograficzne*. Wrocław: Ossolineum.
———. 1973. *Naród a państwo w polskiej myśli historycznej*. Warsaw: PIW.

Shafir, M., 2011. 'Competitive Martirology in Post-communist States. The Holocaust-Gulag Competition', a public lecture in Cluj-Napoca. Retrieved 15 August 2011 from http://dsh.ceu.edu/node/22123.

Sherr, J. 1997. 'Russia-Ukraine Rapprochement? The Black Sea Fleet Accords', *Survival: Global Politics and Strategy*, 39(3): 33–50.

Shevel, O. 2011. 'The Politics of Memory in a Divided Society: A Comparison of Post-Franco Spain and Post-Soviet Ukraine', *Slavic Review* 70(1): 137–164.

Shöpflin, G. 1990. 'The End of Communism in Eastern Europe', *International Affairs* no. 66, 1 January, 3–16.

Siddi, M. 2012. 'Russia and the Forging of Memory and Identity in Europe', *Studia Diplomatica* no. 65/4, 77–103.

Sigona, N. and N. Trehan. 2009. 'Introduction: Romani Politics in Neoliberal Europe', in *Romani Politics in Contemporary Europe: Poverty, Ethnic Mobilization and the Neoliberal Order*, N. Sigona and N. Trehan (eds). Basingstoke: Palgrave Macmillan.

Silberman, M. and F. Vatan (eds). 2013. *Memory and Postwar Memorials: Confronting the Violence of the Past*. Basingstoke: Palgrave Macmillan.

Simhandl, K. 2006. '"Western Gypsies and Travellers" – "Eastern Roma": The Creation of Political Objects by the Institutions of the European Union', *Nations and Nationalism* 121.

Skarga, B. 1995. 'Tożsamość i pamięć', *ZNAK* no. 5, 4–18.

Skoczyński, J. and Woleński, J. 2010. *Historia filozofii polskiej*. Krakow: Wydawnictwo WAM.

Sloterdijk, P. 2006. 'Die thymotische Revolution', in *Zorn und Zeit*, P. Sloterdkijk (ed.). Frankfurt a.M.: Suhrkamp.

Smith, A.D. 1986. *The Ethnic Origins of Nations*. Oxford: Blackwell.

———. 1999. *Myths and Memories of the Nation*. Oxford: Oxford University Press.

———. 2003. *Chosen Peoples: Sacred Sources of National Identity*. Oxford: Oxford University Press.

Smolar, A. 2008. 'Władza i geografia pamięci', in *Pamięć jako przedmiot władzy*, P. Kosiewski (ed.). Warsaw: Fundacja im. Stefana Batorego.

Snyder, T. 2010. *Bloodlands: Europe Between Hitler and Stalin*. London: Basic Books.

Speckmann, T. 2005. 'Renaissance des Themas in den Medien', in *Flucht, Vertreibung Integration* – publication for exhibition under the same name. Bonn: Stiftung Haus der Geschichte der Bundesrepublik Deutschland, 175–179.

Stauber, R. and R. Vago. 2007. 'The Politics of Memory: Jews and Roma Commemorate their Persecution', in *The Roma: A Minority in Europe. Historical, Political and Social Perspectives*, R. Stauber and R. Vago (eds). Budapest and New York: Central European University Press.

'Steinbach hat Kriegsschuldfrage nicht bezweifelt', *FAZ.NET*, 09.09.2010. Retrieved from http://www.faz.net/aktuell/politik/inland/eklat-in-unionsfraktion-steinbach-hat-kriegsschuldfrage-nicht-bezweifelt-11042941.html

Steinlauf, M.C. 2001. *Pamięć nieprzyswojona. Polska pamięć Zagłady*, trans. A. Tomaszewska. Warsaw: Wydawnictwo Cyklady.

Steinlauf, M. 1996. *Bondage To The Dead: Poland And The Memory Of The Holocaust*. Syracuse: Syracuse University Press.
Stekl, H. and E. Mannová (eds). 2003. *Heroen, Mythen, Identitäten. Die Slowakei und Österreich im Vergleich*, Vorlesungen, Konversatorien und Studien. Band 14. Vienna: WUV.
Stewart, M. 2010. 'The Other Genocide', in: *Multidisciplinary Approaches to Romani Studies*, M. Stewart and M. Rövid (eds). Budapest: Central European University Press.
Stobiecki, R. 2003. 'Wprowadzenie', in *Dzieje historiografii*, A.F. Grabski (ed.). Poznań: Wydawnictwo Poznańskie, I–XIX.
Stöckl, K. 2010. 'Modern Trajectories in Eastern European Orthodoxy: Responses to the Post-totalitarian and Post-Cold War Constellation', in *Domains and Divisions of European History*, J.P. Arnason and N. Doyle (eds). Liverpool: Liverpool University Press.
Stola, D. 2012. 'Poland's Institute of National Remembrance: A Ministry of Memory?' in *The Convolutions of Historical Politics*, A.I. Miller and M. Lipman (eds). Budapest and New York: Central European University Press, 45–58.
Stone, D. 2003. *Constructing the Holocaust: A Study in Historiography*. London and Portland, Oregon: Vallentine Mitchel.
Stranga, A. 2009. 'A Few Words about Collective Memory in Europe', in *Europe 70 Years after the Molotov-Ribbentrop Pact*. Vilnius: Margi raštai.
Stråth, B. 2008. 'Constructionist Themes in the Historiography of the Nation', in *Handbook of Constructionist Research*, J.A. Holstein and J.F. Gubrium (eds). New York: Guilford Press. 627–642.
Sułek, A. 2011. 'Pamięć Polaków o zbrodni w Jedwabnem', *Nauka* no. 3, 43–44.
Szacka, B. and A. Sawisz. 1990. *Czas przeszły i pamięć społeczna*. Warsaw: Instytut Socjologii Uniwersytetu Warszawskiego.
Szacka, B. 1983. *Przeszłość w świadomości inteligencji polskiej*. Warsaw: Wydawnictwa Uniwersytetu Warszawskiego.
———. 1995. 'O pamięci społecznej', *Znak* no. 5, 68–76.
———. 2000. 'Pamięć zbiorowa i wojna', *Przegląd Socjologiczny* no. 2, 11–28.
———. 2003. 'Historia i pamięć zbiorowa', *Kultura i Społeczeństwo* no. 4, 3–16.
———. 2006. *Czas przeszły – pamięć – mit*. Warsaw: Wydawnictwo Naukowe Scholar.
Szacki, J. 2004. 'Is There Such a Thing as the Sociology of Nation?' *Polish Sociological Review* 145, no. 1, 3–14.
Szacki, W. 2009a. 'Poplątana pamięć o II wojnie', *Gazeta Wyborcza*, 18 August 2009. Retrieved 22 August 2009 from http://wyborcza.pl/2029020,75248,6936373html?sms_code
———. 2009b. 'Sondaż. Nasza duma i wstyd', *Gazeta Wyborcza*, 19 August 2009. Retrieved 22 August 2009 from http://wyborcza.pl/2029020,75248,6940133htm l?sms_code
Szarota, T. 1996. 'Wojna na pocieszenie', *Gazeta Wyborcza*, 6 September.
Sznaider, N. 2013. 'European Memory: Between Jewish and Cosmopolitan' in *Memory and Theory in Eastern Europe*, U. Blacker, A. Etkind and J. Fedor (eds). Palgrave Macmillan, 59–80.

Sztompka, P. 1994. *The Sociology of Social Change*. Oxford: Blackwell.
——. 2000. 'Cultural Trauma: The Other Face of Social Change', in *European Journal of Social Theory* 3, no. 4, 449–466.
Szűcs, J. 1983. 'The Three Historical Regions of Europe: An Outline', *Acta Historica: Revue de l'Académie des Sciences de Hongrie*, 29, 131–184.
Śpiewak, P. 2005. *Pamięć po komunizmie. Idee i polityka*. Gdansk: Słowo.
'Tabachnik khochet sdelat' uchebniki po istorii 'gumannymi' 2010. Retrieved 1 October 2013 from http://news.liga.net/news/N1010709.html
Tarkowska, E. 2013. 'Collective Memory, Social Time and Culture: The Polish Tradition in Memory Studies', *Polish Sociological Review* 183, no. 3, 281–296.
TASS (the Soviet Government Press Agency) statement given on Friday, 13 April, 1990 at 14.30. 1990. *Zeszyty Katyńskie*, no. 1.
Ther, P. and A. Siljak (eds). 2001. *Redrawing Nations: Ethnic Cleansing in East-Central Europe, 1944–1948*. Lanham, MD: Rowman & Littlefield.
Ther, P. 2006. 'The Burden of History and the Trap of Memory'. Retrieved from http://www.eurozine.com/articles/2006-08-21-ther-en.html
——. 2011. *Die dunkle Seite der Nationalstaaten.»Ethnische Säuberungen« im modernen Europa*. Göttingen: Vandenhoeck & Ruprecht.
Thomas, W.I. and F. Znaniecki. 1918–1920. *The Polish Peasant in Europe and America*, vols. I–V. Boston: Richard G. Badger, University of Chicago Press.
Tibi, B. 1998. *Europa ohne Identität? Leitkultur oder Wertebeliebigkeit*. Munich: Siedler.
Tismaneanu, V. 1998. *Fantasies of Salvation: Democracy, Nationalism, and Myth in Post-Communist Europe*. Princeton, NJ: Princeton University Press.
TNS OBOP. 2000. 'Obraz II wojny światowej w pamięci Polaków', report from research conducted on 29–31.01.2000.
——. 2002. 'Polacy o zbrodni w Jedwabnem', report from research conducted on 23–25.11.2002.
——. 2003. 'Wołyń 1943–2003', report from research conducted on 05–07.07.2003.
——. 2006. 'Polska – Niemcy – Rosja', report from research conducted on 03–06.08.2006.
——. 2009. 'Kolektywna pamięć i nie załatwione sprawy z II wojny światowej', report from research conducted on 06–09.08.2009.
——. 2010. 'Auschwitz in Collective Consciousness of the Poles in 2010', report from research conducted on 7–10 January 2010.
Todorov, T. 2003. 'The Lunchbox and the Bomb', *IWM Newsletter* 3.81.
Todorova, M. 1997. *Imagining the Balkans*. New York, Oxford: Oxford University Press.
——. 2006. 'The Mausoleum of Georgi Dimitrov as Lieu de mémoire', *The Journal of Modern History* 78, 377–411.
Todorova, M. and Z. Gille (eds). 2010. *Post-communist Nostalgia*. New York: Berghahn Books.
Tolczyk, D. 1999. *See No Evil: Cover-Ups and Discoveries of the Soviet Camp Experience*. New Haven: Yale University Press.
——. 2009. *Gułag w oczach Zachodu*. Warsaw: Prószyński i S-ka.

Tomaszewski, A. and D. von Winterfeld (eds). 2001. *Wspólne dziedzictwo. Polsko-niemiecka wspólpraca konserwatorska 1970 – 2000 / Das gemeinsame Kulturerbe. Die deutsch-polnische Zusammenarbeit in der Denkmalpflege 1970–2000*. Gniezno: Agencja Reklamowo-Wydawnicza A. Grzegorczyk.
Tomaszewski, A. 2005. 'Polskie miejsca pamięci według Adama Miłobędzkiego', *Rocznik Historii Sztuki* XXX, 285–290.
Traba, R. 2003. *Kraina tysiąca granic. Szkice o historii i pamięci*. Olsztyn: Wspólnota Kulturowa Borussia.
———. 2007. 'Czy Europa istnieje?', *Gazeta Wyborcza* no. 187, 11 August 2007, 21–22.
———. 2011. 'Gdzie jesteśmy? Nowe otwarcie w polskich badaniach pamięci zbiorowej i ich europejski kontekst', *Kultura i Społeczeństwo* 45: 4, 3–10.
Tracevskis, R.M. 2010. 'Mission Siberia', *The Baltic Times*, 26 June.
Troebst, S. 2005. *Postkommunistische Erinnerungskulturen im östlichen Europa/ Bestandsaufnahme, Kategorisierung, Periodisierung / Postkomunistyczne kultury pamięci w Europie Wschodniej*. Wrocław: Wydawnictwo Uniwersytetu Wrocławskiego.
———. 2006. 'Jalta versus Stalingrad, GULag versus Holocaust. Konfligierende Erinnerungskulturen im größeren Europe', in *Transformationen der Erinnerungskulturen in Europa nach 1989*, B. Faulenbach (ed.). Essen: Klartext.
———. 2008. '"1945". Ein(gesamt-)europäischer Erinnerungsort?', *Osteuropa* 58(6), 67–76.
———. 2009. '"1945" Ogólnoeuropejskie miejsce pamięci?', *Odra* 9, trans. K. Juchniewicz and M. Zybura.
———. 2010a. 'Meso-regionalizing Europe: History versus Politics', in *Domains and Divisions of European History*, J.P. Arnason and N. Doyle (eds). Liverpool: Liverpool University Press.
———. 2010b. 'Halecki Revisited: Europe's Conflicting Cultures of Remembrance', in *A European Memory? Contested Histories and Politics of Remembrance*, M. Pakier and B. Stråth (eds). New York: Berghahn Books.
——— (ed.). 2010c. *Postdiktatorische Geschichtskulturen in Süden und Osten Europas: Bestandsaufnahme und Forschungsperspektiven*. Göttingen: Wallstein Verlag.
———. 2011. 'Halecki Revisited: Europe's Conflicting Cultures of Remembrance', in *Cultural Memories. The Geographical Point of View*, P. Meusburger (ed.). Dordrecht-Heidelberg: Springer, 145–154.
———. 2012. '23 August: The Genesis of a Euro-Atlantic Day of Remembrance', *Remembrance and Solidarity Studies*. Retrieved August 2012 from http://www.enrs.eu/studies/StefanTroebst_EN.pdf
———. 2013. *Erinnerungskultur – Kulturgeschichte – Geschichtsregion. Ostmitteleuropa in Europa*. Stuttgart: Franz Steiner Verlag.
Troebst, S. and U. Brunnbauer (eds). 2006. *Zwischen Nostalgie, Amnesie und Allergie: Erinnerung an den Kommunismus in Suedosteuropa*. Cologne, Weimar and Vienna: Bohlau Verlag.
Trojański, P. 2012. 'Upamiętnianie ofiar Auschwitz na terenie Państwowego Muzeum Oświęcim-Brzezinka w latach 1947–2000. Zarys problemu', *Krakowskie Studia Małopolskie* 17.

Trumpener, K. 1992. 'The Time of the Gypsies. A "People without History" in the Narratives of the West', *Critical Inquiry* no. 18.
Tuan, Y.-F. 1977. *Space and Place: The Perspective of Experience*. Minneapolis: University of Minnesota Press.
Tunander, O. 1997. 'Post-Cold War Europe: A Synthesis of a Bipolar Friend-Foe Structure and a Hierarchic Cosmos-Chaos Structure?' in *Geopolitics in Post-Wall Europe. Security, Territory and Identity*, O. Tunander, P. Baev and V.I. Einagel (eds). London: PRIO-SAGE.
Tyndall, A. 2004. 'Memory, Authenticity and Replication of the Shoah in Museums: Defensive Tools of the Nation', in *Re-presenting the Shoah for the Twenty-First Century*, R. Lentin (ed.). New York and Oxford: Berghahn Books.
Tyszka, S. 2010. 'Holocaust Remembrance and Restitution of Jewish Property in the Czech Republic and Poland after 1989', in *A European Memory? Contested Histories and Politics of Remembrance*, M. Pakier and B. Stråth (eds). New York and Oxford: Berghahn Books.
Uhl, H. 2009a. 'Konkurrierende Erinnerungskulturen in Europa: Neue Grenzen zwischen "Ost" und "West"?', in *Kulturen der Differenz – Transformationsprozesse in Zentraleuropa nach 1989. Transdisziplinäre Perspektiven*, H. Fassmann, W. Müller-Funk and H. Uhl (eds). Göttingen: Vienna University Press.
———. 2009b. 'Conflicting Cultures of Memory in Europe: New Borders between East and West?' *Israel Journal of Foreign Affairs* 3, no. 3, 59–71.
Urban, T.U. 2005. 'Vertreibung als Thema in Polen', in *Flucht, Vertreibung Integration* – publication for exhibition under the same name. Bonn: Stiftung Haus der Geschichte der Bundesrepublik Deutschland, 157–165.
Urry, J. 1990. *The Tourist Gaze: Leisure and Travel in Contemporary Societies*. London: Sage.
Velmet, A. 2011. 'Occupied Identities: National Narratives in Baltic Museums of Occupation', *Journal of Baltic Studies* 42(2): 189–211.
Vendina, O. 2010. 'Ukraina mezhdu Rossiei i Pol'shei: protivorechiia transgranichnogo sotrudnichestva', *Vestnik instituta Kennana v Rossii* no. 17.
Venikeev, E. 1983. *Arkhitektura Sevastopolia*. Simferopol: Tavria.
Verdery, K. and G. Kligman. 2011. 'How Communist Cadres Persuaded Romanian Peasants to Give Up Their Land', in *East European Politics and Societies* 25(2): 361–387.
Verdery, K. 1999. *The Political Lives of Dead Bodies: Reburial and Postsocialist Change*. New York: Columbia University Press.
Vermeersch, P. 2006. *The Romani Movement: Minority Politics and Ethnic Mobilization in Contemporary Central Europe*. New York: Berghahn Books.
Viola, L. 1999. *Peasant Rebels under Stalin: Collectivization and the Culture of Peasant Resistance*. New York: Oxford University Press.
Von Plato, A., T. Vilimek, P. Filipkowski and J. Wawrzyniak (eds). 2013. *Opposition als Lebensform. Biografien von Dissidenten in der DDR, der CSSR und in Polen*. Berlin: LIT Verlag.

Vos, C. 2001. 'Breaking the Mirror: Dutch Television and the History of the Second World War', in *Television Histories: Shaping Collective Memory in the Media Age*, G.R. Edgerton and P.C. Rollins (eds). Lexington, Kentucky: The University Press of Kentucky, 123–142.

Vukov, N. and S. Toncheva. 2006. 'Town Squares and Socialist Heritage: The Reworking of Memorial Landscapes in Post-socialist Bulgaria', in *The Politics of Heritage and Regional Development Strategies: Actors, Interests, Conflicts*, S. Schroder-Esch and J.H. Ulbricht (eds). Weimar: Bauhaus Universität, 128.

Vukov, N. 2009. 'Protean Memories, "Permanent" Visualizations: Monuments and Museums in Post-Communist Eastern Europe', in *The Burden of Remembering: Recollections and Representations of the 20th Century*, E. Koresaar, K. Kuutma and E. Lauk (eds). Helsinki: Finnish Literature Society, 119–159.

Wæhrens, A. 2011. 'Shared Memories? Politics of Memory and Holocaust Remembrance in the European Parliament 1989–2009', *DIIS Working Paper*.

Walicki, A. 1982. *Philosophy and Romantic Nationalism: The Case of Poland*. Oxford: Clarendon Press.

———. 1994. *Poland between East and West: The Controversies over Self-definition and Modernization in Partitioned Poland*. Cambridge MA: Harvard University Press. Ukrainian Research Institute.

Waniek. K. 2012. *Polish Immigrants to Germany: Biographical Analysis of Narrative Interviews with Young People who Left for Germany between 1989 and 1999*. Łódź: Wyd. Uniwersytetu Łódzkiego.

Wasilewski, W. 2009. 'Pamięć Katynia. Działania opozycji', *Biuletyn IPN* no. 5/6.

Watson, R.S. 1994. *Memory, History, and Opposition under State Socialism*. University of Chicago Press.

Wawrzyniak, J. 2009. *ZBoWiD i pamięć drugiej wojny światowej 1949–1969*. Warsaw: Wydawnictwo Trio, Fundacja Historia i Kultura.

Wawrzyniak, J. and M. Pakier. 2013. 'Memory Studies in Eastern Europe: Key Issues and Future Perspectives', *Polish Sociological Review* 183, no. 3, 257–280.

Weber, M. 2006. 'Zur historiographischen Bearbeitung der Stellung Schlesiens zwischen dem Heiligen Römischen Reich und den Königreichen Polen und Böhmen', in *Reiche und Territorien in Ostmitteleuropa. Historische Beziehungen und politische Herrschaftslegitimation*, D. Willoweit and H. Lemberg (eds), Völker, Staaten und Kulturen in Ostmitteleuropa 2. Munich Oldenbourg Wissenschaftsverlag, 13–33.

Weber, M., B. Olschowsky, I.A. Petranský, A. Pók and A. Przewoźnik (eds). 2011. *Erinnerungsorte in Ostmitteleuropa – Erfahrungen der Vergangenheit und Perspektiven*, Schriften des Bundesinstituts für Kultur und Geschichte der Deutschen im östlichen Europa, Bd. 42, Schriften des Europäischen Netzwerks Erinnerung und Solidarität, Bd. 1. Munich.

Weinbaum, L. 2002. 'Penitence and Prejudice: The Roman Catholic Church and Jedwabne', *Jewish Political Studies Review* 14, 3–4.

Weissberg, L. 1999. 'Introduction', in *Cultural Memory and the Construction of Identity*, D. Ben-Amos and L. Weissberg (eds). Detroit: Wayne State University Press.

Welsh, H.A. 1996. 'Dealing with the Communist Past: Central and East European Experiences after 1990', in *Europe-Asia Studies* vol. 48, no. 3, May, 413–428.
Wengraf, T., P. Chamberlayne and J. Bornat. 2002. 'A Biographical Turn in the Social Sciences? A British-European View', in *Cultural Studies ↔ Critical Methodologies* 2, no. 2, 245–269.
Werner, M. and B. Zimmermann (eds). 2002. 'Vergleich, Transfer, Verflechtung. Der Ansatz der Histoire croisée und die Herausforderung des Transnationalen', *Geschichte und Gesellschaft* vol. 28, 607–636.
———. 2004. *De la comparaison à l'histoire croisée*. Paris: Seuil.
Wierzbicki, A. 1993. *Spory o polską duszę: Z zagadnień charakterologii narodowej w historiografii polskiej XIX i XX w.*, 2nd edn. Warsaw: Muzeum Historii Polski, Wydawn. Trio, Collegium Civitas.
Wigura, K. 2011. *Wina narodów. Przebaczenie jako strategia prowadzenia polityki*. Warsaw: Scholar.
Wippermann, W. 2005. *'Auserwählte Opfer?' Shoah und Porrajmos im Vergleich. Eine Kontroverse*. Berlin: Frank & Timme.
Wiszewski, P. 2008. 'Dla wszystkich starczy miejsca pod wielkim dachem historii', *Zapiski Historyczne poświęcone historii Pomorza i krajów bałtyckich* LXXIV2–3, 119–125.
Wolf, G. 2000. 'Proektăt "Raduil" – ethnolozhko izsledvane na seloto mezhdu "mikroistoriya", "prezhivyana istoriya" i "sobstven zhivot"', *Bălgarska etnologiya* 26, 4, 5–16.
———. 2003. '"Vlast" i "Svoenravie". Kam analiza na realniya sotsialisticheski zhiznen svyat', in *Sotsializmăt: Realnost i ilyuzii*, R. Ivanova, A. Luleva and R. Popov (eds). Sofia: EIM – BAN. 120–132.
Wolff, L. 1994, 1997. *Inventing Eastern Europe: The Map of Civilization on the Mind of the Enlightenment*. Stanford: Stanford University Press.
Wolff-Powęska, A. 2005. 'Zwycięzcy i zwyciężeni. II wojna światowa w pamięci zbiorowej narodów', *Przegląd Zachodni* no. 2. Retrieved from http://www.pz.iz.poznan.pl/folder2/dokumenty/2005_2/artykul. 2_2005.htm
Wójcik, A., M. Bilewicz, and M. Lewicka. 2010. 'Living on the Ashes: Collective Representations of Polish–Jewish History among People Living in the Former Warsaw Ghetto Area', *The International Journal of Urban Policy and Planning*, 27(4): 195–203.
Wóycicka, Z. 2005. 'Zur Internationalität der Gedenkkultur. Die Gedenkstätte Auschwitz-Birkenau im Spannungsfeld zwischen Ost und West 1954–1978', *Archiv für Sozialgeschichte* Band XLV.
———. 2009. *Przerwana żałoba. Polskie spory wokół pamięci nazistowskich obozów koncentracyjnych i zagłady 1944–1950*. Warsaw: Wydawnictwo Trio, Fundacja Historia i Kultura.
Wydra, H. 2010. 'Shifting the Gravity of Memory in Europe', *East European Memory Studies* no. 2, November, 3–6.
———. 2012. 'The Dynamics of Memory in East and West: Elements of a Comparative Framework', *Remembrance and Solidarity: Studies in 20th Century European History* no. 1, 1, 125–149.

Wygnańska, J. 2011. 'Tożsamość zorientowana na heterogeniczność. Dyskurs postjugosłowiańskiej serbskiej tożsamości narodowej a idea członkostwa Republiki Serbii w Unii Europejskiej', in *Integracja europejska a przemiany kulturowe w Europie*, K. Kaźmierska and K. Waniek (eds). Łódź: Wydawnictwo Uniwersytetu Łódzkiego. 169–188.

Wysiedlenia, wypędzenia i ucieczki 1939–1959. Atlas ziem polskich. 2008. Warsaw: Demart..

Yamashita, N. 2005. 'Empire or Post-Empire? The Concept of "Long Century" and the Consequences of Globalization', in *Emerging Meso-Areas in the Former Socialist Countries: Histories Revived or Improvised?* K. Matsuzato (ed.). Sapporo: Slavic Research Center, 335–348.

Yancheva, Y. 2012. 'Self-identification Through Narrative: Reflection on Collectivization', in *The European Review of History/Revue Européenne d'histoire* 19, no. 5, 789–808.

Yates, D.E. 1949. 'Hitler and the Gypsies. The Fate of Europe's Oldest Aryans', *Commentary* (8) (November): 455–459.

Yekelchyk, S. 2004. *Stalin's Empire of Memory: Russian-Ukrainian Relations in the Soviet Historical Imagination*. Toronto: University of Toronto Press.

Young, C. and D. Light. 2006. '"Communist Heritage Tourism": Between Economic Development and European Integration', in *Heritage and Media in Europe – Contributing towards Integration and Regional Development*, D. Hassenpflug, B. Kolbmüller and S. Schröder-Esch (eds). Weimar: Bauhaus Universität, 249–263.

Young, C., and S. Kaczmarek. 1999. 'Changing the Perception of the Post-socialist City: Place Promotion and Imagery in Łódź, Poland', *Geographical Journal* 165, 183–191.

———. 2008. 'The Socialist Past and Postsocialist Urban Identity in Central and Eastern Europe: The Case of Łódź, Poland', *European Urban and Regional Studies* 15(1): 53–70.

Young, J.E. 1993. *The Texture of Memory: Holocaust Memorials and Meaning*. New Haven and London: Yale University Press.

Zajda, J. and R. Zajda. 2003. 'The Politics of Rewriting History: New History Textbooks and Curriculum Materials in Russia', *International Review of Education*, 49(3–4): 363–384.

Zaremba, M. 2001. 'Urząd zapomnienia', *Polityka* no. 412319.

Zaszkilniak, L. 2008. 'Nacjonalizacja historii: państwo i historiografia we współczesnej Ukrainie', in *Pamięć i polityka historyczna. Doświadczenia Polski i jej sąsiadów*, S.M. Nowinowski, J. Pomorski and R. Stobiecki (eds). Łódź: Instytut Pamięci Narodowej, 27–34.

Zawadzki, P. 2003. 'Czas i tożsamość. Paradoks odnowienia problemu tożsamości', *Kultura i Społeczeństwo* 47(3): 5–16.

Zernack, K. 1977. *Osteuropa: Eine Einführung in seine Geschichte*. Munich: Beck.

Zhurzhenko, T. 2007. 'The Geopolitics of Memory', *Eurozine*. Retrieved October 2008 from http://www.eurozine.com/articles/2007-05-10-zhurzhenko-en.html

———. 2010. *Borderlands into Bordered Lands: Geopolitics of Identity in Post-Soviet Ukraine*. Stuttgart: ibidem-Verlag.

Zimmermann, M. 2001. 'The Wehrmacht and the National Socialist Persecution of the Gypsies', *Romani Studies* 5, vol. 11, no. 2.

———. 2006. 'The National Socialist Persecution of the Jews and Gypsies: Is a comparison Possible?' in *The Gypsies during the Second World War*, vol. 3: *The Final Chapter*, D. Kenrick (ed.). Hatfield: University of Hertfordshire Press.

———. 2007a. 'The Berlin Memorial for the Murdered Sinti and Roma: Problems and Points for Discussion', *Romani Studies* vol. 17, no. 1.

———. 2007b. 'Jews, Gypsies and Soviet Prisoners of War: Comparing Nazi Persecutions', in *The Roma: A Minority in Europe. Historical, Political and Social Perspectives*, R. Stauber and R. Vago (eds). Budapest and New York: Central European University Press.

Ziółkowski, M. 2000. 'Four Functions of Memory', *Polish Sociological Review* 131, no. 3, 291–308.

———. 2002. 'Memory and Forgetting after Communism', *Polish Sociological Review* 137, no. 17–24.

Znaniecki F. 1973 [1952]. *Modern Nationalities. A Sociological Study*. Westport, CT: Greenwood Press.

Znepolski, I. 2001. 'Les malheurs de l'histoire du temps présent: usage postcommuniste de la mémoire', *Divinatio* no. 13, 73–90.

———. 2004. 'Le communisme – un lieu de mémoire sans point d'appui consensuel', *Divinatio* no. 19, 29–40.

Żakowski, J. (ed.). 2002. *Rewanż pamięci*. Warsaw: Wydawnictwo Sic!

Żukowski, T. 1997. 'Świadomość historyczna Polaków w połowie lat dziewięćdziesiątych', in *Ofiary czy współwinni. Nazizm i sowietyzm w świadomości historycznej. Praca zbiorowa*. Warsaw: Oficyna Wydawnicza Volumen, Fundacja im. Friedricha Eberta, 65–76.

Zwangsumsiedlung, Flucht und Vertreibung 1939–1959. Atlas zur Geschichte Ostmitteleuropas. 2010. Bundeszentrale für politische Bildung, Schriftenreihe 1015. Bonn.

INDEX

1939, 1, 27, 92, 102, 105, 110, 115, 117, 118, 121, 130, 143, 179, 190, 233, 234, 235, 240, 241, 243, 271, 274
1945, 5, 24, 27, 42, 43, 48, 50, 51, 52, 69, 102, 112, 115, 116, 117, 130, 131, 132, 133, 135, 147n1, 161, 162, 166, 168, 190, 220, 224, 232, 234, 235, 236, 240, 241, 246, 263, 267, 268, 269, 272, 274, 290, 291, 311
1989, 2, 3, 4, 9, 13, 18, 19n3, 20, 43, 44, 60, 67, 74, 76, 103, 109, 116, 131, 134, 135, 136, 137, 138, 147n1, 148n8, 148n13, 150, 151, 153, 155, 159, 160, 161, 162, 163, 164, 165, 166, 168, 212, 232, 243, 245, 258, 260, 265, 266, 267, 268, 272, 277, 281n3, 300, 301, 302, 305, 313n4, 313n7, 315n21

agricultural collectivization, 19, 154, 283–298
Alexy II, Patriarch of Moscow (Alexey Ridiger), 176
Allies, 24, 81, 232, 241, 242, 243, 251, 261
America/American. *See* United States
amnesia/forgetting/oblivion, 3, 7, 17, 24, 27, 28, 29, 30, 31, 35, 37n1, 44, 45, 46, 48, 63, 70, 77, 81, 93, 98, 101, 102, 106, 109, 119, 126, 127, 131, 133, 134, 147n7, 151, 161, 162, 163, 164, 165, 238, 239, 240, 271, 299, 301, 302, 312, 313. *See also* erasure of memory
Anders, Władysław, 240
army of, 118
anti-communism/anti-communist, 12, 43, 50, 134, 161, 162, 163, 194, 195, 214, 232, 250, 296, 301, 302, 303, 304, 305, 306, 307, 309, 310, 311, 312, 313n6, 313n7, 314n16
anti-Gypsyism, 84, 88, 312
anti-Semitism, 25, 41, 117, 118, 120, 121, 125, 126, 127, 128, 209n15, 256, 264
archives, 25, 26, 37, 148n17, 203, 217, 259, 302, 303, 307, 308
Arendt, Hannah, 132
army/armed forces, 42, 48, 81, 91, 118, 169, 173, 177, 178, 181, 183, 186, 187, 191n6, 197, 200, 205, 207, 209n13, 210n25, 215, 232, 236, 238, 240, 244, 247, 248, 250, 251, 264, 269, 271, 290, 291, 302, 307, 313n4
Assmann, Aleida, 6, 8, 19n1, 41, 45–49, 51, 52, 55n4, 56n10, 68
Assmann, Jan, 19n1, 68
Assorodobraj-Kula, Nina, 68
Augé, Marc, 64

August 23rd, 47, 110n6, 121, 143, 163, 185, 315n25
Auschwitz/Auschwitz-Birkenau, vi, 18, 42, 47, 91, 118, 143, 233, 240, 246–263
Austria/Austrian, 25, 37n3, 63, 72, 90, 118, 129, 192, 266, 272, 339
Avakov, Arsen, 186
Avineri, Shlomo, 121, 160
Avižienis, Jūra, 137

Bandera, Stepan, 199–201, 204, 210n17, 210n18, 210n25
Bartosz, Adam, 82
Bartov, Omer, 5, 129n9
Bauer, Yehuda, 99, 121, 129n10
Bauman, Zygmun, 88
Belarus/Belarusian, 12, 102, 104, 107, 108, 109, 111, 115, 118, 134, 138, 139, 147n3, 174, 175, 191n5, 237, 238, 249, 252
Belgorod, viii, 169, 170, 172–79, 181, 183, 185, 186, 189, 191, 191n5, 191n6, 191n7
Benjamin, Walter
  le flâneur, 214
Berlin, 42, 133, 240, 269, 278, 280, 314n17
Berlin Wall, 267
Black Sea Fleet, 212, 223, 226n19
Blacker, Uilleam, 4
Boia, Lucian, 70
Bonaparte, Napoleon, 62, 191n2
borderland, vi, 14, 18, 102, 103, 105, 106, 112, 133, 169, 170, 174, 179, 183, 190, 192, 233
border(s), 5, 11, 14, 17, 26, 27, 32, 49, 53, 59, 67, 73, 74, 101, 102, 103, 133, 147, 154, 169, 170, 173, 174, 176, 178, 179, 192, 216, 220, 236, 248, 261, 268, 280, 303
Bratislava, 51, 72
Brezhnev, Leonid
  empire of memory, 171
British, 12, 258, 269
Brussels, vi, 42, 43, 47, 51, 53, 116, 131, 140, 141, 142, 144, 146, 147

Bucharest, 303, 304, 313n4, 316
Budapest, 63, 66, 214
Bulgaria, vii, viii, 12, 19, 61, 90, 139, 147, 168n2, 283–298, 299–301, 305–316

canon, 6, 9, 16, 19n1, 96, 105, 179, 182, 183, 196, 208, 223, 240
capitalism, 83, 163, 174, 216, 301
Catherine II
  commemoration of, 221
Catholic/Catholic Church, 159, 165, 179, 257, 258, 262
censorship, 40, 109, 135, 150, 218, 244, 253, 261
Central Eastern Europe/Central and Eastern Europe, v, vi, x, xiii, xiv, 16, 19, 19n2, 20, 59, 60, 61, 62, 64, 65, 66, 67, 68, 70, 71, 73, 74, 75, 76, 96, 98, 108, 109, 110, 134, 140, 152, 153, 155, 168
Centre against Expulsions, Berlin, 269, 278. *See also* expulsion/deportation
Christianity, 117, 223, 260
Churchill, Winston, 24
citizenship, 34, 97, 109, 201, 206, 330, 337
civic, 66, 109, 119, 126, 173, 196, 201, 206, 208, 209, 274, 305, 313, 332
clash, cultural/of memory cultures, 10, 32, 47, 131, 186, 218, 254, 268, 290, 294, 295
class
  social, 48, 158, 159, 255, 314 n17
  struggle, 31, 154, 248
Cohen, Shari J., 78
Cold War, 15, 24, 25, 34, 54, 88, 132, 147, 255, 265, 268, 271
collaboration, 26, 44, 118, 138, 171, 183, 210, 239, 251, 302
coming to terms with the past/ reckoning with the past, 6, 7, 8, 12, 13, 16, 17, 24, 32, 43, 45, 116, 121, 128, 137, 150, 153, 155, 160, 161, 162, 164, 272, 299
commemoration, ix, 1, 6, 7, 8, 9, 13, 15, 17, 24, 28, 34, 36, 41, 55n3, 66, 72, 80, 93, 95n1, 119, 125, 127, 136, 138,

139, 140, 144, 151, 165, 167, 186, 194, 195, 196, 201, 232, 253, 256, 282n7, 301, 309, 311, 312
commemorative, 13, 42, 43, 82, 184, 186, 198, 202, 213, 217, 311
culture, 42, 170, 190, 213. *See also* memory culture
discourse, 82
practice(s), 82, 195, 196, 202
politics/policy, 169, 186, 187, 191. *See also* politics of memory
project/model, 42, 45, 185, 187, 190
rituals, 50. *See also* ritual
communism/communist past, vi, vii, xiii, 1, 7, 10, 11, 12, 15, 20, 24, 43, 47, 50, 65, 70, 78, 81, 82, 83, 93, 96, 102, 103, 104, 105, 109, 117, 118, 119, 121, 123, 128, 129n2, 129n4, 131, 133, 134, 135, 137, 138, 139, 141, 142, 143, 147n1, 147n4, 148n10, 150, 152, 153, 154, 155, 156, 157, 158, 159, 160, 162, 163, 164, 165, 166, 167, 176, 177, 178, 181, 186, 194, 195, 196, 200, 205, 208, 214, 232, 237, 240, 241, 243, 245, 246, 264, 280, 283, 286, 293, 294, 299–316
collapse of, 8, 18, 47, 75, 93, 116, 117, 135, 136, 150, 15, 153, 160, 172, 193
crimes of, *see* crimes Communist/Soviet/Stalinist
memory of/coming to terms with, 8, 12, 13, 15, 18, 19, 43, 50, 54, 67, 141, 153, 160, 161, 162, 163, 167, 299, 300, 304, 317
Communist parties, 55n3, 177, 196, 198, 199, 287, 289, 292, 293, 294, 297, 301
compensation, 9, 83, 95n4, 151, 157, 158, 159, 160, 165, 167, 210n20, 233, 271, 296, 315n23
complicity, 120, 138, 142, 314
concealment, 45, 111n7, 250, 251, 252, 253, 256, 258. *See also* amnesia/forgetting/oblivion, erasure of memory

concentration camp, 32, 90, 236, 237, 238, 239, 247, 250, 254, 255
Crimea, 206, 207, 208n7, 212–228
Crimean Tatars, 174, 208, 212, 220, 221
crimes, 24, 27, 28, 31, 36, 41, 45, 48, 82, 141, 194, 208n4, 260, 276
Communist/Soviet/Stalinist, 120, 121, 132, 140, 142, 143, 145, 148n9, 148n13, 148n20, 161, 162, 163, 167, 232, 233, 249, 252, 258, 259, 260, , 304, 309, 310, 311, 314n11, 314n12, 315n21, 315n24
Nazi, 45, 91, 121, 252, 260, 261, 264, 266, 268, 269, 272, 273, 276, 278
Croatia, 91, 168n2
Csáky, Moritz, 71–74
Czarnowski, Stefan, 68
Czech Republic, vi, 9, 11, 13, 63, 81, 121, 134, 139, 150–168, 208n1, 265, 266, 269, 274
Czechoslovakia, 65, 67, 154, 161, 255, 256

dark past, 8, 18, 117, 119, 121, 123, 124, 126, 127, 128, 266
Davies, Norman, 103, 110n2
De Certeau, 213, 220
Desbois, Patrick, 116
diaspora, 127, 129, 197, 210n25, 216, 259
Diner, Dan, 142, 148n15, 151, 152, 159, 280
Dobkin, Mikail, 187
Donskis, Leonidas, 121
Donskoy, Dmitriy, 181
Duchardt, Heinz, 29

Eastern Bloc, 1, 3, 7, 15, 25, 255, 261
England/English, 6, 11, 37n6, 37, 60, 62, 85, 92, 97, 168, 18, 225n4, 226
Enlightenment, 83, 84, 86, 88
entangled history, 32, 73, 267, 273
Esbenshade, Richard, 78, 129n1
Etkind, Alexander, 4, 14, 51
Estonia, 13, 42, 68, 69, 110n6, 122, 134, 140, 148n20, 168n2, 208n2, 208n4, 209n14, 210n17

ethnic/ethnicity, 1, 3, 7, 24, 53, 71, 75, 78, 81, 82, 83, 87, 90, 95, 99, 102, 107, 108, 109, 111n13, 117, 118, 122, 125, 126, 133, 146, 154, 155, 164, 169, 182, 197, 198, 205, 208n5, 208n7, 208n8, 209n10, 209n15, 212, 248, 249, 256, 257, 265, 267, 278, 283, 311
  cleansing, 41, 243
ethnography, 63, 89, 207, 208n5, 214, 289, 298
European Commission, 47, 140, 143, 149
European Parliament, 47, 121, 140, 142, 143, 146, 148n11, 198, 199, 308, 311, 315n25
European project/Europeanization, 1, 4, 5, 8, 10, 20, 71, 109, 110, 141, 148n12. *See also* European identity, European memory
European Union, ii, 4, 7, 32, 36, 40, 41, 45, 46, 49, 110, 120, 124, 131, 142, 143, 210n17, 279, 288
exclusion, 9, 85, 86, 108, 111n12, 160
expulsion/deportation, 8, 32, 34, 41, 50, 12, 134, 136, 137, 140, 143, 144, 145, 147n7, 148n9, 155, 232, 250, 265, 266, 269, 271, 272, 273, 278, 279, 282n7, 282n8

Fabian, Johannes, 87
fascism, 15, 41, 42, 81, 132, 172, 207, 217, 253, 311, 339
Fedor, Julie, 51
Filipkowski, Piotr, 11
film, 13, 20, 26, 118, 144, 145, 148n18, 234, 259, 264, 274, 276, 304, 343
Finnin, Rory, 14, 51
Foucault, Michel, 39, 85
France/French, ii, x, xi, 6, 11, 15, 25, 29, 39, 59, 60, 61, 62, 63, 64, 65, 70, 71, 72, 74, 75, 76n2, 76n6, 81, 92, 116, 135, 148, 153, 167, 208n3, 224, 225n4, 241, 242, 243
François, Étienne, 61
Friedländer, Saul, 26, 79, 80

Gauck, Joachim
  Institute. *See* institutes of national memory
genocide, 9, 24, 48, 66, 81, 82, 84, 87, 88, 89, 90, 92, 93, 95, 120, 121, 122, 126, 129n9, 154, 197, 198, 199, 201, 202, 205, 208n3, 210n21, 239, 246, 250, 255, 268
Gensburger, Sarah, 6
Germany/German/Germans, ii, vi, x, xi, 6, 24, 25, 26, 27, 32, 33, 36, 37n3, 40, 41, 42, 45, 46, 49, 50, 60, 62n63, 66, 70, 79, 80, 81, 85, 90, 91, 92, 103, 104, 105, 106, 121, 125, 126, 129n10, 134, 142, 144, 148n16, 154, 168n2, 176, 193, 205, 210n25, 232, 236, 237, 238, 241, 242, 243, 244, 245, 246, 248, 250, 251, 252, 255, 257, 261, 264, 265, 266, 267, 268, 269, 270, 270, 271, 272, 273, 274, 275, 276, 277, 278, 279, 280, 281, 281n2, 282, 282n3, 282n9, 314n17
Giesen, Bernard, 128
globalization, 1, 18, 193, 224
Goli Otok, 138
Golubets, Ivan, 219, 226n19
Gombrowicz, Witold, 62
Grabski, Andrzej Feliks, 69
Grachova, Sofia, 171
Great Britain, 75, 135, 241, 242
Great Famine, 1932–32, 9, 185, 186, 194–211
Great Patriotic War, vi, 32, 106, 169, 170, 171, 172, 177, 181, 182, 183, 185, 186, 189, 190, 191, 195, 196, 197, 199, 207, 208n6, 209n11, 219
Gross, Jan T., 118, 124, 232, 273
guided tours/walking tours, 213, 214, 217, 218
guilt, 8, 27, 32, 36, 41, 45, 51, 120, 121, 138, 142, 160, 162, 169, 250, 264, 269, 271, 273, 278, 302, 313n10, 315n23
Gulag, 10, 18, 42, 47, 49, 55, 115, 120, 131–149, 246
Gyáni, Gábor, 66

Hackmann, Jörg, 11, 73, 146
Hahn, Heinz Henning, 14, 29
Halbwachs, Maurice, 14, 19 n1, 63, 97, 152, 153, 285
Halecki, Oskar, 12, 49, 133
Hancock, Ian, 91
heritage, ix, 5, 36, 51, 96, 109, 111n13, 128, 131, 144, 157, 172, 179, 200, 212, 214–27, 265, 270, 273, 274, 275, 307, 314n14
hero, 32, 71, 100, 125, 170, 177, 178, 181, 199, 201, 206, 210n16, 216, 217, 222, 224, 226n19, 231, 240
heroism/heroic, 8, 13, 30, 34, 36, 42, 44, 46, 103, 124, 165, 176, 178, 181, 183, 197, 199, 209n13, 210n25, 215, 217, 239, 241, 245. *See also* heroic narrative
Heuss, Herbert, 84–86
historians, ix, 5, 15, 16, 26, 32, 33, 60, 63, 64, 66, 68, 69, 70, 72, 75, 81, 117, 118, 122, 123, 132, 165, 179, 187, 203, 204, 207, 209n9, 234, 247, 259, 272, 273, 274, 278
historical consciousness, 60, 70, 75, 109, 121, 123, 126, 128, 137, 254, 262
historical culture, 70
historiography/historical discourse, 12, 52, 61, 64, 69, 72, 75, 76, 76n8, 94, 100, 118, 119, 150, 174, 191n2, 211, 261, 265, 268, 269, 274, 277, 278, 280, 300
Hitler, Adolf, 26, 48, 143, 183, 244, 252, 271, 315n26
Hitlerites, 82
Hobsbawm, Eric, 75
Hofer, Tamás, 63
Hoffman, Eva, 79
Holocaust, 17, 18, 20, 24, 25, 26, 30, 33, 34, 36, 41, 42, 43, 44, 47, 49, 50, 55n2, 56n10, 77–96, 110n5, 115–130, 142–145, 170, 185, 190, 198, 208n3, 209n15, 210n25, 232, 233, 239, 240, 243, 246–263, 264, 268, 271, 281n1
Holodomor. *See* famine, Ukrainian
Home Army (AK), 232, 264

Huener, Jonathan, 256
human rights, 31, 33, 36, 46, 88, 115, 150, 158, 159, 200, 313n8
Hungary, 11, 12, 13, 50, 63, 67, 120, 121, 134, 140, 147n3, 168n2, 208n2, 266
Husserl, Edmund, 85

identity, ix, 1, 4, 5, 7, 29, 30, 34, 37, 44, 46, 50, 52, 62, 64, 69, 73, 75, 82, 84, 85, 87, 90, 91, 94, 95, 99, 100, 108, 123, 127, 129n7, 139, 141, 146, 165, 174, 187, 193, 194, 205, 213, 222, 225, 239, 291
collective, 66, 68, 70, 87, 96, 97, 98, 101, 103, 106, 108, 109, 110n1, 111n8, 112, 165, 171, 194, 239, 291, 301
East European, 10, 15, 44, 139, 142
European, 4, 46, 53, 110, 279
local, 183, 219, 222
national, 46, 74, 90, 96, 102, 109, 111n11, 12, 122, 128, 129n2, 138, 160, 169, 171, 187, 194, 234, 240, 270
politics of, 94, 192
regional, 139, 174, 183, 189
Western, 87
immigrants/immigration, 2, 8, 9, 50
institute(s) of national memory, 13, 65, 66, 140, 144, 146, 151
'Gauck Institute', 65, 66
Polish, 65, 140, 144, 208n1
Romanian, 208n4, 310, 314n12
Slovak, 65
Ukrainian, 194, 203, 204, 207, 209n9
International Auschwitz Council, 256
Internet, 34, 201, 220, 235, 244, 347
Iron Curtain, 16, 67, 88, 140, 148n8, 246, 260, 299
Italy, 20, 37n3, 63, 76, 135, 168, 242

Janion, Maria, 69
Japan, xi, 249
Jarausch, Konrad, xiv, 6, 35, 53
Jaruzelski, Wojciech, 55n3, 55n4, 253, 259
Jasiewicz, Krzysztof, 118, 119, 129n5

Jedlicki, Jerzy, 7, 69
Jedwabne, 25, 46, 118, 122–26, 130, 168n7, 232, 233, 273
Jews/Jewish, 2, 3, 8, 9, 17, 20, 26, 34, 35, 41, 46, 48, 53, 54, 62, 71, 79, 81, 86, 90, 91, 92, 94, 95, 106, 112, 115, 116, 117, 118, 119, 120, 121, 122, 123, 124, 125, 126, 127, 128, 129n6, 129n7, 129n11, 129n12, 130, 138, 154, 159, 160, 185, 190, 199, 205, 209, 209n15, 214, 217, 221, 232, 239, 240, 242, 243, 245, 247, 249, 253, 254, 255, 256, 257, 259, 260, 262, 263, 268, 271, 272, 273
Jobbik party, 117
John Paul II, 62, 118, 259
Judeo-communism/Red Jews, 117, 118, 119, 121, 129n4
Judt, Tony, 1, 6, 78, 120, 133, 142

Kaelble, Hartmut, 74
Kaliningrad, 267
Kalniete, Sandra, 10, 42, 55, 140, 247
Kansteiner, Wulf, 6
Kapralski, Sławomir, 255, 260
Katyn, vi, 14, 19, 102, 104, 105, 111n8, 138, 190, 232, 233, 246, 247, 248, 249, 250, 251, 252, 253, 254, 257, 258, 259, 260, 261, 262, 262n1, 262n2, 262n3
Kelam, Tunne, 140
Kharkiv, viii, 169, 170, 171, 173, 174, 176, 182, 183, 184, 185, 186, 187, 189, 190, 191, 191n3, 192, 252
Khersones, 219, 220, 223, 224
Khmelnytskyi, Bogdan, 174
Kiliánová, Gabriela, 71, 72
Kizwalter, Tomasz, 69
Kligman, Gail, 283
Kłoskowska, Antonina, 96
Klykov, Viacheslav, 179
Knesebeck, Julia von dem, 80
Kolbe, Maksymilian, 240, 260
Kończal, Kornelia, 11, 14, 17, 59
Konev, Ivan. *See* memorials
Kozielsk, 247

Kresy, 62, 102, 103, 104, 105, 106, 111, 118, 233
Kuchma, Leonid, 171, 176, 186, 201, 203
Kucia, Marek, 261
Kundera, Milan, 139
Kurhajcová, Alina, 11
Kurtyka, Janusz, 66, 253
Kushnarev Evhen, 186, 187
Kutuzov, Mikhail, 181
Kyiv, 171, 194, 196, 202, 205, 206, 208, 211, 212

Laczó, Ferenc, 11
Landsbergis, Vytautas, 140
Latvia, 13, 42, 107, 110n6, 122, 134, 140, 148n20, 168n2, 209n14, 09n15, 210n17, 347
Lavabre, Marie-Clare, 6
Lebiedieva, Natalia, 252
Le Goff, Jacques, 64
Leggewie, Claus, 6, 8, 41, 49–51
Lehrer, Erica, 79, 129n7
Lejeune, Philipe, 99
Lemon, Alaina 83
Lenin, Vladimir
    monuments of, 177, 199, 207, 221, 304, 305
Lepsius, Rainer Mario, 27
Levy, Daniel, 6, 9, 26
Lewicka, Maria, 64
Lewy, Guenther, 91
lieux de mémoire/realm of memory, 13, 14, 19n1, 28, 29, 59–76, 80, 143, 280, 290, 295. *See also* site of memory, place of memory
Lindenberger, Thomas, 6, 53
Lipták, Ľubomír, 71, 72, 76n8
literature, 1, 4, 11, 37, 69, 98, 131, 135, 138, 160, 195, 235, 258, 265, 276
Lithuania, 13, 42, 66, 102, 107, 110n6, 121, 122, 134, 137, 139, 140, 141, 144, 145, 146, 148n9, 148n20, 168n2, 194, 209n2, 209n14, 237
Lotman, Juri, 68
Lübbe, Hermann, 24
Luhansk, 205, 207

Lukashenka, Alexander, 176
Łysakowski, Piotr 252

Mach, Zdzisław, 257
Macura, Vladimír, 69
Maidan. *See* revolution
Maier, Charles S., 6, 7, 9, 52, 138
Makuch, Janusz, 120
Małczyński, Jacek, 64
Mannheim, Karl, 105
Mannová, Elena, 71
Margalit, Avishai, 33, 34, 37n5
Margalit, Gilad, 33, 34, 37n5, 81, 91, 92
Mark, James, 12
martyrdom, 65, 82, 83, 103, 104, 115, 121, 237, 239, 240, 249, 250, 253, 254, 256, 257
Max, Frederick, 80
media/mass media, ii, 4, 13, 14, 20, 26, 37, 38, 50, 62, 70, 95n6, 117, 139, 173, 87, 191, 193, 196, 224, 232, 234, 244, 260, 261, 264, 265, 267, 268, 269, 270, 271, 272, 274, 275, 276, 279, 282n3, 300, 312, 315n24
Meier, Christian, 24, 47
melancholia/melancholic, 9, 78, 79, 80
  melancholic remembrance, 9, 78, 79
memorabilia, 235, 236
Mencwel, Andrzej, 69
memorial laws, 38,
  amnesty law, 28
  law of historical remembrance, 28
  lustration law, 65, 302, 307, 308
  restitution laws, 9, 158, 159, 160, 167, 168n2, 307
memorial regimes, 301, 313 n2
memorial(s), 83, 270, 301. *See also* museums, monuments
  Georgi Dimitrov's mausoleum in Sofia, 306, 307
  Holocaust memorial *Drobitskyi Yar*, 185
  Holodomor memorials, 194, 196, 202, 209n12
  Lontsky Prison National Memorial Museum in Lviv, 194, 203–204, 210

Marshal Konev Height near Kharkiv, 187–190
Memorial cemetery of Polish victims of NKVD in Kharkiv, 185
Memorial to Roma victims in Szczurowa, 82
Memorial to the Heroes of the Kursk Battle, 177
Memorial to the victims of communism in Lodz, 166
Memorial to the victims of communism in Prague, 166
Memorial to the victims of communism in Sofia, 311
Prokhorovka memorial in the Belgorod region, 175–176, 179–182
Sighet Memorial, 303–304, 313n5
memory(ies). *See also* remembering, remembrance, historical culture, historical consciousness, history, identity
  abundance of, 78, 79
  asymmetry of, 46, 50, 98, 101, 102, 104, 105, 106, 107, 108, 111, 246, 264
  authorized, 218
  auto-/biographical, 12, 98–110, 288
  boom, ix, 3, 54, 74, 122, 231
  collective, x, 4, 11, 12, 17, 42, 46, 47, 50, 56, 62, 64, 66, 67, 70, 72–75, 83, 96–98, 101–110, 111n12, 123, 141, 142, 146, 151–153, 164, 169, 173, 185, 186, 190, 193, 233, 235, 239, 244, 250, 275, 284, 297, 299, 300, 301, 313n3
  commodification of, 217
  communicative, 28, 93, 99, 100, 102, 103, 105, 235, 244
  conflicts of, 16, 24, 43, 75, 78, 147, 167, 298, 305
  cultural, 6, 13, 100, 219, 221, 222, 227
  culture, 8, 12, 16, 23, 31, 48, 53, 153, 161, 162, 165, 166, 169, 170, 173, 183, 186, 191, 225, 279
  dialogic, 8, 16, 28, 32, 33
  erasure of, 44, 79, 80, 83. *See also* amnesia/forgetting/oblivion

memory(ies) (*cont.*)
  East European/Central and East
    European, 10–15, 17, 19n3, 43,
    45–55, 78, 83, 87, 88, 110, 140–147,
    148n10, 148n12, 246, 262
  European, 4–10, 35, 36, 40, 41, 45–55,
    131, 246, 262, 279, 312
  frameworks of, xi, 4, 5, 14, 15, 23, 25,
    31
  and history, 38, 56n9, 99. *See also*
    history
  and identity, 84, 123, 142. *See also*
    identity
  individual/private, x, 46, 55, 98, 119,
    See also biographical memory
  national/nationalist, 13, 25, 27, 30, 32,
    33, 49, 66, 128, 146, 147, 151, 162,
    164, 165, 195, 280. *See also* nation/
    national, nationalism/nationalist
  patriotic, 65
  politics of, x, 5, 6, 18, 41, 42, 44, 54,
    56 n9, 72, 143, 146, 155, 165, 169,
    172, 173, 176, 181, 193–195, 207,
    210 n 25. *See also* politics of history
  policy of, 28–34, 49, 139, 141
  monologic, 34
  official, 6, 13, 105, 107, 300
  public, 8, 9, 10, 38, 43, 51, 81, 123,
    126, 128, 136, 151, 165, 166, 173,
    186, 187, 249, 284, 298, 300, 302,
    304, 310, 312, 313n2
  practices of, 214, 225
  performative, 222
  postcommunist. *See* postcommunist
    memory
  prosthetic, 93
  regional/regional frameworks of/
    regions of, xi-xii, 14–15, 169, 173
  restoration of, 116, 119
  semantics of, 67
  site of, 12, 19 n1, 65, 177, 179, 189,
    194, 198, 199, 220. *See also lieux de
    mémoire*/realm of memory
  social, 4, 20, 31, 77, 84, 90, 98, 124,
    125, 246, 247
  transnational, 6, 12, 14, 15, 29, 31, 34,
    36, 41, 49, 52, 73, 145, 146

  turn, 61, 70, 138
  vernacular, 233, 243, 244, 245
  walking, 213, 214, 218, 223–225
  West European, 1, 17, 34, 42, 45–55,
    140, 142, 143, 246
Michnik, Adam, 36
milieu(x) de mémoire, 80, 312
Miłosz, Czesław, 62
Mink, Georges, 6
minority
  ethnic, 8, 9, 29, 117, 118, 120, 122,
    123, 124, 126, 127, 160, 221. *See also*
    ethnic/ethnicity
  national, 9, 29, 117, 122, 146, 160,
    267, 305, 307, 308. *See also* nation/
    national
Misztal, Barbara, 285
modernity, 61, 84, 85, 86, 87, 132,
  147–148n8
Moldova, 147 n3, 265, 298
monument(s), 6, 26, 51, 65, 79, 166, 174,
  177–179, 181, 186, 198–200, 202,
  205, 207, 210 n18, 213, 219, 221,
  252–254, 256, 257, 259, 299, 302,
  308, 309, 311, 312
  living monument, 64
  See also memorial(s)
Moscow, 68, 81, 133, 171, 176, 177,
  191n5, 191n6, 209n13, 214, 215,
  224, 226n 27
mourning, 27, 44, 78–80, 94, 135, 177,
  185, 202, 206
Müller, Michael G., 133, 134, 282n5
museum(s), 6, 13, 41, 79, 140, 144,
  146, 217, 270, 301, 313. *See also*
  memorials
  Diorama museums in Sevastopol,
    219
  Ethnographic Museum at the
    Bulgarian Academy of Sciences, 289
  Gulag Museum in Perm, 148n17
  Gulag: Museum on Communism
    (virtual), 148n17
  Holocaust Memorial Museum in
    Washington, 81
  House of Terror in Budapest, 66,
    208n2, 214

Kursk Battle Museum in Belgorod, 177
Museum of Communism in Prague, 208n2
Museum of Ethnography in Budapest, 63
Museum of Military Glory of Russia's Third Battlefield in Prokhorovka, 182
Museum of the Memory of Siberia, 145
Museum of the Second World War in Gdansk, 233
Occupation Museum in Riga, 66, 214
Occupation Museum in Tallinn, 66, 208n2, 214
Panorama museum in Sevastopol, 219
State Museum of Auschwitz-Birkenau, 95n1, 254–257, 259–260
Warsaw Uprising Museum, 165, 190, 208n2
Müller, Jan-Werner, 6
myth/mythology, 7, 8, 10, 17, 33, 41, 71, 77, 83, 84, 86–89, 93, 94, 95n6, 100, 117–120, 128, 138, 170–173, 177, 183, 186, 189, 195, 206–208, 215, 218, 225, 251, 268, 280, 297, 302–304
national, 29, 30, 45, 46, 68–70, 75, 123–125, 183, 195, 197, 199, 202, 210n25. *See also* nation

Najder, Zdzisław, 63
Nakba, 34
Nakhimov, Pavel
  monument of, 219, 221
narrative(s) of the past, 8, 11, 12, 13, 15, 29, 30, 38, 40, 44, 67, 82, 85, 89, 94, 102, 115, 150, 151, 155, 167, 174, 227n28, 232, 256, 284
  auto-/biographical/personal, 98, 102, 104, 105, 107, 110, 111n8, 284, 288, 290, 291, 294, 295, 297
  European, 2, 5, 6, 8, 9, 11, 49, 54, 89, 131, 142, 145, 148n12

Great Patriotic War, 106–109, 169, 170–176, 178, 183, 185, 187, 189, 190, 191, 216
Gulag, 135, 136, 139, 142
heroic, 165. *See also* heroism
Holocaust, 9, 80, 89, 92–94, 115, 116, 117, 256
Holodomor, 185, 202, 209n15. *See also* Holodomor
national, 5, 26, 29, 33, 40, 44, 47, 66, 81, 82, 102–104, 117, 118, 121, 123, 128, 137, 170, 173, 183, 216, 231–245, 246–262, 264–281
tour guide, 219–221, 224
victimhood/martyrdom, 115, 142, 151, 165, 167, 272, 273, 279
nation/national, xi-xiii, 4–8, 11, 13–15, 25, 27, 29–33, 36, 40, 43–50, 52–54, 56n10, 60, 62, 68–75, 79, 83, 84, 87, 90, 91, 93, 96–98, 103, 108, 109, 111n13, 116, 117, 119, 122–128, 131, 133, 134, 137, 139, 142, 144–147, 147n1, 147n2, 151, 152, 157, 165, 167, 169–191, 193, 194, 197, 198, 209n10, 213, 216, 220, 225, 226n23, 300, 303, 305, 310–312. *See also* national identity, national minority, national memory(ies), national myths, national narrative(s) of the past
nationalism/nationalist, 1, 29, 41, 53, 78, 82, 83, 94, 109, 117, 132, 136–138, 146, 148n9, 148n20, 160, 193–208, 208n7, 210n21, 210n25, 255, 299
civic, 206, 208, 210n10
political, 87
ethnic/ethnonationalism, 117, 118, 121, 127, 205, 278. *See also* ethnic/ethnicity
Nazis/Nazism, xiii, 6, 7, 15, 24, 27, 41, 47, 92, 138, 144, 244, 247, 248. *See also* national socialism
Neumayer, Laure, 6
NKVD, 185, 248, 259
Nora, Pierre, 13, 19n1, 29, 42, 59, 60–76, 80

Novitch, Myriam, 80
Nuremberg Laws, 85

occupation, 27, 133
  German/Nazi, 4, 104, 111n9, 125, 154, 155, 166, 183, 185, 190, 214, 246, 248, 249, 250, 253, 254, 260, 261, 265, 266, 268, 270, 271, 272, 275
  Soviet, 42, 47, 102–105, 111n8, 111n9, 118, 154, 190, 214, 232, 237, 246, 248, 255, 272. *See also* crimes
Odesa, 189, 198, 201
Offe, Claus, 7
Olick, Jeffrey K., 143n3, 285
Olšáková, Doubravka, 11
oral history, 13, 20
Organization of Ukrainian Nationalists (OUN), 197, 199, 205, 206, 210n24, 210n25
orientalism/orientalizing, 77, 132, 140
orthodox/Orthodox Church, 174, 175, 176, 177, 178, 179, 181–183, 188, 189, 191, 222, 299, 302, 309, 310
Ostaszków, 249
Outhwaite, William, 78
Oz, Amos, 33

Pakier, Małgorzata, iii, v, viii, xiv, 1, 2, 3, 6, 8, 13, 14, 20, 246
patriotism/patriotic, 172, 178, 181, 225, 248, 251, 260
  education, 178, 181, 215, 217, 218, 225
  memory. *See* memory
People's Republic of Poland (PRL), 104, 164, 166, 232, 240, 243, 251, 253, 272
Petranský, Ivan, 66, 280
photography, 236,
pilgrimage, 62, 144, 190, 216, 217, 225, 260
Pinto, Diana, 79
Piper, Franciszek, 260, 262n1
place/space, memory and, 2, 4, 8, 10, 16, 30, 33, 42, 46, 53, 61, 64, 65, 71, 73, 79, 83, 87, 103, 107, 120, 129 n3, 131, 133–138, 145, 152, 153, 160, 165, 169, 177, 179, 183–186, 190, 206, 212–225, 241, 248–254, 256, 257, 261, 284, 295, 301, 304, 305–310, 309
Plokhy, Serhii, 215
Poland/Polish, 2, 3, 7, 9, 11, 12–14, 26, 29, 32, 33, 42, 45–47, 50, 51, 53, 54, 55n3, 61–74, 79, 80, 82, 83, 90, 91, 95n6, 96, 97, 99, 102–107, 110n2, 110n3, 110n6, 111, 117, 118, 120, 122–127, 129n11, 129n12, 134, 136, 137–139, 145, 147nn3–7, 148 n10, 148n12, 148n20, 150, 151, 153–155, 158–161, 163–168, 185, 190, 194, 199, 203, 205, 210n25, 208n2, 209n14, 231–245, 246–262, 264–281
Polishness, 69, 103
political party(ies), 13, 117, 173, 201, 203–205, 207, 208, 293, 300, 309
  All-Ukrainian Union *Svoboda*, 206
  Bulgarian Communist Party, 287, 289–294, 297, 301, 305, 306, 314n17
  Bulgarian Socialist Party, 306, 307, 312, 314n18, 315n19
  Communist Party of the Russian Federation, 177
  Communist Party of the Soviet Union, 199
  Communist Party of Ukraine, 186, 196, 198
  Homeland Union–Lithuanian Christian Democrats (*Tėvynės sąjunga - Lietuvos krikščionys demokrat*ai), 148
  Jobbik, the Movement for a Better Hungary, 117
  Our Ukraine, 186
  Party of Regions (Ukraine), 171, 186, 187, 197, 198, 200, 201, 203–205, 208
  People's Movement of Ukraine (*Narodny Ruch*), 186
  Polish United Workers' Party, 55n3, 252, 255
  Romanian Communist Party, 301
  Socialist Party of Ukraine, 186

Union of Democratic Forces (Bulgaria), 305–307, 314n16, 315n20
United Russia, 191
political correctness, 38, 39, 40, 51, 55, 55 n1, 104
politics, 4, 12–14, 18, 24, 29, 53, 54, 94, 109, 141, 161, 162, 165, 169, 171, 174, 186, 187, 191, 204, 207, 231, 248, 265, 268, 270, 307, 313
  historical/of history, 51, 56n9, 64–67, 75, 151, 164, 165, 193, 194, 197, 200, 203, 205, 272. *See also* memory politics; memory policy; history policy
  of regret, 13
postmemory, 19 n1, 93, 246
postcommunism/postcommunist, 79, 136–138, 150, 153, 155, 156, 160, 164, 193, 302, 314n14. *See also* postsocialism
  memory/dealing with the past, 1, 3, 12, 14, 18, 43, 65, 77, 78, 106, 115–120, 122, 123, 126–129, 129n2, 131, 140, 142, 151, 152, 162, 194, 245, 299–313
  society, 1, 12, 14, 119, 123, 142, 151, 156, 300, 314n14
press, 135, 234, 250, 253, 262n3
prisoner(s), 32, 104, 144, 150, 166, 170, 183, 185, 240, 247, 248, 249, 252–256, 303, 304, 313n7
property, 18, 84, 152, 156–161, 167, 236, 283, 290, 294. *See also* revolution
  nationalized/nationalization of/ 150, 153, 154, 156, 157, 159, 162–165
  collectivization of, 291, 292, 296
  post-German, 154, 270
  post-Jewish, 154, 155, 159
  private, 152
  restitution of/return of, 9, 150–156, 158–160, 162, 163, 165–168, 288
  rights, 151–157, 159, 236
Prussia, 265, 268, 272
  East(ern) Prussia, 53, 265, 267, 270, 273, 274
  West Prussia, 267

psychoanalysis, 78, 97
public debate/discourse, 9, 12, 13, 25, 26, 66, 86, 104, 109, 110, 115, 117, 119, 120, 122, 134, 139, 147, 148n11, 151, 153, 160, 163, 165, 171, 194, 231, 232, 233, 237, 244, 254, 259, 297, 300, 301, 313n10
public opinion, 125, 160, 233, 261, 275, 309
Pushkin, Alexander
  poems by, 219, 223
Putin, Vladimir, XX, 55n3, 175–177, 191, 207, 225n2

Qualls, Karl, 215, 216

racism, 269
Ray, Larry, 78
Reading, Anna Marie, 81
reconciliation, 13, 31, 38, 78, 79, 137, 140, 167, 232, 266, 277, 278, 281, 282n7, 282n8, 302, 308, 310
Red Army/Soviet army/troops/ military, 42, 48, 81, 91, 107, 169, 173, 181–183, 187, 191n7, 200, 215, 232, 238, 240, 244, 252, 269, 307
  veterans, 42, 107, 111, 170, 172, 176, 182, 185–187, 190, 197, 198, 200, 217
region(s)/regional, xi, xii, xiii, 1, 4, 5, 7, 10–12, 14, 15, 29, 33, 34, 45, 46, 59–62, 64, 65, 67–71, 73–75, 83, 90, 92, 110n1, 111n13, 115, 116, 118, 119, 120, 124, 126–129, 132–134, 136, 138, 139, 142, 144–147, 147n1, 148 n 20, 150, 153, 155, 156, 169–174, 176–179, 183, 185–187, 189–191, 194, 196–201, 203, 207, 208, 212, 213, 221, 226 n 26, 232, 234, 237, 265, 267, 268, 271, 273, 276, 279, 280, 283, 285–288, 297, 311. *See also* memory
rehabilitation, 28, 66, 150, 161, 195, 210n17, 221, 289, 304, 313n7
religion/religious, 1, 28, 29, 34, 35, 53, 71, 75, 78, 83, 116, 117, 127, 128, 159, 167, 169, 170, 178, 181, 249, 260, 267, 306, 309, 311

remembering, 1, 7, 14, 23–25, 28, 30–32, 36, 47, 48, 73, 83, 98, 116, 126–128, 151, 235, 283, 284, 289, 293, 299, 312. *See also* melancholic remembrance, remembrance, ritual remembrance
remembrance, 6, 8, 9, 12, 14, 15, 28, 31, 32, 36, 47, 49, 73, 77–80, 83, 87, 93, 95n2, 121, 122, 134, 140, 141, 144, 146, 148n12, 152, 153, 161–163, 173, 213, 255, 256, 259, 260, 280, 281, 301, 311. *See also* melancholic remembrance, remembering, ritual remembrance
representation(s), ix, 14, 15, 29, 93, 117, 119, 125, 131, 170, 194, 196, 199, 202, 209n15, 213, 247, 278, 285, 199, 301, 305, 313n2
resistance, 13, 81, 142, 171, 236, 237, 240, 249, 258, 266, 283, 287, 289, 303, 310, 311, 313n6
myth(s)/narrative(s) of, 303
restitution. *See* property restitution
revitalization, 195
revolution(s), 31, 152
    1956 in Hungary, 67
    1989–1991, 116, 129n1, 147–148n8, 302
    French, 153, 167
    Maidan Revolution, 206, 207
    Orange Revolution, 176, 186, 187, 196, 198, 200
    property, 152–154, 161, 163, 284, 290
    socialist, 307
Ribbentrop-Molotov Pact, 47, 102, 110n6, 121, 143, 315n26
Richardson, Tanya, 214
Ricœur, Paul, 64
Riga, 53, 66, 145
Rioux, Jean-Pierre, 70, 76n6
ritual(s)/ritualization of, 176, 179, 195, 203
    of remembrance/of memory/ commemorative, 9, 13, 17, 28, 41, 50, 80, 83, 100, 128, 138, 144, 206, 301, 309. *See also* remembering, remembrance

Roma (Gypsies), 8, 17, 77, 81–94, 95n1, 95n4, 95n5, 247, 249
Romania/Romanian, 12, 13, 61, 63, 67, 69–71, 81, 90, 111n6, 115, 119, 120, 134, 140, 146, 147n3, 147n20, 168n2, 208, 265, 283, 299, 300, 302–305, 308, 310, 312, 313, 313n1, 312nn6–8, 312n10, 313n11, 313n12, 313n14
Rublev, Andrey, 181
Rüsen, Jörn, 69
Russia/Russian, 12–14, 16, 32, 33, 39, 42, 43, 47, 50, 51, 61, 62, 68, 69, 92, 101, 103, 105, 107, 108, 111n8, 111n12, 117, 137, 139, 145, 148n17, 169–175, 176–179, 181–183, 186, 187, 189–191, 191n2, 191n4, 191n5, 194, 198–200, 202, 203, 205, 207, 208n7, 209n14, 210n17, 210n20, 210n21, 212, 213, 215–225, 225n4, 226n12, 226n13, 226n18, 226n22, 226n23, 226n25, 226n28, 232, 236–238, 241–243, 245, 249, 252, 253, 265, 267, 268, 272, 279, 283
Ryzhkov, Nikolai, 179, 182

Said, Edward, 29, 30, 33, 132
Samuel, Raphael, 75
Samuels, Shimon, 94
Saryusz-Wolska, Magdalena, 64
Savchenko, Evgeniy, 176
Schwan, Gesine, 6
Second World War, x, xi, 6, 8, 10, 12, 13, 33, 34, 37n4, 40, 41, 47, 50, 54, 65, 81, 82, 87, 88, 90, 94, 102, 105, 111n12, 116, 117, 121, 124, 125, 132, 134, 141, 142, 148n12, 153, 154, 159, 161, 166, 167, 169–172, 176, 179, 183, 185–187, 189–191, 191n7, 197, 204, 208n6, 210n25, 231–245, 247, 249, 252, 253, 259–26, 264–276, 279, 282 n7, 303
self-critical approach to history/ reckoning with the past, 27, 53, 142, 272
semiotics, 68, 69
Semprún, Jorge, 32

Sendler (Sendlerowa), Irena, 240
Serbia/Serbian, 12, 83, 265
Serejski, Marian Henryk, 69, 76n5
Sevastopol, 212–225, 225n1, 225n5, 225n7, 226, 226n11, 226n17, 226n18, 226n23, 226n24, 226n27, 226n27
Siberia/Siberian, 102, 131, 135–138, 140, 143–145, 147, 147n4, 147n7, 147n18
Sigona, Nando, 87
Sikorski, Władysław, 240
silence/silencing of, 24, 27, 28, 31, 45, 48, 77–79, 81, 83, 93, 95 n2, 104, 134, 135, 151, 159, 160, 167, 171, 226n23, 238, 250, 253, 258, 302
Simferopol, 189
Simhandl, Katrin, 87
Sinti, 87, 95n1, 95n7, 247, 249
Skarga, Barbara, 99, 147n5
Skoczyński, Jan, 67
Sloterdijk, Peter, 30
Slovak National Uprising, 66, 72
Slovakia/Slovakian, 11, 50, 71, 134, 139, 146, 194, 208 n1, 265, 266
Slovenia, 148 n10, 168 n2, 265
Słowacki, Juliusz, 62
Smith, Anthony, 75
Snyder, Timothy, 5, 48, 110n1, 133, 247, 262, 274
socialism/socialist, 132, 133, 138, 214, 272, 286, 288, 289, 291, 294–297, 305, 307, 308
   humane socialism, 305, 306
   national socialism, 81, 90, 266, 279, 282n7
   post-socialism, 214
   real socialism, 15
   state socialism, 147n1
Sofia, 51, 306, 307, 311, 312
Solidarność/Solidarity (movement), 66, 164, 259
Soviet
   aggression/attack on Poland, 147n6, 148n20
   army. See Red Army

anti-Soviet, 171, 252
authorities/system/policy/power, 32, 101, 102, 107, 171, 179, 195, 259
bloc/dependency/domination/rule/sphere of influence, 15, 49, 55, 61, 110, 133, 135, 139, 179, 183, 194, 226 n 12, 243, 272, 283
commemorative culture, 111n12, 169–172, 174, 177, 183, 184, 186, 188, 189, 191, 191 n6, 194–196, 199, 200, 202, 203, 207, 208, 214, 216
communism, 8, 174n1
empire/state/regime, 48, 118, 121, 171, 186, 194, 220
era/history/past/period/times, 171–173, 181, 183, 195, 198, 205, 212, 215–217, 223
experience, 215
ideology/propaganda/narrative/education, 15, 104, 105, 170, 172, 176, 178, 181, 185, 187, 191, 205, 215, 216, 218, 225, 250, 251
modernization, 174
people/population/society, 171, 252, 268
post-Soviet, 39, 50, 169–172, 174, 185, 187, 190, 212, 215–217, 220, 225
pro-Soviet, 118
republics, 176, 249
totalitarianism, 32, 140, 244, 262. See also totalitarian
See also crimes; occupation; USSR/Soviet Union
space. See place/space
Śpiewak, Paweł 137
Stalin, Josef/Stalinism, 32, 48, 121, 143, 171, 181, 204, 251, 256, 315n26
monument of, 200
Stalinism, 47, 132, 138, 144, 145, 259
Stalinist crimes/repressions, 132, 140, 143, 170, 259, 268
Stalinist labour camps, 143
Stalinist terror, 81
Starobielsk, 252
Steinlauf, Michael, 260
Stekl, Hannes, 72

stereotype(s), 68, 69, 75, 117, 118, 127, 132, 198, 205, 208, 234, 239, 243, 273, 279
Stewart, Michael, 92
Stråth, Bo, ii, 6, 8
survey(s)/poll(s), 124–126, 129, 210n22, 233–235, 239, 241, 261, 262n5, 275, 276, 304, 311, 314n12, 315n26
  survivors, 82, 95n2, 119, 120, 129, 135, 148n9, 170
Świebocka, Teresa, 249
Szacka, Barbara, 64, 76n3
Sznaider, Natan, 6, 9, 19n1, 26, 53, 54
Szűcs, Jenö, 12

television, 234, 264, 274, 313n5
testimonies, 36, 80, 110n7, 118, 135, 136, 139, 303
theatre, 81, 217, 220, 223, 224, 276, 294
Ther, Philipp, 5
Third Reich, 6, 81, 238, 242, 248, 269, 322
Tismaneanu, Vladimir, 83
Todorova, Maria, 14, 61, 62, 63, 132
Tőkés, László, 140
Tolstoy, Lev, 219
  Sevastopol Sketches, 219, 223
Tomaszewski, Andrzej, 66, 273
Toporov, Vladimir, 68
totalitarian/totalitarianism, 10, 15, 36, 44, 47, 48, 50, 106, 108, 131–133, 136, 137, 140, 141, 143, 148n10, 148n11, 152, 166, 167, 171, 194, 198, 241, 246, 247, 262, 275, 279, 280, 303, 306, 311, 315n25. *See also* Soviet totalitarianism
Traba, Robert, 7, 8, 11, 14, 29, 265
tradition, ix, 5, 26, 34, 70, 85–87, 89, 103, 109, 124, 128, 164, 170, 181, 182, 190, 191n6, 193, 194, 201, 209n11, 216, 225, 249, 268, 273, 278, 294, 314n11
transitional justice, 24, 150, 161–163
trauma/traumatic past/traumatic memories, ix, 4, 23, 25, 28–32, 34–36, 40–44, 46–48, 50–52, 55, 78, 86, 107, 136, 147, 152, 169, 183, 238, 239, 272, 284, 290, 291, 297–301, 305
travelling concept, 59, 60
Trehan, Nidhi, 87
trente mémorieuses, 70
Tripartite Pact, 242
Troebst, Stefan, 12, 49, 55n3, 133, 134, 147n1
Trojański, Piotr, vi, 13, 18, 263
Trumpener, Katie, 86, 89
Tuan, Yi-Fu, 213
Tyndall, Andrea, 79
Tyszka, Stanisław, 9, 18, 150

Ukraine/Ukrainian, 9, 12, 13–15, 51, 62, 102, 115, 117, 121, 122, 134, 138, 139, 169–176, 179, 183, 185–187, 189, 190, 191n3, 191n4, 191n5, 193–208, 208n5, 208n7, 208n8, 209n9, 209n10, 209n15, 210n17, 210n18, 210n20, 210n21, 210n25, 212, 213, 216, 218, 219, 221, 223–225, 226n23, 226n25, 226n26, 232, 237, 238, 242–245, 249, 252, 272, 303
Ukrainian Insurgent Army (UPA), 186, 187, 191n7, 197, 199, 203, 205, 209n11, 210n17, 210n24, 238
  veterans, 199, 209n11
United Nations, 2
United States (USA), xi, 8, 11, 19, 26, 56n10, 70, 74, 84, 85, 135, 138, 148n17, 210n17, 224, 231, 241, 242, 243, 252, 253, 255, 268, 273, 311, 313n6, 319, 325, 326, 327, 328, 337, 343, 344, 351
uprising. *See* Slovak National Uprising; Warsaw Uprising; Warsaw Ghetto Uprising
Ushakov, Fyodor, 219, 222, 226n18
USSR/Soviet Union, 37n4, 90, 102–104, 107–109, 111n12, 116, 117, 121, 147n7, 170–172, 177, 178, 182, 193, 210n16, 215–217, 226n19, 241–243, 247–249, 251–253, 255, 261, 267, 268, 272, 283, 303, 314n17. *See also* Soviet; crimes; occupation

Verdery, Katherine, 283
veterans. *See* Red Army, UPA
victim(s), 6, 8, 9, 13, 15, 26, 28, 30, 31, 33, 35, 37n4, 39, 41–44, 47, 48, 65, 78, 81–84, 90–92, 94, 121, 125, 126, 129n11, 135, 136, 139, 141–146, 148n11, 150, 158, 160, 162, 165–167, 169–171, 183, 187, 195, 198, 202, 205, 206, 209n15, 231, 242, 243, 247–249, 251–254, 256–258, 260–262, 266, 269–273, 278, 279, 290, 303, 304, 306, 308, 310–312, 313n10, 315n25
victimhood, 124, 142, 148n21, 150, 160, 161, 165–167. *See also* narratives of victimhood
victory, 42, 55n3, 107, 170–172, 176–179, 181, 183, 187, 191n2, 200, 201, 217, 222, 240, 241, 246, 268, 294
Viola, Lynne, 283
violence, 5, 15, 23–25, 28, 30–33, 35, 36, 38, 44, 65, 67, 78, 83, 88, 94, 118, 135, 136, 148n20, 152, 187, 231, 283, 289, 290, 295, 298
Vilnius, 51, 105, 145
Vladimir the Great, (Ukr. Volodymyr), 223
 monument of, 179

Waldheim, Kurt, 25
Wałęsa, Lech, 66
Walicki, Andrzej, 69
Warsaw, xiii, 2–4, 19, 76n2, 166, 235, 237, 241, 242, 244, 250, 258, 270, 271, 273, 275, 276
Warsaw Ghetto, 2, 259
 Warsaw Ghetto Uprising, 33
Warsaw Uprising, 33, 165, 190, 237, 239, 240, 275

Wasilewski, Witold, 258
Wawrzyniak, Joanna, iii, iv, v, xiv, 1, 11, 19n3, 20, 110n4
Wehrmacht, 238
Weitz, Eric D., 5
Weizsäcker, Richard von, 27, 246
Western Europe/West, x, 1, 10, 12, 15, 27, 34, 40, 42, 44–46, 49–51, 53–55, 59, 60, 67, 70, 71, 74, 78, 86–88, 91, 93, 97, 109, 110, 111n13, 131, 133, 134, 139–143, 145, 146, 215, 231, 246, 267, 315n19. *See also* West European memory, Western identity
Wierzbicki, Andrzej, 69
Wigura, Karolina, 13, 14
Wippermann, Wolfgang, 91
Wolff, Larry, 4, 39, 88, 132

xenophobia, 1

Yalta, 42, 43, 47, 141, 143
Yanukovych, Victor, 186, 187, 200, 201, 202, 203, 204, 210n21, 223
Yates, Dora, 80
Yeltsyn, Boris, 179
Yoasaf bishop (Yakim Gorlenko), 179
Yugoslavia, 7, 109, 111n13, 138
Yushchenko, Victor, 171, 186, 188, 196, 197–205, 208, 209n9, 210n20, 210n22, 210n24, 223

Zapatero, José Luis, 28
Zernack, Klaus, 12, 133
Zimmermann, Michael, 90, 91, 92
Znaniecki, Florian, 96
Zombory, Máté, 11, 63
Zhukov, Georgiy
 monument of, 181